Why We Lost the ERA

Why
We Lost the
ERA

Jane J. Mansbridge

University of Chicago Press
Chicago and London

Most of Chapters 7 and 8 appeared in "Who's in Charge Here? Decision by Accretion and Gatekeeping in the Struggle for the ERA." *Politics and Society* 13 (1984): 343–82.

The University of Chicago Press, Chicago 60637
The University of Chicago Press, Ltd., London

95 94 93 92 91 90 89 88 87   5 4 3

Library of Congress Cataloging-in-Publication Data

Mansbridge, Jane J.
  Why we lost the ERA

  Bibliography: p.
  Includes index.
  1. Women's rights—United States. 2. Equal rights
amendments—United States. 3. Feminism—United States.
I. Title.
HQ1236.5.U6M37 1986   305.4'2'0973   86-6954
ISBN 0-226-50357-7
ISBN 0-226-50358-5 (pbk.)

Contents

List of Tables and Figures   vii

Preface   ix

1   Why We Lost the ERA   1

2   A Very Brief History   8

3   Rights versus Substance   20

4   The Amendment Process   29

5   59 Cents   36

6   The Court Catches Up   45

7   The ERA and the
    War Powers Clauses   60

8   A Decision by Accretion   67

9   Of Husbands and Toilets   90

10   Ideology and Activism   118

11   Reaction in the Legislature   149

12   Organizing in Illinois:
    A Case Study   165

13   A Movement or a Sect?   178

14   Requiescat in Pace   187

*Appendix: Support for
the ERA, 1970–1982*   201

Notes   219

Index   311

List of Tables
and Figures

Table 1:   Traditionalists Support the ERA, 1977   21

Figure 1:   Americans Are Not as Traditional as
            They Were: Trends in Women's
            Labor Force Participation and
            Attitudes toward Women's Roles,   24
            1930–1982

Figure 2:   The Growing Class Divergence regarding
            Housework, 1957/1962–1976/1978   106

Table A1:   Percent Favoring the ERA, 1970–1982   206

Table A2:   Characteristics That Make Little
            Difference: Percent Favoring the
            ERA in 1982, by Gender, Race,
            Class, and Catholicism/Protestantism   212

Table A3:   Characteristics That Make a Difference:
            Percent Favoring the ERA in 1982,
            by Religion, Number of Children,
            Age, Rurality, and Region   213

Table A4:   Support and Opposition to the ERA in
            Unratified States, 1975–1981   214

Table A5:   Support and Opposition to the ERA in
            Illinois, 1976–1982   214

Table A6:   Support and Opposition to the ERA in
            Oklahoma, 1978–1982   215

Table A7:   Party Activism and Support for the ERA
            Nationwide, 1981   215

Table A8:   Party Activism and Support for the ERA
            in California, 1981   215

Table A9:   Attitudes of Men, Women in the Labor
            Force, and Homemakers toward the
            ERA and Nontraditional Roles,
            1974–1982   216

Table A10: Liberal Trends, 1972–1985   217

Table A11: Conservative Trends, 1972–1985   218

Preface

More than a decade ago Pauline Bart and Linda Frankel advised social scientists not to study their own organizations, since social science usually involves showing that appearances are deceptive.[1] Because what appears on the surface is, in part, what we—individually or organizationally—have decided to let appear, investigations that go deeper often hurt the organization or cause we love.

I thought Bart and Frankel were right when I first read their advice. For this, among other reasons, I put aside the file drawers full of data that I had collected from a Women's Center to which I belonged, and which I had planned to include in my book *Beyond Adversary Democracy*. I did not think, however, that their argument applied to a phenomenon as "public" as the struggle for the Equal Rights Amendment (ERA), so I later began to study the ERA movement despite the fact that I was also a participant.[2]

As the work progressed, I discovered that my optimism had been unfounded. I began with a deep conviction that the Equal Rights Amendment should be ratified, and I still have this conviction. Yet if I had published this manuscript earlier, the political result might well have been to weaken support for that Amendment. If I had studied the STOP ERA movement as closely as I studied the pro-ERA movement, my revelations might have weakened the opposition instead. These thoughts did not buoy me as I wrote.

Today, the federal Equal Rights Amendment is—at least for the near future—politically dead. The ERA failed to win ratification in 1982, and an effort to start the process anew in 1983 failed to win a two-thirds majority in the House of Representatives. The ERA is unlikely to accumulate such a majority in Congress in the near future, and even if it does, its chances of ratification at the state level are almost nil. I knew defeat was likely from the time I started to work on this book, but it still depressed my spirits as I worked. The solidity of that defeat means, however, that what I write about the ERA is not likely to do the cause serious harm. It is beyond harm now. At this point, I believe, the story of the ERA is important mainly because of the lessons it provides for any political effort, feminist or otherwise, in the future. It is to these lessons that this book is directed, in the hope that we learn from defeat.

My participation in the struggle to ratify the ERA poses interpretative as well as personal and political problems. Several readers have been unsettled by the way what I have written tries to combine both scholarly disengagement and political advocacy. After outlining what I see as possible options for the pro-ERA movement, for example, I pause to say what I personally would have done (e.g., p. 89). Unsettling as this mixture may be, I believe that clarifying my own position makes the book more useful. The interjections will, I hope, encourage the reader to reflect, at that point, on what he or she might have done. They also make more obvious than is usual in works like this the stance from which I have chosen the events I report.

Who, then, is the "we" of the title? First of all, it designates those who supported the ERA—both the 50–60 percent of the population who reported on surveys (whose limits I will come to shortly) that they "favored" the ERA, and the more committed minority who told interviewers that they favored it "strongly." But the "we" also represents the entire American citizenry, including those who opposed the ERA and those who did not care. Almost everyone involved in the ERA struggle was primarily concerned with the good of the country rather than with personal self-interest. Thus, since I believed both that the principle involved in the ERA was a good one and that the justices of the United States Supreme Court, working with a good principle, would have done more good than harm for the nation as a whole over the long run, I cannot escape the conclusion that even the opponents were "really" among the losers when the ERA went down to defeat.

This book several times gives instances in which the ERA activists' positions in the larger social and economic structure heavily influenced the way they saw issues affecting the ERA and the way they acted on their perceptions. The analysis applies equally to myself. As a political scientist, I have adopted ways of looking at the world and ways of accruing professional credit that differ from those of, say, a legal scholar, an activist with her eye on a potential political career, or a nurse trying to eke out some time for political work from a life already crowded with the demands of a paying job and work in the home. We must view the universe from particular vantage points. While multiple perspectives are helpful for organizations, no individual can see the world from more than two or three vantage points without suffering from blurred vision. We can try to note the ways in which our perspectives and the incentives built into our positions color what we see. We can be relatively humble about the amount of the elephant we have got hold of when our perspective clashes with someone else's. But on an issue like the ERA, analysis from any perspective is a political act, and one must, as a political being as well as a scholar, take responsibility for it.

I could not have written this book without the consistent moral and monetary support of the Center for Urban Affairs and Policy Research at Northwestern University. An interdisciplinary haven from the pressures of departmental life, the Center encourages academic work that might have a practical impact. The intelligence, interest, and integrity of my colleagues at the Center sustained me at many points. I am also grateful to Northwestern University for a series of small grants that enabled me to conduct many of my interviews in person and to have the transcripts typed. I would like to thank the Rockefeller Foundation for funding a year's leave that allowed me to bring the book almost to the point of completion, and the National Endowment for the Humanities and the Institute for Advanced Study in Princeton for the half of my year at the Institute that I spent on this book. Finally, I would like to thank the many people who read and commented on various drafts—Judith Areen, Stephen Bendich, Pauline Bart, Janet Boles, Arnold Feldman, Leslie Friedman Goldstein, Susan Goodman, Edwin Haefele, Susan Horn-Moo, David Lyon, Ronald Mansbridge, Donald Mathews, Pamela Rothenberg, Leonard Rubinowitz, Kay Lehman Schlozman, Gilbert Steiner, Arthur Stinchcombe, the anonymous referees from the University of Chicago Press, and several of the people I interviewed for this book, who must also remain anonymous—as well as Martha Field, Ruth Bader Ginsburg, Sylvia Law,

Leon Friedman, Steven Smith, and Cass Sunstein, who all read specific chapters. It is particularly important in this book to point out that their reading implies neither agreement nor the claim to having checked my facts. I alone have to take responsibility for ideological orneriness, conceptual blindness, and empirical error. It is impossible to thank adequately Christopher Jencks, who edited the manuscript more than once, puzzled with me through many of the problems, took a fully equal share of the maintenance of our daily lives, and continued to contend, in my moments of depression, that the work deserved to be done.

This work, funded as much out of my own pocket as by any other source, has relied heavily not only on the Center for Urban Affairs and Policy Research but also on the Federal Work-Study Program for both typists and research assistants. I would like to thank Caryl Athanasiades, Ronald Brown, Joanna Brownstein, Elizabeth Burr, Elizabeth Foulser, Deborah Gerner, Melissa Orlie, Janet Soule, Shimon Wagner, and Trudy Williams, who worked with me under these auspices, for all their help. I would particularly like to thank Gary Winters, who worked on almost every table in the book, for the concern and intelligence he displayed in the cause of "getting it right."

1 Why We Lost the ERA

1. Equality of rights under the law shall not be denied or abridged by the United States or by any
   State on account of sex.
2. The Congress shall have the power to enforce, by
   appropriate legislation, the provisions of this
   article.
3. This amendment shall take effect two years after
   the date of ratification.

   —Complete text of the Equal Rights Amendment

In March 1972 the Equal Rights Amendment to the United States Constitution—the ERA—passed the Senate of the United States with a vote of 84 to 8, fifteen votes more than the two-thirds required for constitutional amendments. In the ensuing ten years—from 1972 to 1982—a majority of Americans consistently told interviewers that they favored this amendment to the Constitution. Yet on June 30, 1982, the deadline for ratifying the amendment passed with only thirty-five of the required thirty-eight states having ratified.

How did this happen?

This book will argue that if the ERA had been ratified, the Supreme Court would have been unlikely to use it to bring about major changes in the relations between American men and women, at least in the foreseeable future. Nor did the American public want any significant change in gender roles, whether at work, at home, or in society at large. The groups that fought for the ERA and the

1

groups that fought against it, however, had a stake in believing that the ERA *would* produce these kinds of changes. With both the proponents and the opponents exaggerating the likely effects of the ERA, legislators in wavering states became convinced that the ERA might, in fact, produce important substantive changes—and the necessary votes were lost. Considering the large number of legislative votes required to amend the Constitution, the puzzle is not why the ERA died but why it came so close to passing.

Contrary to widespread belief, public support for the ERA did not increase in the course of the ten-year struggle. In key wavering states where the ERA was most debated, public support actually declined. Much of the support for the Amendment was superficial, because it was based on a support for abstract rights, not for real changes. Many nominal supporters took strong antifeminist positions on other issues, and their support evaporated when the ERA became linked in their minds to feminist positions they rejected.

The irony in all this is that the ERA would have had much less substantive effect than either proponents or opponents claimed. Because the ERA applied only to the government and not to private businesses and corporations, it would have had no noticeable effect, at least in the short run, on the gap between men's and women's wages. Furthermore, during the 1970s, the Supreme Court began to use the Fourteenth Amendment to the Constitution to declare unconstitutional almost all the laws and practices that Congress had intended to make unconstitutional when it passed the ERA in 1972. The exceptions were laws and practices that most Americans approved. Thus, by the late 1970s it was hard to show that the ERA would have made any of the substantive changes that most Americans favored.

While the ERA would have had few immediate, tangible effects, I nonetheless believe that its defeat was a major setback for equality between men and women. Its direct effects would have been slight, but its indirect effects on both judges and legislators would probably have led in the long run to interpretations of existing laws and enactment of new laws that would have benefited women. The lack of immediate benefits did, however, deeply influence the course of the public debate. Because ERA activists had little of an immediate, practical nature to lose if the ERA was defeated, they had little reason to describe it in a way that would make it acceptable to middle-of-the-road legislators. As a consequence, the most influential leaders in the pro-ERA organizations and many of the activists in those organizations chose to interpret the ERA as delivering radical results.

Most proponents contended, for example, that the ERA would require the military to send women draftees into combat on the same basis as men. ERA proponents adopted this position even though it reduced their chances of achieving the short-run goal of passing the ERA and despite the fact that the Court was not likely to interpret the ERA as having this effect. They did so in part because their ideology called for full equality with men, not for equality with exceptions. In a somewhat similar manner, certain feminist lawyers argued in state courts that state ERAs required states to fund medically necessary abortions if they were funding all medically necessary services for men. Such arguments also reduced the chances that legislators in the key unratified states would vote for the federal ERA.

The struggle reveals how impossible it is, even in the most favorable circumstances, to dispense with "ideology" in favor of practical political reasoning when the actors in the drama give their energies voluntarily, without pay or other material incentives. Volunteers always have mixed motives, but most are trying to do good and promote justice. As a result, most would rather lose fighting for a cause they believe in than win fighting for a cause they feel is morally compromised.

Because the ERA offered its supporters no tangible benefits, activists worked hard for it only if they believed strongly in equality for women. They had no reason to "betray" that principle by compromise for compromise offered no concrete benefits, either to them personally or to women generally. ERA opponents took relatively extreme positions for similar reasons. But their "radicalism" cost them less, because they had only to disrupt an emerging consensus, not to produce one.

Refusing to compromise is, of course, often better than winning. It is not the focus on principle rather than practice that should give the reader of this story pause. It is the difficulty both sides had assimilating information about the struggle in which they were engaged. This institutionalized deafness meant that neither the activists nor the general public could make even an informed guess about what passage of the ERA would accomplish. As a result, there was no serious national debate about whether the Amendment was the best way of accomplishing what the proponents sought or whether it really threatened the values that opponents sought to defend. Nor did the proponents, who ran the gamut from feminist lawyers to grass-roots activists, ever engage one another in a wide-ranging discussion of strategy.

The only possible way to have persuaded three more state legislatures to ratify the ERA would have been to insist—correctly—that it would do relatively little in the short run, and to insist equally strongly—and correctly—on the importance of placing the principle in the Constitution to guide the Supreme Court in its long-run evolution of constitutional law. In addition, the pro-ERA movement would have had to develop an ongoing, district-based political network capable of turning generalized public sympathy for reforms that benefit women into political pressure on specific legislators in the marginal unratified states. But even this strategy might not have worked. Comparatively few state legislators were open to persuasion on this issue, and the troops for district-based organizing were often hard to mobilize—or keep mobilized.

The movement away from principle and the increasing focus on substantive effects was probably an inevitable result of the ten-year struggle for the ERA. Inevitable or not, the shift did occur. In the near future, therefore, the only way to convince legislators that the ERA would not have undesirable substantive effects would be to add explicit amendments limiting its application to the military, abortion, and so on. No principled feminist, including myself, favors an ERA that includes such "crippling" amendments. In the present political climate, therefore, the future of the ERA looks even dimmer than its past.

The death of the ERA was, of course, also related to broader changes in American political attitudes. Two of these changes were especially relevant: growing legislative skepticism about the consequences of giving the U.S. Supreme Court authority to review legislation, and the growing organizational power of the new Right.

Suspicion of the Supreme Court, and of the role of lawyers and judges generally, certainly played a significant role in the ERA's demise. For its advocates, the ERA was a device for allowing the Supreme Court to impose the principle of equality between the sexes on recalcitrant state legislators. For legislators, that was precisely the problem. They did not want their actions reviewed, much

less reversed, by federal judges whom they did not even appoint.
There was a larger problem as well. The ERA embodied a principle, which was supposed to apply, without exception, to specific
pieces of legislation. But most people—including most legislators—
do not derive their preferences from principles. Instead, they derive
their principles from their preferences, endorsing principles they
associate with outcomes they like. Because the justices of the
Supreme Court of the United States put somewhat more weight
than ordinary citizens do on the principles they have evolved from
the Constitution, they often find themselves taking controversial or
even unpopular stands. As a result, much of the public has come to
view the Court as "out of control." Although the Court's unpopular
decisions have not yet reduced its power, they took their toll on the
ERA. If the primary cause of the ERA's defeat was the fear that it
would lead to major changes in the roles of men and women, a
major subsidiary cause was legislative backlash against "progressive" Court decisions, starting with the 1954 school desegregation
decision. Many state legislators were unwilling to give the Court
"new words to play with," rightly fearing that this could eventually
have all sorts of unforeseeable consequences they might not like
and would not be able to reverse.

The same sense of impotence in the face of national changes
that fueled the reaction against the Court also fed the conservative
backlash against feminism and the growth of the "new" Right. For
many conservative Americans, the personal became political for
the first time when questions of family, children, sexual behavior,
and women's roles became subjects of political debate. Leaders of
the "old" Radical Right, who had traditionally focused on national
defense and the Communist menace, became aware of the organizing potential of these "women's" issues only slowly. Once assimi-
lated, however, the "new" issues turned out to have two great
organizational virtues. First, they provided a link with fundamentalist churches. The evangelizing culture and the stable geographic base of the fundamentalist churches made them powerful
actors in state legislatures once they ventured into the political
process. Second, "women's issues" not only gave a focus to the
reaction against the changes in child rearing, sexual behavior, divorce, and the use of drugs that had taken place in the 1960s and
1970s, they also mobilized a group, traditional homemakers, that

had lost status over the two previous decades and was feeling the psychological effects of the loss. The new women's issues, combined with improvements in computer technology that reduced the cost of processing large numbers of names, made it feasible for the first time to contact by direct mail and thus bring into concerted political activities many who had previously been concerned only with a single issue or not been involved in politics at all.

State legislators were predisposed to oppose a constitutional amendment that gave the federal government power in one of the few areas that was still primarily in the province of the states, namely, family law. The entry of new conservative activists into the political process enhanced this "natural" resistance. As fundamentalist women became more prominent in the opposition, the ERA came to be seen as an issue that pitted women against women and, moreover, women of the Right against women of the Left. Once the ERA lost its aura of benefiting all women and became a partisan issue, it lost its chance of gaining the supermajority required for a constitutional amendment.

There are two lessons to be learned from the story told here. The first is a lesson about the politics of promoting "the common good." We have known for a long time of the extraordinary inequities built into the way different groups can influence legislators in a pluralist democratic system. We have also known that because it is harder to organize for the general interest than for particular interests, the general interest will—all other things being equal—count less in the political process than most people want it to. The story of the ERA struggle reveals a third, less widely recognized, obstacle to promoting the common good. Organizing on behalf of the general interest usually requires volunteers, and mobilizing volunteers often requires an exaggerated, black or white vision of events to justify spending time and money on the cause. Ironically, the greatest cost in organizing for the public interest may be the distortion, in the course of organizing, of that interest itself.

A second, practical lesson follows from the first. While organizations that depend on volunteers to promote the common good seem to have an inherent tendency toward ideological purity and polarized perceptions, they can develop institutions that help correct these tendencies, ranging from small-group techniques through formal systems of representation. Although ongoing organizations are susceptible to the temptations of speaking only to themselves, they are also our main repositories of past experience and our main mechanism for avoiding the endless repetition of past errors. Effectively promoting the common good thus requires that we keep such organizations strong and consistently funded, while at the same time trying to ensure internal dialogue on substantive issues.

2 A Very Brief History

The major women's organizations were able to persuade two-thirds of the states to approve women's suffrage in 1920. In the same year these organizations began to discuss an Equal Rights Amendment. Alice Paul and her militant National Woman's Party had gained national notoriety by picketing the White House and staging hunger strikes for women's suffrage. Now the same group proposed a constitutional amendment, introduced in Congress in 1923, that read: "Men and women shall have equal rights throughout the United States and in every place subject to its jurisdiction. Congress shall have power to enforce this article by appropriate legislation."[1]

From the beginning, "equal rights" meant "ending special benefits." An ERA would have made unconstitutional the protective legislation that socialists and social reformers like Florence Kelley, frustrated by the lack of a strong working-class movement in America, had struggled to erect in order to protect at least women and children from the worst ravages of capitalism. Against Kelley and women like her, the National Woman's Party leaders, primarily professional and upper- or upper-middle-class women,[2] argued that "a maximum hour law or a minimum wage law which applied to women but not to men was bound to hurt women more than it could possibly help them." Kelley in turn dubbed the ERA "topsy-turvy feminism," and declared that "women cannot achieve true equality with men by securing identity of treatment under the law."[3]

After a 1921 meeting between Alice Paul, Florence Kelley, and

8

others, the board of directors of the National Consumers' League voted to oppose the Equal Rights Amendment. The League, a powerful Progressive organization of which Kelley was general secretary, thereafter made opposition to the ERA a consistent plank in its program.[4] The strong opposition of Progressive and union feminists meant that when the Equal Rights Amendment was introduced in Congress in 1923 it was immediately opposed by a coalition of Progressive organizations and labor unions. And although the Amendment was introduced in every subsequent Congress for the next twenty years, opposition from this coalition and from most conservatives ensured its repeated defeat.

During the 1930s, the National Association of Women Lawyers and the National Federation of Business and Professional Women's Clubs (BPW) decided to sponsor the ERA, and in 1940 the Republican party revitalized the ERA by placing it in the party's platform. In 1944, despite strong opposition from labor, the Democratic party followed suit.[5] Nonetheless, the ERA never came close to passing until 1950 and 1953, when the U.S. Senate passed it, but with the "Hayden rider," which provided that the Amendment "shall not be construed to impair any rights, benefits, or exemptions now or hereinafter conferred by law upon persons of the female sex."[6] In both years the House of Representatives recessed without a vote. Because the women's organizations supporting the ERA knew that special benefits were incompatible with equal rights, they had tried to block the amended ERA in the House and were relieved when their efforts succeeded.[7]

Support widened during the 1950s—primarily among Republicans, although among the Democrats Eleanor Roosevelt and some other prominent women dropped their opposition to the ERA in order to support the United Nations charter, which affirmed the "equal rights of men and women."[8] In 1953 President Dwight Eisenhower replaced the unionist head of the Federal Women's Bureau with a Republican businesswoman who, having sponsored Connecticut's equal pay law, moved the bureau from active opposition into a neutral position regarding the ERA. In later speeches Eisenhower also stressed the pro-ERA planks of both parties and stated his support for "equal rights" for women.[9] In 1963, however, labor struck back when President John Kennedy's Commission on the Status of Women—created under labor influence partly to siphon off pressure for an ERA—concluded that "a constitutional amendment need not now be sought in order to establish this principle [equal rights for women]."[10]

The crucial step in building progressive and liberal support for the ERA was the passage of Title VII of the Civil Rights Act of 1964, which prohibited job discrimination on the basis of sex. Title VII had originally been designed to prevent discrimination against blacks, but a group of southern congressmen added a ban on discrimination against women in a vain effort to make the bill unacceptable to northern conservatives. Initially, Title VII had no effect on "protective" legislation. Unions, accordingly, continued to oppose the ERA because they thought it would nullify such legislation. In 1967, when the newly formed National Organization for Women (NOW) gave the ERA first place on its Bill of Rights for Women, several union members immediately resigned.[11] But by 1970 both the federal courts and the Equal Employment Opportunity Commission (EEOC) had interpreted Title VII as invalidating protective legislation, and had extended most traditional protections to men rather than removing them for women. With their long-standing concern now for the most part made moot, union opposition to the ERA began to wane.[12]

In 1970, the Pittsburgh chapter of NOW took direct action. The group disrupted Senator Birch Bayh's hearings on the nineteen-year-old vote, getting Bayh to promise hearings on the ERA the following spring.[13] This was the moment. Labor opposition was fading, and, because few radical claims had been made for the ERA, conservatives had little ammunition with which to oppose it. In April, the United Auto Workers' convention voted to endorse the ERA.[14] In May, Bayh began Senate hearings on the ERA, and for the first time in its history the U.S. Department of Labor supported the ERA.[15] In June, Representative Martha Griffiths succeeded in collecting enough signatures on a discharge petition to pry the ERA out of the House Judiciary Committee, where for many years the liberal chair of the committee, Emanuel Celler, had refused to schedule hearings because of the persistent opposition by labor movement traditionalists. After only an hour's debate, the House of Representatives passed the ERA by a vote of 350 to 15.

The next fall, the ERA came to the Senate, which, after several days of debate, added by a narrow majority a provision exempting women from the draft.[16] This provision eliminated the only consequence proponents claimed for the ERA that might not have received support from a majority of Americans. However, having consistently insisted on bearing the responsibilities of citizenship as well as the rights, the women's organizations promoting the ERA had decided that women must be drafted. Because an ERA amended to exempt women from the draft was not acceptable to any of the organizations promoting the ERA, Senator Bayh did not bring it to a vote. Instead, without consulting those organizations, he proposed a new wording for the ERA that mirrored the words of the Fourteenth Amendment: "Neither the United States nor any State shall, on account of sex, deny to any person within its jurisdiction the equal protection of the laws." Bayh described his new wording as "recognizing the need for a flexible standard" and "meeting the objections of [the ERA's] most articulate critics,"[17] and he said in a subsequent press interview that the new wording would permit excluding women from the draft.[19] Fearing, on the basis of these remarks, that Bayh would be too flexible in his interpretation of this new wording, the major women's organizations told him that this substitute was not acceptable to them.[19]

In the spring of 1971, the House Judiciary Committee returned to the original 1970 wording of the ERA but adopted the "Wiggins amendment," which said that the ERA would "not impair the validity of any law of the United States which exempts a person from compulsory military service or any other law of the United States or any state which reasonably promotes the health and safety of the people."[20] The women's organizations supporting an ERA concluded, correctly, that the standard of "reasonably" promoting health and safety was no more stringent than the standard the Supreme Court was already using to judge constitutional many laws discriminating against women. Accordingly, they opposed the Wiggins amendment, and under their urging the House rejected it,[21] voting 354 to 23 to adopt the original ERA.

Having passed the House, the ERA went to the Senate, where the Subcommittee on Constitutional Amendments, chaired by ERA opponent Senator Sam Ervin, adopted another substitute: "Neither the United States nor any State shall make any legal distinction between the rights and responsibilities of male and

female persons unless such distinction is based on physiological or
functional differences between them."[22] A majority of the full Committee on the Judiciary, chaired by Senator Bayh, rejected this
attempt, so similar to the previous two, and adopted the original
wording of the ERA in its definitive March 1972 report.

In the immediately ensuing Senate debate, Senator Ervin introduced eight amendments to the ERA relating to draft and combat,
marital and family support, privacy, protections and exemptions,
and homosexuality. His goal was twofold. First, he hoped to tempt
a majority in the Senate into adopting one or more of the amendments, which would have divided the ERA proponents and at the
very least would have delayed the ERA's passage. Second, if the
ERA did pass in the Senate, he hoped to focus the upcoming
debates in the states on the potentially unpalatable substantive
consequences of the ERA. According to Catherine East, an active
participant in these events, "proponents could not accept any
amendment, even innocuous ones, since an amended ERA would
have had to have gone to conference, where hostile House Committee members would most likely have killed it. (Senator Ervin knew
this.)"[23] Bayh succeeded in pursuading a majority to vote down all
the Ervin amendments. On March 22, 1972, the ERA passed the
Senate of the United States with a vote of 84 to 8.

As soon as the Senate voted, a secretary in the office of the
senator from Hawaii contacted the Hawaii legislative reference
bureau, and within twenty minutes the president of the Hawaii state
senate presented a resolution to ratify. Five minutes later the resolution, unanimously passed, came before the Hawaii house, receiving equally quick and unanimous treatment.[24] Thus on the very
day that the U.S. Senate passed the ERA, Hawaii became the first
state to ratify. Delaware, Nebraska, and New Hampshire ratified
the next day, and on the third day Idaho and Iowa ratified. Twenty-
four more states ratified in 1972 and early 1973. The very earliest
states to ratify were all unanimous, and in the other early states the
votes were rarely close. Moreover,

> rules were suspended in order to avoid referral to committee. Fre-
> quently no or only perfunctory hearings were held on the subject.
> Floor debate too was brief. . . . Even in those states where open
> hearings were held, it was not uncommon for only proponents of the
> amendment to appear as witnesses.[25]

By late 1973, however, the ERA's proponents had lost control of the ratification process. While the national offices of the various pro-ERA organizations could relatively easily coordinate their Washington activities to get the ERA through Congress, they were slow in organizing coalitions in the states. At the end of the 1973 state legislative sessions, only a few states even had active ERA coalitions.[26]

Moreover, in 1973 the Supreme Court decided, in *Roe v. Wade,* that state laws forbidding abortion violated the "right to privacy" implicit in the Constitution. Although the ERA had no obvious direct bearing on whether "abortion is murder," the two issues nonetheless became politically linked. The *Roe* decision took power out of the hands of relatively parochial, conservative state legislators and put it in the hands of a relatively cosmopolitan, liberal U.S. Supreme Court. The ERA would have done the same thing. Furthermore, both were sponsored by what was at that time still called the "women's liberation" movement. Traditionalists saw the "women's libbers" both as rejecting the notion that motherhood was a truly important task and as endorsing sexual hedonism instead of moral restraint. The *Roe* decision seemed to constitute judicial endorsement for these values. Since NOW was not only the leading sponsor of the ERA but the leading defender of abortion on demand, conservative activists saw abortion and the ERA as two prongs of the "libbers' " general strategy for undermining traditional American values.[27] Unable to overturn the *Roe* decision directly, many conservatives sought to turn the ERA into a referendum on that decision.[28] To a significant degree, they succeeded.[29] The opponents began to organize and convinced the first of several states to rescind ratification—a move that had no legal force but certainly made a political difference in unratified states.

Three more states ratified in 1974, one in 1975, and one—Indiana—in 1977, bringing the total to thirty-five of the required thirty-eight. No state ratified after 1977 despite the triumph of ERA proponents in 1978 in getting Congress to extend the original 1979 deadline until 1982.[30] In 1982 this extension ran out, and the Amendment died. Alabama, Arizona, Arkansas, Florida, Georgia, Illinois, Louisiana, Mississippi, Missouri, Nevada, North Carolina, Oklahoma, Utah, and Virginia had not ratified. All were Mormon or southern states, except Illinois, which required a three-fifths majority for ratifying constitutional amendments and which had a strongly southern culture in the third of the state surrounded by Missouri and Kentucky.[31]

Public Opinion

The first time a polling organization asked the American public about the ERA, in 1970, 56 percent of the people interviewed said they favored ERA. From 1970 to 1982, when the struggle for ratification ended, a majority of adult Americans consistently supported the ERA. Table A1 in the Appendix gives the percentage of American adults favoring the ERA in all the important national surveys that asked about the ERA more than once. More respondents favored passage than opposed it in every survey. Fifty percent or more favored passage in every survey but one. While responses differed according to the wording of the question, the "average" survey found 57 percent for the ERA, 32 percent opposed, and 11 percent with no opinion.

These surveys, however, were a poor guide to how people would actually act. Time after time in the referenda on state ERAs, feminists experienced the agony of seeing survey support as high as 60 or 65 percent turn, after a brief but bitterly fought campaign, into defeat. In the fall of 1975, two independent polling organizations reported that a majority of people who planned to vote on the state ERAs in the upcoming referenda in New York and New Jersey said they would approve an ERA in their respective states.[32] But in the actual vote on November 4, both state ERAs failed, with 57 percent voting against in New York and 51 percent in New Jersey.[33] In Florida in 1978, preelection surveys showed the state ERA winning by "two to one," but in the referendum it lost by the same margin— two to one.[34] In a 1980 Iowa survey one month before the referendum, 48 percent of likely voters favored a state ERA and only 23 percent opposed it, but in the referendum itself the state ERA lost by 55 to 45 percent.[35] Finally, in Maine in 1984, a survey taken a month before the referendum indicated that 62 percent of the registered voters would vote for a state ERA; in the election 63 percent voted against it.[36]

Although the ERA was bitterly contested, the conflict did not follow the expected demographic lines. Observers often assumed, for example, that because most ERA activists were women, and because the Amendment was supposed to help women, women would support it more often than men did. In fact, men and women differed hardly at all on the ERA (see table A2, Appendix). Activists also believed that differences between men and women on the ERA had an important effect on the "gender gap" in the 1980 Presidential election. But these views came from looking at their own friends, since among the highly educated and politically active, women did support the ERA more than men. In the population as a whole, however, men supported the ERA almost as much as women and voted against Reagan on the basis of their ERA support just as much as women did. Contrary to the activists' beliefs, therefore, the ERA had only a very small effect on the gender gap in the 1980 presidential election.[37]

There were also several reasons to expect the middle class, particularly among women, to have supported the ERA more than the working class. First, people with more education tend to take "progressive" stances regarding "cultural" innovations in gender roles, sexual practices, drug use, and so forth. To the degree that the ERA was a similar "cultural" issue, one would have expected differences by education on the ERA as well. Second, while the ERA affected only governmental laws and practices and not the private sector, 56 percent of the women in the experienced labor force who had college degrees worked for the government in 1970, as did 64 percent of the women with graduate training.[38] (These figures become less startling when one realizes that the governmental sector includes all public school and public university teachers, nurses in public hospitals, and social workers and secretaries at any level of government administration.) One might conclude, on this basis, that middle-class women had a greater stake in the ERA's passage than working-class women. Third, and most important, the activists for the ERA were predominantly middle class, both in comparison with the general population and, to a much lesser degree, in comparison with the anti-ERA activists.[39] (The activists on both sides were predominantly white.)[40] But in spite of all these reasons for expecting predominantly white middle-class support for the ERA, both the working class and blacks were at least as likely to support the ERA as the middle class and whites (table A2). In another upset of the ERA-WASP stereotype, Catholics were more likely than Protestants to support the ERA (table A2).[41]

Support for the ERA, however, did split along lines that would become familiar in the new politics of the 1980s: religious fundamentalists and heavy churchgoers against agnostics and Jews, people with many children against those with none, old people against young, country against city dwellers, and nationwide, southerners against people on the East and West Coasts. (table A3). The battle against the ERA was one of the first in which the New Right used "women's issues" to forge a coalition of the traditional Radical Right, religious activists, and that previously relatively apolitical segment of the noncosmopolitan working and middle classes that was deeply disturbed by the cultural changes—especially the changes in sexual mores—in the second half of the twentieth century.

The bitterly fought ratification campaign did not, on the best available evidence, have any effect, either positive or negative, on public support for the ERA in the nation as a whole. The 1970 survey question was never repeated, but we have more or less comparable data from 1975 to 1982. With one exception, no survey organization ever found any clear trend in public support for the ERA over this period. The exception was Louis Harris's survey organization. After showing no trend for seven years, Harris suddenly reported a huge leap in support, from 50 to 63 percent, in April 1982. Harris portrayed this thirteen-point change as evidence of a last-minute surge in popular approval for the ERA. In syndicated newspapers across the country, under the headline, "ERA Support Soars as Deadline Nears," Harris declared:

> With less than two months to go before the time allowed for ratification will run out, support for the Equal Rights Amendment has soared to 63–34 percent nationwide, an increase of 13 points just since last January when a much closer 50–46 plurality favored passage of the ERA.[42]

At first glance this increase is puzzling, since none of the other organizations asking comparable questions (Gallup, NBC/Associated Press, and CBS News) found much change in this period. But on closer inspection the explanation becomes clear. Right before its traditional question on the ERA, the Harris organization's April survey asked a new question:

> As you know, the Equal Rights Amendment to the Constitution is being debated across the country. Let me read you the actual wording of that Equal Rights Amendment: "Equality of rights under the law

shall not be denied or abridged by the United States or any state on account of sex." Do you favor or oppose that Equal Rights Amendment to the Constitution?

Like other questions that include the actual wording of the Amendment, this one produced a resounding 73 percent approval rate. Harris then asked its traditional "balanced" question about the ERA:

> Many of those who favor women's rights favor the Equal Rights Amendment to the Constitution. This Amendment would establish that women would have rights equal to men in all areas. Opponents argue that women are different from men and need to be protected by special laws which deal with women's status.

The question ended with almost the same words as the preceding question: "Do you favor or oppose the Equal Rights Amendment?" (questions X and XI, table A1). By asking its traditional question right after a question worded so that most respondents committed themselves to the ERA, Harris altered people's answers to the traditional question. When one does not have a strong opinion—and about two-thirds of the people who had an opinion on the ERA said they did not favor or oppose it strongly—a desire to be consistent in one's responses can overwhelm a tentative impulse pro or con.

Since polling is a difficult art, and the Harris organization is not one of its more meticulous practitioners, I would ordinarily attribute this particular gaff to incompetence rather than a deliberate desire to deceive. But the story does not end here. In August 1983, *BusinessWeek* reported,

> Ironically, support for the ERA began to gather new momentum in 1982, just as the campaign for the failed version of the amendment was foundering in state legislatures. The Harris organization, which has polled on the issue several times, reported 50% support for the ERA in January, 1982. By April, when legislatures in key states were in session, pro-ERA sentiment rose to 63%, and support has remained rock-solid.[43]

In 1984, *Ms.* magazine reported, also on the basis of a Harris poll, that "sixty-four percent of American women favor passage of the

ERA; a major change from the 48 percent of women who favored it in 1975.''[44] What neither *Business Week* nor *Ms.* reported, presumably because Harris had neglected to tell them, was that in the post-1982 polls—from which they derived the belief that support was now "rock-solid" at about 63 percent—Harris had substituted a new question that included three arguments for the ERA instead of one, and stressed economic discrimination, which many strategists agreed was the best way to sell the ERA.[45] Harris often fails to note changes in wording. But Louis Harris is a good liberal and is married to a feminist activist. If a change in wording had produced an apparent *decline* in public support for the ERA, Harris would almost certainly have tried to figure out why and noted the problem. The same is true of ERA activists generally. If Harris had produced a decline of this magnitude, women with experience in survey research would undoubtedly have noticed that no other survey organizations had found such a decline and they would have discounted the Harris results. But because the results matched both their desires and expectations, ERA activists believed them.

In fact, however, even the stable picture painted by most national survey organizations masked a growing gap between the ratified and the unratified states. By 1977 the opponents of the ERA had effectively blocked ratification in the states. Between 1976–1977 and 1980–1981 there was a significant increase in public opposition to the ERA in the unratified states. Those who had previously no opinion were turning from apathy to opposition (table A4). In some unratified states support for the ERA also dropped. In two key unratified states, Illinois and Oklahoma, public opposition actually exceeded support by June 1982 (tables A5 and A6). Thus, when conservative representatives in the unratified states reported increased opposition to the ERA in their districts in 1977, 1978, and 1982, they were probably right.[46] The national ERA leaders, most of whom lived either in Washington, D.C., or in states that had ratified the ERA, seldom were aware of these developments. Because their friends and acquaintances all supported the ERA, and opinion polls told them that the general public supported it, they tended to dismiss legislator's reports of local opposition as self-serving distortions.

In the late 1970s, attitudes toward the ERA also polarized along party lines. The percentage of Republicans supporting the ERA in the Illinois House of Representatives, for example, fell from 54 percent in 1975 to 41 percent in 1978 to 34 percent in 1982, while the percentage of Democrats supporting the ERA rose from 71 to 73 and finally to 78 percent.[47] In 1980, in a reversal of the party stances that had prevailed in the 1950s and early 1960s, the Republican Presidential candidate and party platform opposed the ERA while the Democrats supported it. By 1981, support or opposition to the ERA had become strongly related to party activism. Democratic activists were much more likely to support the ERA than were Democrats among the public, and Republican activists were much more likely to oppose the ERA than Republicans among the public. Moreover, the closer activists came to a position of party leadership, the more likely they were to take the party position on the ERA (tables A7 and A8). This pattern of polarization among party leaders and activists holds for a wide range of partisan issues.[48] But a constitutional amendment needs an overwhelming majority, so once it becomes a partisan issue its chances of passing are minimal.

3 Rights versus Substance

Why did the states stop ratifying in 1973? Why did public support in the unratified states begin to decline? The campaign against the ERA succeeded because it shifted debate away from equal rights and focused it on the possibility that the ERA might bring substantive changes in women's roles and behavior. In this era, the American public, though changing in its outlook, still objected to any major changes in traditional roles of men and women. To the degree that the opposition could convince people that the ERA would bring about such changes, it eroded support for the ERA.

Much of the apparent support for the Equal Rights Amendment in surveys came from a sympathetic response to the concept of "rights," not from a commitment to actual changes in women's roles. In 1977, exactly half-way through the campaign for ratification, the National Opinion Research Center's General Social Survey (GSS) asked a representative sample of Americans both whether they favored or opposed the ERA (question V, table A1) and how they felt about women's roles. Among the people who claimed to have heard or read about the ERA, a strong majority—67 percent—favored it, while 25 percent were opposed, and 8 percent had no opinion. Yet, as table 1 shows, many in the same sample also had quite traditional[1] views about women's roles, especially in the economic sphere. Two-thirds of the sample thought that preschool children were likely to suffer if their mothers worked, 62 percent thought married women should not hold jobs when jobs were scarce and their husbands could support them, and 55 percent thought it more important for a woman to advance her

20

TABLE 1
Traditionalists support the ERA, 1977

	Percent of Sample Taking Traditional Position on Women's Roles[a]	Percent of Traditional Group Favoring ERA[a]
1. A pre-school child is likely to suffer if his or her mother works. (Agree)	66	68
2. If there is a limited number of jobs, do you approve or disapprove of a married woman holding a job in business or industry when her husband is able to support her? (Disapprove)	62	67
3. It is more important for a wife to help her husband's career than to have one herself. (Agree)	55	65
4. A working mother can establish just as warm and secure a relationship with her children as a mother who does not work. (Disagree)	49	64
5. Do you think it should be possible for a pregnant woman to obtain a *legal* abortion if she is not married and doesn't want to marry the man? (No)	48	68
6. Most men are better-suited emotionally for politics than are most women. (Agree)	42	64
7. Women should take care of running their homes and leave running the country up to men. (Agree)	37	55
8. If the husband in a family wants children, but the wife decides that she doesn't want children, is it alright for the wife to refuse to have children? (No)	32	68
9. If your party nominated a woman for President, would you vote for her if she were qualified? (No)	20	49

[a]"Don't know" responses excluded; N = ca. 1500.

husband's career than to have one of her own. The sample was about evenly divided regarding abortion on demand and women in politics. Only on questions about a wife's right to refuse to have children or voting for a woman Presidential candidate—questions that raise libertarian issues of personal privacy and equal opportunity—did a sizable majority take a "feminist" position. This pattern held for both men and women.

These traditional attitudes are not surprising. The surprise is that in almost every case a substantial majority of those who took traditional positions on women's roles *favored* the ERA (table 1, column 2). Among the majority who disapproved of a married woman working when jobs were limited, for example, 67 percent still favored the ERA. Even among the diehard 20 percent who could look a female interviewer in the eye and tell her that they would not vote for a qualified woman their party had nominated for President, 49 percent favored the ERA. This pattern had not changed appreciably by 1982.[2]

Pro-ERA activists found the character of ERA support among the public hard to understand. When I interviewed activists, I often showed them the findings in table 1 and asked if they could explain why a majority of the people who believed that "a woman's place is in the home" supported the ERA. The activists' most common response was some version of, "Jesus, that's incredible!" or "I don't know why they would support the ERA—the two don't seem to correspond!" or simply, in real bewilderment, "I don't know . . . I don't know." They assumed, as I had before I saw these numbers, that people who supported the ERA must have a real commitment to bringing about substantive changes in women's roles.[3] Yet the explanation for these figures is quite simple: Americans can favor abstract rights even when they oppose substantive change.

In the period 1972–1982, Americans were highly ambivalent regarding the appropriate role for women. The percentage of women in the paid work force had risen steadily after 1950 (fig. 1.A),[4] and attitudes toward women in business and government had changed correspondingly. More Americans have become willing to vote for a qualified woman for President if their party nominated her (fig. 1.B),[5] and more had come to approve of married women earning money in business or industry (fig. 1.C).[6] The women's movement that took shape in the late 1960s and legitimated itself in the 1970s also brought important changes in public attitudes toward women (fig. 1.D).[7] If we had more long-term data on attitudes toward women's roles, we would probably find that most attitudes followed the same pattern as willingness to vote for a woman for President: a gradual change after World War II, a dramatic change after the women's movement began to get national publicity in 1969, and some leveling off toward the end of the 1970s.

Figure 1 makes clear that when the Equal Rights Amendment went to the states for ratification in 1972, attitudes toward women were in the midst of rapid change. As a consequence, positions were not firmly held and much depended on the wording of a question. When a survey organization worded a question so as to stress freedom of choice, this greatly increased the proportion of "feminist" responses. Asked to agree or disagree with the statement, "There is no reason why women with young children shouldn't work outside the home if they choose to," 84 percent of the American public agreed in 1981. Superficially, this response seems to *favor* mothers of young children working. But given the statement, "A woman with young children should not work outside the home unless financially necessary"—a statement that did not stress free choice and provided a useful "unless" escape clause—76 percent of the public again agreed, thus taking almost the opposite position and seeming to come out *against* mothers of young children working.[8]

In the same way, when a survey worded a question so as to stress general principles rather than substantive role changes, it usually produced more egalitarian responses. In one 1980 survey, 62 percent of American men said they favored "an equal marriage of shared responsibility in which the husband and wife cooperate on work, homemaking and childraising."[9] But in the same year, 69 percent of American men said they disapproved of the changes in women's traditional roles that they had observed, primarily because "the husband has to spend more time on household chores he doesn't like."[10] Because people had acquired their new "egalitarian" attitudes recently and had not worked them into a stable set of rules to live by, egalitarian principles could coexist with traditional sexist expectations about how the world should run from day to day.

This tension between support for the principle and opposition to the practice helps explain how Harris generated its 1982 leap in support for the ERA. Survey questions that told people what the

A. *Female labor force as a percentage of the female population.*

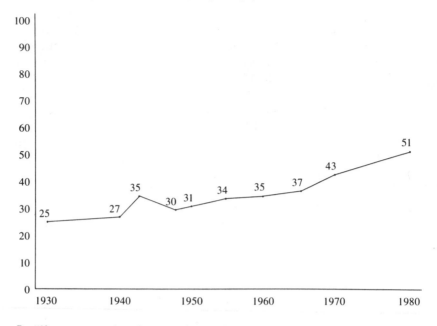

B. *"If your party nominated a woman for President, would you vote for her if she were qualified for the job?" Percentage responding "yes."*

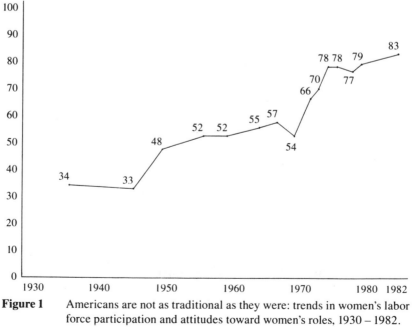

Figure 1   Americans are not as traditional as they were: trends in women's labor force participation and attitudes toward women's roles, 1930 – 1982. Sources: see footnotes 4 - 7, chapter 3.

C. *"Do you approve or disapprove of a married woman earning money in business or industry if she has a husband capable of supporting her?" Percentage responding "approve."*

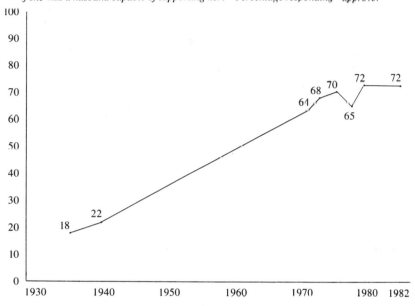

D. *"There has been much talk recently about changing women's status in society today. On the whole, do you favor or oppose most of the efforts to strengthen and change women's status in society today?" Percentage resonding "favor."*

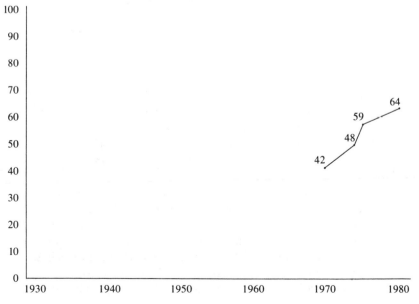

Amendment actually said—a statement of principle regarding equal rights—always produced greater approval than questions that simply identified the ERA as an Amendment to the Constitution or suggested possible consequences of its passage. This pattern was not confined to the Harris poll. Even in Mormon Utah, a bastion of anti-ERA sentiment, 58 percent endorsed the words of the ERA when these words were read and not identified with "the Equal Rights Amendment." But only 29 percent of the same sample approved of the Equal Rights Amendment as an actual constitutional amendment.[11] The same pattern appeared in Oklahoma.[12]

Americans have always favored "rights" in the abstract. The principle that government should not deny anyone "equal rights" commands widespread approval. But citizens who approve this principle are often conservative in practice. They support the principle of "equal rights" only insofar as they think it is compatible with the status quo. Focusing on the principle, by reading the extremely general words of the ERA, therefore produced much more support than asking people, either without a prelude or with "balanced" arguments on both sides, whether they wanted the Constitution of the United States to be amended.

Active supporters of the ERA presumably understood this dynamic, at least unconsciously, when they chose an "equal rights" amendment as a vehicle for bringing about substantive changes in men's and women's lives. Their implicit strategy was to get people to agree to the principle of equal rights, enshrine that principle in the Constitution, and then let the Supreme Court decide what this principle actually meant in practice.

The problem with this strategy is that very few Americans *want* the Supreme Court to tell them how to live on the basis of abstract principles, even when the principles themselves seem unexceptional. Few people derive their preferences deductively from general principles. Rather, they infer their principles from their particular preferences. People may approve of "democracy," for example, not because they espouse the principle of equal power to each citizen but because they like many things that they connect in some way with what we loosely call "democracy." Thus in the late 1950s from 95 to 98 percent of the public agreed that "democracy is the best form of government," but 54 percent believed at the same time that "if a communist were legally elected mayor of this city, the people should not allow him to take office," and 79 percent believed that "in a city referendum deciding on tax-supported undertakings, only tax payers should be allowed to vote."[13] This everyday pattern of "practical" thinking contributes to public distrust both of lawyers and of the Supreme Court, which the public often sees as taking principles to "unreasonable" lengths.

So it was with the ERA. The men and women of America approved the principle of equal rights only so long as it did not change much in practice. But ERA proponents had something more substantive in mind. They wanted real changes in the lives of both men and women. Admitting women to an all-male organization like the Boy Scouts, for instance, would be a "right" for women but would change the character of the male organization. A woman's "right" to take a combat job in the armed forces would change the military and, eventually, the way men and women acted toward one another in everyday life.

The tension between rights and substance was particularly strong from 1972 to 1982, because the Supreme Court had recently applied many principles enshrined in the Constitution of the United States in controversial ways. The cases legalizing pornography that began in 1957,[14] the decisions beginning in 1961 that set convicted criminals free if the police had not conformed to certain standards in arresting them,[15] the 1963 decision against school prayer,[16] the school busing decisions that began in 1969,[17] and the abortion decisions that began in 1973[18] had all evoked strong liberal support and strong conservative opposition. Their crucial feature, however, was that they reinforced the popular view that federal judges could and would use superficially innocuous principles to achieve substantive results that many conservative and middle-of-the-road citizens opposed. If "equal protection" could mean busing white children to black neighborhoods, if "due process" could bar punishing people who everyone agreed had committed serious crimes, and if the "penumbra" of the Bill of Rights gave women a right to abortions, one did not have to be a certifiable paranoid to suppose that guaranteeing men and women "equality of rights under the law" might turn out also to have substantive consequences that legislators who supported the Amendment had not anticipated and that many of would them have opposed.

Liberal scholars have, on occasion, worried that the Supreme Court would lose its legitimacy if it went too far in unpopular directions.[19] The Court, after all, has claimed only by custom jurisdiction in most of the matters it decides. Congress could, perfectly legally, strip the Court of most of its powers, or reduce or add to its members. But while public confidence in the Court has fallen sharply since the mid-1960s, it has fallen no more than has confidence in other institutions.[20] The Court's unpopular decisions have so far produced no significant congressional attempt to change the Court but only growing public sentiment for a constitutional convention, which might curb the Court in various ways. In the absence of such a convention, power has bred only more power. The more often the Court has made important and often unpopular decisions, the more it has come to seem, to each succeeding generation, that that is its job. Far from draining the Court's "pool of prestige" and making it vulnerable to curbs from Congress, the unpopular decisions have instead sanctified the Court as a keeper of the anti-majoritorian flame.

But unpopular Supreme Court decisions did take their toll on the ERA. Unlike other recent amendments to the Constitution, the ERA spelled out a broad statement of principle, in language much like that of the First, Fifth, or Fourteenth Amendments—those amendments on which the civil liberties of the nation largely rest. But many mainstream legislators had been burned too often by the Court's interpretation of the broad principles incorporated in those amendments. While it was not true, as opponents often claimed, that the ERA would give the Supreme Court a "blank check," it was true that the Supreme Court had used other seemingly unexceptional principles to generate highly unpopular substantive results. It seemed, then, that the ERA would give the Court another set of words to work with. By calling the ERA a "Pandora's Box" the opponents used imagery that captured the way many state legislators already felt about the First, Fifth, and Fourteenth Amendments. Given the relative ease with which a determined minority can block a constitutional amendment in America, the analogy was fatal.

4 The Amendment Process

The framers of the Constitution did not want their handiwork tampered with. Any amendment must win the votes of two-thirds of the members of both houses of Congress and be ratified by three-quarters of the states. As a consequence, an amendment that evokes strong opposition has little chance of passing. Once Phyllis Schlafly had organized the opposition to the ERA and begun to argue that the Amendment would lead to major substantive changes, the ERA became "controversial." No really controversial amendment has passed since Prohibition was repealed.

The Constitution has been amended five times since World War II. These amendments limited Presidents to two terms, allowed residents of the District of Columbia vote in Presidential elections, prohibited poll taxes in federal elections, regulated Presidential succession, and gave eighteen-year-olds the vote. While these amendments were not all wildly popular, none evoked strong, organized opposition. Establishing Presidential voting for the District of Columbia was widely perceived as a technical solution to a problem in constitutional engineering, and so far as I can discover no polls were conducted about it. Changing Presidential succession also was seen as a largely technical issue. Only a bare majority of the public had heard of the amendment at the time it passed, and many of these had no opinion about it.[1] Limiting Presidents to two terms caused some controversy within the federal and state legislatures, but little stir among the public. The Democrats, opposing the amendment largely because it seemed to be a posthumous attack on Franklin Roosevelt's four terms, explicitly argued that there was "no demand from the people" for it. One senator said he had received "no letter, no telegram, no telephone call, not one word from anyone, about such a constitutional amendment,"[2] and others entered in evidence their almost equally empty mailboxes. But surveys showed there was public support for limiting Presidential tenure: 59 percent of the public favored the change in 1947, the year the amendment won two-thirds of the vote in Congress.[3] When the Republicans gained more seats in the state legislatures in 1950 and 1951, three-quarters of the legislatures ratified the amendment.

The Twenty-fourth and Twenty-sixth Amendments provided somewhat closer parallels to the ERA. The Twenty-fourth Amendment enlarged citizen rights by prohibiting states from levying a poll tax on the act of voting, while the Twenty-sixth Amendment gave the vote to citizens between eighteen and twenty-one. Yet even these amendments did not cause enough public controversy for a major survey organization to consider it important enough to ask the public what it thought about them, although occasionally surveys did ask what the public thought about the policies that these two amendments sought to change. The amendment abolishing the poll tax, a fee for the privilege of voting, passed Congress in 1962 and was ratified in 1964. Neither the Gallup nor the Harris surveys asked the public its opinion on this issue during these two years. In 1941, 1948, and 1953, however, surveys had asked the public: "Some Southern states require every voter to pay a poll tax amounting to about a dollar a year before they can vote. Do you think these poll taxes should be abolished?" Of those queried, 63 percent wanted the tax abolished in 1941, 65 percent in 1948, and 71 percent in 1953.[4] This trajectory suggests that by the early 1960s, when the amendment came before the states, opposition to poll taxes was probably even more widespread.

Support for the eighteen-year-old vote was less strong. When first asked in 1939 about lowering the voting age to eighteen, only 17 percent of the American public favored the idea. This percentage rose to just above a majority during the Second World War, dropped again after the war, rose to between 58 and 63 percent after the Korean War, and appeared again at that level when the public was surveyed during the Vietnam War. In 1970, the year of the amendment's passage through Congress, public opinion ranged from 57 to 60 percent in favor of giving eighteen-year-olds the vote. (Unfortunately, surveys did not ask about the amendment itself.)[5]

The amendment was ratified by three-quarters of the states within a year.

These poll data, limited as they are, suggest that the percentage of the public supporting policies promoted by these successful amendments was probably no greater than the 43 to 74 percent who supported the ERA in various polls between 1970 and 1982 (table A1). But unlike the successful amendments, the ERA generated intense, tenacious, and politically organized opposition. No amendment that inspired such opposition has passed for over half a century.[6]

Recent constitutional history gives several examples of the power of intense veto groups to block an amendment. The Child Labor Amendment of 1924 presents an instructive, almost eerie, parallel with the ERA. This amendment was the product of the National Child Labor Committee (NCLC), one of the many organizations in the Progressive movement. In 1924, under pressure and persuasion from the NCLC, the House of Representatives (by a vote of 297 to 69) and the Senate (by a vote of 61 to 23) passed and sent to the states the following amendment:

> Section 1. The Congress shall have power to limit, regulate, and prohibit the labor of persons under 18 years of age.
>
> Section 2. The power of the several States is unimpaired by this article except that the operation of State laws shall be suspended to the extent necessary to give effect to legislation enacted by Congress.[7]

When the amendment went to the states, it met the vigorous opposition of a small but intense far-right group called the Sentinels of the Republic, and of a far-right newspaper, the *Woman Patriot*, founded by Mrs. Arthur Dodge, past leader of the National Association Opposed to Woman Suffrage. These two well-funded, though very small, organizations distributed "reams of propaganda" to stop the child labor amendment.[8] They were aided by a division within the working class itself, with some southern mill workers opposing the amendment. The Catholic church was divided, with the cardinals of New York and Boston and many leading bishops opposing the amendment as an attack on parental authority. The legal profession was divided, with the conservative American Bar Association president appointing a Special Commit-

tee to Oppose Ratification. Finally, the opposition had the backing
of employers in general and the National Association of Manufacturers in particular. The opposition was able to activate these allies
by stressing the issues of federal interference in the family and in
state government. Only twenty-eight of the forty-eight states
ratified the amendment. In 1937 the NCLC decided to abandon
efforts to ratify. Instead, it pushed for federal legislation regulating
child labor without any constitutional change, hoping that, with
increasing pressure from public opinion and a changing composition, the Supreme Court would not rule this legislation unconstitutional.[9] This strategy worked. Congress passed the Fair Labor
Standards Act in 1938, and in 1941 the Supreme Court, overruling
its earlier interpretations, declared the act constitutional.[10]

More recently, the School Prayer Amendment has also been
stymied by minority opposition. This amendment, introduced in
Congress in 1963, reads:

Section 1. Nothing in this Constitution shall be deemed to prohibit the
offering, reading from, or listening to prayers or biblical scriptures, if
participation therein is on a voluntary basis, in any governmental or
public school, institution or place.

Section 2. Nothing in this Constitution shall be deemed to prohibit
making reference to belief in, reliance upon, or invoking the aid of
God or a Supreme Being in any governmental or public document,
proceeding, activity, ceremony, school institution, or place, or upon
any coinage, currency, or obligation of the United States.

Section 3. Nothing in this article shall constitute an establishment of
religion.[11]

After the amendment was introduced in the House, Emanuel
Celler, chair of the House Judiciary Committee, refused to let it out
of committee, just as he did with the ERA. A discharge petition to
force the amendment out of committee got only 157 of the 218
signatures necessary to constitute a majority.[12] But if we turn to
public opinion, we see strong support for this amendment. A 1974
survey asked, "What are your views on the reading of the Lord's
Prayer or Bible verses in public schools? Do you think it should be
required in all public schools, not allowed in any public schools, or
that it should be up to each state or local community to decide?"

Only 8 percent supported the Supreme Court's ban on prayer and Bible reading in the public schools. The words "up to each to decide" apparently appeal to the laissez-faire streak in American public opinion, for 58 percent of the public answered that it should be up to the states and local communities to decide, while 31 percent thought that prayer should be required, and 3 percent had no opinion. The same survey asked another question worded less favorably to the amendment: "The United States Supreme Court has ruled that no state or local government may require the reading of the Lord's Prayer or Bible verses in public schools. What are your views on this—do you approve or disapprove of the court ruling?" In its answers to this question, 66 percent of the public disapproved of the Supreme Court ruling, with only 31 percent approving and 3 percent having no opinion. When the question is asked this way, the percentages disapproving of the Supreme Court ruling have declined slightly since 1974—to 62 percent in 1976, 64 percent in 1978, 60 percent in 1982, and 57 percent in 1983.[13] Yet when asked more directly, "Do you favor or oppose a constitutional amendment to allow daily prayers to be recited in school classrooms?" 69 percent of the public in 1982 said it favored such an amendment, with 28 percent opposing and 3 percent not sure.[14] Thus in 1982 there was even greater public support for the school prayer amendment than for the ERA. In spite of this potentially strong support from the public, however, the school prayer amendment had not even reached the point of being sent to the states. It failed because it met intense resistance among the minority opposing it. As a result, legislators were anxious to avoid voting either way on an issue bound to alienate some of their constituents, and they tacitly agreed to let the amendment die.

It is unclear whether the minority opposed to the school prayer amendment could organize a resistance comparable to that of Phyllis Schlafly and STOP-ERA either in Congress or in the states if that amendment were ever to get out of committee. Once put in the position of having to declare themselves, many representatives and senators would have to vote for such an amendment, regardless of their private reservations, just the way some voted for the ERA because they thought explaining their opposition to their constituents would be too difficult.

The proposed "balanced budget" amendment also enjoys strong popular support but has never gotten out of committee.[15]

Other more technical amendments, like state representation for the District of Columbia and Presidential election by popular vote, have majorities in the opinion polls as well.[16] However, the proposed constitutional amendment to ban legalized abortion does not command majority support in opinion polls.[17] It has remained a live issue only because its advocates feel so passionately about it, while many opponents are ambivalent. If the anti-abortion movement were to produce an amendment with greater mainstream appeal, perhaps decentralizing control to the states, the balance of popular opinion might change, and such an amendment might get through Congress. In this case pro-choice forces would be in much the same position as STOP-ERA. By organizing intense opposition at the state level, they well might be able to prevent the amendment from attracting a majority of state legislators in the thirteen most liberal states.

For resistance to an amendment to be successful, it helps if the resistance is concentrated in a relatively small number of states—so long as that number exceeds one quarter of the states in the union. If the minority opposing an amendment were spread evenly over all the states, it could not produce a majority against ratification in any one of them. Opposition to the ERA had, to some extent, this advantage of geographical concentration. It centered in the fundamentalist South, including southern Illinois, and in the Mormon states of Utah and Nevada, where the Mormon church actively fought the ERA. Opposition was strongest in the poorest states, in those with a conservative, populist tradition, and in those that have traditionally hesitated to adopt any kind of innovation.[18] These were the states in which opposition forces had the greatest advantage in persuading conservative legislators that ratifying the ERA did not amount simply to endorsing the principle of equality, but would actually change the way women and men acted toward one another in the United States.

The framers of the Constitution meant to give intense, sizable minorities a near veto on constitutional amendments, and they succeeded. This raises a democratic paradox. We sometimes think of the rights-oriented amendments to the Constitution as having the function of protecting politically disadvantaged groups from the power of the majority. Yet the Constitution requires much more than a majority to pass these amendments. How, politically, can one persuade not only a majority but a supermajority to thwart its own will, or the will of future majorities? The only way to get the public to pass what amounts to a self-denying ordinance is to stress the principle involved in an amendment rather than the specific substantive ways it would prevent the majority from doing what it wants to do. Proponents almost managed to have the ERA ratified by using this strategy. But once debate shifted to its substantive effects, it was doomed.

5 59 Cents

The ERA was remarkably ill-suited to bring about major changes in anyone's life, at least in the near future. Even in 1972 the ERA would have had relatively little immediate substantive impact on the lives of either American women or American men, and it would have had almost no effect on the gap between women's and men's wages.

The early literature and themes of the pro-ERA effort hardly mentioned the impact of the ERA on the gap between women's and men's wages. Rather, the early effort focused on the general principle of equality. In the 1975 referendum campaign for a State of New York ERA, the ERA Coalition issued red, white and blue buttons with the slogan, "All *people* are created equal." According to the Coalition's director, however, the slogan "didn't work very well. Our natural constituency [feminists] wasn't turned on by it, and the average person on the street didn't understand what we were getting at."[1] By the late 1970s the central theme had become more concrete—women's wages. Asked what was the most important argument for the ERA, officials of the National Organization for Women immediately responded with some version of "Equal pay for equal work. That's the strongest argument for ratifying."[2] Women lobbying for the ERA in state capitols wore buttons with the sole message: "59¢." This was meant to remind legislators that American women who work full-time outside the home still typically earned only 59 cents for every dollar men earn—a ratio that has changed little since the federal government first began publishing such statistics in the 1950s.[3] It was also supposed to suggest that the ERA would help narrow the wage difference between men

36

and women. NOW's most widely distributed pamphlet in the last years of the campaign made this argument explicit. It began, "The Equal Rights Amendment is much more than a symbol. It is a bread-and-butter issue. It means dollars and cents for women."[4] When STOP ERA women distributed home-baked bread to state legislators, pro-ERA women countered by handing out butter, to show that ERA was a "bread-and-butter" issue.

Yet anyone who read the Amendment carefully could see what the problem was with regard to women's job prospects or pay. The ERA would have kept the United States or any state from legally denying or abridging "equality of rights *under the law*" (my emphasis). The *law* however, was already almost gender blind in its treatment of workers in 1972. In order to help women workers, the ERA would have had to do more than just make the law gender blind. It would have had to forbid discrimination by *private* organizations and individuals. This it did not do.

Furthermore, even before Congress approved the ERA in 1972, it had passed other legislation that did not only what the ERA would have done for women's wages but far more. Until the 1960s, for example, a number of states had "protective" legislation instituting higher minimum wages for women. Such legislation obviously made employers less likely to hire women for certain jobs. By 1972, when Congress passed the ERA, the U.S. Department of Labor had already interpreted the Equal Pay Act of 1963 as invalidating laws of this kind and held that if such laws remained on the books they must be extended to male as well as female employees.[5]

A number of states also traditionally had laws limiting the number of hours employers could require women to work, the weights employers could require women to lift, and so forth—laws that, like a higher minimum wage, made employers less likely to hire women. Some states even had laws completely barring women from certain occupations, such a coal mining and bartending. By 1972 the Equal Employment Opportunity Commission (EEOC) had interpreted Title VII of the Civil Rights Act of 1964 as making such legislation unenforceable,[6] and the federal courts had upheld this interpretation.[7] While such laws remained on the books in a few states, they had only the force of tradition, with no legal sanction behind them. This would have remained true under an ERA.

An ERA would, of course, have made it harder for any future Congress to reinstate "protective" legislation. If, for example,

Congress were to repeal the Equal Pay Act and Title VII, an ERA would have ensured that "protective" legislation remained unenforceable. This would have been a useful function, although the likelihood that even a conservative Congress would repeal the Equal Pay Act or Title VII seems low. But the key point is that not even the Equal Pay Act and Title VII together have had much effect on "59 cents."[8] Thus it is hard to see how the ERA, which was far less sweeping than these two laws, could have done much in the short run for women's earnings.

The Equal Pay Act and Title VII have had relatively little impact on the gap between women's and men's wages for several reasons. First, discrimination, though pervasive, is usually difficult to prove with hard evidence in a court of law. Even the most blatant cases take considerable legal, statistical, and investigational talent. The ERA would not have changed this situation.

Second, explicit discrimination in pay is not as important in lowering women's earnings as is occupational segregation, by which women are channeled into "women's jobs." While a constitutional statement that Americans believed in equality for women might have had some effect on women's occupational channeling, it is hard to believe this effect would have been significant.

Finally, social and cultural traditions keep women's pay low. For example, although almost all couples assume they will have children, most men and women also assume that the mother will take much more responsibility for raising these children than will the father. Accordingly, most women expect either to interrupt their careers or to take jobs that make minimal demands when their children are young. This is one source of occupational segregation. The demands of single-sex child care seem to play some role in explaining women's low pay: women who have worked uninterruptedly since leaving school earn 75 percent of what similar men earn.[9]

Even when women are as able to commit themselves to their careers as men, they face other handicaps that equal pay legislation cannot touch. As we have seen, in this period 20 percent of the population said it would not vote for a woman for President, and the percentages were similar for many lower-level elected offices. We do not have comparable data on the percentage of executives who would oppose putting a woman in a position of authority, but in the 1960s and 1970s female executives aroused even more opposition than female presidents.[10] This opposition arises when the woman in question is presumed acceptable on all other grounds. In practice, women are usually seen as less competent than men even when they perform identically. In academic settings, for example, readers are less likely to believe that an article is "competent," "valuable," "profound," "effectively written," and "persuasive" if it is written by "Joan McKay" rather than by "John McKay."[11] Many women still feel that being "feminine" involves deferring to men, and even those who consciously reject this view are still likely to be affected by it. Most men are brought up to expect such deference, at least unconsciously, and see women who refuse to provide it as "aggressive." As a result, some women find it easier not to compete with men at work, while others find their competitiveness punished. Federal pressure on private firms to engage in affirmative action is intended to help remove these forms of discrimination, and the increasing number of women in positions of authority suggests that such pressure has had an effect, even though it has not altered the ratio of female to male wages. But whereas Title VII of the Civil Rights Act of 1964 provides the government with authority for monitoring private employers' behavior, the ERA, standing alone, would not have applied to most private employers. It would have applied only to the actions of governments and to those private activities that involve "state action." As a specific guarantee against discrimination at work, therefore, the ERA, without further statutory implementation, was far weaker than Title VII.

Title VII is subject to three important limitations, but the ERA would not have dealt effectively with any of them. First, Title VII exempts employers of fewer than fifteen people. But since the ERA would only have covered government, or government-related, employment, not private employment, and since few governments or government-related industries employ fewer than fifteen people, the ERA would not have done much about this limitation in private industry.

Second, Title VII does not cover those staff members of elected officials who serve at the pleasure of their boss rather than having civil service protection. The President, for example, is under no legal obligation to consider women (or blacks) for the Cabinet or sub-Cabinet positions, and the same is true of governors. But while these jobs are of considerable symbolic importance, they do not involve a great number of people. In any event women have done at least as well in these jobs as in "covered" employment, precisely because these jobs *are* so visible.

A third limitation of Title VII is that it does not cover jobs for which an applicant's sex is a "bona fide occupational qualification" (BFOQ). Using this standard, states have continued to require male guards in male prisons, for example, and the Supreme Court has upheld this practice as legitimate.[12] The ERA would not have required the Court to act differently on this issue from the way it does now, even in the cases involving government employees. Nor would it have required the Court to reverse the burden of proof in Title VII cases, as many activists believed it might.[13]

As a practical matter, then, it is hard to see how passing an ERA would have helped American women improve their pay or promotion opportunities in the short run. Title VII covers far more jobs than the ERA would have, and it imposes more stringent requirements on employers. Since Title VII has not been able to change the ratio of female to male earnings, it is hard to see how the ERA, which would have covered only a handful of jobs not covered by Title VII, could have done so. Nor would an ERA have protected most working women if Congress or the EEOC decided to weaken Title VII, since it would only have covered women who worked for the government. It is conceivable that some future Supreme Court might hold that the ERA required Congress and the President to provide adequate funds for enforcing statutes like Title VII, but even this seems quite unlikely.

At some future date the Supreme Court might also broaden its interpretation of what constitutes "state action," extending the ERA's guarantees to a significant part of the private sector.[14] Liberal and radical lawyers have repeatedly urged the Court to treat private organizations that carry out a governmental purpose as being subject to the same restrictions as the government itself. Thus, it is conceivable that the Court might at some point have decided that guarantees available to government workers under the ERA also covered those who worked for government contractors. But in the period from 1972 to 1982, the Supreme Court acted to narrow rather than to broaden the definition of state action.[15] It is hard to imagine the Court extending the definition of state action to cover more of the private sector if the overall political climate were becoming more conservative, as one must assume it would be for Congress to repeal or significantly weaken Title VII. In foreseeable circumstances, therefore, an ERA would not provide much of a "safety net" when Title VII came under attack.

The most likely place in which the Court might have extended the ERA's guarantees from the public to the private sector was in heavily regulated realms like insurance. The Supreme Court has already held under Title VII that gender-based classifications in pensions are discriminatory.[16] Were the Court to consider insurance rates, which are extensively regulated by the states, to be sufficiently suffused with state action to come under the ERA, the industry would no longer be able to set separate rates for men and women in automobile insurance, life insurance, and annuities not related to employment. But because women generally pay less than men for auto and life insurance, unisex rates in these areas would not be to their advantage, as they are in the case of pensions.[17]

Another possible benefit of the ERA, to which feminists have recently devoted considerable attention, would have been to provide a constitutional basis for requiring governments to pay men and women equally if they were engaged in occupations of "comparable worth." Rather than simply emulating the private sector in setting wages for "men's occupations" higher than wages for "women's occupations," governments under an ERA, in this view, would have to establish some independent criteria for setting wages, based on skill, effort, responsibility, and working conditions.

For the ERA to have played a dispositive role in legal battles over comparable worth, however, one of two conditions would have had to be met. One possibility would be for the Supreme Court to have concluded that Congress intended the ERA to mandate equal pay for male and female government employees engaged in equally valuable activities. Since there is no evidence that Congress had this intention, it seems unlikely that the Court would have concluded that it had a Congressional mandate for imposing the doctrine of comparable worth on federal, state, and local governments.

Alternatively, the Supreme Court might have concluded that the doctrine of comparable worth, while not necessarily so intended by Congress, was in some sense implicit in the ERA and was sound public policy. But the notion that the ERA would require governments to establish comparable pay scales for male and female occupations of comparable worth rests on the larger notion that the

ERA would require governments to scrutinize their actions not just for discriminatory intent but for discriminatory results.[18] In the period from 1972 to 1982, the Supreme Court moved away from a results-oriented interpretation of the Fourteenth Amendment's equal protection clause.[19] In the same period, the Court also moved away from results-oriented interpretations of existing federal prohibitions in other areas. For example, during the early 1970s, when dealing with discrimination in federally funded programs, the Court appeared to hold that Title VI of the 1964 Civil Rights Act required the courts to review the impact of a given practice, not just the intent of the practitioners. By 1982, the Court had backed away from this position, interpreting Title VI as prohibiting primarily those practices and policies that had discriminatory intent.[20] Given this history in several areas of statutory and constitutional interpretation, it is hard to believe that the Court would soon move in exactly the opposite direction when interpreting the ERA. If, on its own initiative, the Court did move toward an "impact" analysis of the ERA, it would presumably also move this way on Title VII, which affects many more employees. The ERA itself would not require the Court to make any move toward comparable worth.

In the long run, of course, the Supreme Court might begin to take a more expansive view of all legislation that prohibits discrimination, especially if the mood of the country became more hostile to discriminatory outcomes. But the Court would not need the authority of an ERA to justify such a change in policy. It could simply invoke Title VII or the Equal Pay Act, either of which would have a much more sweeping impact, since both cover private as well as public employment.

The most important way the ERA would have helped women in the labor force was as a public statement of moral commitment. Legislators would surely have interpreted passage of the ERA as implying strong public support for equality between the sexes. They might therefore have been more reluctant to oppose legislation that feminists supported, including legislation dealing with the problems of women in the paid labor force. Judges probably also would have taken ratification as a mandate for stronger action in discrimination suits, where actual intent to discriminate is usually hard to prove and much depends on judicial interpretation of the facts. Most crucially, ratification would probably have encouraged judges to interpret Title VII, the Equal Pay Act, and the equal protection and due process clauses of the Constitution in ways that would benefit women. Thus in the long run and indirectly, through the encouragement of its general mandate, the presence of the ERA in the Constitution might have helped bring about dramatic changes, like comparable worth, that could have had a significant effect on 59 cents.

One of the most important indirect effects might have been the effect on the public. The Constitution has an important symbolic place in American life. If women knew that the Constitution guaranteed them equal rights, they would probably be more inclined to demand such rights. A woman who encounters discrimination at work may well feel more entitled to complain if she thinks she has the Constitution on her side. The fact that the Constitution would not, in fact, protect her rights as a private employee is, from this perspective, quite irrelevant. The situation is analogous to that of private employees who are willing to fight for the right to say things their employer doesn't want said, because they believe that "the Constitution guarantees free speech, doesn't it?" The fact that the Constitution doesn't guarantee a job to those who exercise their right to free speech may make the First Amendment legally irrelevant in such cases, but it does not make it psychologically irrelevant. To the degree that having an ERA in the Constitution would remind Americans that equality for women ought to be an important goal in their everyday lives, and to the degree that increased commitment to this value would result in changed behavior on practical issues like who takes care of children, the ERA might have reached beyond the law to the social and economic patterns that produced most of the 59-cents gap.

Nonetheless, nobody who looked carefully at the question concluded that passing the ERA would have a significant direct impact on women's pay or job opportunities, at least in the short run. No feminist lawyer believed the ERA would have a significant impact on laws governing employment, and neither did any feminist economist. Publications that discussed the issue carefully were almost unanimous in their conclusion that the impact would be negligible.[21]

In these circumstances, we must ask why ERA supporters, and especially those associated with NOW, made the benefits of the ERA for women's wages their main argument for passing the Amendment. One reason is that, unlike most other alleged benefits of the ERA, "equal pay for equal work" was an almost universally accepted slogan, as unassailable as home and motherhood. Even in 1945, 76 percent of the public believed that women should receive the same rate of pay as men for the same work.[22] By 1954 the percentage favoring equality in pay was 87 percent,[23] and it had undoubtedly risen even higher by 1972.[24] "Equal pay for equal work" was safe ground, and when juxtaposed to the persistent inequality between men's and women's wages, it provided an obvious focus for ERA advocacy.

Most important, however, the wish was mother to the fact. Most ERA activists worked in the paid labor force, had done so recently, or expected to do so soon. Knowing that the ERA would generally strengthen women's constitutional position, the activists expected to see the greatest payoff in the workplace, where they themselves had often experienced discrimination. As a political judgment, NOW's decision to focus on "59 cents" may well have been correct. But it inevitably forced proponents of the ERA to keep their arguments vague, since the short-term benefits of the ERA for working women were almost exclusively symbolic, and the long-term benefits were both hypothetical and uncertain.

6 The Court Catches Up[1]

LCP: . . . can you explain why, when the polls
       consistently show majority support for the
       ERA, it still hasn't translated into a victory?
DY: I think what it really boils down to is a lack
       of credibility that the ERA would mean any-
       thing to the average woman's life.
       . . . People think: if it isn't going to mean
       that much, why knock yourself out?
LCP: Are you saying that we were unsuccessful at
       explaining the *practical* effects of constitu-
       tional protection?
DY: There was a lack of credibility.

       —*Letty Cottin Pogrebin, Interview
       with Daniel Yankelovitch, May 1982*[2]

By the late 1970s ERA activists had a real problem
explaining how the ERA would benefit women, at least in the short
run. This had not always been true. In 1970, when the ERA first
reached the floor of Congress, a significant number of laws and
official practices still denied women "equality of rights under the
law." A few laws and official practices also denied men rights
available to women. Furthermore, while the Supreme Court had
used the Fourteenth Amendment to strike down statutes that denied individuals equal rights because of their race, national origin,
or citizenship, it had refused to extend this logic to laws that
discriminated on the basis of sex. Thus, when proponents argued

that the United States needed an ERA to eliminate laws that discriminated against women, they were clearly right.

But the political changes that led Congress to pass the ERA inevitably affected the Supreme Court as well. In 1971 the Court began to look more closely at laws that treated men and women differently. In 1973 the *Frontiero* decision[3] came close to designating gender a "suspect" classification, analogous to race. Finally, in 1976, the *Craig* decision[4] established a new set of standards for reviewing laws that treated men and women differently. As we shall see, these standards, based on the Fourteenth Amendment's "equal protection" clause, were not as demanding as the standards the Court would probably have applied if the ERA had passed, but the differences were both subtle and unpredictable. *Frontiero* and *Craig* made most of the statutes and official practices that the ERA would have eliminated in 1972 presumptively unconstitutional even in the absence of an ERA. This development meant that when opponents said that the ERA was unnecessary it was much more difficult to refute their arguments than it had been earlier.

The change brought about by these cases had important, if little noticed, political consequences. The new standard of scrutiny made it extremely likely that the Court would strike down any statute or official practice that most Americans regarded as discriminating against women. The one arguable exception was that the Court let stand a Massachusetts law giving veterans absolute preference for most state jobs, even though this had the practical effect of excluding women from many of these jobs. But even the ERA might not have invalidated this law, because it contained no direct reference to gender. The only important statute that explicitly distinguished between men and women and survived under the post-1976 standard of scrutiny was one that most Americans favored—the all-male draft. As a result, when opponents of the ERA challenged its supporters to point to specific benefits that would result if it passed, supporters either had to equivocate or else had to point to changes that were quite unpopular. This situation may help explain why no state ratified the ERA after January 1977.

It is hard to tell how important the Supreme Court's expanded reading of the Fourteenth Amendment was in reducing enthusiasm for the ERA in the state legislatures. By 1980, when I did my interviewing, many legislators, both for and against the ERA, answered my question on its impact by saying that they thought the

ERA would have very little impact. This suggests that the Court's evolution had significantly affected the way they thought about the ERA. Yet its effect on their thinking seems to have rested largely on hearsay rather than familiarity with the legal cases. Only one of the legislators I talked with specifically mentioned the Supreme Court's evolution between 1972 and 1980. And in the Illinois legislative debates on the ERA, no one brought up the Court's evolution until 1980. In that year one legislator referred briefly to the way "the Supreme Court and the federal courts have more and more gone to the Fourteenth Amendment to give equal protection of the law,"[5] and another mentioned the Fourteenth Amendment "being used increasingly to cover cases of sex discrimination."[6] One of these legislators said he had changed his vote and now opposed the ERA because he had come to believe there was now no need for it,[7] but I do not know how accurately he reported his motives, much less whether others were similarly influenced.

More important than its direct effect on the legislators, I believe, was the indirect effect that the Court's evolution had in shaping the debate on the ERA. The fact that the ERA would have had no significant immediate tangible impact on most women's lives dramatically influenced the ways that both pro- and antiforces thought about and argued for the ERA. First, the dearth of tangible effects helped focus attention on the question of women in combat, since this was almost the only concrete change both advocates and opponents agreed the ERA would bring. (As we will see, both sides were probably wrong, but that is another story.) Second, the dearth of tangible benefits encouraged advocates to focus on the "symbolic" and "long-term" effects of the ERA. Focusing on such issues strengthened the hand of opponents, who argued that the ERA was a "blank check for the Supreme Court." Third, and most important for this analysis, the dearth of immediate benefits made feminists reluctant to compromise on issues of principle, like the ERA's implications for women's role in the military. People seldom compromise their principles, after all, unless they think they will get something tangible in return.

The remainder of this chapter begins by documenting how the Supreme Court's changing interpretation of the Fourteenth Amendment left little room for the ERA to affect decisions regarding laws that explicitly distinguish between men and women. It then turns to the possible effects of the ERA on the Court's interpreta-

tion of laws and practices that are neutral on their face but work to
women's disadvantage in practice, where the ERA would not have
had much effect in the short run but might someday have proven
very important. Readers who are willing to accept my claims about
these legal matters on faith may want to turn directly to Chapter 7.

Laws That Treat Men and Women Differently

The Fourteenth Amendment says that no state "shall deny to any
person within its jurisdiction the equal protection of the laws." But
laws must, by their very nature, treat people unequally. The law
must distinguish thieves from honest citizens, those who need
medical treatment from those who do not, children from adults, and
so on. The question, therefore, is *which* persons the law must treat
equally, and which persons the law can legitimately distinguish. The
Fourteenth Amendment is silent on this point.

Until World War II the Supreme Court held that laws violated
the equal protection clause only if they were "arbitrary" and bore
"no fair and substantial relation" to a legitimate governmental
interest.[8] Since legislatures are not usually made up of complete
lunatics, almost any law has *some* relation to *some* legitimate governmental interest. For example, in 1948 the Court held constitutional a law prohibiting all women except wives and daughters of
bar owners from tending bar, on the grounds that this distinction
was rationally related to the state's legitimate interest in protecting
women from the "moral and social problems" that might arise from
bar tending.[9]

But as early as 1944 the Court began to evolve a doctrine that
required a government to show "pressing public necessity" when
the law prescribed different treatment for certain categories of
people rather than just showing some "rational relation" between
the law and a governmental interest. When the Court upheld in-
terning Japanese-Americans during World War II, it suggested that
a stricter standard of judicial review might be required for some
classifications, like classifications based on race:

> All legal restrictions which curtail the civil rights of a single racial
> group are immediately suspect. That is not to say that all such restric-
> tions are unconstitutional. It is to say that courts must subject them to

the most rigid scrutiny. Pressing public necessity may sometimes justify the existence of such restrictions; racial antagonism never can.[10]

Since the Court went on to conclude that "pressing public
necessity" had, in fact, justified putting Americans of Japanese
descent in concentration camps, this argument did not set an important legal precedent. But in 1964 the Court again asserted that laws
involving racial distinctions were "constitutionally suspect" and
went on to hold the relevant law unconstitutional, stating that a law

> which trenches upon the constitutionally protected freedom from
> invidious official discrimination based upon race . . . bears a heavy
> burden of justification . . . and will be upheld only if it is necessary,
> and not merely rationally related, to the accomplishment of a permissi-
> ble state policy.[11]

Later, the Court would formalize as "suspect classifications"
subject to "strict scrutiny" all classifications based on national
origin and foreign birth as well as race.[12] The result was to create an
extremely strong presumption that laws or official practices that
distinguished persons on the basis of race, national origin, or foreign birth were unconstitutional. The Court did not, however,
include gender among its "suspect classifications."

In 1971, while the Senate was still debating the ERA, the Court
for the first time struck down a law that treated men and women
differently. The offending statute had required probate courts to
appoint the father rather than the mother as executor of a dead
child's estate when both were equally qualified on other grounds. In
Reed v. Reed, the Court concluded that while the state's desire to
simplify the choice of estate administrators was "not without some
legitimacy," requiring the Court always to choose the father over
the mother did not have "a fair and substantial relation to the object
of the legislation."[13] While the justices appeared to be using the
traditional "rational basis" test to reach this conclusion, most
observers agreed that it was applying the test more stringently than
it would have done if the law had used some basis other than sex
(like age) to choose estate administrators.[14] While the Court no-
where suggested that sex was a "suspect" classification, it seemed to
be treating it as "somewhat suspect" in practice.

After 1971 the Supreme Court quickly evolved an interpretation of the equal protection clause that made most laws that distinguish men from women unconstitutional. This development was
codified in 1976 in *Craig v. Boren,* when the Court created what
became known as an "intermediate" test for constitutionality in
sex-discrimination cases—a test harder for a state to meet than the
simple "rational basis" test, but easier than the "strict scrutiny" test
used with suspect classifications. In *Craig* the Court decided that
states could classify individuals on the basis of sex only when it
could show that the classification had a "substantial" relationship
(more than a simple "rational" relationship but less than the
"necessary" relationship required for suspect classifications) to an
"important" governmental objective (more than a "legitimate"
governmental objective but less than the "compelling" objective
required for suspect classifications).[15]

The ERA, by contrast, would almost certainly have made sex at
least a "suspect" classification. Indeed, Supreme Court Justices
Powell, Burger, and Blackmun assumed in 1973 that in deciding on
the ERA the state legislatures were deciding whether or not to
make sex a suspect classification.[16] Because an "intermediate" test
is at least in theory weaker than a "suspect" classification test, it
seems likely that the Court will hold at least *some* laws constitutional under the intermediate test that it would not have upheld
under the ERA. The only example since *Craig* of the Court uphold-
ing a law or practice that explicitly distinguished between men and
women and seemed to favor men is its 1977 decision allowing
Philadelphia's Central High School to exclude women.[17] In this
case, an evenly divided court let stand a lower court decision—a
procedure that sets no precedent. All the other statutes that distinguished between men and women and survived the intermediate
test appeared on their face to discriminate against men. The most
important such statute was the all-male draft.[18] The others dealt
with matters that would have little immediate practical impact on
the lives of most American women, like restricting the crime of
statutory rape to men,[19] denying the fathers of illegitimate children
the same legal standing regarding their children as that of illegitimate mothers,[20] and temporarily instituting certain gender-based
provisions in the Social Security law in order to protect legitimate
expectations.[21] After 1976 these were the kinds of cases ERA pro-

ponents had to point to in order to argue that the ERA would have some direct effect on laws and governmental practices that distinguished between men and women.[22]

Barbara Brown, Thomas Emerson, Gail Falk, and Ann Freedman, authors of an oft-cited 1971 *Yale Law Journal* article on the ERA (hereinafter called simply the "Yale article"), argued that the ERA would have done more than make sex a "suspect" classification. In their interpretation, the ERA would have made sex a "prohibited" classification. They singled out, however, two exceptions: laws protecting the right to privacy and laws involving physical characteristics unique to one sex. With these exceptions, the ERA as they saw it would make unconstitutional any law, public policy, or governmental practice that distinguished in any way between men and women.[23]

Looking at the way courts actually act, however, it seems unlikely that the Supreme Court would have interpreted the ERA in this way.[24] First, three justices went on record in 1973 as believing that the ERA would have made sex a suspect classification. Second, little in the legislative history suggests that Congress intended to make sex a prohibited classification. While sponsors of the ERA in the House and Senate sent the Yale article to their colleagues, they stopped citing that article as soon as they realized its implications for the military (see Chapter 7). Statements by the floor leaders in the House and Senate in the crucial 1971 and 1972 debates are ambiguous. The Senate Judiciary Committee's Majority Report, which takes no clear position on the issue, also produced an analysis somewhat different from that of the Yale group.[25] State legislators did not interpret the ERA as making sex a "prohibited" classification. Virtually nothing in the Illinois legislative debates, for example, suggests that state legislators who backed the ERA thought it would make sex a prohibited classification.[26]

Finally, conscious of the problems of unintended consequences, most Supreme Court justices tend to proceed slowly when they can. Nothing in the language of the ERA required them to interpret it as making sex a "prohibited" classification. Treating sex merely as a "suspect" classification would have left them free to strike down any statute involving sex discrimination that did not in their view have a compelling justification, while leaving them free to uphold any statute that they thought did have compelling justification. To have deliberately tied their own hands by instead calling sex a "prohibited" classification would have been atypical judicial behavior.

If the justices were to have taken the unlikely step of viewing gender as a "prohibited" classification under the ERA, that step would have rendered more laws unconstitutional than if they had interpreted the ERA as simply making gender a suspect classification.[27] However, while this might have had a great impact on certain symbolic distinctions in the law, even this radical interpretation would not have had a major effect on most women's everyday lives.

Regardless of whether the Supreme Court would have interpreted the ERA as making sex a "suspect" or a "prohibited" classification, or would have devised some other interpretation, there is no doubt that the ERA would have strengthened the standard of scrutiny applied to statutes that treated men and women differently. The legislative history of the Amendment would, for example, almost certainly have led the Supreme Court to interpret the ERA as requiring Congress to draft women on the same basis as men. Without the ERA, the Court in 1980 upheld Congress's right to require only men to register for the draft.[28] The ERA probably also would have led the Court to declare some other laws unconstitutional that it has (and will) let stand under the "intermediate" principle. But how many laws fall into this "in-between" category is a matter of speculation.[29] All we can say for sure is that while there would probably have been some effect, the effect would have been far smaller in 1982 than in 1972.

Laws That Are "Neutral on Their Face"

When the ERA was debated in the Senate in 1972, its advocates characterized it as a device for eliminating laws and official practices that drew formal distinctions between individuals on basis of sex.[30] Proponents said very little about laws that drew no legal distinction between men and women but operated in practice so as to put one sex at a disadvantage relative to the other.[31] Such laws are both more numerous and far more onerous than those that draw formal distinctions between the sexes. If the ERA had been used to invalidate these laws, it could have had a major effect.

The present Social Security system, for example, does not value a wife's contribution to a marriage as highly as her husband's, if the wife is a homemaker. Social Security provides disability and retirement benefits both to those who contributed to the system while they were working and to their spouses. The benefits available to nonworking spouses are, however, less comprehensive than the benefits available to former workers. Since nonworking spouses are typically women, while working spouses are typically men, husbands end up with more benefits than their wives. Congress has ordered the Social Security Administration to study the possibility of eliminating this kind of discrimination against homemakers by crediting half of a couple's total earnings to each spouse, regardless of who earned the money, but there is no assurance that Congress will actually decide to do this.

Similarly, as we saw in Chapter 5, governmental pay practices that "neutrally" mirror market rates produce pay scales for different kinds of jobs that work to the disadvantage of women, who are disproportionately clustered in the poorly paid jobs. If the Court were to have used the ERA to invalidate apparently neutral governmental practices like this, on the grounds that they had a discriminatory impact on women, its effect could have been substantial.

Such possible consequences of the ERA clearly loomed large in the minds of its conservative opponents. They feared that the Supreme Court would use the ERA in a multitude of unforeseeable ways, just as it has used the Fourteenth Amendment in ways no one foresaw when that amendment was being debated in the 1860s. The Supreme Court's decisions since the early 1960s had made many legislators and members of the public wary of the way the Court might interpret the ERA.

The ERA's legislative proponents were silent on this issue in 1972, presumably because they thought raising this possibility would arouse more opposition than support. But after the *Frontiero* and *Craig* decisions, the case for the ERA, like the case against it, rested largely on its potential effect on laws that were "neutral on their face," since laws that explicitly distinguished men from women were for the most part unconstitutional even without the ERA. Unless the ERA affected the constitutionality of laws that were neutral on their face, its importance was almost exclusively symbolic.[32]

Prior to 1976 the Supreme Court had used the equal protection

clause of the Fourteenth Amendment to strike down several statutes that were neutral on their face but hurt blacks more than
whites. Most lawyers assumed that if the ERA passed the Court
would apply the same principles when interpreting the ERA that it
applied when interpreting the Fourteenth Amendment's implicit
guarantees for blacks and other "protected" groups. Until 1976,
therefore, it seemed reasonable to assume that the Court might use
the ERA to strike down statutes that were neutral on their face but
bore more heavily on women than on men. In 1976, however, the
Court decided in *Washington v. Davis*[33] that when a law was neutral
on its face it violated the Fourteenth Amendment only if it could be
shown to have had discriminatory intent. The mere fact of a discriminatory result was not sufficient to make a law violate the equal
protection clause. This ruling made it far less likely that the Court
would strike down laws that simply worked in practice to women's
disadvantage.

The critical question posed by *Washington v. Davis* is how the
Court will interpret "intent." During the late 1970s, the Burger
Court construed intent quite narrowly, showing little inclination to
use the Fourteenth Amendment to overturn laws that were neutral
on their face just because they worked to a protected group's
disadvantage. For example, in *Personnel Administrator of Massachusetts v. Feeney* (1979), the Court held that a Massachusetts law
giving absolute veterans' preference for civil service jobs did not
show intent to discriminate against women. It reached this conclusion even though it conceded that the legislature was perfectly
aware at the time it passed the law that this form of veterans'
preference worked significantly to women's disadvantage, and
further conceded that the *federal* law limiting women to 2 percent of
the armed forces prior to 1967 had been discriminatory in intent as
well as result.[34] Nonetheless, the Court concluded that the Massachusetts legislature's "intent" was to reward veterans, not hurt
women. So long as the Court interpreted intent in this narrow way,
it would not have struck down absolute veterans' preference even if
the ERA had passed. If absolute veterans preference does not
involve "intent" to discriminate, few other statutes that are "neutral on their face" can be said to do so.

If we look to the future, however, the ERA might eventually
have made an important difference. A more liberal Supreme Court
might well construe legislative intent more broadly. Of course, if

the Court construes intent more broadly, it could also use its "post-*Craig*" interpretation of the Fourteenth Amendment to do almost anything it could have done under the ERA. But passing the ERA would have been a clear signal to the Court that the country wanted a relatively strict review of laws that had different effects on men and women. This might well have encouraged the Court to construe "intent" somewhat more liberally in cases involving gender than it would otherwise have done. Thus, one could plausibly argue that, if the ERA had passed, the Court might have concluded that absolute veterans' preference did show intent to discriminate and was therefore unconstitutional. One could make this political argument even though there was nothing in the formal logic of the Court's opinion suggesting that it would have acted differently if the ERA had passed.

In the short run, then, the Supreme Court's decision in *Washington v. Davis,* like its decision in *Craig v. Boren,* meant that the ERA would have far less immediate impact on constitutional law than most of its advocates had assumed back in 1972. In the long run, it was still possible that passing the ERA would eventually have had a political impact on the Court, leading it to apply more demanding standards than it now applies to laws that are formally neutral between men and women.

The Impact of an Impending ERA on the Supreme Court's Evolution

It is difficult to determine whether or not the Supreme Court would have broadened its interpretation of the Fourteenth Amendment to include women as rapidly as it did had Congress not passed the ERA in 1972.

On the one hand, the favorable climate for change produced by the ERA debates in the House and Senate may well have led the Court to begin in 1971 the series of changes that eventuated in the "intermediate" standard of *Craig v. Boren.* Certainly, in the year after the ERA passed the Senate, Justice Brennan, with Justices Douglas, White, and Marshall, used the ERA, along with the Equal Pay Act of 1963 and Title VII of the Civil Rights Act of 1964, to indicate Congress's "increasing sensitivity to sex-based classifications." Brennan argued in *Frontiero v. Richardson* that "Congress itself has concluded that classifications based upon sex are inher-

ently invidious, and this conclusion of coequal branch of Government is not without significance to the question presently under
consideration."[35]

On the other hand, the Supreme Court may have stopped at the
"intermediate" standard precisely because the ERA was under
consideration in the states. In the congressional hearings on the
ERA, Professor Leo Kanowitz had warned that the ERA, if it did
not pass, might actually reduce the chances of the Court on its own
making sex a suspect classification, by encouraging the Court to
defer to the upcoming—or defunct—ERA.[36] This seems to have
been exactly what happened. In *Frontiero* Justices Brennan, Douglas, White, and Marshall wanted to conclude "that classifications
based on sex, like classifications based on race, religion and national origin," were "inherently suspect and must therefore be
subjected to strict judicial scrutiny."[37] They needed only one additional justice to make a majority. But while Justice Powell, with
Chief Justice Burger and Justice Blackmun joining him, voted with
Brennan et al., they refused to make sex a suspect classification at
that point. Justice Powell did not take a stand *against* considering
sex inherently suspect. Rather, he argued that making sex an inherently suspect classification in 1973 would be "reaching out to
preempt by judicial action a major political decision," namely, the
state legislatures' decision whether or not to ratify the ERA. In
Powell's view, the ERA "if adopted will resolve the substance of
this precise question" of whether the Court should consider sex a
suspect classification.[38] If the ERA had not been before the states,
Justice Powell, Burger, or Blackmun might have gone along with
the idea of making sex a suspect classification in 1973. This step
would have made the ERA almost entirely symbolic.

In Brief: The 1972 Claims and the Court's Evolution

One way to summarize how rapidly the legal situation changed
between 1972 and 1982 is to review the claims made in behalf of the
ERA by its Senate proponents in 1972.

Some of the evils cited by proponents in 1972 had been declared
illegal by Congress or the federal courts even at that time. In the
1972 Senate debate, for example, proponents argued that the ERA
would invalidate dual pay schedules for men and women performing the same job,[39] laws excluding women from certain jobs and

professions,[40] and laws limiting weights and hours that had a disproportionate impact on women.[41] As we have seen, the ERA would have had practically no immediate effect in any of these areas. It was already illegal for any employer of more than fifteen people to pay men and women different wages for the same work. Although five states continued to prohibit women from working in mines or selling alcoholic beverages, and many states kept their maximum hours and weight-lifting laws on the books, these laws were also unenforceable under existing federal statutes.

Most of the other laws that ERA advocates cited as evils in the 1972 debates became presumptively unconstitutional between 1972 and 1982. For example, Senate proponents argued that the ERA would abolish "quotas and steeper entrance requirements that excluded women from public colleges, universities and professional schools."[42] This was true enough in 1972. But because public institutions with quotas of this kind almost all received some federal funding, Congress had the power to prevent them from discriminating against female applicants even without an ERA, and Congress did precisely this only a few months after it voted for the ERA.[43]

ERA supporters also argued in 1972 that the ERA would eliminate state statutes that automatically exempted women from serving on a jury.[44] Again, the claim was correct when it was made in 1972, but it became moot after 1975, when the Supreme Court declared such exemptions unconstitutional on the grounds that they violated the Fourteenth Amendment.[45]

Senate proponents of the ERA also argued that it would abolish restrictions on the legal capacity of married women, like their right to establish a domicile, hold a driver's license in their own names, or go into business for themselves; provisions in family law giving greater responsibility to the husband and presuming dependence in the wife; and presumptions in divorce that the wife should care for the children or receive alimony.[46] The Supreme Court's broadened interpretation of the Fourteenth Amendment's equal protection clause led it to strike down almost every law of this kind that it accepted for judgment between 1972 and 1982. The Court would probably have ruled unconstitutional those that remained on the books in 1982, if anyone had challenged them, even without the ERA.

ERA advocates also argued in 1972 that the amendment would eliminate gender differences in state and federal pension and Social

Security benefits.[47] The ERA would almost certainly have eliminated differences in retirement benefits that were explicitly based
on sex, but the Supreme Court had eliminated almost all such
distinctions even without the ERA by 1977.[48] While in 1972 there
was, as we have seen, some reason to think that the Supreme Court
might use the ERA to invalidate facially neutral Social Security
provisions that discriminated against homemakers, this became
unlikely after the *Washington* decision in 1976.

In 1972 Senate proponents also argued that ERA passage
would eliminate laws establishing different sentences for the same
crimes.[49] A number of laws of this kind were still on the books at the
time of the Senate debate. Georgia, for example, gave men fixed
sentences while giving women indeterminate sentences for certain
crimes, and indeterminate sentences usually turn out to be longer
than fixed sentences. But the courts had struck down a number of
similar laws in the late 1960s on the grounds that they violated the
equal protection clause of the Fourteenth Amendment. The Supreme Court's heightened standard of scrutiny of such laws during
the 1970s almost certainly meant that by the late 1970s they would
all have been ruled unconstitutional if they had been appealed.[50]

Finally, in the 1972 Senate debate proponents argued that the
ERA would abolish restrictions on women entering and advancing
in the armed forces.[51] As we shall see, the Supreme Court would
probably not have interpreted the ERA as applying fully to the
military.[52] Thus, it is not clear that the Court would even have
required the military academies to admit women. Congress, however, did require them to do so shortly after it passed the ERA.[53]
The Supreme Court might well have held that the ERA required
equal treatment of women in military jobs that were essentially
civilian in character, but Congress did this even without the ERA.
Congress did not require women to register for the draft, and
neither did it change the laws excluding women from combat-
related jobs. Congressional reluctance to move in these areas
reflected the fact that these measures were extremely controversial.
Even in 1972, therefore, few politically sensitive supporters of the
ERA emphasized these possible consequences of its passage. Not
surprisingly, the Supreme Court between 1972 and 1982 did not rule
the male-only draft or combat rules unconstitutional under the
Fourteenth Amendment. Instead, as we shall see, the Court explicitly refused to make this move. The claim regarding the ERA's

effects on the military thus became the only claim that proponents had made for the ERA in the Senate debate in 1972 that the Supreme Court had not already implemented by 1982. For obvious reasons, however, proponents rarely used this claim as an argument for the ERA, while opponents publicized it heavily.

Consequences

The fact that by the mid-1970s the ERA promised few immediate, tangible benefits for women was not, I believe, even in 1982, a strong reason against voting the ERA into the Constitution. As I argued earlier, the ERA undoubtedly would have encouraged legislators and judges over the long run to take the problems of women more seriously and to be more sensitive to the patterns of disadvantage that impair women's lives. This chapter and the preceding one stress the dearth of immediate benefits not to argue against ratification but rather to lay the groundwork for explaining why the activists who promoted the ERA were likely to exaggerate even its unpopular potential effects. Because women stood to gain so few immediate, practical benefits from ratification, activists had little incentive to sacrifice principle for expediency. No potential beneficiaries made the case that if the proponents did not moderate their claims for the ERA's effects, and the ERA lost as a consequence, then they personally would lose important benefits that otherwise they would have gained.

7 The ERA and the War Powers Clauses

By 1982, the Supreme Court had left the ERA only two important potential roles. First, the Amendment could have acted as a symbol of the nation's commitment to women's rights—a symbol that would probably have had important practical effects both in encouraging legislators and judges to take this mandate into account, and in encouraging citizens to bring civil suits demanding their rights. Second, the Amendment could have committed the American government to particular substantive applications of the general principle of equal rights that a majority of the still traditional, still ambivalent, still sexist American public would not have voted for in a referendum.

Chapter 6 argued that, while the Supreme Court might at some point try to bring about changes that a majority of the American public opposed, passing the ERA would have made this only marginally more likely in the foreseeable future. The justices would probably have decided that the ERA made gender a "suspect" classification, but except for the draft they probably would have interpreted this in almost the same way as the "intermediate" classification they had already established under the Fourteenth Amendment. However, both proponents and opponents of the ERA insisted that the Supreme Court would interpret the ERA as making important changes, including requiring Congress not only to draft women but also to send women draftees into combat on the same basis as men.

How likely was this outcome? The operative section of the Equal Rights Amendment stated:

60

> Equality of rights under the law shall not be denied or abridged by the United States or any State on account of sex.

Taken at face value, this language seems to require the military to assign male and female draftees to jobs on a sex-blind basis. But appearances can be deceptive. Had the ERA been ratified, the Supreme Court could still have decided that these words did not require the sex-blind assignment of draftees to combat. It could have done so by invoking the "war powers" clauses of the Constitution, which it has often interpreted as partially exempting the military from the Bill of Rights. The Supreme Court did not have so much discretion in the case of the draft itself, because the legislative history made it clear that despite wavering on the part of the Senate floor leader Congress expected the ERA to make women subject to the draft. On the issue of combat, however, the legislative history was ambiguous. This left the Court in the enviable position of easily being able to decide the issue either way.

On the side of requiring sex-blind assignment to combat was an interpretation of the ERA that I will call "egalitarian." Barbara Brown, Thomas Emerson, Gail Falk, and Ann Freedman, the authors of the *Yale Law Journal* article on the ERA, summarize this view as follows:

> [The] principle of the Amendment must be applied comprehensively and without exceptions. . . . the prohibition against the use of sex as a basis for differential treatment applies to all areas of legal rights. To the extent that any exception is made, the values sought by the Amendment are undercut. . . . Only an unequivocal ban against taking sex into account supplies a rule adequate to achieve the objectives of the Amendment. . . . the constitutional mandate must be absolute.[1]

As we have seen, their interpretation allowed only two exceptions to the absolute ban on taking gender into account: laws dealing with physical characteristics unique to one sex (e.g., laws concerning wet nurses) and laws guaranteeing privacy to the two sexes (e.g., laws separating the sexes in public rest rooms or the sleeping quarters of prisons). Regarding the military, the Yale authors commented, " . . . the Amendment permits no exceptions for the military. Neither the right to privacy nor any unique physical characteristic justifies different treatment of the sexes with respect to voluntary or involuntary service."[2] As for the "claim that women are physically incapable of performing combat duty," they contended,

> The facts do not support this conclusion. . . . In order to screen out those of both sexes incapable of combat service, it will be permissible to measure ability to do the requisite physical tasks. . . . The test will have to be closely related to the actual requirements of combat duty. There will be many women able to pass such a test.[3]

On the side of allowing Congress or the military to exclude women draftees from combat was the interpretation, which I will call "deferential," that, because of the war powers clauses in the Constitution, the Supreme Court would defer to military judgment in military matters. Because of the war powers clauses, soldiers already have fewer rights—of free speech, association, and so forth—than do civilians. In congressional testimony and in a law journal article supporting the ERA, William Van Alstyne argued that the Supreme Court had used the war powers clauses to modify the meaning of provisions "fully equivalent" to the ERA elsewhere in the Constitution, like the free speech provision in the First Amendment:

> The first amendment is quite absolute in the expression of its central premise respecting one's freedom of speech . . . however, the first amendment is acknowledged to be subject to construction in light of certain enumerated powers of Congress including, most importantly, the war powers.[4]

Sometimes, when two interpretations are equally plausible, the Court looks to the legislative history to decide which of the two should prevail. But in this case, the legislative history was, perhaps deliberately, murky. The 1972 Majority Report from the Senate Judiciary Committee, which was the closest thing to an official interpretation of the ERA's meaning, began its discussion of the ERA's effects in a way that seemed to support the Yale authors' egalitarian position, by citing the senior author, Thomas Emerson, on the "fundamental proposition that *sex should not be a factor* in determining the legal rights of women or of men."[5] However, the report never cited the *Yale Law Journal* article itself, and in its section on the military the report stressed the discretion that army commanders would have in assigning tasks, implying that those commanders might not assign women to combat: "Once in the service, women, like men, would be assigned to various duties by their commanders, depending on their qualifications and the service's needs."[6] In support of this position it quoted Representative Martha Griffiths, primary sponsor of the ERA in the House. In response to what she called "all of this nonsense about the Army," Representative Griffiths had said:

> [T]he draft is equal. That is the thing that is equal. But once you are in the Army you are put where the Army tells you you are going to go.[7]

The report did not quote her next sentence, in which she said, "The thing that will happen with women is that they will be the stenographers and telephone operators." By omitting this remark, the report left the door ajar for an egalitarian interpretation. It then quoted Representative Don Edwards, who chaired the House Subcommittee Hearings on the ERA. According to Edwards,

> Women in the military would be assigned to serve wherever their skills or talents were applicable and needed, in the discretion of the command, as men are at present.[8]

Again, while this comment emphasized the "discretion" of commanding officers, and thus seems to support a deferential interpretation of the Amendment, it did not completely rule out an egalitarian interpretation. Finally, the Senate Majority Report pointed out that although in Israel women were required to serve in the defense forces, "they are not, however, assigned to combat posts, nor are they required to engage in physical combat."[9] The report did not say that the ERA necessarily would have the same effect in America, but it certainly implied the possibility.

Once the ERA was reported out of the Senate Judiciary Committee, Senator Birch Bayh, the floor leader for the Amendment, specifically addressed the question of whether the ERA would require Congress to send women into combat on an equal basis with men. In the debate over Senator Sam Ervin's suggested amendment to the ERA exempting women from combat duty, Bayh argued that with the Vietnam War over and the Senate seriously considering an all-volunteer army, there would soon be no draft; further, if there were a draft, any parent could be exempted, or any parent "who has the primary duty of rearing the children or caring for the home"; further, sex-neutral standards of physical competence for combat would probably exclude more women than men. Finally, regarding what he considered the less than 1 percent of women in the pool of eligibles who might actually be drafted, Bayh asked: "[W]ould they be assigned to combat duty?"

> Admittedly, there is no way we can guarantee they would not be, but in the judgment of the Senator from Indiana, they would be assigned to duty as their commanders thought they were qualified to serve. Just as 85 percent of those who are in the armed services and who are men are not assigned to combat duties, so the commander would not need to send a woman into the front trenches if he felt that it would not be in the best interests of the combat unit to make such an assignment.[10]

Bayh then pointed out again that Israel did not send women into combat and entered into the *Record* a letter from the Israeli embassy saying that although in the Israeli army the "girls" are assigned to combat units, they fill noncombatant posts, are not given the same combat training as the "men," and are not required to engage in physical combat. "It is our expectation," Bayh concluded later, "that few if any [women] will be in combat."[11]

Other supporters of the ERA agreed with Bayh. "The amendment," said Senator Gurney, "does not require that women become combatants in the Armed Forces although it will subject them to the draft."[12] Or, in Senator Humphrey's somewhat more cautious words, the ERA "would not mean that women would serve in every aspect of our military effort: if some military jobs, such as certain aspects of combat action, had requirements that eliminated women, then so be it. Women would not serve in those jobs."[13] When Senator Ervin, the foremost opponent of the ERA in the Senate, proposed an amendment to the ERA specifically exempting women from combat, Bayh countered by trying to reassure his colleagues that this was not an issue. As Senator Hiram Fong argued when urging his colleagues to support Ervin's amendment, "[m]ost proponents of the Equal Rights Amendment say it is supposed to mean" that women will not be involuntarily assigned to combat.[14] This was true. Only one ERA proponent, Senator Cook, urged his fellow senators to vote against Ervin's amendment on the grounds that men and women should, in fact, be eligible for combat on the same basis.[15] Most proponents argued only that Ervin's amendment was unnecessary. Thus, one cannot argue that the defeat of Ervin's amendment (by a vote of 71 to 18) demonstrated that the Senate actually wanted to send women into combat.[16] All the Senate wanted was to close off debate and agree on a text identical to that adopted by the House, so it could move on to other matters.[17]

In the face of this ambiguous legislative history, the Supreme Court might reasonably be expected to look to other indications of congressional intent. Nothing in the 1972 debate suggested that Congress *wanted* women draftees assigned to combat roles. Indeed, in 1980 Congress refused to support even President Carter's mild proposal to *register* young women in case Congress should ever decide to draft them for noncombat assignments.[18]

If the President, Congress, and the military were to decide, especially in wartime, that it was in the military interests of the country not to send women draftees into combat on the same basis as men, the justices of the Supreme Court would be unlikely to order such an outcome if there were a plausible constitutional reason for not doing so. The Court's deference to the military in the past and the legislative history of the Amendment clearly gave the Court such an alternative. Without even looking at the legislative history or public opinion, and without confining his remarks to draftees, William Van Alstyne concluded that, if Congress decided not to allow women in combat units, "it is unimaginable to me that the Supreme Court would apply the Equal Rights Amendment in contradiction to that determination by Congress. . . . I have no professional hesitation at all in suggesting to you that that cannot become a problem if [the ERA] is adopted."[19]

Neither supporters nor opponents of the ERA paid much heed to the evidence suggesting that the ERA could leave Congress free to legislate as it saw fit regarding combat assignments for women draftees. It is easy to see why the opponents claimed that the ERA would require Congress to put women draftees into combat, just as one can see why they claimed that the ERA would require unisex public toilets. Public opinion was solidly against sending women draftees into combat in the years between 1972 and 1982. Less than a quarter of the adult population favored sending women draftees into combat in 1980, although a majority might have favored allowing women to volunteer for combat jobs.[20] Recognizing this, Senator Ervin repeatedly said that the ERA would send women into combat, "where they will be slaughtered or maimed by the bayonets, the bombs, the bullets, the grenades, the mines, the napalm, the poison gas, or the shells of the enemy."[21] (He always listed these weapons alphabetically.) Opponents in the state legislatures returned to the subject again and again, particularly when the ERA was first introduced during the Vietnam War, and after 1980, when the revival of draft registration for men and the subsequent election of President Reagan made the public worry more about the possibility of another draft and perhaps another war. In the 1978 Illinois hearings on the ERA, when proponents lined up prestigious business and union leaders, lawyers, priests, ministers, rabbis, and nuns to testify for the ERA, the opponents simply sent in a host of teenage girls, one from each district in the state, to tell the legislators that they did not want to be drafted and sent into combat.[22]

Yet, as the struggle for the ERA progressed, most supporters of the Amendment also claimed that it would require Congress to send qualified women draftees into combat along with qualified men. This stance requires fuller explanation.

8 A Decision by Accretion

Judy Baar Topinka, the only woman in the Illinois House of Representatives uncommitted on the ERA, represented a mixed-class, strongly ethnic district. In the late 1970s she asked a pro-ERA speaker from NOW to debate Phyllis Schlafly in her district. This is how Topinka remembered the pro-ERA speaker's performance:

> She gets herself hung up on women should be in the military. Women are smaller, they'll fit well in tanks, is the comment that I remember.— And that was the end of the argument. I mean, that was it!

The ERA speaker had lost her audience on the issue of women in combat. Topinka, every inch the old politician, shook her head in disbelief at what she called the "marketing" of the ERA: "That one never ceases to amaze me. I've never seen a more incredible political botching of an issue than ERA."[1]

Two things had happened between 1970, when the major ERA organizations first articulated formal positions on the effect of the ERA on women's role in the military, and 1982, when the ERA went down to defeat.

First, the idea that the ERA would require not just drafting qualified women but sending them into combat had become a powerful substantive objection to the Amendment. Second, the organizations campaigning for the ERA had come to insist more and more strongly that the Amendment would do exactly this. The result almost guaranteed that when a NOW speaker spelled out NOW's analysis of the ERA's effect on the draft and combat to

Topinka's local group, Topinka would conclude, ". . . that was it!"
Feminists could have chosen an interpretation of the ERA that
would have allayed concern on this issue. Instead, they chose an
interpretation unpalatable to mainstream voters and legislators.
But few ERA activists made the choice consciously. Their choices
were embedded in a movement-wide "decision by accretion,"[2] in
which even the most influential actors seldom realized the full
impact of their actions. Key decisions taken by a few actors struc-
tured the information available to the rank and file. Those key
decisions—and the decision by accretion of which they were a
part—were shaped by the ideology of the activists who promoted
the ERA, by the pressures for philosophical consistency in the
public stands of the major women's organizations, and by the larger
concerns of feminist constitutional lawyers.

Ideology

In order to understand why, almost unconsciously, ERA supporters chose the egalitarian over the deferential interpretation, we
must begin by recognizing that in the ERA movement, as in all
social movements, ideology was critically important. Within the
larger women's movement, the groups that originally sponsored the
ERA and later provided the primary financial and political support
for its ratifications were deeply committed to *legal* equality for
women. While radical feminist collectives were arguing for the
supremacy of women's culture and urging the complete restructur-
ing of patriarchal society, the National Federation of Business and
Professional Women (BPW) and the National Organization for
Women (NOW) were demanding an end to "protective" legislation
and beginning to organize for the ERA.[3] For these legalistic groups,
exceptions to the general principle that the law should be blind to
gender were deeply disturbing.[4]

But no feminist, whether committed to legal egalitarianism or
not, could help being repelled by the kinds of arguments habitually
advanced for keeping women out of combat. In particular, every
feminist needed to reject, in her own psyche and in society, the
image of women as victims and incompetents. When army tests
showed women equaling or bettering men in combat skills, stamina,
endurance, and motivation, and when the Vietnam experience in
guerrilla warfare indicated that a small but agile soldier could often
do a better job than a large and heavy one, no feminist could feel

anything but fury when a general argued sarcastically, "But imagine, if you will, a news photo distributed worldwide showing American diplomats cowering behind their desks while women marines try to defend them. It could happen tomorrow."[5]

Phyllis Schlafly's entire case against the ERA revolved around women's continuing need for male protection. As she put it, "Women want and need protection. Any male who is a man—or gentleman—will accept the responsibility of protecting women."[6] Schlafly, following the Western custom since the Middle Ages, saw the powerful male protecting the defenseless female as the only alternative to treating women as chattel. But feminists saw Schlafly persuading women to connive in their own subordination, and understood this dynamic as lying at the heart of women's continuing oppression. The protectionist position could not be better put than in a poem Senator Ervin quoted on the Senate floor in the middle of the ERA debate, a poem he said he loved, about a "little" bride ("little" repeated three times in the poem), who after the wedding guests have gone is left alone "with him, her lord." At that moment, as the bride looks "up" at her new husband, the poet addresses her and tells of her "nameless fear," which, combined with "wordless joy,"[7]

> . . . calls the tear
> In dumb appeal to rise,
> When, looking up on him where he stands,
> You yield up all into his hands,
> Pleading into his eyes.

The protectionist position led both men and women to expect women to be passive victims. Victims they became. As the NOW "Position Paper on the Registration and Drafting of Women in 1980" pointed out, in America in the 1980s,

> One rape occurs every five minutes. One out of every four American married women is a victim of wife beating. . . . When the word "protection" is used, we know it costs women a great deal.[8]

In rejecting protectionism, feminists urged women to stand on their own feet and wield power on their own right.

Feminists also suspected that public and legislative antipathy to women to combat derived less from concern for the lives of women (or even for the efficiency of the army) than from a cultural rejection of the idea that women should ever be aggressive or powerful. This suspicion finds support in survey data and in the remarks of state legislators. In the most thorough survey to date of public attitudes toward women in the military, 94 percent of a sample of Americans thought it acceptable for a trained woman to be assigned to the job of "nurse in a combat zone," but only 59 percent thought a trained woman should be assigned to the job of "air defense missile gunner in the United States."[9] Since the danger of both death and capture is infinitely greater in a combat zone than in the United States, and since the upper body strength that provides men's chief physical advantage is, if anything, more useful for a nurse in a combat zone than for the person who activates a missile in the United States, one can only conclude that the huge difference in approval rating between the two jobs derives from little more than public disapproval of women in the role of "gunner," which is both aggressive and nontraditional.

The same set of prejudices appears in legislative speeches like that of Representative Webber Borchers of Illinois, who, oblivious to the often repeated fact that only qualified members of either sex would be sent to the front lines, assured his listeners that,

> . . . based on actual observation of women in combat with the French underground, the French collaborationists and Germans, German women in combat, I know in my heart that women would be slaughtered. I would assure you, women in combat, any more than a random football team, that picked the boys and a number of girls, the boys would beat the girls. We have a different relationship to our physical ability. That difference is the difference between life and death in combat. I do not want, I would never want women to be alongside of me in combat. I couldn't bear the thought of the responsibility and knowing from experience what would happen. . . . I tell you that they would never be able to survive the hardships, the battle and the troubles of a front line. It is impossible.

When Representative Edward Bluthardt, an ERA supporter, retorted that in combat "I met women Russian soldiers that would make Borchers run like hell," Borchers replied, laughing, that he too had "met the Russian women soldiers. One look was enough; Representative Bluthardt is absolutely right, I would run like hell."[10] In short, it did no good for NOW or Women's Equity Action League (WEAL) to keep pointing out that women nurses, mechanics, and technicians had "performed bravely and competently under hostile fire" in World War II, or that army tests of women in war games, simulated combat, guerrilla warfare, airborne assault, and loading and firing heavy artillery howitzers (the "heaviest, noisiest job in the army") showed women performing as well or better than men.[11] Representative Borchers and his brethren still concluded either that women couldn't do the job or that, if by chance they could do it, such aggressive behavior would make them so physically repellent as to destroy the possibility that a man might be attracted to them.

These deep-seated attitudes toward women led feminists from every part of the political spectrum to sympathize with a policy that treated women and men equally in regard to combat. As some of the many pacifists in the women's movement concluded, at least this way women as well as men would have the right to resist induction.[12]

Nonetheless, feminist opposition to the military also made it difficult for some in the ERA movement to take the combat issue seriously. Most feminists opposed the draft. The argument that a volunteer army thrust the burden of military service on the working and lower-middle classes, making it even less costly for the dominant classes to engage in aggressive warfare, rarely surfaced in the feminist press. Many feminists simply opposed the draft and ended their analysis there. When grass-roots movements in NOW challenged the arguments in NOW's 1980 Position Paper on registration and the draft, they wanted to substitute not a deferential interpretation of the ERA but total opposition to the draft, with no further statement on the role of women if Congress were in fact to institute a draft. This strong antidraft sentiment, combined with the assumption that arguments against the ERA never had much rational basis, led many feminists to lump combat and unisex toilets together as "red herrings." Some even spoke on occasion of "the sharing toilets/combat issue" as if it were one thing, not noticing the major difference that while the ERA would *not* require unisex toilets, their own organizations often said it *would* require women in combat.

Spillover from Other Commitments

During the course of the ERA campaign, egalitarian and feminist principles forced several national women's organizations to address themselves, sometimes rather unwillingly, to the inequalities that plagued women in the military. When Congress ended the draft in 1973 and established the All-Volunteer Force, few people realized how heavily the military services would come to depend on women recruits. Because of the low pay, unattractive working conditions, and perhaps the potential risk, not enough men with high school diplomas volunteered for the armed forces. To meet the need for more recruits with a high school education, the services turned more and more to women, who joined primarily because military pay was typically about 40 percent more than such women would have earned in the civilian labor force.[13] These newly recruited women soon became aware of the institutionalized discrimination in the armed forces where both the law and explicit military policy prevented women from taking most jobs designated as "combat-related." Jobs with this label included not only actual hand-to-hand combat jobs in the infantry but also prestigious and highly paid jobs like fighter pilot in the Air Force, jobs involving combat support, and jobs that seemed to have nothing whatever to do with combat but were reserved for combat-ready soldiers in order to give these soldiers something to do while they waited for mobilization. In 1980, 73 percent of the jobs in the military were off-limits to women, primarily because the jobs involved potential combat.[14] The jobs from which women were excluded were, by and large, the highest paying jobs and also those that led to the most powerful arenas of command. As a consequence, exclusion from combat stunted the careers of women who stayed in the military. Exclusion from combat also effectively ensured that no woman would ever reach the very top positions in the armed services. So long as this policy regarding combat continues, military decisions that affect the future of our civilization will continue to be made exclusively by men, and, less important, the honor and potential political stature that goes with making such decisions will also be reserved for men.

Because of the obvious consequences for women in the armed forces, women's organizations like the Women's Equity Action League (WEAL) and the National Federation of Business and Professional Women (BPW), often prompted by women in the upper levels of the services or women in the Office of Equal Opportunity in the Department of Defense, began to subject the "combat-related" job classification to closer scrutiny. They began asking, for example, whether the physical qualifications that were used to exclude women from many jobs had any more relation to the actual tasks performed than the physical qualifications that police and fire departments used to exclude women—qualifications that had been held invalid under some state ERAs. Those were clearly legitimate questions. But as women's organizations pressed such challenges on behalf of the *volunteer* women in the services, conservatives inevitably began to doubt that the military would be able to come up with any sex-neutral physical standard that would prevent women *draftees* from being sent into combat.

In November 1979, the House of Representatives held hearings on the Carter administration's proposal to remove existing statutory prohibitions against women in combat and combat-related positions in the air force, navy, and marines. The administration proposed to make assignment in all branches of the All-Volunteer Force depend only on internal military policy rather than congressional policy, as was already the case in the army. The administration was *not* proposing to open all jobs in the military to qualified women, but it was proposing a step in that direction. On behalf of organizations like WEAL, BPW, and the American Association of University Women (AAUW), the executive director of the National Coalition for Women in Defense testified.

> We cannot escape the conclusion that large numbers of women, who are properly selected and trained, are mentally and physically capable of serving in the entire range of military occupational specialties.[15]

In response to a question, the executive director stated that she personally believed that "if women can meet the standards for military combat that men can meet . . . they should be assigned to that kind of duty."[16] Diana Steele, a feminist lawyer from the American Civil Liberties Union, argued even more forcefully that "combat duty, horrendous as it may seem to all of us, must be assigned to persons on a gender-neutral basis."[17]

NOW was not an official member of the National Coalition for Women in Defense (although NOW's offices were used for the meetings), and NOW did not testify at these hearings, probably because so many of the NOW's members opposed any involvement with the military. Nevertheless, within a year Congress had drawn NOW into the fray. Overriding President Carter's desire to register women for noncombat service, Congress decided to register only men.[18] Since NOW had always espoused a gender-neutral draft, it had to take a public position opposing Congress's move. Accordingly, after a national NOW meeting which discussed the issue and arrived at the organization's position, Judy Goldsmith presented an official NOW Position Paper on the subject in congressional hearings in March 1980. The Position Paper reiterated NOW's opposition to "the registration and drafting of anyone," along with its belief that "if a draft and registration is instituted . . . it must include women," and its conviction that "under the ERA men and women would register and be drafted according to their ability."[19] Then, on the basis of evidence on women's performance in the All-Volunteer Force, it added:

> There is no reason behind the blanket assumption that "bigger is always better" in the military arena. The proliferation of advanced equipment installed in planes, ships, tanks, and other land vehicles is turning "elbow room" into a scarce commodity. A soldier with a smaller physique becomes a valuable asset in these situations. In many situations, it is the small, lithe and agile soldier who can do the job more proficiently, escape the space more easily, and better fit the needs of today's (and tomorrow's) armed forces. . . . Thus, it is clear that there are no genuine reasons to exclude women from combat.

As the Position Paper summarized the issue,

> War is senseless. Neither the lives of young men nor young women should be wasted. But if we cannot stop the killing, we know we cannot choose between our sons and daughters. The choice robs women as well as men. In the long and short run, it injures us all.[20]

All-male registration also reactivated and brought to the Supreme Court a lawsuit that had lain dormant in the lower courts since the discontinuation of the draft in 1973. In *Rostker v. Goldberg,* several males of draft age challenged the constitutionality of an all-male draft under the Fifth Amendment "due process" clause, which states, "No person shall . . . be deprived of life, liberty, or property, without due process of law." The due process clause of the Fifth Amendment has for some time been interpreted as imposing essentially the same standards on Congress that the Fourteenth

Amendment's "equal protection" clause imposes on the states. WEAL, joined by Federally Employed Women (FEW), the AAUW, BPW, and other women's organizations, submitted an amicus brief arguing that the Supreme Court, having recently reinterpreted the Fourteenth Amendment to ban analogous forms of sex discrimination in civilian life, should apply the same standard to the military and ban an all-male draft.[21] In addition, the WEAL brief suggested that "when this Court finally considers the reasons for the exclusion of women from combat and combat-related positions, those reasons will not provide an adequate justification for the combat bars."[22] NOW, in a separate amicus brief in *Rostker,* concentrated on how excluding women from registration reinforced sex-role stereotypes of women as weak and unfit to serve their country. Like NOW's earlier Position Paper, it argued that

> differences in strength and physical conditioning narrow and disappear when women receive adequate training, and it is a simple fact that some women are stronger than some men. Moreover, size and strength are not always synonymous. A person trained in martial arts can defeat a larger opponent. Technological advances also continue to diminish the importance of brute strength. A soldier with a smaller physique can perform certain tasks in today's planes, ships and tanks more proficiently than a larger person.
> . . . the evidence is overwhelming—indeed, undisputed—that women are capable of filling current positions that bear "combat" labels.[23]

The Supreme Court rejected these arguments, using the war powers clauses to conclude that the Fifth Amendment did not require gender-neutral registration for the draft. After the *Rostker* decision, the likelihood that the Court would adopt a "deferential" interpretation of the ERA became even higher. But the Court's support for the deferential interpretation in this case was of far less significance politically than the fact that the major organizations promoting the ERA had publicly rejected that interpretation. From 1980 on, no lawyer from any of these women's organizations could, in good conscience, argue for deferential interpretation of the ERA.

Thus events beyond the control of the major women's organizations—the problems of women in the All-Volunteer Force and the legal strategy most likely to win the *Rostker* case—combined to lure these organizations into accepting their opponents' major argument against the ERA. But the decision was not contentious. Eleanor Smeal, who was president of NOW from 1977 to 1980, told me that rejecting the deferential position was "not a major decision. From the proponents' side, the egalitarian issue was the only issue" ("issue" in this context meaning "appropriate stance"). As she saw it, "NOW's position on the draft was well developed. We took a position on *Rostker* that extended to combat in that case, and did it in national conference, with votes and so forth. It would have been inconsistent to go with a deferential position on the ERA."[24]

The Lawyers

Feminist constitutional lawyers played a critical role in ERA proponents' adoption of an "egalitarian" rather than a "deferential" reading of the ERA. Although divided on many issues—including the importance of the ERA, the benefits of eliminating gender distinctions in the law, and the legitimacy of the very language of rights—these lawyers were unanimous in never mentioning the deferential interpretation, except to say that it was irrelevant or incorrect.

Experts exert disproportionate influence on many decisions. But the influence of the feminist lawyers in the ERA movement was unusual because the decentralized structure characteristic of social movements made them even less accountable to other participants than experts usually are. Most of these feminist lawyers taught at law schools or worked for public interest groups like the ACLU. They saw their job not as serving an organized constituency or client but as making America a better society. As a consequence, their first loyalty was to their own political and legal principles, not to a specific political "cause," like passing the ERA, or to a specific organization, like NOW. Even those lawyers who worked directly for NOW or WEAL on specific cases like *Rostker* identified socially and politically with the larger community of feminist lawyers, not with the NOW or WEAL leadership, much less with NOW's local activists. Some of these lawyers became involved in the political struggle for the ERA, and in the name of getting the Amendment ratified found themselves, on issues other than combat, opposing friends who took a "purer" ideological line. Others were unwilling to compromise their principles to help the ERA, especially after the Supreme Court's decisions in *Frontiero* and *Craig* convinced them that the ERA would do little more than the Fourteenth Amendment to protect women's rights.

Yet, whatever their political and emotional relation to the ERA, feminist constitutional lawyers were all liberal or radical in their broader legal perspectives. By temperament and training they disliked the military and wanted nothing to do with the war powers clauses. The Supreme Court's most famous recent use of the war powers clauses was, after all, to allow the government to imprison citizens of Japanese descent during World War II, simply on the basis of their race and ancestry.[25] Constitutional interpretation of the war powers is now in flux, and the Court would probably no longer sanction rounding up civilians in time of war on the basis of their race or ancestry alone. But the Court still interprets the war powers clauses as limiting the scope of the Bill of Rights within the military. Radical lawyers usually argue that citizens' rights should be no less in the military than in civilian life. To argue that the war powers clauses would keep the ERA from applying with full force to the military would give these clauses a legitimacy that few liberals and no radical lawyers felt it deserved.

The lawyers' total antipathy to the war powers clauses shows itself at every point in the ratification history, beginning with the 1971 *Yale Law Journal* article that made the issue of combat so central to the ERA debate. That article, "The Equal Rights Amendment: A Constitutional Basis for Equal Rights for Women," was written by three Yale law students "active in the women's movement"[26] (Barbara Brown, Gail Folk, and Ann Freedman) and by Thomas Emerson, a distinguished Yale law professor who specialized in civil liberties. Emerson had advised the pro-ERA women's organizations during the early House and Senate fights, and had been involved in their decision not to accept Senator Ervin's 1970 amendment to the ERA exempting women from the draft. Emerson assumed that this decision implied a commitment to integrating women fully into every aspect of the military, and the other authors did not disagree. Accordingly, their article, which was meant to benefit the ERA by eliminating uncertainty regarding its meaning, never raised the possibility of a deferential interpretation.

When I interviewed all four authors a month after the ERA's

defeat in June of 1982, not one of them realized that their article had been crucially important in making combat per se a major talking point for the opposition. As I described how the Senate opposition had begun to focus on combat after their article, one author responded that this news was "fascinating. It didn't occur to us that we were injecting a new issue. Amazing!" As for the political consequences of the combat issue, she remembered, "We didn't even focus on it. We had many more problems with rape laws, homosexuality, and pregnancy."

The authors had also assumed, in 1971, that the ERA would pass. They thought its chance for passage through Congress were "excellent," and as one of them told me, reflecting with some sadness on her own youthful trust in the power of lawyers:

> None of us thought of the country as being different from that. If you could get it through Congress, that would be it. [In those days] the way the world was, you remade it. You wrote articles, they were distributed to members of Congress, and that was it.

However, even with the wisdom of hindsight, only one of the authors said she would have changed her interpretation of the Amendment in a more conservative direction in the hope that then it would have passed. Two stated firmly that they would not have changed their stands even to save the ERA. In the first place, they strongly resisted giving greater recognition to the war powers clauses for any purpose. As one put it, "National security considerations do not override constitutional protections. You might have a total collapse into martial law, but otherwise the military has to operate within the constitutional structure, or you don't have a democracy."

In the second place, both of these authors believed that allowing qualifications regarding the military would, as one put it, open the door to the Court's "fussing around with every possible exception." Or, in the other's words, "If the war powers, why not the powers over interstate commerce?" In 1971, the four authors had even debated whether to allow in the "privacy" qualification itself and had only decided in its favor on account of "mixed conceptual and political considerations." Indeed, by 1982 two authors had begun to have doubts about the "unique physical characteristics" qualification.

One of the authors had further become convinced, since she wrote the original article, that in American society women could never be accepted fully and into the highest echelons of public life without being fully integrated into those parts of the military involving combat.

Finally, all four authors still believed, for feminist reasons, in their original strict egalitarian interpretation of the ERA. As they had said in their article,

> no one would suggest that combat service is pleasant or that women who serve can avoid the possibility of physical harm and assault. But it is important to remember that all combat is dangerous, degrading and dehumanizing. That is true for all participants. As between brutalizing our young men and brutalizing our young women there is little to choose.[27]

Because the Yale interpretation was a logical one, given a combination of liberal or radical legal principles and feminist egalitarianism, the other law journal articles that took up the issue at this time all echoed the egalitarian position.[28] One of these—Joan Wexler's "The ERA and the Military" (also in the *Yale Law Journal*)—touched upon the deferential interpretation, but it did so only to proclaim that interpretation incorrect.[29] It was not until William Van Alstyne's congressional testimony in 1977 in favor of extending the ERA ratification deadline, and his subsequent article in the *Washington University Law Quarterly,* that the possibility of a deferential interpretation was made "public."

At this point, the influence of some feminist constitutional lawyers began to reach into the actual politics of ratification. When the women's organizations had to send lawyers to testify for the ERA at legislative hearings in the unratified states, a highly placed woman in one of these organizations phoned a friend to see whether a professor who supported the ERA would be willing to testify in those states. She also suggested that they try to get Van Alstyne. Her friend remembers that

> they were going to recruit Van Alstyne. And I was really furious. I said that that war powers jazz was nonsense—although that was the way the Court would go in *Rostker.* . . . I was opposed to the idea that you could *ever* have a sex-based ban.

The woman organizing the testimony confirmed this account: "We had an issue on whether Van Alstyne should testify, [because] some things he wrote were not fully the party kind of line." But, she says, she called and asked him to testify anyway, on the grounds that "for him to present that kind of testimony would not prevent other people from taking the positions they took. So raising this other 'take' on the issue would be okay."[30]

This little flurry seems to be one of the few times that ERA strategists ever consciously compared the virtues of the deferential and the egalitarian positions. They did not do this alone but, as two of the participants confirmed, in consultation with Eleanor Smeal, then president of NOW, and a few of her close advisors. None of those involved consciously intended to preempt discussion of the alternatives within the ERA movement. They were making a quick decision on a limited subject, in a way that to them seemed completely consistent with prior understandings. Because it was difficult for Van Alstyne to travel on the appropriate days, and because no one urged him strongly to attend, he never testified on the ERA except in South Carolina, where it had no chance of passing, and in his own state of North Carolina. Thus a strong version of the deferential position never reached most of the key wavering states. In effect, a few feminist lawyers and the top leadership in one organization had acted as "gatekeepers" in this decision, foreclosing discussion at the grass roots.

At the national-level meetings where the advantages and disadvantages of a deferential interpretation of the ERA might have been discussed in depth, the issue was rarely raised. In one NOW meeting, a few locally based activists mentioned the possibility but felt no one paid attention to their brief remarks. The lawyers themselves seem never to have discussed the issue. In one key "summit meeting," leading feminist lawyers met with the president of NOW to discuss the possible impact of the upcoming draft registration case, *Rostker v. Goldberg,* on the political prospects for the ERA. At this meeting, participants spoke of their hopes regarding *Rostker*. If they won, in the words of one participant, "it would take away one of the major arguments of the opponents—that the ERA would draft women." If they lost the case, they believed it would be "devastating." In an entire meeting devoted to the political effects of *Rostker* on the ERA, no one ever suggested that, if the Supreme Court decided against drafting women on the grounds of deference to the military, this could actually *help* the ERA by reassuring the public that the Supreme Court would defer to the military under the ERA as well. When I raised this possibility with a lawyer who had been at the meeting, she dismissed it instantly with the words, "None of us believed *that!*"

It would not have been ideologically inconsistent for the lawyers, let alone the activists, lobbyists, and legislators who supported the ERA, to have said that, although they personally believed that women draftees should be sent into combat on a sex-blind basis, they realized that the country was not ready for this. Nor would it have been inconsistent to say that, while they personally opposed the war powers clauses, the Supreme Court would probably treat the ERA as having limited application to the military. Certainly, ERA lawyers could have alerted pro-ERA groups to the deferential interpretation after *Rostker* had they believed this would help persuade wavering state legislators. Indeed, if proponents had foreseen the importance of the issue, they could have encouraged Congress to write legislative history in 1972 making clear its intent to give the military discretion in using conscripts in wartime. But no one contemplated any of these strategies. Reliance on the war powers clauses was literally unthinkable for the group of lawyers involved in ERA ratification.

Thus a decision that would have important consequences for the ERA debate in wavering states was taken with very few of the participants realizing that they were taking a major step. The unanimity of the feminist lawyers on the war powers clauses made it almost impossible for anyone not deeply involved in these issues to realize that there was an alternative interpretation. And for the few at the top of the most powerful pro-ERA organization, NOW, the "decision" simply flowed from earlier decisions and premises.

Given the leadership's unanimous commitment to the "egalitarian" interpretation, it is tempting to assume that the whole movement was equally unanimous and that serious debate would have been impossible. But when one looks outside the leadership and the feminist legal community, no such unanimity is apparent. The movement's publicists and pamphlet writers, for example, often took a more or less "deferential" line. These authors probably did not know of the surveys indicating that only 22 percent of the public thought that women should be drafted and eligible for combat. But, writing for a mass audience, they tended to write what they thought the public wanted to read or hear. While not understanding the constitutional basis for the deferential interpretation, they usually echoed the implicitly deferential Senate Majority Report rather than the *Yale Law Journal*'s egalitarian interpretation.

The "National Plan of Action," written by the members and staff of the National Commission on the Observance of International Women's Year and adopted at the National Women's Conference in Houston in 1977, is a good example of this tendency. It categorically stated that the ERA would "not mean that women would automatically be assigned to combat, unless they volunteered for such duties. . . . the decision as to who is best equipped for combat is up to the commanders."[31]

Common Cause, a nonfeminist good-government group, also argued in an early pamphlet that the ERA would not require the military to send women into combat. After mentioning ongoing tests that "will help the military decide which assignments should be open to women and which should continue to be restricted to males for reasons of combat effectiveness," it concluded:

> Should the military decide that by assigning women to certain dut[ies], discipline, morale or effectiveness would be substantially impaired, women could be excluded from such assignments even if the ERA was in effect. In the military, an individual's constitutional rights are balanced against the needs and the responsibility of the armed forces to protect the nation.[32]

This pamphlet also displayed a photograph of Major General Jeanne M. Holm with the caption, "Sees the military making its own decisions," and a quotation from Lieutenant Col. Verna Kellogg: "Just because the ERA is ratified does not mean that [women] will be drafted. The same is true of women in combat. If the Congress and the Courts determine that this is not the proper role for women, they could so rule."[33]

Other organizations had more ambiguous ways of presenting the issue. The Federation of Business and Professional Women, the first major women's group to support the ERA, put out pamphlets that ranged from the strongly deferential ". . . the ERA will *not* . . . put women in combat positions in military service,"[34] through the repeating the Senate Majority Report's vague formulation that women "would be assigned various duties by their commanders, depending on their qualifications and the service's needs,"[35] to an essentially egalitarian position: "As in the past, only those persons—men or women—who can meet the very high physical demands which combat duty imposes would be eligible for such assignments."[36]

Yet, while most pro-ERA pamphlets suggested that the ERA would not require Congress to send women into combat, the pamphlets never explained *why* this might be so in legal terms. Basing their conclusions only on the Senate Majority Report, they never mentioned the war powers clauses in the Constitution, probably because the authors of the pamphlets had never heard of these clauses.[37] As a result, their arguments lacked credibility. The wording of the Amendment itself said nothing about exceptions for the military, and few readers knew about the courts' traditional interpretation of the war powers clauses. Consequently, readers not only had reason to doubt the pamphlets' claims that there would be a military exception but also had reason to fear that if the Supreme Court made a military exception it could make all sorts of other exceptions too. For proponents who got their information from these pamphlets, therefore, the military exception looked extremely dangerous, since it seemed the first step down a slippery slope. Had the pamphlets invoked the war powers clauses, the unique character of the military exception would have become clear. Activists would have no trouble explaining the distinction to most Americans, who are quite used to soldiers not having the same rights as civilians.

The importance of the constitutional foundation for a military exception was evident to the sophisticated activists who happened upon it. One woman prominent in a governmental commission dealing with the ERA stumbled over the deferential interpretation of the ERA in Joan Wexler's *Yale Law Journal* note on the ERA and the military, even though Wexler's note had explicitly tried to discredit that interpretation. Discovering the deferential interpretation changed her understanding of the ERA's effect. Looking back, she concluded,

> I wish somebody had done more research on the assignment of women in the military at the time of the Senate debates. We should have made it clearer that it was entirely up to the military.
> What I didn't realize, and none of the people working on it—

including Tom Emerson's people who wrote the *Yale Law Journal* article—didn't realize, was how great discretion the military had. *Rostker* clarified that . . . the military would have full authority to authorize hand-to-hand combat.

Later, it was [Wexler's] *Yale Law Journal* article on the ERA and the military that pointed that out. Once I read that article I never had any doubt. We just failed to do enough research.

The Result

Because the pamphlets were vague, the feminist lawyers unanimous, and the top leadership of NOW implicitly committed to the egalitarian interpretation, local speakers in behalf of the ERA seldom adopted the deferential interpretation, despite its political advantages. In part, this was because they themselves usually preferred an egalitarian interpretation. Neither the feminist lawyers nor the top leadership of NOW could have been as effective as they were in promoting their interpretation of the ERA unless most of the activists who were working for the ERA's passage—both in the national leadership and in the rank and file—shared many of their values. However, the stance of local activists also reflected the fact that when opponents charged that the ERA would send women draftees into combat, they could see no persuasive counterargument. Merely citing pamphlets was not helpful. Instead, the speakers told their audiences of the infinitesimal chance that any individual woman would ever be drafted for combat, of the fact that Congress already had the authority to send women into combat, of the possible consequences in a nuclear age of a military made up exclusively of men, and, most powerfully, that full citizenship required equal responsibility. Frequently, ERA speakers said that as mothers they loved their daughters and their sons equally, and would be equally devastated if either child were killed in combat. At least in Illinois, I know of no ERA speaker—including those from the more conservative pro-ERA organizations—who told her audience that the ERA probably would not, if there were a draft, require women draftees to be sent into combat on the same basis as men.

Because none of the ERA organizations consistently and actively promulgated a deferential interpretation based firmly on the war powers, most state legislators had no access to this interpretation. They heard a lot of testimony that strongly supported an egalitarian interpretation[38] and a little testimony that weakly and obscurely supported an interpretation somewhat deferential to the military.[39] When I mentioned the deferential interpretation to the one Illinois legislator most likely to have understood the legal nuances of the Amendment, that legislator paused a while before responding, "I don't ever remember hearing that." After further thought, this long-time supporter of the ERA concluded, "I would have used it, frankly."

Without access to the deferential interpretation, most state legislators who supported the ERA simply decided not to meet the issue head-on. In the 1980 debate on the ERA in the Illinois House of Representatives, six opponents and three supporters of the ERA addressed the issue of the ERA's effect on the military. The six opponents all raised the specter of "combat" and "front line trenches." The three supporters all praised the justice of an equal draft and remained totally silent on combat.[40]

The fact that most feminists claimed the ERA would send qualified women draftees into combat on the same basis as men made mainstream conservative legislators reluctant to support it. But even more important than the issue itself was the perfect example it provided of the conservative legislators' greatest fear— that this seemingly innocuous amendment might in fact give rise to a host of radical, unintended, and unwanted consequences that the legislators would no longer be in any position to control. Middle-of-the-road legislators had seen the Supreme Court interpret other apparently innocuous principles embodied in the Bill of Rights as forbidding prayer in the schools, requiring judges to release criminals when police made procedural errors, and requiring school boards to bus students into neighborhoods where they did not live and were not wanted. Such legislators thought it quite possible that the ERA, while not doing much good, could produce a lot of harm by making it impossible for state legislators like themselves to design what they thought were reasonable laws regarding gender. Under the ERA, if scouting groups used public buildings, the Boy Scouts and the Girl Scouts might have to be integrated; women's and men's sports in public schools might have to be integrated, with the probable result that in most sports, which were orginally designed for men, few women would make either first or second string and would lose all opportunity for competition; prisons might have to be integrated, except for the sleeping quarters; abortions might have to be funded by the state. Some proponents of the ERA had in fact argued that it would have all of these consequences, although until 1982 most proponents denied any effect on abortions. In short, combat for drafted women, important in itself, had its greatest effect as a vivid symbol of the possibility that the Supreme Court might intepret the ERA, like other "rights oriented" amendments, as requiring consequences the public strongly opposed.

As President Carter's renewal of registration for the draft and President Reagan's hard line in foreign policy made Americans more aware of the possibility of future wars, opponents of the ERA began to focus more and more on the issue of women in combat. Phyllis Schlafly's 1972 "The Right to Be a Woman" had devoted only four short paragraphs to the draft and combat and had concentrated largely on a wife's supposed right to support and other "family" issues.[41] By 1980, the draft and combat had become, along with abortion, her central themes. All the earlier issues—unisex toilets, the right to support, and homosexual marriages—took a distinctly subordinate role. As the ERA deadline neared, Schlafly became fond of posing for publicity photographs holding a pamphlet on women in combat.[42] She arranged that out of the eleven people testifying against the ERA in Illinois in 1982, eight would be simply mothers, daughters, and local notables telling the assembly how awful it would be if women were drafted and sent into combat.[43] To a journalist she concluded that the proponent's decision to interpret the ERA as mandating qualified women in combat "put the nails in ERA's coffin."[44] A feminist writer, summing up the last vote on the ERA in Oklahoma, called the draft and combat "a really decisive issue in the ERA's defeat."[45]

Was It a Mistake?

Was the decision to choose the egalitarian over the deferential interpretation a mistake? The question of whether in principle it would be a good thing to draft qualified women for combat duty, should an emergency arise in the next few years, is too complex to treat fully here. Feminists have only just begun to think seriously about the nuances and effects of using conscripted women as combat troops, and their conclusions are not unanimous.[46]

Nor is it possible to consider adequately here the question of whether, if drafting women for combat were a good thing, a constitutional amendment would be the appropriate vehicle to this end. If even feminists are not agreed on the subject, it may be unwise to write into the Constitution a strict mandate one way or the other. Moreover, untried experiments with potentially severe consequences are not particularly suited to the dichotomous categories inherent in the liberal conception of "rights." In the language of rights, either something is a right, and the individual "possesses" that right in all its fullness, or something is not a right, and the individual has no claims at all. Almost by definition, this approach to women's roles in the military would make incremental experiments impossible. A blanket prohibition on the legal mention of gender would probably render unconstitutional combat units composed entirely of women, for example, even if such units were to prove more mutually supportive or more effective in the field than all-male or mixed units.[47]

If one concludes that it would have been desirable to write into the Constitution gender-blind standards for selecting combat troops, still one must ask whether the attempt was a political mistake at the historical moment when it was attempted. It was clearly a gamble that lost, but that does not mean it was a foolish gamble.

First, as we have seen, very little of immediate practical benefit to women was lost through the ERA's failure to pass. The Supreme Court's extension of the equal protection clause of the Fourteenth Amendment to include women meant that by 1982 the Court had declared unconstitutional, either directly or presumptively, almost all the laws that proponents in the 1972 Congressional debates had said the ERA would change.[48] The major exceptions were all-male draft registration, which because of the ERA's legislative history would almost certainly have been declared unconstitutional if the ERA had been ratified, and certain laws designed to benefit women rather than men. Because there was little of substance to be lost, no one worried that if the egalitarian interpretation killed the ERA women would lose concrete benefits.

Second, because the ERA's primary importance was as a symbol of the nation's commitment to women's rights, it served best as a strong symbol. Even if sending women into combat was not in itself good for women, as some feminists believed, it might, as a vivid symbol of equality, still have benefits that outweighed the more direct costs. The very extent of public opposition to women draftees in combat indicates how powerful a public statement it would have been if women had been treated equally with men not only in the military but in that most "masculine" of arenas, combat itself. Within the movement itself, the ERA had particular symbolic importance. Here was a strong constituency for an ERA that an activist could believe in, an ERA that refused to compromise, an ERA that had at least some radical edge. The women who gave up hours, weeks, months, and years of their lives to work for the ERA made these sacrifices in the service of an ideal. Compromising that ideal would have meant diminishing their ardor and weakening the ERA movement.[49]

Finally, although the best political compromise on the issue might have been for the ERA to require the military to assign *volunteers* to combat on a sex-blind basis while allowing it to assign *conscripts* any way it wished, there was no obvious way of interpreting the ERA as requiring this result. The only way to achieve such a compromise in practice was to argue that the ERA did not apply fully to the military. Under the Carter administration, the military was moving toward allowing women volunteers in combat positions. That movement was stopped in part by congressional fear that if Congress lowered the combat bar at all, the courts would leave it no further discretion in the matter.[50] A deferential interpretation of the ERA might have encouraged Congress to allow women volunteers into combat on a trial basis. The problem with this approach was that interpreting the ERA to allow military discretion would have meant that any change of administration, circumstance, or public sentiment could bring a retrogression in policy with no legal means of redress. This is just what happened under the Reagan administration. It was a risk many feminists did not want to take.

Because of these considerations, many active members of NOW and some members of the other major pro-ERA organizations would undoubtedly have decided for the egalitarian interpretation of the ERA even if they had faced the issue explicitly with full knowledge of the alternatives. In 1970, when the Senate amended the proposed ERA to stipulate that it would not apply to the draft, the ERA leadership decided that the whole Amendment should be withdrawn. Clearly, they were ready at that point to risk not getting an ERA rather than settling for one with "crippling" amendments. The same thing happened again in 1983. When the Democrats brought up a new ERA in the U.S. House of Representatives, the Republicans made clear that they would not support it unless it included language exempting laws relating to the draft and combat, along with language stipulating that it would not create a right to funding for abortions. The Democrats, with the support of the pro-ERA organizations, refused to allow votes on these proposals. As a result, the Amendment failed to get the required two-thirds vote.[51]

There is, of course, an important symbolic and practical difference between accepting explicit, permanent, constitutional exceptions to the ERA and merely accepting the likelihood that today's Supreme Court would make such exceptions. Many feminists, including myself, would oppose a specific provision in an ERA that permanently exempted the draft or combat from its coverage. A constitutional guarantee of rights should, in this view, be a clear and simple statement of principle, like the other guarantees in the Bill of Rights. But in 1972 I would have favored creating a legislative history that made clear Congress's assumption that the ERA would not require the military to assign women draftees to combat on the same basis as men. After 1976, when the practical costs of losing diminished, I would have been inclined to gamble on an egalitarian interpretation, on the grounds that if one is going to fight for a symbol, it is better to lose fighting for a good symbol than to win fighting for a bad one. Unfortunately, there is no way of knowing how other ERA activists felt about this issue, since the choice never came up for debate.

9 Of Husbands and Toilets

> The laws of every one of the 50 states now require
> the husband to support his wife and children. . . .
> The Equal Rights Amendment will remove this sole
> obligation from the husband, and make the wife
> equally responsible to provide a home for her family,
> and to provide 50 percent of the financial support of
> her family.
>
> —*Phyllis Schlafly Report (November 1972):1*

While the proponents exaggerated the effect of the ERA on equality at work and in the military, the opposition was hard at work producing exaggerations in a multitude of realms. This chapter will look at two such claims—that ERA would hurt homemakers, and that it would require integrating public toilets.

The opposition's claim that ERA would hurt homemakers was about as farfetched as the proponents' claim that it would help working women. The ERA might, on balance, have helped homemakers in 1972. By 1982 it probably would have had little effect either way. Yet just as the ERA's proponents had found in working women a "natural constituency" angry at its relative deprivation vis-à-vis working men, so the ERA's opponents found in homemakers a "natural constituency" angry at its relative deprivation vis-à-vis working women. This led the anti-ERA forces to stress the home issue, in much the same way that the pro-ERA organizations stressed 59 cents.

Because the home was a symbol as unassailable as equal pay for equal work, the opponents' exaggerations probably helped their cause rather than hurting it, much as the proponents' claims about 59 cents probably helped them. However, the opponents' claims about unisex toilets hurt them badly. Organizational dynamics like those that led the proponents to argue that the ERA would send women draftees into combat also led opponents to argue that the ERA would require unisex toilets, even though this claim had the practical result of weakening their credibility in the legislatures. Like the pro-ERA activists, the anti-ERA activists wanted to believe that the ERA would have massive effects. They needed the drama and symbolism of unisex toilets for its effect on their own troops, regardless of its effect on legislative opinion.

The ERA and Family Law

Unlike most modern legislation governing economic life, legislation governing the family has often made important distinctions between family members based solely on their sex. These laws have had little practical importance so long as families stayed together, but when family members separate, laws that define a husband's and father's rights and responsibilities differently from a wife's and mother's rights and responsibilities can become very important. The ERA would have invalidated almost all such laws. In the early 1970s this would have led to noticeable revisions in family law, some of which would have worked to the homemaker's advantage, and others, indirectly, to the homemaker's disadvantage. By the late 1970s, these laws had almost all been changed, struck down as unconstitutional under the Fourteenth Amendment, or become unenforceable because they were presumptively unconstitutional.

The most important laws that differentiated husbands from their wives were those affecting support obligations, control over property, the "tender years presumption," and laws symbolizing secondary status, like those that prevented a wife from choosing her legal domicile or name and that restricted the right to marry without parental consent. I will begin by reviewing the situation in 1972, when Congress passed the ERA, and will then discuss the changes that took place while the states were debating the ERA from 1972 to 1982. (Tired readers may skip to p. 98).

Support Obligations

Under the common law, which we inherited from England and which remains in force in each state until modified by statute or judicial decision, a husband is obliged to support his wife during marriage. In return, a wife is obliged to do housework and care for children. Schlafly and other ERA opponents argued that the ERA would end a husband's obligation to support his wife, leaving home-makers with no legal claim on their husbands.

Few lawyers took this argument seriously, for two reasons. First, American courts have never enforced a husband's obligation to support his wife so long as the two continued to live together.[1] Judges have only been willing to become involved in a couple's financial arrangements after the marriage has broken down and the partners have separated. At this point, the common law presump-tion about a husband's obligations is superseded by specific state laws covering separation and divorce. Second, past precedent makes it almost certain that judges would not interpret the ERA as invalidating the husband's traditional obligation to support his homemaking wife. Instead, judges would simply assume that the ERA extended this obligation to wives in marriages where the wife worked and the husband did not.[2]

When we turn from common law to legislation, the obligations of spouses to support one another after they separate usually de-pend on their financial situation, not their sex. But there were still some exceptions in 1972. Alimony obligations, for example, were often phrased as something men might owe to women, but not the other way around.[3] In addition, some states phrased the parental support obligation as requiring only a father—but not a mother—to support their children.[4]

The ERA would have invalidated all these laws, forcing legisla-tures to make support obligations depend on ability to pay instead of sex. This change would have cost a few affluent women some money. The losers would have been women who had both ne'er-do-well husbands and either well-paid jobs or inherited money. But because women on the average earn 59 cents to the average man's dollar and the number who earn a great deal more than their husbands is small, only a handful of women would have been affected.

What really worried homemakers about the ERA was not its

direct effect on women who earned more than their husbands, but its indirect effects—the way it seemed to promote a public image of women having the same needs and economic capacities as men. Judges, for example, were already awarding alimony, as distinct from child support, in fewer cases and in smaller and smaller amounts. Many feared that the ERA would accelerate this trend by legitimating the fiction that women were the equals of men not only in rights but in their ability to support themselves. Alimony, of course, was seldom ordered and even more seldom paid even in 1972.[5] By and large, the harm had already been done. While the ERA might have been responsible for a small further decline by symbolically fostering an image of independent womanhood, it probably would have made up for this by giving symbolic support to the compensatory principle that the wife in a marriage has earned during the marriage a right to a certain percentage both of the physical property and of her husband's salary.[6] This principle, based on recognizing the homemaker's contribution, may in time provide a divorcing full-time homemaker with more support than the principle of alimony, now almost defunct for reasons far larger than the ERA.

As for the mother's obligation to support her children, since the few states that imposed child-support obligations exclusively on fathers in 1972 were those that usually awarded custody to the mother, the fact that women in these states were not legally obligated to support their children usually had little practical meaning. Among the middle-class, most support settlements were negotiated, and among the working class and poor, fathers often simply disappeared. In all classes, mothers in fact had to contribute much of the child support because child support allocations were so small, and because they had few ways to make their ex-husbands live up to their legal obligations.

Marital Property

In 1972, eight states treated all property that a couple bought with their earnings during marriage as "community property," and these states normally gave the husband managerial control over such property.[7] The ERA would have forced these eight states to establish joint control over marital property, a move that would undoubtedly have benefited the homemaker.

In the other forty-two states, spouses were presumed to own whatever property they personally had paid for. If a couple brought no assets to their marriage, and if the husband worked for pay while the wife did the housework and raised the children, the husband was presumed to have paid for, and therefore in some sense to "own," all the couple's assets.[8] Whether this arrangement would have violated the ERA was unclear in 1972, because these laws were neutral on their face. Until the 1976 *Washington v. Davis* decision, some family lawyers assumed that the Court would use a disparate impact analysis under the ERA to force the remaining states to shift to some arrangement more like community property, with joint control over assets. After the *Washington* decision, this was not likely.

Even if the court had not ruled disparate impact irrelevant in *Washington v. Davis,* the actual effect of forcing all states to adopt some variant of community property was unclear. Within the marriage, joint legal control would have helped homemakers primarily psychologically, through knowing that their unpaid contribution to the marriage would now entitle them to half the physical product of that marriage. Since most couples decide on their internal financial arrangements informally, and the courts do not interfere in an ongoing marriage, joint control would be of little importance except in case of divorce. At the point of divorce, the ERA's effect under a disparate impact analysis was hard to predict. Working-class couples seldom had much in the way of capital assets. Middle-class couples rarely owned more than a partly paid-for house. In the "separate property" states, the woman sometimes got more than half the property, because she got the house along with custody of the children. In "community property" states, the tendency was to divide the house, or the money from its sale, equally. Lawyers disagreed about which system was best for women.[9]

Because of these uncertainties, even in 1972 the greatest effect of the ERA on marital property would probably have been not its strict legal effect but the effect of its presence in the Constitution on the nation's judges. Experience with state ERAs suggests that on balance the presence of an ERA in the constitution encourages judges to take steps that enhance women's property rights in divorce settlements, like calculating the forgone earnings and the development of marketable skills that a wife might have sacrificed on agreeing to manage the home while the husband took a paid job. Presumably, a federal ERA would have had similar effects.

Custody

Even in 1972, when parents split up, custody of the children was supposed to be arranged so as to protect the "best interests of the child." This neutral standard is clearly consistent with the ERA. But if, as was often the case, statutes specified that in the child's "tender years" it was always in the best interests of the child to give the mother exclusive custody regardless of the child's actual relationship to each parent, aggrieved fathers could have successfully challenged this practice under the ERA. Few homemakers would have considered this a benefit.

Domicile, Names, and Marriage Age

In 1972, most states required a married woman to assume her husband's legal domicile, no matter where she actually lived. Although these laws had few practical effects, in some situations they hurt the wife's interests.[10] All these laws would have become unconstitutional if the ERA had passed, and both the psychological and the practical gains would presumably have benefited homemakers.

In 1972, a number of states still required wives to use their husband's name for certain official purposes. In Alabama, for example, wives had to use their husband's name rather than their own maiden name to get a driver's license.[11] The ERA would have ended such requirements.

In 1969, when Leo Kanowitz surveyed the law, thirty-nine states allowed women to marry at a younger age than men without their parents' consent.[12] From the average teenager's viewpoint, no doubt, such laws appear to discriminate in favor of women. But because early marriage typically means early withdrawal from school and substantially increases the likelihood of divorce, it is not obvious that letting women marry younger than men is a favor to women. One might argue that legislatures allowed women to marry at a younger age than men without parental consent because male legislators thought it less important to protect women from their own folly than to protect men. Whatever the legislators' motives, the ERA would have forced them to set uniform age standards for prospective spouses.

Conclusions as of 1972

Summing up, we can say that in 1972 the ERA would have given wives in community property states a veto over their husband's disposition of joint assets. By indirect influence it might also have helped give wives a fairer share of marital property in separate property states. It would have protected wives from having to assume their husband's legal domicile if it was not their actual domicile, and from having to assume their husband's name if they did not want to. It would probably have encouraged judges when deciding the terms of a divorce settlement, to consider a homemaker's contribution to the marriage as well as her forgone earnings and skill development, although it might also have encouraged them to award less traditional alimony. On the cost side, the ERA would have required affluent women to assume the same obligations vis-à-vis their ex-spouses and children that men with comparable income assume. It would also have allowed husbands to challenge the assumption that when parents separated the mother was better able to care for the children than the father. In short, in 1972 the balance for or against the ERA from the point of view of homemakers was ambiguous. Most of them probably would have benefited financially but at the cost of their presumptive right to custody of young children.

The Law in 1982

The law changed substantially in all of the foregoing areas between 1972 and 1982, and all the changes reduced the likely impact of the ERA on homemakers.

Support Obligations

In 1979, the U.S. Supreme Court struck down as a violation of the equal protection clause the Alabama statute requiring husbands but not wives to pay alimony.[13] In 1975, it also struck down the Utah statute requiring parents to support sons until they reached twenty-one but daughters only until they reached eighteen.[14] At the state level, Colorado and Georgia courts upheld laws requiring fathers but not mothers to support their children in 1974,[15] but, in light of the Supreme Court's 1979 alimony ruling, it seems that the U.S. Supreme Court would strike down these laws if they were challenged in federal court today. At the moment, no such case appears to have reached the federal courts.

Custody

Even without an ERA, litigation under the equal protection clause of the Fourteenth Amendment has led the courts to declare unconstitutional any statute or practice that under a "tender years" doctrine equates the "best interests of the child" with maternal custody. In practice, moreover, more courts are awarding joint custody, and fathers tend to get more visitation rights than they did a decade ago.

Marital Property

By 1982 most community property states voluntarily changed their laws to require joint control over joint assets. Louisiana did not, but in 1981 the U.S. Supreme Court struck down under the equal protection clause the Louisiana statute making the husband "head and master" of the household and giving him the sole control over community property.[16] Likewise, by 1982 most of the separate property states had required courts to "equitably" apportion at divorce all property accumulated during marriage.[17]

Domicile, Names, and Ages

Under the equal protection clause, state and federal courts have invalidated several laws requiring wives to assume their husband's domicile.[18] If such a case came to the Supreme Court today, it seems virtually certain that the Court would rule that a wife could, if she wished, establish her legal domicile wherever she actually lived, regardless of where her husband was legally domiciled.

Although the Supreme Court has not yet recognized any constitutional right of wives to retain their original surnames,[19] other federal and state courts have been more responsive. If the Supreme Court were now to accept such a case, the obligation to use one's husband's name would probably not survive under the interpretation of the equal protection clause that the Court has evolved since 1972.[20] Of the thirty-nine states that in 1969 required parental consent for marriage at different ages for men than for women, all but one (Arkansas) had established a uniform age by 1981.[21] The states acted in response to Supreme Court decisions under the equal protection clause invalidating similar statutes.[22] The Arkansas statute would almost surely be struck down if it were to reach the federal courts today.

Taking all these changes together, it is hard to avoid the conclusion that while the ERA would have changed quite a lot in 1972, by 1982 most of this had been accomplished by other means.

The Perceptions of Homemakers

If the ERA promised at least as much benefit as harm for homemakers before 1976, and if it would have had little short-term impact either way after 1976, how are we to account for the fact that so many homemakers saw it as a threat and that so many legislators claimed to see it the same way? One answer, popular among feminists, was that homemakers had been misled by "Phyllis Schlafly's lies." While there is some truth in this charge, we must still ask why these particular lies seemed credible to these particular people. The answer, I think, is threefold. First, while the ERA would not have had any direct negative effect on family life, it was nonetheless a by-product of a movement that was profoundly opposed to traditional conceptions of how families should be organized. Second, homemakers as a group were ripe for such an appeal because they had recently lost considerable status in society. Third, the ERA would in fact have deprived homemakers of some traditional protections and benefits (like the tender years presumption). While feminists intended to raise new and presumably better protections in place of the old, these were not strictly mandated by the ERA. Homemakers could feel, therefore, that they were being asked "to relinquish tangible benefits in exchange for a vague promise of dubious value."[23]

Feminists against Homemaking

From the very beginning of the modern women's movement in the mid-1960s,[24] feminists had been ideologically opposed to, or at best ambivalent about, homemaking as a full-time career. In turn, homemakers had been ideologically opposed to, or at best unenthusiastic about, important planks in the feminist platform. NOW's founding statement of purpose, in 1966, stated:

> We believe that a true partnership between the sexes demands a different concept of marriage, an equitable sharing of the responsibilities of home and children and of the economic burdens of their support.[25]

While NOW's word "equitable" was not nearly as strong as the more radical groups' demands for "equal" sharing, NOW's "different concept" of marriage still implied an androgynous division of labor, in which men took half the responsibility for child care and housework and women took half the responsibility for bringing in money. This position became not just an implication but an article of faith for later feminists. Such a position always implies a criticism of life as a full-time homemaker.

It is true that NOW's founding members were careful not to take a formal position against the homemaker. Not only did they use the phrase "equitable sharing," which could cover a 100/0 percent division if sufficient "credit" were given the person who did 100 percent of the child care and housework, but they laced the founding statement with other phrases and sentences that gave support to the full-time homemaker.[26] NOW, however, was originally one of the more conservative feminist groups.[27] Other groups gave the life of a homemaker shorter shrift. When the women in Students for a Democratic Society (SDS) first got together in 1967 to work for what later became "women's liberation," they suggested that the organization "work on behalf of all women for communal childcare, wide dissemination of contraceptives, easily available abortions, and equal sharing of housework."[28] Most other women's groups also pushed for reforms—like day-care centers, shared housework, and legal abortion—that would help women cast off their traditional role of full-time homemaker and join the paid labor force.

The conflict between feminists and homemakers was a genuine conflict of interest, which could not easily be resolved by compromise. The very existence of full-time homemakers was incompatible with many goals of the women's movement, like the equal sharing of political and economic power. Women can never hold half the economically and politically powerful positions in the country if a greater proportion of women than men withdraw from competition for those positions. More important, if even 10 percent of American women remain full-time homemakers, this will reinforce traditional views of what women ought to do and encourage other women to become full-time homemakers at least while their children are very young. If women plan to drop out of the labor force while their children are young, they will choose careers that are interruptible, that convert easily to part-time work, that do not demand either long hours or geographical mobility, and that whenever possible have some connection to the tasks of motherhood (like teaching or nursing). Occupations that have these characteristics will remain stereotyped as "women's occupations," and for the forseeable future they will pay less than men's occupations that require comparable training. As we have seen, about half the difference between men's and women's wages is due to the sex segregation of occupations, age (women are in the paid labor force when they are young or old, not in their prime productive years), and interrupted careers.[29] If women disproportionately take time off from their careers to have children, or if they work less hard than men at their careers while their children are young, this will put them at a competitive disadvantage vis-à-vis men, particularly men whose wives do all the homemaking and child care. This disadvantage will show up especially clearly in the most powerful and best paid positions in the society.[30] Thus, the more full-time homemakers there are, the harder it will be to break traditional expectations that homemaking ought to be a woman's career. This means that no matter how any individual feminist might feel about child care and housework, the movement as a whole had reasons to discourage full-time homemaking.

Most feminists also had personal reasons for rejecting the notion that women should "specialize" in housework and child care.

The women who founded NOW were mostly professional women,[31] and those who began "women's liberation" in the Student Non-violent Coordinating Committee (SNCC) and SDS were usually college-educated community organizers. Very few of these women saw homemaking as their primary identity. Yet their husbands or lovers often expected them to do the housework. Recognizing these unequal expectations regarding housework as a source of personal oppression, radical feminists began to inquire into the historical character of marriage and the family. Discovering how recently women had been the property of their husbands, and how recently women had been the ones in the marriage ceremony who promised to "obey," radical feminists concluded that the traditional nuclear family oppressed women. Because conventional images of marriage are permeated by scenes of male domination and female subordination, they concluded that married life would always be shaped by this legacy. An "egalitarian marriage" was thus a contradiction in terms. No matter how "liberated" she was, a woman who defined herself as "married" would inevitably slide into roles that carried an inegalitarian heritage, and would adopt, without fully thinking them through, symbols like the bridal veil, or lingerie at the "shower," that reinforced the inegalitarian tradition. In this analysis, if a married woman were to have any hope of developing self-respect or self-confidence, she would have to be at least as independent of her husband as he was of her. This meant having a job as interesting, as demanding, and as well paid as his, not being his unpaid housekeeper and babysitter.

For radical feminists, one of the most popular, personally helpful pamphlets of the late 1960s was Pat Mainardi's "The Politics of Housework," which catalogued the many excuses middle-class men gave for not doing an equal share of the housework and "explained" their underlying meaning. Here is one such excuse, and Mainardi's explanation of its meaning:

> "I don't mind sharing the housework, but I don't do it very well. We should each do the things we're best at."

> Meaning: Unfortunately I'm no good at things like washing dishes or cooking. What I do best is a little light carpentry, changing light bulbs, moving furniture (how often do you move furniture?).

Also meaning: Historically the lower classes (black men and us) have had hundreds of years experience doing menial jobs. It would be a waste of manpower to train someone else to do them now.

Also meaning: I don't like the dull stupid boring jobs, so you should do them.

Here is another:

"I hate it more than you. You don't mind it so much."

Meaning: Housework is garbage work. It is the worst crap I've ever done. It is degrading and humiliating for someone of my intelligence to do it. But for someone of your intelligence. . .

Remember, wrote Mainardi, "the measure of your oppression is his resistance." The pamphlet was funny. For couples who were both in school, or who, like Mainardi, could say, "We both had careers, both had to work a couple of days a week to earn enough to live on,"[32] it was also much to the point.

The feminist analysis of marriage led to demonstrations like one at the Marriage License Bureau in New York, where a group called The Feminists distributed a leaflet entitled "Women: Do You Know the Facts about Marriage?" The leaflet began:

DO YOU KNOW THAT RAPE IS LEGAL IN MARRIAGE?

According to law, sex is the purpose of marriage. You have to have sexual intercourse in order to have a valid marriage.

DO YOU KNOW THAT LOVE AND AFFECTION ARE
NOT REQUIRED IN MARRIAGE?

If you don't have sex with your husband, he can get a divorce or annulment. If he doesn't love you, that's not grounds for divorce.

DO YOU KNOW THAT YOU ARE YOUR
HUSBAND'S PRISONER?

You have to live with him wherever he pleases. If he decides to move someplace else, either you go with him or he can charge you with desertion, get a divorce and, according to the law, you deserve nothing because you're the guilty party. And that's if he were the one who moved![33]

At a metropolitan bridal fair, a guerrilla theater group called WITCH distributed a pamphlet beginning, "Marriage is a dehumanizing institution—legal whoredom for women."[34] On Mother's Day, a WITCH group solemnly incanted these stanzas from a "card by Hellmark":

> Every year we set aside
> a very special day
> to remind you, Martyr Dear
> that home is where you stay.
> While hubby challenges the world
> his wonders to perform
> you cook his meals, clean his home
> and keep his bedside warm.
> Now look upon your daughter
> will she too be enslaved
> to a man, a home, and family
> or can she still be saved?[35]

The founders of NOW and the early proponents of the ERA were a good deal more staid than the Feminists, WITCH, or even Pat Mainardi, and they were seldom as hostile to the family. Indeed, both radical and liberal feminist literature includes a lot of writing sympathetic to mothers, mothering, home life, and more recently even marriage. The nurturant, care-taking role has consistently been central to the cultural strands of feminism, which focus on women's particular gifts for giving love.[36] But every feminist, radical or otherwise, still knows that when people start talking about the home as women's "special sphere," they are constructing a rationale for excluding women from economic and political power. Gaining economic and political power thus requires some attack on the idea that a woman's place is in the home. This made antagonism between homemakers and feminists almost inevitable.

Opponents of the ERA were acutely aware that its sponsors were generally opposed to homemaking as a career. Phyllis

Schlafly's very first salvo against the ERA, "What's Wrong with 'Equal Rights' for Women?" identified the ERA with *Ms.* magazine, which she characterized as

> anti-family, anti-children, and pro-abortion. It is a series of sharp-tongued, high-pitched, whining complaints by unmarried women. They view the home as a prison, and the wife and mother as a slave. To these women's libbers, marriage means dirty dishes and dirty laundry. One article lauds a woman's refusal to carry up the family laundry as "an act of extreme courage." Another tells how satisfying it is to be a lesbian. . . .
>
> Women's lib is a total assault on the role of the American woman as wife and mother, and on the family as the basic unit of society.
>
> Women's libbers are trying to make wives and mothers unhappy with their career, make them feel that they are "second-class citizens" and "abject slaves." Women's libbers are promoting free sex instead of the "slavery" of marriage. They are promoting Federal "day-care centers" for babies instead of homes. They are promoting abortions instead of families.[37]

Right-wing state legislators were impressed by such arguments and often echoed them. In Illinois, for example, one argued that the ERA was

> really an attack on the home. It is an attack on motherhood. It says that for a woman to have to be a mother and have to be a housewife is somehow degrading.[38]

Older rural legislators made speech after speech along these lines,[39] rarely specifying how the ERA would hurt homemakers but stressing its "guilt by association" with feminism and the tension between feminism and homemaking. This was a promising strategy. In 1977, 42 percent of American women saw the women's movement as a major cause of family breakdown.[40] If the women's movement was behind the ERA, and if the women's movement was a cause of family breakdown, then the ERA must be a potential cause of family breakdown too.

Homemakers' Perceptions of Women
Who Work Outside the Home

Even if there had been nothing in feminist ideology to threaten a homemaker, and even if every feminist had kept silent about her anger at being forced to do more than half the housework, some homemakers would probably have suspected the ERA, simply because its sponsors billed it as an effort to improve the position of women who work outside the home. By the late 1970s, many full-time homemakers had come to see women who worked for pay as "the enemy," regardless of whether those women were feminists or not. This perception was not as quixotic as women who worked outside their homes thought. It reflected the fact that the social respect once accorded to homemakers was eroding. While this erosion may have been partly traceable to feminist attacks on housework, its primary cause had nothing to do with ideology. Full-time homemaking lost status primarily because high-status women abandoned it.

In 1962, only 37 percent of all wives worked for pay outside the home. The wives of high school–and college-educated men were hardly more likely to work for pay than the wives of men with only a grade school education. Between 1962 and 1978 the proportion of wives working for pay rose from 37 to 58 percent. This growth was concentrated among wives with highly educated husbands, for whom the economic pressures to work were lowest. Among women whose husbands had only a grade school education, 34 percent worked for pay both in 1962 and in 1978. Among women whose husbands had attended college, 38 percent worked for pay in 1962, but this had grown to 65 percent by 1978 (fig. 2.A).[41]

The growing class divergence in whether a married woman worked for pay was matched by a growing class divergence in how women felt about housework. Between 1957 and 1976 there was no change in the percentage of homemakers with a grade school education who said they "enjoyed" housework. In both years it was about 76 percent. Among those who had attended high school, the percentage who said they enjoyed housework fell from 66 to 54 percent. Among homemakers who had attended college it fell from 67 to 38 percent (fig. 2.B).[42] The same pattern emerges when one looks at career aspirations. Among grade school–educated homemakers,

A. *Percent of married women working outside the home.*

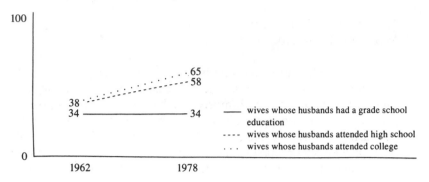

B. *Percent of homemakers who say they "enjoy" housework.*

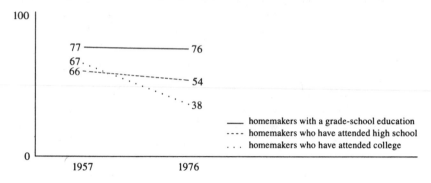

C. *Percent of homemakers who say they once wanted a career.*

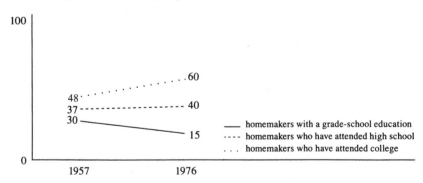

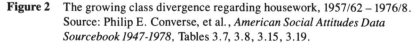

Figure 2 The growing class divergence regarding housework, 1957/62 – 1976/8.
Source: Philip E. Converse, et al., *American Social Attitudes Data Sourcebook 1947-1978,* Tables 3.7, 3.8, 3.15, 3.19.

the percentage who said that they had at some point wanted a career actually fell from 30 percent in 1957 to 15 percent in 1976. Among high school educated homemakers it rose only slightly, from 37 to 40 percent. Among college-educated homemakers it rose from 48 to 60 percent. (fig. 2.C).[43]

The rise of careerism and the declining attraction of housework among educated women was partly a response to changes in job opportunities. For a woman with only a grade school education, homemaking was usually a more pleasant, autonomous, growth-inducing profession than waitressing, cleaning other people's houses, or working as a factory operative, and these alternatives did not improve during the 1960s and 1970s. For women with a college education, homemaking was often more attractive than teaching school or being a secretary, which were the main alternatives in 1960. But homemaking was often far less attractive than the options that had opened up by the late 1970s.

These changes meant that women became less likely to share the same common experiences. At the beginning of the contemporary women's movement, in 1968, women of all classes found themselves in something like the same boat. Their structural positions either as homemakers or as lower-level employees were similar, and they expressed much the same feelings about their work and their home lives. By 1982, when the ERA went down to defeat, one of the bonds of sisterhood—a common experience in the home—was breaking. When employers opened good jobs to women, the beneficiaries were highly educated women who had decided not to become full-time homemakers. The more educated a woman was, the more she benefited from these changes. For less-educated women, homemaking remained the job of choice, but it lost social standing as high-status women abandoned it.

The decision of most college-educated women to pursue careers other than homemaking raised to public consciousness the many disadvantages of work in the home. Highly educated women were tastemakers for their sisters. In the 1950s, to preserve their own self-esteem, they extolled the virtues of work in the home. By 1980, they saw matters quite differently. A job once perceived as noble now seemed distinctly plebeian. Thus, homemakers suffered a tremendous loss in social prestige in two decades. Sociologists call this phenomenon "status degradation." It had happened to these homemakers through no fault of their own. As the paid labor force offered urban, educated women attractive options, the more rural, less-educated women found that the world judged the traditional job of homemaking less attractive. Middle-class women who chose to stay in the home began to feel déclassé. Women's magazines began to print outraged letters from homemakers who now found that they had to describe themselves as "only" a housewife, not only to men but to other women.[44]

Prestige is an important social reward for almost everyone. Since homemakers have never received direct monetary rewards for their work, prestige is especially important to them. During the late 1960s and 1970s they experienced a severe "pay cut" in prestige. Naturally, they were resentful. And consciously or unconsciously they blamed the people who were, at least in part, responsible—their sisters who had deserted the home for paid careers, making the now empty homestead look shabby.

The Loss of Protections

Homemakers not only lost a lot of status in the course of the decade preceding the ERA struggle, they lost a number of their traditional protections as well. The divorce rate was increasing, and alimony was decreasing. Many states had instituted "no-fault" divorce laws, which reduced social blame on the husband who tired of his family, and even put pressure on some nurturant women to go along with their husbands' desire to abandon ship. A new ethic had arisen for men, in which hedonistic egoism was no longer encumbered by responsibility.[45] Society was beginning to condone a man leaving his family on the sole grounds that living with them and providing for them made him unhappy.

The old common-law contract between the sexes held that if a woman did the housework, raised the children, and obeyed her husband, he had to support her. As we have seen, this contract had little practical force, but the ERA would have undermined its symbolic force as well. As Barbara Ehrenreich put it, "What was at stake in the battle over the ERA was the *legitimacy* of women's claim on men's incomes, and for this there was reason enough to fear—and to judge from the intensity of the opposition, fear enough to abandon reason."[46] It was the ERA's symbolic meaning that frightened the opposition. When Phyllis Schlafly said of loveless marriages, "Even though love may go out the window, the obligation should remain. ERA would eliminate that obligation,"[47] any reader would assume she meant the ERA's legal effect. But she spelled out her concerns more clearly when she "insisted that the ERA would say, '[B]oys, supporting your wives isn't your responsibility anymore,' and then they could no longer see it as their duty."[48] It is what the ERA would "say," not what it would do, that really concerned Schlafly and the rest of the opposition. In this deep sense the struggle over the ERA was indeed a "struggle over symbols."[49] When a proponent of the ERA argued on a televised debate with Schlafly that "[t]he idea that a woman can sit home and be supported by her husband has long died out," she was not only wrong as a matter of fact but was reenforcing doubts about the ERA among the millions of women whose husbands *were* supporting them.[50]

Homemakers have always been somewhat more conservative than men or working women, perhaps partly because they are less exposed to a cosmopolitan world. This conservatism does not show up on all issues,[51] but on matters that involved sexual relations, the family, and women's roles, homemakers were noticably more conservative than either men or working women in the years from 1974 to 1982 (table A9). Furthermore, on interracial marriage, homosexuality, and abortion, the gap between homemakers and working women increased markedly over these years (table A9, col. 4).[52]

These concerns meant that homemakers were less likely than working women to join feminist organizations like NOW. When NOW did a sample survey of its members in 1974, only 17 percent described themselves as homemakers, whereas 52 percent of all women over eighteen in the United States described themselves that way in that year.[53] During 1973 and 1974 NOW launched five direct-mail campaigns to solicit funds. Of these five, the only one that failed to pay for itself involved subscribers to *Redbook* and *McCalls,* both of which are aimed at homemakers.[54]

While feminist groups found it hard to restructure their thinking to appeal to homemakers, the homemakers' precarious social position made them a natural resource for groups that wanted to turn back the clock on the sexual, legal, and labor-force trends that had undermined the patriarchal basis of the family in the decades before the ERA struggle. Indeed, the resurgence of the New Right in the 1970s was based largely on "women's issues" such as abortion and the ERA.

Schlafly Courts the Homemaker

Many people who followed the struggle over the ERA believed—rightly in my view—that the Amendment would have been ratified by 1975 or 1976 had it not been for Phyllis Schlafly's early and effective effort to organize potential opponents. Schlafly seems to have stumbled on the ERA issue almost by accident. In 1964 she had written a campaign biography of Barry Goldwater *(A Choice, Not an Echo)* that attacked the elite East Coast Republican establishment for selling out to the Russians and neglecting American defense. In 1972 she was writing a monthly newsletter, the *Phyllis Schlafly Report,* which focused mainly on military preparedness and the dangers of Communism. Her first attack on the ERA appeared in February 1972, before the Amendment passed the Senate, but did little more than damn the Amendment by association with *Ms.* and "women's lib" while praising the privileges women had derived from the Christian Age of Chivalry. In this first article, Schlafly urged women who did not like their lot to "take up your complaint with God."[55]

After the Senate passed the ERA, Schlafly entered the fray in earnest. She devoted her entire November 1972 *Report* to an attack on the ERA, stressing the substantive changes that the ERA might make in men's and women's lives.[56] To her potential audience of homemakers, she began by arguing that the ERA would abolish the husband's duty to support his wife. Quoting *American Jurisprudence,* she defined this as a level of support

> in accordance with the station in life to which he has accustomed his family . . . in the light of [the] normal living of persons, the particular estate, social rank and condition of the husband and wife . . . without reference to the wife's separate estate [or] what she can earn by her own labor.

This information seems to have come from her own research. The rest of the article summarized anti-ERA articles by Paul Freund of the Harvard Law School and Philip Kurland of the University of

Chicago Law School, both of which Senator Ervin had inserted in the *Congressional Record* during the 1971 and 1972 Senate debates. From Freund, for example, she concluded that if the ERA were passed, and if child-care centers were made available, "a wife with small children would no longer be 'unable' to support herself through employment, and so . . . would lose the right of support from her husband."

While her focus was clearly on the concerns of the homemaker, Schlafly also touched on other substantive changes that she knew were likely to appall a conservative, or even mainstream, audience. She quoted Freund as saying the ERA would mean that

> women must be admitted to West Point on a parity with men; women must be conscripted for military service equally with men; . . . girls must be eligible for the same athletic teams as boys in the public schools and state universities; . . . and life insurance commissions may not continue to approve lower life insurance premiums for women (based on greater life expectance)—all by command of the Federal Constitution.

"Thus," added Schlafly, "the Equal Rights Amendment will positively make women subject to the draft and for combat duty on an equal basis with men. Most women's libbers admit that this is what they want." (Note that Freund, writing in 1971, had said nothing about combat. Schlafly presumably picked this up from Senator Ervin's 1972 remarks in the Senate after reading the *Yale Law Journal* article on the ERA.)

According to Schlafly, Freund concluded that the ERA (1) might make separate athletic competitions for men and women illegal; (2) would "presumably" reduce certain Social Security retirement benefits for women to the same level as those available to similarly situated men; (3) might abolish freedom of choice between boys' schools, girls' schools, and coed schools; (4) might eliminate separate physical education classes for girls and boys in public schools; (5) might abolish separate prison cells for men and women; and even (6) might make illegal separate public rest rooms for the different sexes.

Schlafly ended her *Report* with another pitch to homemakers, pointing out that the Civil Rights Act of 1964 already guaranteed equal pay for equal work. She concluded by describing the "two very different groups of women lobbying for the Equal Rights Amendment":

> One group is the women's liberationists. Their motive is totally radical. They hate men, marriage and children. They are out to destroy morality and the family. They look upon husbands as the exploiters, children as an evil to be avoided (by abortion if necessary), and the family as an institution which keeps women in "second-class citizenship" or even "slavery."

The second group was business and professional women who "have felt the keen edge of discrimination in their employment. Many have been in a situation where the woman does most of the work, and some man gets the bigger salary and the credit." Citing her own experience with this kind of discrimination, she said she supported this group in their effort to eliminate injustice, but she argued that everything necessary could be done through the Civil Rights Act and the Equal Employment Opportunity Act, which would not "take away fundamental rights and benefits from the rest of women."

This issue of the *Report* was aimed at homemakers (and their husbands), and the tactic was a startling success. To be sure a majority of homemakers in the United States continued to support the ERA,[57] as did a majority of every other major demographic group. But the anti-ERA forces drew much of their active support from homemakers. Just as an exaggeration of the ERA's effect on working women became the major argument for the proponents, because it appealed not only to the general public but to a particular large and angry constituency, so an exaggeration of the ERA's effect on homemakers became, for the same reasons, the first major argument of the opponents.

Freund, Schlafly, and Toilets

While Phyllis Schlafly's exaggerations regarding the husband's duty of support and other "family" issues may well have helped her cause, the exaggeration that hurt her most, and became a major weapon in the hands of her enemies, was the issue of unisex toilets. Schlafly devoted only one sentence to the "toilet" issue in "The Right to be a Woman," but the wording of that sentence was crucial. Professor Paul Freund, she wrote, "indicates that [if the ERA is adopted] we must assume that rest rooms segregated by sex would be prohibited by the courts just as the courts prohibit color-segregated rest rooms." Her phrase "we must assume" suggests considerable certainty. The truth was exactly the opposite to her claim. It was true that in 1971 Paul Freund had raised the issue of integrated toilets. However, he had done so at the end of a paragraph in which he pointed out the difficulties produced by assuming that the principles established in the struggle for racial equality were also applied to sexual equality. All he had said was this:

> One of the prime targets of the equal-rights movement has been the color-segregated public rest room. Whether segregation by sex would meet the same condemnation is at least a fair question to test the legal assimilation of racism and "sexism."[58]

Freund wrote his article before the 1971–1972 debates in the House and Senate had produced a legislative history on the ERA. Precisely because of Freund's comments and the opposition's subsequent interest in this point, every proponent who addressed the issue in those debates insisted that the "right to privacy" in the Constitution meant that the ERA would not require sex-integrated washrooms. This understanding was also explicit in the Senate Majority Report. Even the *Yale Law Review* authors developed the point at length. Such unanimous and unambiguous legislative history would have made it hard for the Supreme Court to interpret the ERA as requiring integrated restrooms, even in the extremely unlikely event that it wanted to do so. Yet, seemingly without compunction, Schlafly turned Freund's weak suggestion into a claim that the Court would in fact take this step. This contention then provoked local campaigns against the Amendment highlighted by women dressing up as outhouses labeled "Theirs," and leaflets telling voters to reject the ERA, "also known as the Common Toilet Law."[59]

The unisex toilet issue fed the fervor of the anti-ERA forces by giving them something absolutely outrageous to focus on. It could conjure up visions of rape by predatory males. It could symbolize the stripping away of all traditional protections in an androgynous society where women could no longer claim special treatment from the more powerful male simply on the grounds that they were women. In the South it recalled vividly the historical trauma of racial integration. Indeed, as we shall see, unisex toilets became one of the four major themes that activists speaking to reporters and writing in the newspapers stressed as central to their opposition.

But while this issue strengthened the morale of the activists, it had mixed results among the public and backfired in the legislatures. Among the public nationwide, the argument was probably counterproductive. Even among those members of the public who opposed the ERA, less than 3 percent gave unisex toilets as either a first, second, or third reason for their opposition.[60] While there is no way of proving that this or any other argument hurt the opposition, the fact that in another survey 76 percent of the public thought that the ERA would not even increase the likelihood of integrated toilets[61] suggests a widespread skepticism that normally would undermine credibility.

In the four key unratified states of Illinois, Oklahoma, Florida, and North Carolina, the overall effect on public opinion of the opposition's focus on toilets is less clear. Having lived through the racial integration of public toilets, the citizens of Florida and North Carolina may have been psychologically more susceptible to claims that the ERA would integrate toilets sexually, with the connotations of rape, defilement, and vulnerability that that image implies.[62] But so few people anywhere gave integrated toilets as a reason for opposing the ERA that it is hard to see this issue as a frequent source of opposition even in the key unratified states. It is more likely to have appealed almost exclusively to the already convinced.[63]

In the legislatures, the issue served to solidify the conviction of middle-of-the-road legislators that the opposition was irrational. In Illinois, pro-ERA legislators, aware of the effects on opinion of the toilet issue, were the only legislators to bring it up. They used unisex toilets over and over to imply that all other arguments against the ERA were equally exaggerated. Indeed, the pro-ERA forces jumped on the unisex toilet issue as quickly as the anti forces jumped on combat. This one massive and obvious distortion of the truth allowed them to label all the opponents' arguments as lies, irrelevancies, and scare tactics not worthy of serious consideration.

Schlafly herself came to understand the negative effect of this issue in the course of the ten years between 1972 and 1982. After her

early salvos, she rarely mentioned unisex toilets again. After she entered law school in 1975, her speeches became a little more careful in other respects as well. She was learning, both from her new training and from experience, what worked with the mainstream audience. As one Illinois legislator commented, "I heard her in her first arguments, which were sloppy at times—incendiary, you know, not very, very good. She is so smooth now, I mean, she's got it down to an art form. I think she is totally unbeatable."

The STOP ERA forces were relatively hierarchically organized, with Schlafly herself at the apex of the hierarchy, but, in managing the activists who volunteered to help oppose the ERA, Schlafly still had to contend with the decentralized character of all social movements. Local groups could and did mount actions that highlighted the common toilet issue, and Schlafly could do little to stop them without diminishing their enthusiasm. This decentralization of responsibility was probably helpful with the public on some issues, because local groups could raise completely false arguments against the ERA without anyone having to take responsibility for them. (Schlafly herself, faced with some extreme anti-ERA propaganda, demurely told state legislators, "That is not one of my arguments against the ERA. . . . I think I can back up anything I write. And I am also very tolerant. I let people be against ERA for the reason of their choice.")[64] Yet the opponents' cause must have suffered somewhat with middle-of-the-road legislators when proponents could testify that more than 90 percent of the allegations in some anti-ERA pamphlets were false.[65]

Anti-ERA legislators usually avoided the most inflamatory charges. An analysis of newspaper reports on the ERA in six states indicates that while pro-ERA legislators gave the papers much the same reasons for supporting the ERA as the pro-ERA rank and file, anti-ERA legislators usually advanced reasons quite different from those of the anti-ERA activists. The opposition legislators' most frequent point in these newspaper stories was that the ERA would remove powers from the states. Their next most frequent point was that the Amendment was not needed. They were also worried about unforeseen consequences, including the draft and combat. They practically never mentioned toilets. In these same newspapers, activists' opposition to the ERA focused on four issues: first, that women would be drafted; next, that husbands would not be solely liable for the support of their families; third, that the ERA would threaten the family in general; and, finally, that public restrooms would become sexually integrated.[66] In short, except for the draft and combat, opposition legislators and activists were worried about different issues. As for toilets, although one Georgia legislator claimed that the ERA "would absolutely abolish segregated washrooms,"[67] no opposition legislator in Illinois ever raised the issue, either in the ten years of debate on the ERA in the legislature or in interviews with me.

While the parallels are not exact between the proponents' use of "59 cents" and the opponents' use of the husband's right to support, or between the proponents' exaggerations regarding combat and the opponents' exaggerations regarding toilets, these issues illustrate similar dynamics operating within both pro- and anti-ERA movements. Yet, for reasons that should now be obvious, the opponents' exaggerations cost them less in the political struggle.

First, public support for the ERA rested not so much on a calculation of particular costs and benefits as on a generalized commitment to abstract rights. Given this kind of public commitment, almost any move from principle to substance tended to hurt the Amendment's chances. Consequently, once opponents turned public attention to the Amendment's effects, they were already well on their way to winning. Their exaggerations, while incurring some costs in credibility, succeeded in making the substantive effects of the Amendment a central issue in the debate.

Second, because the amendment process requires a near consensus, the opponents had only to create enough doubt about the Amendment to prevent a consensus from forming. As in slander, only some of the dirt had to stick. The ERA's opponents had the framers of the Constitution on their side. Without proving anything, they had only to create an atmosphere of distrust in order to win.

10 Ideology and Activism

       Anyone who followed the debate over the ERA is likely to have been impressed by the fact that it was both grossly oversimplified and extremely antagonistic. This chapter will suggest three explanations for this state of affairs. First, the ERA was a public good (or a "public bad") that had to be promoted or defeated by volunteer activity. Because neither passing nor defeating the ERA promised any immediate tangible benefits to activists, both sides recruited activists by appealing to principle.[1] They also exaggerated the ERA's probable long-run effects. Second, because activists were volunteers, they were not subject to much organizational control. Even when an organization wanted to "rein in" activists for pragmatic reasons, it had few good ways of doing so. Abortion funding became linked to the ERA, for example, in part because the ERA organizations could not fully control all the feminist lawyers. Finally, the adversary nature of the political process never encouraged the gladiators on either side to amass information that might weaken their rhetorical stance. The pro-ERA organizations were a great deal more likely to have done extensive legal research, but even they, as we will see, developed blind spots whenever seeing too much might have undermined their position. On the opponents' side, individual and organizational autonomy provided an opportunity to circulate blatant lies without anyone having to take responsibility for them.

The ERA as a Public Good

The American brand of interest group politics has trouble creating what economists call "public goods."[2] A public good is the kind of

118

good—like national defense, clean air, or an open park—that, once available to anyone, will be available to everyone. An individual good, in contrast, can be divided up and distributed to those who are willing to pay for it. Because public goods cannot be sold to individuals on a fee-for-service basis, organizations that provide them have three choices. The most effective is to force individuals to contribute. When unions help all employees in a firm to win better wages or working conditions, for example, they try to force all these beneficiaries of union largess to pay union dues by creating a "union shop." When governments provide everyone with national defense, they force everyone to pay for it through taxation. In a sense, democratic government is an agreement to be coerced for the purpose of producing a large number of desirable results that would never come about without such coercion.

If an organization has no effective means of coercion at its disposal, it can try to link the public good to an individual good. Workers may join a union to get the funeral benefits provided for members only; their dues then support the union's efforts to get "public goods" like pay raises for all. Senior citizens join the American Association of Retired People to get access to its insurance and other benefits; the association then spends some of its members' money promoting legislation that benefits not only the members but other old people as well. Gun owners join gun clubs primarily to use the private rifle ranges and skeet shoots; because these clubs are usually affiliated with the National Rifle Association, part of their dues then goes to promote what for them is a public good—legal gun sales. But even this strategy for financing public goods has severe limitations, because it is hard to find individual goods so closely linked to the organization that an individual entrepreneur cannot produce them more cheaply by eliminating the extra cost tacked on to finance the public good.

Finally, an organization seeking to produce public goods can rely on moral exhortation. It can claim that people ought to spend their time and energy promoting a public good because it is right and will benefit many others. Organizations that have to rely on such moral appeals are, at least in an individualistic culture, inherently weak. From a strictly selfish viewpoint it is almost always more rational to let others do the work in such organizations and become a "free rider" who enjoys the benefits of others' labor without contributing oneself. While few people are completely selfish all the time, even fewer are completely devoted to the

common good. Organizations that depend on such devotion usually
have a capricious, undependable membership. When an organization cannot count on a stable membership, it must devote a
tremendous amount of time and effort to soliciting and maintaining
the commitment of its members, to the detriment of the time and
effort it can spend promoting the public good itself. In contrast,
organizations based on the sale of individual goods, whose members continue to pay as long as they want the benefits provided, are
usually more stable and have a more predictable flow of funds.

The strength or weakness of a group's organizational base
usually translates into political strength or weakness. Trade associa-
tions like the National Automobile Dealers Association, whose
members gain technical information, access to conventions, and
business contacts from their membership, are organizationally
strong and politically powerful. Comparable consumer organizations, which can offer few individual benefits, are either nonexistent
or organizationally and politically weak.

Although in theory each citizen's interests should count for one
and none for more than one in a democracy, in practice well-
organized interests count for a great deal more than poorly organized ones. The more an organization can count on a stable membership held together by either coercion or individual benefits, the
more it can make its members' interests count in the political
process.

For this reason, the major organizations promoting the ERA
were shaky at their core. The National Organization for Women
(NOW) could offer its members little in the way of individual
benefits. To some members—for example, young women, the
newly divorced, the newly conscious feminist, or the recent migrant
to a new city—the organization could offer new friendships, mutual
support, companionship, and solidarity with others like oneself. It
could also provide one-time participation in a consciousness-raising
group. But members did not need to maintain their formal organizational affiliation to keep getting these benefits. Because NOW
had few ongoing individual benefits to offer, its membership drives
had to rely on emotional identification and moral exhortation.
Whenever women, rightly or wrongly, felt somewhat more
threatened, or whenever the president of NOW happened to write a
particularly moving letter of appeal, membership in the organization would rise. But as the critical moment faded into history,

membership would drop. The organization could offer no individual benefits to make its members feel the rationality of paying their dues consistently year after year.

ERAmerica, and its affiliates like ERA Illinois, had a seemingly more stable base as a coalition of religious, professional, civic, and labor groups. But ERAmerica and its affiliates had the usual problems of broadly based coalitions. Each member organization had priorities different from those of the coalition, few provided consistent financial support, and only one or two tried to enlist their individual members in the work of the coalition—passing the ERA.

The Federation of Business and Professional Women (BPW) had at its disposal the important individual benefit of professional contacts with other women in business, government, and the professions. The League of Women Voters provided relatively isolated homemakers with a chance to maintain adult social contacts, continue their education, and do some good. However, the very emphasis on professional networking and self-help that drew women to BPW also worked against that organization's involvement in state politics—where ERA had to pass—because politics of this sort means conflict, and conflict does not facilitate business contacts. In the same way, the League's specializing in projects that everyone could agree were good (League policy decisions are made by consensus) attracted members who preferred studying "good government" issues to clashing with opposing interests in partisan state politics. Neither BPW nor the League entered easily into the political struggles in state legislatures that the ERA demanded after 1975.

Because the ERA movement had little coercive power and few immediate individual benefits at its disposal, it had to rely on ideological incentives to recruit and maintain activists. People worked for the ERA because they believed in the cause. This meant that the people staffing the organizations that promoted the ERA were not a cross-section of those who favored it. They differed from the rest of the American population in one major respect—they believed in, and wanted to bring about, major changes in the roles of men and women in America.

Because the ERA organizations had to attract their membership primarily with moral and ideological incentives, and because activists were brought into the fray by their sense of injustice rather than by any individual rewards, there were times in which they preferred being right to winning. Moreover, their instincts about which arguments would appeal to legislators and the public were not very reliable.

The STOP ERA movement had a similar problem, for its job was also to promote a "public good." As a result, the STOP ERA organizations were both weak and ideological in their approach. Although this would have made it difficult for them to pass an amendment, it was not fatal when they had only to stop one.

Participatory Decentralization in the Abortion Decision

In a voluntary association, the initiative for action, the sanction for nonperformance, and the manner in which the work is done all depend heavily on the individual actor. Each actor is relatively autonomous, bound only by the constraints of ideology and solidarity—the incentives for working in the first place. To illustrate this phenomenon of "participatory decentralization," it is instructive to look at the role of feminist lawyers again, this time in the context of the debate about whether the ERA would require the government to pay for abortions on the same basis as other medical procedures.

In theory, feminist lawyers could relate to the ERA in quite diverse ways. When organizations like NOW, League of Women Voters, BPW, or ERAmerica paid a lawyer to act as general counsel or as a consultant, she was supposed to see herself as accountable to the organization's leadership in the same way that any lawyer would be accountable to a client. When a lawyer did unpaid volunteer work, she nominally had the same formal responsibility to her clients, but expected greater autonomy. When there is no quid pro quo, the donor inevitably feels free to consider aspects of a situation other than the client's needs. When a lawyer contributed to the ERA movement through articles in law journals, she was even more autonomous. She was still likely to be deeply committed to the feminist cause, since otherwise she would not commit her academic energies to relatively low-status "women's" subjects which did not give her much academic credit. But she was accountable only to the scholarly community for the accuracy and clarity of her analysis, and was unlikely to feel that her broad commitment to feminism required her to weigh all her words for their possible effects on the ERA's chances of passing.

In practice, these distinct roles often blurred. The small community of Washington and Washington-related feminist lawyers discussed issues among themselves both formally and informally, and many played all the roles I have described at one time or another. As a consequence, even the paid staff lawyers thought of themselves as serving a broader "public" interest, or at least a "feminist" interest, rather than thinking of themselves simply as advocates for their client's own interest, narrowly construed. This helps explain why no staff lawyer, even for the more conservative ERA organizations, raised the possibility of a deferential interpretation of the ERA on the military. In the community of feminist lawyers within which she was operating, that approach was ruled out for reasons that had relatively little to do with the ERA per se.

Toward the end of the ERA campaign, some feminist lawyers also acted relatively autonomously in linking abortion to the ERA. These lawyers were certainly not primarily responsible for the link. Given the strength of support for both the ERA and abortion within NOW, it was impossible after 1973 to keep the two issues entirely separate either in the mind of the public or within NOW. Toward the end of the ERA struggle, for example, Illinois NOW sent a questionnaire to the candidates for reelection to the state legislature, asking for their positions both on the ERA and on abortion. One black woman legislator who supported the ERA criticized this questionnaire sharply:

> [The pro-ERA forces] confused the issues with abortion and ERA. That [abortion] would have been an issue that I would have stayed completely away from. Even though I may be pro-abortion or anti-abortion, it has nothing to do with it [the ERA]. . . . They use their own tactics—[really] the *anti*-ERA people's tactics— to defeat themselves! . . . And you couldn't get them to understand that. . . . Why be concerned on the *same* questionaire with the ERA and the abortion issue so heavily into it?

Despite mistakes like this, however, most NOW activists, and certainly the more conservative pro-ERA activists, consciously tried to keep the issues of abortion and ERA separate.

Like the combat decision, the series of decisions linking the ERA and abortion involved both feminist lawyers and external events not within the control of the ERA organizations. In this instance, the key event came in 1973, when Justice Blackmun, speaking for seven of the nine justices of the Supreme Court in *Roe v. Wade*, distinguished among the three trimesters of pregnancy, and made the right to an abortion in the first three months a matter of personal autonomy, protected by a right to private decision making that the Court derived from the Constitution's due process guarantee.[3] Foes of abortion immediately launched a counterattack and succeeded in getting the U.S. Congress and several state legislatures to pass legislation denying public funding to any abortion that did not involve rape, incest, or the potential death of the mother.

Feminist organizations and feminist lawyers did what they could to repel this counterattack. What feminist lawyers could do most easily was to bring suits arguing that federal and state laws that restricted abortion funding were unconstitutional under the Fifth and Fourteenth Amendments of the Constitution, under comparable guarantees in the state constitutions, and under various state ERAs.

For some feminist lawyers, the ERA-abortion connection posed a major political and ethical problem. On the one hand, their commitment to equality for women, to publicly funded abortions, to their clients, and—much less important—to winning important cases and setting judicial precedent all encouraged them to use every argument in their constitutional arsenal against restricting access to abortions. Some believed strongly that the best argument against cutting off abortion funding was that this denied women the equal protection of the laws under the Fourteenth Amendment so long as the government funded other medical procedures for both sexes or for men. Not making that argument when the issues were being litigated for the first time, in the late 1970s and early 1980s, ran the risk of setting a series of possibly irreversible precedents. If the ERA had not been before the states, these lawyers could have proceeded without external hindrance in trying to persuade the Court of their interpretation of the Fourteenth Amendment's equal protection clause. But with the ERA before the states, and with state legislators asking more and more often about the substantive effects of the ERA, the lawyers had to be careful not to frighten potential legislative proponents by suggesting that the equal protection clause—in theory a weaker protection than the ERA—could be linked substantively to abortion. Those feminist lawyers who believed that the ERA added little to the equal protection clause in any case wanted to press ahead with the equal protection analysis, ignoring the political consequences for the ERA. However, in Washington, against some resistance, Eleanor Smeal persuaded the feminist lawyers in the federal abortion funding case not to make this argument.[4] In this way Smeal hoped to keep the ERA and abortion funding separate.

Smeal was less successful in the states. Here, local legal organizations made their own autonomous decisions and based their arguments for abortion funding not only on the potentially dangerous equal protection clause but also, in some states, on the state equal rights amendments. This strategy obviously jeopardized the political future of the federal ERA in the unratified states. In 1978, feminist lawyers in the Hawaiian chapter of the American Civil Liberties Union (ACLU) argued unsuccessfully in the case of *Hawaii Right to Life, Inc. v. Chang* that "[a]bortion is a medical procedure performed only for women; withdrawing funding for abortions while continuing to reimburse other medical procedures sought by both sexes or only by men would be tantamount to a denial of equal rights on account of sex." Withdrawing abortion funding, they argued, would violate not only Hawaii's due process and equal protection clauses, but also its equal rights amendment, which, like the proposed federal ERA, provided that "equality of rights under the law shall not be denied or abridged on account of sex."[5]

In 1980, the lawyers defending federal abortion funding in *Harris v. McRae* lost their case. A majority of the Supreme Court concluded, among other things, that the Constitution's Fifth Amendment (and, in a parallel state case, the Fourteenth Amendment) did not invalidate legislative restrictions on abortion funding. The majority's grounds were that (*a*) Congress had a "legitimate" interest in "protecting potential life," (*b*) restricting funding for abortion bore "a direct relationship" to this legitimate purpose, and (*c*) the classification of poverty (the distinction between "indigent" women and other women) was not a suspect classification requiring a test stronger than that congressional action be rationally related to a legitimate governmental interest.[6]

Once the Court's majority had shown that for them the Fourteenth Amendment's equal protection clause did not bar legislative

restrictions on abortion funding, the ACLU would no longer hold
back. As the executive director of the Civil Liberties Union of
Massachusetts wrote in its newsletter:

> Because a strong coalition is being forged between the anti-ERA
> coalition and the anti-abortion people, it was our hope to save Medic-
> aid payments for medically necessary abortions through the federal
> court route without having to use the state Equal Rights Amendment
> and possibly fuel the national anti-ERA movement. But the loss in
> *McRae* [the federal abortion funding case] was the last straw. We now
> have no recourse but to turn to the State Constitution for the legal
> hook to save Medicaid funding for abortions.[7]

Accordingly, the ACLU argued in the Massachusetts case of *Moe v.
Secretary of Administration* that both the Massachusetts state ERA
and its due process clause made restricting funding for abortions
unconstitutional. Anxious ERA proponents in the key unratified
states rejoiced in 1981 when the Massachusetts Supreme Court
declared the funding restrictions unconstitutional under the due
process clause of the Massachusetts Constitution rather than invoking the state ERA.[8]

ERA supporters in the key nonratified states sometimes felt
that they were engaged in a race with the local feminist lawyers who
were bringing abortion funding cases in the more liberal ratified
states. But no state court actually decided a case regarding abortion
funding on the basis of a state ERA prior to the ratification deadline
in June 1982. In Connecticut, a lower court found the feminist
lawyers' argument that restrictions on abortion funding violated the
state ERA "very persuasive," but invalidated those restrictions on
other grounds.[9] In Pennsylvania, the courts did not decide on the
feminist challenge to state restrictions on abortion funding until
after the deadline for ratifying the federal ERA had passed. When
the Pennsylvania lower court did finally rule on abortion funding, it
struck down the restrictions under the equal protection clause of its
state constitution. But it also commented that the argument under
the state ERA was "meritorious and sufficient in and of itself to
invalidate the statutes before us in that those statutes do unlawfully
discriminate against women."[10] This wording, stronger than any
prior to June 1982, gave the opposition valuable ammunition in the
1983 Congressional hearings on a new ERA.

In the 1983 House and Senate hearings on the ERA, Ann
Freedman, an author of the original *Yale Law Journal* article interpreting the ERA, stated—I believe correctly—that "as a practical
matter" the U.S. Supreme Court was unlikely to base its future
decisions about abortion funding on the ERA. Rather, the Court
would be likely in such cases to continue its elaboration of the right
to privacy that provided the basis for *Roe v. Wade*.[11]

Moreover, as Freedman pointed out several times in the Senate
hearings, on ambiguous matters the legislative history could be
crucial. In 1983, the Congress probably had the power to influence
heavily the way any future Supreme Court would decide on this
issue. Freedman argued that

> the Senate and the House of Representatives control the meaning. . . .
> You are the legislators. . . . If the amendment is adopted, it is what the
> proponents say it means and what the majority reports or any reports
> supporting the adoption of the amendment in either House say. And if
> they are clear about what the amendment means, that will be
> controlling.[12]

Yet, while it was true as a practical matter that the Supreme
Court was unlikely to use the federal ERA to strike down legislative
restrictions on abortion, the arguments that feminist lawyers had
made in the state courts for an ERA–abortion link were immediately picked up by ERA opponents.[13] These feminist arguments
claimed that the ERA would require government funding for abortion at a moment when more than half the public support for the
ERA came from people who opposed abortion on demand.[14] In
such circumstances, a credible claim that the ERA would mandate
abortion funding almost guaranteed that the ERA would neither
pass Congress nor be ratified in the states. But when Ann Freedman
testified in the House and Senate Hearings that the Supreme Court
of the United States would not be likely to use the ERA to mandate
funding for abortions, several feminist lawyers treated her testimony as a betrayal.

Here, as on combat, some feminist lawyers had taken a position
that would have detrimental consequences for ratification. Both the
parallels to the combat decision and the differences from it are
striking. In both cases some feminist constitutional lawyers were
arguing a position that the Supreme Court of the United States was,

as a practical matter, unlikely to take. And in both cases the position they were arguing severely hurt the cause of the ERA in the unratified states. But in the abortion decision, unlike the combat decision, the participants were well aware of the issues. Lawyers who linked the ERA to abortion funding made their decision quite consciously, often after discussion with legal and political leaders in Washington. As might have been predicted, the lawyers most closely connected to the ERA movement argued that there was no practical link. Lawyers in the already ratified states were the ones who made the connection. They knew they were reducing the ERA's chances of passing, but since they thought it unlikely to pass no matter what they did, they decided to proceed.

The Prohibited Classification Decision and Homosexual Marriages

More like the combat decision was the implicit decision in the ERA movement to follow the *Yale Law Journal*'s lead in claiming that the ERA would make gender a "prohibited" rather than a "suspect" classification. According to this interpretation of the ERA, legislators would be absolutely prohibited from making laws that distinguished according to gender—the only exceptions being laws relating to privacy and to unique physical characteristics. This interpretation of the ERA was accepted by many feminist lawyers and supported at least passively by most of those who were conscious of the issue in the ratification movement.

As in the combat decision, arguments could have been made for both the "suspect" and the "prohibited" interpretations. Moreover, as in the combat decision, the Supreme Court would probably have chosen the "suspect" rather than the "prohibited" interpretation.[15] But as in the combat decision, the ERA movement, following its lawyers' lead, decided on the more sweeping interpretation.

The "prohibited classification" interpretation of the ERA had less direct effect on the ratification process than did the combat decision, because few legislators or members of the public ever raised the issue. Conservative supporters of the ERA in the state legislatures met little challenge when they declared in speeches and interviews that the ERA would simply make gender a "suspect" classification. Nevertheless, the decision did have a small direct effect. At least one conservative Oklahoma legislator was sufficiently disturbed upon hearing the "prohibited classification" interpretation to change his vote on the Amendment.[16] The decision also had a pervasive indirect effect, by encouraging ERA proponents to suggest that the ERA would produce consequences, like sending women draftees into combat and legalizing homosexual marriage, that mainstream legislators wanted to prevent.

Lawyers outside the ERA movement played an autonomous role in linking the ERA to homosexual marriages. In 1973, Samuel T. Perkins and Arthur J. Silverstein, two Yale law students, wrote a Note in the *Yale Law Journal* arguing that the ERA would legalize homosexual marriage. A claim for state marriage licenses by homosexual couples, they wrote, "would almost certainly be vindicated under the proposed Equal Rights Amendment."[17] Their analysis of the ERA rested on the assumption, current at Yale at the time, that the Court would interpret the ERA to make gender a prohibited classification.[18] To make their argument, they had to discount heavily the explicit statement of Senator Birch Bayh, chief sponsor of the ERA in the Senate, who said on the Senate floor that under an ERA state prohibitions against homosexual marriage would not constitute impermissible discrimination so long as licenses were denied equally to both male and female pairs.[19] When I asked whether they had expected their article to have any effect on the political fortunes of the ERA, one of the authors answered, "Absolutely not. We were strict scholars, and naive ones at that." Indeed the only reaction they got at the time was that some of their fellow students erroneously concluded that they might be homosexual. Asked whether he had supported the ERA at the time of writing the article, one author commented, "I can't remember— that was eleven years ago." The other described himself as, at the time, a "supporter, but not an active supporter." In this case the ERA movement was at the mercy not of its own active suppporters, who believed the Amendment would pass and exaggerated the Amendment's effects to make it more effective,[20] but of two law students who submitted a publishable article to get elected to the prestigious board of the *Yale Law Journal*.

Participatory Decentralization in the States

The ERA movement depended not just on national experts like lawyers but on every spark of local energy it could inspire. And autonomous action on the local level often affected the course of

local debate. Civil disobedience provides the most obvious example. The decision of seventeen women to chain themselves to the
rotunda in the Illinois state capitol for four days sprang from individual initiative. So did the much publicized thirty-seven-day fast in
the same state. These actions affected the ratification debate in a
way that no ERA organization could easily alter. Throughout the
ERA struggle individuals took actions like these on their own
initiative, almost on the spur of the moment, and with as much
concern for the personal testimony embodied in the act as for its
practical effect on the ERA's chances for ratification.[21]

The costs and benefits of civil disobedience for ratification are
hard to calculate. While some of these acts may have reduced the
public popularity of the ERA in the short run,[22] the testimony they
embodied rekindled the fire in every activist's heart. And because
acts like this inspire others in the future, the gain for the movement
as a whole may have outweighed small momentary losses in public
approval. Certainly the harm to the movement if it had tried to
quench such heartfelt gestures would have been incalculable.

The ERA movement had virtually no collective control over
any of these acts of civil disobedience. But unlike the lawyers'
decisions on what the ERA should be alleged to mean, the pros and
cons of visible civil disobedience were discussed at length among
the rank and file. If most activists had felt that such actions were
hurting the movement, they could have made that conclusion
known, either informally or by bringing it up explicitly in their
organizations and publications. Because it was a visible, widely
understood issue, we can assume that the absence of formal debate
on civil disobedience within the organizations reflected widespread
acceptance of the tactic.

Pro-ERA marches and demonstrations also provided important opportunities for autonomous action. In the early days of the
ERA struggle, pro-ERA demonstrations were open to all. As a
consequence, almost every demonstration had a socialist and a
lesbian contingent, with banners proclaiming their identities as well
as their support for the ERA. After considerable debate, NOW
decided not to allow socialist and lesbian banners in its ERA
demonstrations. While many disagreed with this decision, it was
explicit and relatively participatory.

Here, as in so many other decisions, the initiative first came
from peripheral extraorganizational actors, who often simply

joined public ERA demonstrations carrying their banners. But in this case the eventual decision was made after lengthy discussion by workers on the front lines. Most pro-ERA organizations first took an activist-pleasing stance and allowed the banners. When the opposition began to publish photographs of these banners and the women carrying them,[23] the pro-ERA groups reversed their policy, often instituting not only a ban on visible lesbian and socialist participation but also a dress code for demonstrations. Although each state followed a slightly different course,[24] the pattern was usually to allow visible socialist and lesbian participation until local evidence convinced most activists that such a course would hurt the ERA. In these decisions, the pressures for ideological purity were the same as in the decisions on combat, the prohibited classification, and abortion funding, but participants eventually had accurate information regarding the alternatives, and personal knowledge of the practical effects of allowing the purists to have their way. Right or wrong, the result was not a decision by accretion.

From the point of view of the movement as a whole, each organization, as well as each individual, was also an autonomous actor. As we will see in Chapter 12, NOW could not keep the president and vice-president of ERA Illinois from attending a Republican fund-raising dinner. ERA Illinois could not keep NOW from calling a demonstration in the last days of the legislative session. By virtue of its size and resources, NOW became the center of the ERA struggle toward the end of this ten-year period. Realizing that it could not maintain its own active membership and at the same time engage in continual compromises with more conservative groups, NOW formally decided in 1978 to discourage coalition activity and to work with other pro-ERA organizations only when those organizations chose to co-sponsor specific actions that NOW had initiated, or when NOW wanted to co-sponsor specific actions initiated by other organizations. This stance freed NOW from whatever control the other pro-ERA organizations had previously exercised over it.

In a system of participatory decentralization, many individuals act relatively spontaneously, subject only to the sanctions of their peers and their consciences. Such a system has the great advantages of flexibility, adaptability, promoting innovation, and generating commitment.[25] But the advantage of not requiring a common line, which encourages innovation, brings with it a corresponding disadvantage: being able to avoid the internal dialogue necessary to hammer out that common line. When individuals and organizations can take action that affects the movement after consulting only their friends, they can avoid many hard questions and have less opportunity to acquire information from outside their group.

In these circumstances, each subgroup reinforces its members' perceptions of reality. Activists fighting for the ERA in the states, for instance, began to see the ERA as an end in itself. Each argument with an angry opponent, each attempt to convince an uncertain neighbor, each phone call to a talk show or letter to the editor, each visit to an irritated legislator made a little scar on the soul, healed only, if at all, by the recounting of similar experiences, the sympathy, and the reaffirmation of the goal that one's friends could provide. As the small but emotionally poignant costs cumulated,[26] and each friend reinforced the other's experience, it is no wonder that for the grass-roots activists the ERA became much more than a practical instrument for improving the lives of American women, much more than a symbol that would inspire women throughout the ages—it became a public symbol of the meaning of one's own life.

These emotional forces sometimes made local activists (including myself, who was only minimally active) care even more about winning than about being right. Getting something *called* the ERA through the legislature, somehow capturing those last two or three votes, became a goal in its own right, worth almost any sacrifice, including perhaps some of the instrumental character of the ERA itself.

Meanwhile, other actors in other parts of the drama were reinforcing in the same way the collective perceptions of their fellows. A number of feminist lawyers believed after 1978 that the ERA was both a lost cause in the states and a minimal addition to constitutional protections. They therefore placed little weight on the way their actions might affect the political fortunes of the ERA. Objectively, they may well have been right. Other lawyers, who thought the ERA meaningless unless it was uncompromising, may also have been right. But they all were living in a different world from the activists on the front lines, just as some activists were living in different worlds from one another. The problems of communicating across the boundaries of these worlds were not just the classic problems of individual autonomy versus the collective good; they were problems of the autonomy of small groups, whose members felt responsible to one another, in a movement that spanned the continent.

The Leadership Question

STOP ERA was able to overcome some of the problems of participatory decentralization by accepting, at least in theory, a relatively hierarchical chain of command centering on one person— Phyllis Schlafly—without whom the opposition would probably not have been able to prevent ratification.

Concentrating much of the responsibility for public debate in one person also meant that Schlafly could perfect her technique, while her opponents, who debated her only once or at the most two or three times, remained comparative amateurs on the ERA issue. Noting Schalfly's increasing skill in debate on the ERA over the years, one state legislator concluded that the pro-ERA forces should also have created a single "spokesman," like Schlafly, who could have honed to perfection the pro-ERA debating position.

Among the ERA forces, the decision not to organize hierarchically was explicit, conscious, and almost unanimous. While one woman sponsor grumbled that "the antis were able to take orders better," most proponents firmly believed in a participatory democracy that spread power among as many different individuals as possible. "Empowering women" was a goal as important as winning the ERA, and empowering women meant, among other things, giving instant responsibility even to the very inexperienced.

As one local NOW leader voiced the dilemma,

NOW LEADER: To some extent, some of our principles prevent us from doing some things that Phyllis [Schlafly] has been able to do.

JM: What are some of those principles?

NOW LEADER: Well, for example, her never-changing leadership. We think it is very important for lots of people to learn how to do these things. An interesting fact about NOW is that many NOW members are not joiners; they've joined virtually nothing in their lives and probably won't join anything else once they're in NOW. And they don't know basic things about organizations.

. . . What we're about is helping people, empowering them, helping them take control of their own lives, and to the extent that we impose a kind of "follow us to the ends of the earth" kind of mentality or emotional framework on what we're doing, we weaken what we're trying to do. And it's a short-term gain for a long-term loss. I mean, it's something we're not willing to do. Phyllis doesn't care if the people who follow her ever learn anything. She's content to have them ignorant; we're not. And there's a price you pay for that in media recognition.[27]

When I asked Susan Catania, a key sponsor of the ERA in the Illinois House of Representatives, whether there was anything she thought the pro-ERA forces could have done differently, she expressed almost the same sentiments:

I doubt it. The temptation is to say that either I should have insisted that I be the one to call the shots, or insisted that Eugenia Chapman be the one to call the shots, or insisted that Giddy Dyer do it, because it is so much easier to get it done when one person is making the final decision about everything that is going to happen. But so many women and some men have become politically aware, trained, astute, capable, because of their work for ERA ratification that I don't think I would change it.

As frustrating as it is to have new people coming in constantly, all those people are learning a great deal about how it happens. . . . [But in some ways it is an] uncontrollable mess. It would be much more efficient to have one person running the whole show.

However, while the kinds of people who came to work for the ERA may well have had to learn by doing, Schlafly's hierarchical techniques also seemed to create commitment, release energy, and promote learning, at least for her constituency. Far from indifferent to whether "the people who follow her ever learn anything," Phyllis

Schlafly held each year a training conference for members of her Eagle Forum, climaxing in a banquet Saturday evening at which the STOP ERA "commander" formally addressed "her lieutenants." Begun the year after Schlafly lost her bid for president of the National Federation of Republican Women, these conferences had as their goal teaching her stalwarts how to prevent liberal control of Republican party conventions. At first, the conferences attracted only Schlafly's own loyalists in the Republican party, but after the Senate ratified the ERA and it went to the states, they began to attract more and more women.

> The training ran the gamut from how to get your anti-ERA message on the "boob-tube," mount an effective letter-writing campaign, testify at public hearings, hold a press conference, set up a phone bank, hold a fund raiser (Schlafly recommended brunches to avoid selling alcohol), infiltrate the feminist camp to learn ERA strategy.
>
> A video room was open at all hours so participants could watch tapes of Phyllis debating Barbara Walters and Phil Donahue and Birch Bayh and Betty Friedan and a multitude of others. The purpose was not to provide entertainment or a much-needed break. The next day Phyllis would evaluate the women's performance in mock ERA debates. . . . [In workshops] Each woman would be videotaped making a two-minute speech and then watch "instant replays."
>
> At another session a Schlafly aide handed women evaluation forms as they entered the room. Schlafly commanded a leader from every state to stand before the group and, in precisely two minutes, summarize a year's worth of STOP ERA and other "pro-family" activity. Speakers ultimately got their evaluation forms back, on which their peers anonymously evaluated their appearance, the content of their knowledge, poise, hand movements, etc., and then summed it all up with a grade. The person with the highest grade got a prize.[29]

For those who had no principled or emotional objections to the style, hierarchy led to far more learning than ERA proponents imagined.

The worst effect of hierarchy seems to have been the usual one of ignorance of local conditions. Both Ellie Smeal, at the top of a democratic and relatively participatory system, and Phyllis Schlafly, at the top of an autocratic one, experienced this problem. Smeal, for example, told me about the combat issue:

> The whole military issue was not raised in the legislatures. It was used
> by the opposition in campaigns, but it did not cost us votes. The only
> time we had trouble was in Illinois in 1980. So we had Kathleen
> Carpenter testify on our side, and it absolutely blew them away. It
> absolutely wasn't an issue after that.

But Smeal was wrong about combat. Florida, Oklahoma, and Illinois were the only three wavering states that transcribed their debates; in all three, legislators often raised the military issue. And in Illinois, Kathleen Carpenter's 1980 Judiciary Committee testimony was a masterpiece of obfuscation, which left one ERA opponent—a lawyer and a conservative Democrat—saying, "I guess I still do not have an opinion of the bottom line from your testimony about the effect that ERA passage would have with regard to the question of women serving in combat." (This was also my own reaction after reading the testimony several times and even interviewing Carpenter in person to determine her meaning.) Later, the same legislator declared in debate that he was voting against the ERA because on many questions, including that of women in combat, "the bottom line is 'what does ERA do?' The answer in my opinion is no one knows."[30] Nor, as the debates indicate, did combat stop being an issue in the Illinois legislature after Carpenter's testimony. This kind of misperception of local conditions by top leaders sometimes undermined the morale of state activists, who found it hard to get their insights taken seriously at the Washington office.

Similarly, Schlafly had difficulty understanding how to work effectively in states that had no Southern base. In 1984, Maine Right to Life had put together what its president, Sandra Faucher, called a "tasteful" campaign against the state ERA. In the campaign's television commercial a professor or lawyer read the text of the ERA, listed some possible consequences of the Amendment—like eliminating separate sports teams for boys and girls, ending the primary responsibility of the father for the support of children, homosexual marriages, and abortions paid for by tax dollars—and concluded, "We'd like you to read about this." Faucher says that support for the state ERA, which had begun at 61 percent in mid-June, fell dramatically as soon as the ads began, at times by as much as ten percentage points a week. But then Phyllis Schlafly, with her own small organization, Maine STOP ERA, entered the act and, in Faucher's words, "stopped our momentum dead." Schlafly's group ran a newspaper ad showing two men from New York's Gay Pride parade embracing under the headline: "Who Hid the Sex in Six?" (Six was the referendum number of the ERA). The text ran, in part,

> What does the word "sex" [in the language of the ERA] mean? The sex you are, male or female, or the sex you engage in, homosexual, bisexual, heterosexual, sex with children . . . or whatever? . . . One thing is for sure: Militant homosexuals from all over America have made the ERA issue a hot priority. Why? To be able finally to get homosexual marriage licenses, to adopt children and raise them to emulate their homosexual "parents," and to obtain pension and medical benefits for odd-couple "spouses." . . . Vote *NO on 6!* The Pro-Gay E.R.A.

"That almost killed us," said Faucher, "There's a big difference between Iowa's conservative farmland and liberal Maine. . . . [After Schlafly's ad,] our polls showed that we were losing all our upscale better educated Republican types." Faucher was particularly upset because two teenagers had only shortly before this thrown a homosexual man off a bridge, killing him, and sentiment against homophobia was running high in Maine. "She [Schlafly] felt that she knew more than we did," complained Faucher. "But we had *lived* in this state!"[31]

While Schlafly, at the head of an autocratic organization, could simply dismiss information that did not conform to her views, Smeal was constrained by her democratically elected position, her democratically elected board, and her democratic ideals. Smeal's occasional lack of responsiveness to local insight derived in part from the conviction of a charismatic leader that on certain issues she simply knew she was right. It derived in part from the fact that the members of NOW's board and other officials, depending on the president for internal promotion and support in future NOW elections, were sometimes reluctant to contradict her. And it derived in part from the size and diversity of NOW's concerns, which—perhaps in combination with NOW's commitment to involving many people in the day-to-day operations of the organization—made Smeal much more inaccessible to the average member than Phyllis Schlafly was. When I tried to reach Schlafly, for example, it took one phone call.

When I tried to reach Smeal, it took months. This meant that the lines of communication from the front lines to the center and back were often poor in NOW and hardly existed in some of the other pro-ERA organizations.

The Search for Information

Proponents of the ERA did not consciously exaggerate its effects. On the contrary, because of the background of many of the proponents in "good government" and public education projects, one leitmotif of local activity was the effort to gather accurate information on the Amendment's effects. Such efforts failed because local organizations lacked resources, because national organizations practiced conscious or unconscious restraint in publishing information, and because activists maintained a mind-set of belief that withstood the cognitive shifts necessary to grasp the way the situation had changed since 1972.

Local ERA efforts could not generate on their own, for example, the much desired "list of laws the ERA would change." Late in 1980, the board of directors of ERA Illinois decided that "a research effort devoted to reasons why we need the ERA" (i.e., a catalogue of tangible, practical effects) was its highest priority as an organization, outweighing even the priority of "political action working for pro-ERA candidates."[32] But having made this decision, the organization did absolutely nothing to implement it. It turned out that there were no lawyers active in the organization who could volunteer their skills and time for the task. Nor were any other volunteers anxious for this kind of work. The organization could not afford to hire anyone for the job.[33]

In the same year and responding to the same concerns, the president of Women in Communications (a professional women's organization supporting the ERA) wrote from her home in Pennsylvania to women in her organization in twenty-eight of the thirty-five states that did not have a state ERA:

> I need some information and you can help me. One of the charges for our ERA effort this year was to take a look at the laws discriminating against women in states which do not have state ERAs. . . .
>
> What I'd like you to do is contact the state commission on the status of women whose address appears below. Ask how many state

laws still discriminate against women, how many have been brought into compliance with the federal ERA. Get some examples of the types of discriminatory laws. . . .

You may need your reporter's skills to get this information we need. Some governors have appointed those opposed to women's rights to state commissions. Their argument has been that all viewpoints have a right to be heard. For this reason, some commissions make every effort to prevent publication of their findings.

I'm counting on you to succeed. Please send me a report on your state's position as soon as possible.

She received only five replies to her twenty-eight letters, one of which simply stated that "no survey has been done to document laws which still discriminate against women [and] we are not in a position, either fiscally or in terms of staff time, to undertake such an effort."[34]

The national organizations' efforts to document the impact of the ERA were often half-hearted. In 1974, the California Commission on the Status of Women got a substantial grant from the Rockfeller Foundation to study the impact of the ERA on federal and state laws. Yet only seventy-five of the 287 pages in their report, *Impact ERA*, dealt with actual changes in the law that the ERA would bring about, and that discussion was often superficial. Most of the report dealt with the possible indirect social effects of the Amendment, along with other issues.

In the fall of 1981, just ten months before the deadline for ratification, ERAmerica assigned a student intern for three months to collect and codify state laws relating to women. In this limited time the intern was able to acquire records from only twenty-two states, and many of these records were incomplete.

The NOW Legal Defense and Education Fund (LDEF) probably had the best information in the United States on the legal impact of the ERA, but the publicly available information was not helpful for the local activists who wanted a list of discriminatory laws that the ERA would abolish. Although its *ERA Impact Clearinghouse Index and References* manual summarized in useful detail the experience of fifteen states under their state ERAs, this massive and expensive project, indispensable to understanding how legislatures and courts had interpreted state ERAs, covered only states that already had their own ERA.[35] These were, of course, the

states where a federal ERA would change the fewest laws. The
project did not cover federal laws. Nor did it compile information
on the thirty-five states that lacked an ERA.

In 1982 an aide at NOW LDEF told me that "for another
author, under contract, we did a sweep, nearly three years ago, of
most of the laws relating to women: marriage, employment, et
cetera." Although the terms of the contract provided that the work
could not be made public, the aide did say, "I eye-balled it, reviewed it, this summer. We'd been getting so many requests: 'What
are the bad laws? What are the bad laws?' But it's not the kind of
impressive list that people hope for." The meager results presumably did not make it worthwhile for LDEF to repeat the study in
such a way that the results could be made public.

Local efforts to compile a list were made much more difficult by
the mind-set with which almost all nonlawyers and even some
lawyers approached the problem. They (and I include myself here)
all assumed that the task was to identify specific laws that discriminated against women. This seemed to require a review of both the
U.S. Code and the codes of all fifty states to find such laws. This was
a perfectly reasonable definition of the problem in 1972, when the
Supreme Court had not yet shown much inclination to strike down
laws that discriminated against women under the Fourteenth
Amendment. But by the late 1970s the Court had both complicated
and simplified the task. By then such a list would have had to focus
on the subset of discriminatory laws that the Supreme Court could
be expected to hold unconstitutional under the ERA but not under
the Fourteenth Amendment. Had the pro-ERA groups realized
that this was now their task, they would also have realized that the
first step was not to conduct an exhaustive review of state statutes
but to figure out how the principles the Court would use to interpret
the equal protection clause of the ERA would differ from those it
was using to interpret the equal protection clause of the Fourteenth
Amendment. A few telephone calls to competent constitutional
lawyers would then have convinced most ERA supporters that the
difference was likely to be quite modest.

It is tempting to argue that ERA supporters did not reformulate
the problem this way because such a reformulation would not have
served their political interests, and there is undoubtedly some truth
in this claim. But it is important to bear in mind that nobody else
formulated the problem this way either. The ERA's opponents

claimed it was unnecessary, but they did not explicitly invoke the post-*Craig* interpretation of the Fourteenth Amendment to justify their claims. Neither did skeptical legislators. The mind-set that defined the task as identifying discriminatory laws was so nearly universal that it simply did not occur to activists to redefine the problem.[36]

While calculations of political advantage doubtless played some role in the failure of ERA activists to appreciate the way the Supreme Court had narrowed the likely impact of the ERA, there was another important reason that bears directly on the significance of the ERA itself. Look, for comparison, at the Supreme Court's dramatic, clear-cut decision in 1954 on the implications of the Fourteenth Amendment for legal distinctions based on race. Every civil rights activist knew about *Brown v. Board of Education,* even though the activists seldom knew exactly what it said or how subsequent decisions had broadened its implications. Had anyone proposed a constitutional amendment outlawing racial segregation during the 1960s, virtually every activist would have assumed that the *Brown* decision made such an amendment redundant. The court has never made an equally dramatic or clear-cut decision with regard to sex. The "intermediate" standard of scrutiny established in 1976 is extraordinarily complex, reflecting deep divisions within the Court, and its substantive implications were deliberately left ambiguous, allowing the Court to handle future cases on an ad hoc basis. As a result, *Craig v. Boren* never became a well-known symbol of the Court's determination to use the Fourteenth Amendment to outlaw sex discrimination. The invisibility of the *Craig* decision was, in many ways, the strongest argument for an ERA. *Craig* may have made the ERA much less necessary in technical legal terms, but since almost nobody knew about it, it was not a "social fact" in the same way that the *Brown* decision was. Passing the ERA would have made obvious and visible a change in policy that remained tortuous and invisible in the absence of an ERA.

It is clear from this account of the search for information that although resources were limited, resources were not the main problem. The national pro-ERA organizations could have found the monetary resources and legal talent to produce up-to-date information on the practical effects of the ERA if that had been a high priority for them. It never became a priority because the meager results would almost certainly have hurt the cause more than they helped it. Without such a list, most activists remained convinced that the ERA would produce major substantive results.

Ignorance kept up morale among the pro-ERA groups and legitimated the propagation of out-of-date information exaggerating the number of laws the ERA would change. Moreover, that ignorance probably hurt the lobbying effort in the legislatures only slightly, for what counted most in this debate was underlying commitment. A minor incident in Illinois may illustrate this point. On my first visit to the Illinois state capitol to lobby for the ERA in 1980, an apoplectic legislator jumped up behind his desk and shouted at my little group, "Not one of you can point to a single law that the ERA would change!" Not so, I countered, remembering a pamphlet I had read on the bus: there are many laws—for example, the Georgia law that gave women indeterminate sentences. The legislator sneered, "Cite me chapter and verse!" and launched into a torrent of abuse concerning our rationality and integrity. I could not cite chapter and verse, since at that time I had not investigated the legal impact of the ERA with any care. But nothing in this interchange left me or anyone else in my group with the feeling that we would have been able to change this legislator's mind if we had been able to recite Georgia's entire criminal code.

I later discovered that the Georgia law I cited was almost certainly unconstitutional under the Supreme Court's evolved interpretation of the Fourteenth Amendment. As a result, the ERA would probably have had no effect on Georgia women's chances of receiving indeterminate sentences. But I would not have been a much more effective lobbyist if I had known this in 1980. The legislator in question never raised the issue of the Fourteenth Amendment. Nor did he convey the impression that better information would have changed his views. In my interviews, only one Illinois legislator raised the issue of the Supreme Court's progress under the Fourteenth Amendment. Most of the activists who opposed the ERA were equally unforthcoming. Although opponents were quick to call the ERA "unnecessary," specific information on the growing overlap between the ERA and the Fourteenth Amendment during the late 1970s was not a standard part of the debate over the ERA, at least in Illinois.

Among proponents, the low level of discourse was produced in part by the silence of the constitutional lawyers and the few highly informed activists who knew how little the ERA would do for women in the short run. They believed, I think correctly, that the ERA would have a major long-run effect by encouraging legislators and judges to draft and interpret laws in ways that would make it harder to discriminate against women. Given that conviction, they favored the ERA and believed they should do nothing to weaken its supporters' fervor. When they spoke they chose their words carefully, so as to maintain their credibility in the profession but still not disillusion the rank and file activists.

The Opponents

When we turn from the proponents to the opposition, we again find that the level of information was low and that acquiring more information would probably have weakened the opposition's cause. Once again, this ignorance was attributable to the fact that the legal situation changed over the course of the ten-year battle. But once again the more fundamental fact was that the opposition had no incentive to keep track of the legal changes, since doing so would have made clear that the ERA's practical impact in the forseeable future was likely to be minimal. For the opposition, as for the proponents, the ERA's main significance was symbolic. But the opposition could hardly concede this point openly, for while some people opposed equality between the sexes in principle, they were a small minority. The "swing" votes in unratified states were legislators who had no principled objection to "equal rights" but were alarmed about one or another practical consequence they feared might flow from the ERA. Had these ambivalent legislators been persuaded that they were only voting for a symbol with no practical short-term consequences, some would probably have supported the Amendment instead of opposing it.

I have not had the resources to investigate the proponents' decision to promote "59 cents" as an argument for the ERA, except to find out that it was primarily NOW's decision and was heavily influenced by Eleanor Smeal. Nor have I been able to trace the evolution of the many false statements put out by anti-ERA organizations. It is therefore impossible to do more than document with examples my strong impression that, in spite of similar incentives on both sides, the opposition indulged far more often in what appear to have been conscious lies.

An organization called Wake Up, formed to fight the New

York state ERA when it came up for a referendum vote in 1975, distributed leaflets urging voters to reject ERA, also known as the "Common Toilet Law." When the Fair Campaign Practices Commission in Rochester, New York, unanimously ruled that leaflet unfair, Wake Up labeled the commission a "Kangaroo Court," ignored its decision, and said on the phone to a pro-ERA reporter that the "common toilet business was brought up more by proponents than by us."[37] The same reporter spoke to a pro-ERA activist who recalled investigating a claim made by Mary Hober, a Wake Up vice-president, that women in a Bechtel Corporation mining camp in Montana were forced to use the same bathroom as men because of that state's ERA. According to the ERA activist,

> I got letters from the company's lawyer and from the Human Rights Commission in Helena, Montana, saying that this never happened. Not only was there no common toilet at the camp, but there weren't even any women at the camp. I showed Mary Hober one of the letters at a debate one night. She said she was interested and wanted a copy. Then the next day on radio she repeated the very same claim.[38]

Another anti-ERA pamphlet stated that after Maryland passed its ERA, a series of bills requiring common toilets, making women—even pregnant women—part of the state militia, and other highly unpopular measures (not legally entailed by an ERA) immediately "followed." The bills did indeed "follow." They were proposed, usually by ERA opponents trying to get publicity, but they never passed—a point that the anti-ERA pamphlet did not reveal.[39]

In Nebraska, a high-ranking insurance executive sent to all state legislators a piece of literature that declared:

> Under the proposed Equal Rights Amendment, wherever males are accustomed to appear in public, nude above the waist, equal rights are absolutely guaranteed to females. Such places would most certainly include swimming pools, tennis courts and drive-in theaters.[40]

In the continuing controversy after 1982, Schlafly's Eagle Forum put out a pamphlet that proclaimed "The ERA-GAY-AIDS-CONNECTION," and asked whether "if the E.R.A. puts 'sex equality' into the constitution . . . [w]ould police, paramedics, dentists, health personnel and morticians be permitted to take adequate precautions to defend themselves against AIDS and other homosexual diseases?" and "Could we restrict homosexuals from working in the food handling business, such as restaurants and as flight attendants on airlines?"[41]

Compare these allegations to what seems to me NOW's most farfetched claim:

> Without the ERA, women will not have constitutional or economic equality in this century. Without ERA, women will continue to be paid only 59 cents for every dollar paid to men. . . . the Equal Rights Amendment holds the answer for many families, headed by women who now live in poverty—and for families with two full-time wage earners who earn only one-and-a-half incomes simply because of sex discrimination.[42]

The "59 cents" claim is fairly vague, promising a general improvement, which might in fact eventually come about in part because of the general, indirect mandate of the ERA. While the generalized symbolic effects of the ERA might also over time influence community standards regarding, say, topless bathing, the specificity in the opponents' exaggerations produces a different psychological result. The opponents often promised with certainty a host of concrete "horrors" that they claimed would be caused immediately and directly by the ERA. And in some cases, like the Montana mining camp case or the unpopular bills in the Maryland legislature, their claims seem to have involved a reckless disregard for the truth.

In debate, opponents frustrated speakers with their "homey" approach to the issues. Carol Bellamy, then a New York State senator, recalled one of the Wake Up leaders telling "the audience forty-seven terrible things the ERA would do, and when you answered them and proved her wrong, she'd say, 'I'm just a housewife—how do I know?' Then she'd turn around and repeat them all over again."[43] In an early debate with Brenda Feigen, Schlafly charged that in a recent case in Pennsylvania a woman had been shorn of all her support after her marriage because of the ERA. When Feigen, puzzled, asked for the legal citation, Schlafly responded jubilantly, "I have the letter from that woman here in my purse!" For the lawyer, this was no evidence. For the audience, it was sufficient.

It was true, of course, that once the ERA battle reached what Janet Boles has called the "community conflict" stage[44]—involving amateurs in politics, unconventional tactics, personal slander, and overt hostility—the leadership in both camps could no longer control the actions or the tone of the people who contacted the legislators. The legislators soon came to dislike the personalities and distrust the claims of both sides, encouraged, no doubt, by the fact that these amateur lobbyists were women. When Debrah Bokowski asked legislators in several states to "describe and evaluate" the lobbying efforts of both sides of the ERA issue, a little over half the legislators who answered her request portrayed opponents as uninformed, unreasonable, ineffective, extreme, and emotional. Exactly half the legislators portrayed proponents in equally unflattering terms.[45] Some legislators simply dismissed the activists of both sides:

> I think they've both been obnoxious, really. The ladies with the bread and everything else they bring in [the antis] can be just as irritating as the ones who carry the placards [the pros].
> —*Female pro-ERA legislator*

> The activists, the people they [the leaders] bring with them—and this goes for both sides, the pro and the con—are pretty much wild-eyed crazies. You know, they are not professional, in the sense of the professional lobbyists that you, you know, work with normally down there. These people pull at you, yank you, yell, scream, threaten; they all look wild-eyed to me.
> 　. . . These people simply aren't coherent half the time. You can't discuss anything with them. They're just, you know, they just keep at you, and keep at you, and keep at you, just—till you can't get any other work done.
> —*Female anti-ERA legislator*

Even legislators who thought hard about the Amendment discounted the analyses of the citizens on their "side."

> Most of the pro-ERA activists are so radical that they contend a great deal more will be accomplished by passage than I think is realistic to assume.
> —*Female pro-ERA legislator*

I've generally been embarrassed by the [arguments] that I've seen publicized on the negative side. They're more . . . comments about brain-less, bra-less broads than ones based on any legal analysis of what the Fourteenth Amendment has and hasn't done and might potentially do in the future, as compared with what the ERA would accomplish.

—Male anti-ERA legislator

Why should activists whose avowed purpose was to pass or defeat a piece of legislation have behaved in ways that so many legislators regarded as foolish? One answer is that the alternative was very difficult and potentially costly. Predicting the substantive effects of the ERA was a difficult, time-consuming task, requiring a relatively dispassionate analysis of the issue. Those in a position to perform the task seldom knew exactly what the result would be, but they knew enough to see that disseminating such information to activists would be risky, since it would probably convince a lot of activists that they were wasting their time. The benefits of taking this risk were far from obvious, since only a small minority of legislators seemed to care about the Amendment's likely effects. Both sides therefore found it convenient to assume that no one in the legislature cared about the substantive effects and that the ERA's passage or defeat depended entirely on displays of passion and political muscle. Based on my observations in Illinois, I believe this view was probably an overgeneralization. A few waverers really did seem to me to care about what the Amendment would do. But such legislators were certainly a small minority compared to those who had either made up their minds in advance or who responded only to political pressure rather than argument.

However, at a more fundamental level, activists' ignorance about the substantive effects of the ERA was probably an almost inevitable by-product of the way in which they were recruited to the struggle. Because the ERA was a public good, the struggle attracted volunteers with strong ideological preconceptions about its merits and demerits. It promised few immediate changes in anyone's life, so it did not attract pragmatists for whom the tangible short-run costs and benefits were paramount. The volunteers who conducted the battle on both sides could not be subjected to "party discipline" in order to ensure that their actions always promoted the goal of either passing or defeating the ERA. Both sides had to give their volunteers a lot of leeway to do things that made legislative experts on both sides unhappy. In most cases the acts that irritated legislators reflected the fact that working for or against the ERA was not the volunteers' primary goal in life but was, instead, sub-ordinated to a larger agenda. Since legislators seldom shared the agenda of either proponents or opponents, the fact that neither side could conceal these agendas or "stick to the issue" was bound to antagonize legislators who only wanted to get on with their business.

11 Reaction in the Legislature

The state legislators who voted down the Equal Rights Amendment in Florida, North Carolina, Oklahoma, and Illinois ran the gamut from an unbudgeable coterie of far-right bigots through what I have called "mainstream" conservative legislators, usually male, who were not opposed to "equal rights" in principle but were opposed to almost any major substantive change either in the position of women or in other aspects of American life. These "mainstream" state legislators were usually contemptuous of the ignorance of both proponents and opponents of the ERA, equally ignorant themselves, apathetic on women's issues, conservative regarding significant changes of any sort, concerned with preserving the power of state legislatures against the federal government and Supreme Court, distrustful of the Court's recent decisions, anxious to retain local business support for their campaigns, and fearful of intense minorities with long-lasting strongholds in their districts. These legislators voted against the ERA not because of massive organized lobbying by the insurance industry or large corporate contributions to their campaigns but because the cumulative impact of many influences, including district-based organizing by STOP ERA, had led them to believe that voting for the Amendment would cause them more trouble than it was worth.

State legislators are subject to many of the same influences as other political activists. Three factors—selective incentives for joining the legislature, built-in distortions in the way legislators acquire information, and incentives connected with legislators' desires for reelection—all hurt the ERA's chances in the states. For these reasons legislators' votes often failed to reflect the views of the

149

electorate.[1] Nonetheless, state legislators are structurally better placed than almost anyone else to understand how their constituents' views apply to particular matters of policy. As a consequence, activists ought to listen to legislators more carefully than they usually do.

Selecting Legislators

The willingness of legislators to support the ERA in the states varied dramatically by gender, with more than three-quarters of the women legislators supporting ratification, compared to only half the men. Indeed, in the fifteen states that never ratified the ERA, 79 percent of the women legislators supported ratification, compared to 39 percent of the men.[2] In every legislature, however, the legislators were overwhelmingly male. This disparity reflects many factors, including the fact that women find it harder than men to get party support and campaign contributions.[3]

Among men, the incentives to run for legislative office are especially strong in occupations that were particularly hostile to the ERA. Only a few occupations allow legislators to enter politics while keeping their old jobs. Those who sell insurance or real estate or practice noncorporate law find running for public office relatively easy. They are their own bosses and do not have to be constantly present at their place of business. They can give themselves permission to leave and can keep their jobs open for their return. Their jobs require and develop the skills of speaking and persuading. Their work requires the extensive community contacts that facilitate political success. Finally, the visibility and contacts a state legislator usually gains in office facilitate future success in these occupations even if the legislator eventually fails to win reelection.

The single-person firm or small partnership that makes the most effective platform for an interruptable state legislative career also tends to breed support for rugged individualism and nostalgia for a small-business past. People with such sentiments were often strong opponents of the ERA, lumping the ERA in with "affirmative action" programs and other governmental attempts to intervene in "free enterprise."

Perhaps because of its innately conservative character, insurance seems particularly to attract political conservatives, and, among these, the Radical Right is disproportionately represented.

The Radical Right consistently opposed the ERA.[4] Moreover, ERA passage might have forced the insurance industry to change its rate schedules. Insurance rates often differ for men and women, because their driving records, health records, and life spans differ. The Supreme Court has never held that state regulation of insurance rates was sufficient to make these rate schedules constitute "state action." Thus, it has never faced the question of whether dual rate schedules meet the equal protection requirements of the Fourteenth Amendment laid down in *Craig v. Boren.* But if the Court were ever to define insurance rates as state action, which it might well do at some point, it would almost surely strike down dual rates if the Constitution included an ERA. It is unclear whether the insurance industry would actually lose any money by eliminating gender-based distinctions, since lower premiums for one group would be offset by higher premiums for the other.[5] But whatever the magnitude of the potential loss, there is no question that the insurance industry strongly opposed eliminating gender-based distinctions.[6] Although I found no evidence of a conscious insurance industry conspiracy to stop the ERA, the general conservatism of legislators connected with the insurance industry and the particular demands of their own industry meant that such legislators were distinctly more likely than others to oppose the ERA. And because of the selective incentives involved, the insurance industry was more heavily represented in the state legislatures than most other industries—in some cases by a large margin.[7]

Selecting Information

Once in the legislature, distortions in the way legislators collected information on the opinions of their constituents were also, on balance, likely to have hurt the ERA's prospects.

Many legislators seem to assume that the people who come in person to talk with them represent opinion in their district. When I spoke with Illinois legislators, for example, I asked whether they saw any difference between their average pro-ERA or anti-ERA constituents and the activists who came to Springfield to demonstrate for or against the ERA. Thirteen of the twenty-two legislators I asked explicitly denied that the activists differed—either sociologically or in their typical arguments—from the rest of their constituents. Of the nine legislators who reported noticing some

difference, almost all mentioned the somewhat higher socioeco-
nomic status, and sometimes the youth, of the pro-ERA activists.
Several mentioned the greater intensity of the activists' emotions on
both sides. As Chapter 12 shows, a very high proportion of the
anti-ERA demonstrators came from strict fundamentalist churches
and were, in this respect, even less typical of their districts than
pro-ERA activists were of theirs. But only three legislators (all
women who had worked hard for the ERA) in my sample of
twenty-two seem to have realized this fact.[8] Legislators who did not
realize that many of the communications from "typical homemakers" actually came from fundamentalist women were almost certainly misled about the breadth and depth of the opposition.

Legislators also put great weight on their mail, and although
volume—in which the pro-ERA groups did relatively well—was
one major consideration, the STOP ERA groups, with their base in
the fundamentalist churches, had activists with the time to generate
the homey, hand-written letters on personal stationery that legislators count heavily. As one anti-ERA legislator said,

> Well, I'll tell you something about what the pros will send. They'll send
> you a post card. Every card is the same. They sign their name on it and
> maybe their address. The people who are anti will write me a hand-
> written letter. Now, that's the difference.

Another legislator, uncommitted on the ERA, commented, "I
have very few activists who contact me. . . . From pro-ERA? No,
they never bother me. And if I do get something, I get a post card
that's a form letter where they fill in the blanks! Wonderful!"

For some, the chief measure of constituent opinion is introspec-
tion. As one rural legislator said, "I come from my district, and they
were brought up the same way that I am, or was, and worked the
same way I always have." But since legislators are disproportionately male, they are not really brought up in the same way as
at least half of their constituents, who are female. And as we have
seen, legislators are also unlikely to do the same kind of work as
most of their constituents.

The "Trustee" Theory

Once in the legislature, legislators acted both according to their
conception of how a legislator ought to act and according to their

conception of what they needed to do to win reelection. Legislators sometimes acted on the theory that they ought to be "trustees" for their constituents' real long-run interests rather than just mirroring their constituents' present preferences. Indeed, they sometimes saw themselves as trustees for the interests of the whole polity rather than just their particular districts. In some cases, these trustee theories encouraged both proponents and opponents of the ERA to ignore majority opinion in their districts.

For proponents, the case for a trustee orientation was clear. If a representative's constituents opposed the ERA, this was because those constituents had been blinded by "irrational" fears. At the very least, the representative should educate those constituents. At most, he or she should vote against the constituents' short-run preferences for their long-run good. Further, proponents argued that since the ERA was a change in the whole nation's constitution, state legislators should think of themselves as representing the whole nation and not just their own state or district.

For anti-ERA legislators, the case was equally clear. If their constituents supported the ERA, this was because they did not know certain facts—that the ERA would have no substantive consequences they favored, that it gave the federal courts a larger voice in family law, that it might force women into combat, and so on. These legislators believed that by blocking the ERA they could save the country from the ill-considered and politically inspired actions of the U.S. Congress.

The trustee orientations of both proponents and opponents were accentuated by their conviction that activists on both sides were too committed to their cause to see the reality and that the public was almost totally misinformed. In 1976, for example, less than 20 percent of the American public knew both whether the legislature in their own state had considered the ERA and, if so, whether the Amendment had passed or failed. Even in the states where the ERA was a live political issue—where at least one legislative house had had a floor vote on the ERA but had not ratified—only 25 percent of ERA proponents and 40 percent of opponents knew that the ERA had been considered and had failed in their states.[9]

The voters' ignorance was combined with their unwillingness to let the ERA influence their choices in statewide elections. During June 1982, for example, with the deadline for ratification only days away, one group of supporters were fasting in the Illinois capitol and another had chained themselves to the rotunda in order to publicize, among other things, the Republican governor's failure adequately to support the ERA. All this was being heavily publicized. Yet in this month, of a sample of registered Illinois voters, 73 percent said they did not know where the governor's Democratic opponent stood on the ERA, and 44 percent said they did not know the governor's own stand. Moreover, 66 percent of the sample said they thought the gubernatorial candidates' positions on the ERA should not "be a factor in deciding who to vote for in the election this fall."[10] This combination of ignorance and apathy led many legislators to conclude that "the citizens don't give a hoot about the ERA."

Party Politics

Because the legislators' constituents were unlikely to vote for or against them on the basis of their stands on the ERA, constituent opinion on this issue was less important to them than the opinion of party leaders and major campaign contributors. Recognizing this fact of political life about halfway through the campaign, ERA advocates began to pay much more attention to party politics.

The Democratic party leadership, which had a growing partisan commitment to the ERA, was not always successful in persuading its representatives to vote the party line. In Chicago, one pro-ERA legislator told me,

> [They] used all the muscle they could, any way they could, from Mayor Bilandic or Mayor Byrne, to get some of the Chicago legislators who always go along with the wishes of the mayor; but for some reason or other on this issue [those legislators] said, "I don't care who calls; I don't care what they do to me; I am not gonna vote for it." And it was that type of opposition that they ran into that held back the Chicago vote.

However, many did go along, like the black representative who cast his vote for the ERA in 1980 with the curt explanation, "The Assistant Majority Leader who has worked hard on this issue, James Taylor, leaned very hard on me and said he wants this vote, so vote me 'aye'."[11] In the words of one pro-ERA legislator, "Jane Byrne [mayor of Chicago] really put the screws to a lot of Chicago regulars who were not themselves for ratification."

Political parties do not need a machine to exercise power over a legislator. At election time, parties provide money and workers. During a legislator's term of service, the party leadership can arrange appointments to powerful committees. If reelection fails, the party leadership can arrange a judgeship, a paid appointment to a governmental commission, or another place in the governmental machinery. In Illinois, these considerations meant that after 1980, when the Republicans took the ERA out of their national party platform and the Republican Presidential candidate opposed it publicly, many Republican legislators were reluctant to oppose the anti-ERA parliamentary rulings of the Republican Speaker of the House. A few Republican women legislators who had been elected on ERA platforms with the help of ERA volunteers did openly defy the Republican leadership by holding back their votes on an important piece of Republican legislation, in order to "trade" them for a parliamentary ruling that would let the ERA be passed by a majority in the Illinois house. But these "suicidal" antics brought amused scorn from more experienced members of their party.

Contributions

Beyond party, legislators must look to the interests that contribute most to their election campaigns. Local business interests usually make the steadiest contributions to a legislator's reelection campaign fund, while unions and professional organizations contribute to a lesser degree. After a career in the legislature is over, specific corporations can arrange a consultantship, a retainer for a lawyer, a job as a paid lobbyist, or simply a job in the industry. When large contributors speak, therefore, the legislator is likely to listen.

It is impossible to get accurate data on political contributions for and against the ERA in the unratified states. In Illinois, Barbara Brotman analyzed the pattern of politically acknowledged pro- and anti-ERA political contributions and discovered that, although both sides had spent about the same amount of money between 1976 and 1980, the pro-ERA contributions had been inconsistent and scattered, while the anti-ERA contributions, guided by the "single voice" of Phyllis Schlafly, had been predictable, regular and steady.[12]

Brotman concluded that the pro-ERA forces should have consistently rewarded all pro-ERA legislators. However, political strategists do not all agree that across-the-board contributions are better than targeting the most important races. Moreover, in this period the Illinois constitution required a three-fifths majority in each house of the legislature to ratify an amendment to the U.S. Constitution. If ERA proponents had tried to match the opponents' consistent rewards to those who voted with them, they would always have had to spend, as a matter of course, three dollars to their opponents' two. Most important, the specifically earmarked contributions on which Brotman reported were probably only the tip of the iceberg and may not have reflected accurately either the amount or the pattern of ERA-related contributions.

While no one can know how much money each side *spent* on the national scale, comparing the goods each side *bought*—television advertising, pamphlets, and logistical support at demonstrations, for instance—does not suggest that STOP ERA had more money than the pro-ERA organizations. STOP ERA might have used all its money in campaign contributions, but if there had been massive expenditures of this kind over time, one would expect to have heard about it from legislators, who do not turn a deaf ear to gossip involving money.[13]

In the short run, large expenditures can be hidden easily. Moreover, "hidden money" derives in part from general patterns of contribution: the ERA was a liberal rather than a conservative cause, and conservatives usually have a higher and more consistent pattern of giving than liberals. One member of ERA Illinois, who had helped decide how to use an astounding last-minute gift of $30,000 from out of state, spelled out the process:

MEMBER: Now the thing that I felt really good about in that whole election was we plotted all summer, we analysed those districts and looked at the vote totals and in the end it was crystal clear that there were these 16 districts—these were the hot ones. That's where we had to work, that's where we had to make a difference. The Republican Party picked the same 16 districts.

JM: So at least you knew your analysis was right.

MEMBER: See, I figured I had—we did a good job. And did we fight it out! Well, you know, we were giving guys $3,000–$4,000, and the way we lost was the Republican Party and the manufacturers out-spent us.

JM: Now why was it so important for them?

MEMBER: Because, generally the people we were giving money to
          were the liberals, or the more liberals. They were Demo-
          crats, in most cases, or they were liberal Republicans,
          and to the manufacturers it is exceedingly important to
          have conservative men there who will vote the business
          line. And they raise money like—

JM: So your view is it doesn't really have anything to do with
          the ERA; it's that the right-wing Republicans take both
          an "anti" position on the ERA and also a right-wing
          position on the economic issues? Then the businessmen
          support them for the economic issues?

MEMBER: That's right.

JM: And then, along with that comes the ERA?

MEMBER: Uh huh. Now, you know, I would sit—I met Dave
          Wastrom [the names in this account are fictitious] at
          least once a month and we'd sit and go over what was
          happening.

JM: Who is Dave Wastrom?

MEMBER: He's the lobbyist for the Manufacturers Association.
          He's their bag man. And he would come and say,
          "Somebody just gave Jones $5,000 and now I have to go
          raise $10,000!" And then he'd look at me. [She mimicks
          herself, feigning ignorance:] "No, really, somebody just
          gave Jones $5,000?"
              Well, I'd just given Dandridge $5,000, you know,
          that Sandler gave me—and Dandridge almost died when
          we gave him $5,000. He said, "I can't take that much."
          Because he was afraid it was coming from ERA Illinois.
          And [an ERA Illinois board member] said, "It won't
          come from ERA Illinois; it will come directly from the
          donor." He didn't want $5,000 from ERA Illinois on his
          campaign contribution sheet, but Bobby Miller was not
          afraid to have $5,000 from the Manufacturers' Associa-
          tion on *his* campaign disclosure sheet! And the other
          thing, you know, Wastrom is only allowed to give him
          $5,000 or whatever; then Wastrom goes to all the local
          business people and says, "Send him $1,000," and they
          all do.

JM: Individually?

MEMBER: Uh huh. About the disclosure statements, you can't tell,
            because the ERA PAC and the anti-PAC—or what-
            ever—are just a drop in the bucket compared to the
            other stakes that aren't labeled.

Several ERA activists and legislators concluded that the issue
was not dollar amounts but timing and that the key years had been
early, around 1975. This was the year

when pro-ERA senators, for example, suddenly started voting no after
Mrs. Schlafly contributed $300 to their campaigns. In those days, it
took $300 to buy a senator, $100 to buy a representative. . . . It never
occurred to us to give money because we were naive and neophytes.
. . . Idealism and logic were important, not financial contributions.[14]

Continuity

Probably the most important problem lay in the perceptions of
legislators that the proponents' organizations were ephemeral while
the opponents' organizations were enduring. For in spite of the
ERA activists' motto, "We won't go away," that was exactly what
the state legislators expected them to do. The legislators expected,
and often got, sporadic initiatives, intense one-time activity, and
little follow-through. The most dramatic example of this pattern in
Illinois came in 1980, when national NOW organized a massive
ratification campaign, launched two giant demonstrations from a
base in Chicago, set up phone banks around the state, and involved
thousands of women in lobbying efforts. After the ERA was defeated in the Illinois house in 1980, national NOW simply folded up
its Chicago ratification office. Although NOW's regular Chicago
and Illinois chapters continued the struggle after the national
money and recruits had left town, the state legislators felt that the
dramatic decline in activity confirmed their prediction: "Here today, gone tomorrow."

Another example of the off-again, on-again character of pro-
ERA activity came in the proponents' lobbying efforts. If a piece of
legislation is likely to encounter opposition, success usually requires the consistent services of a full-time lobbyist at the state
capitol. A permanent lobbyist can confer with sponsors of the
legislation, sound out possible supporters and opponents, provide

information for supporters, calm the fears of potential opponents, sense what possible deals can be made with wavering potential supporters, and do the behind-the-scenes legwork in positioning the legislation's arrival on the agenda. In 1972, when the ERA first came to the states, there was no strong national organization dedicated solely, or even primarily, to ratification.[15] In most states, ERA supporters had no full-time lobbyist, though lobbyists from several groups did what they could without making the Amendment their primary concern. In Illinois, ERA proponents used five or six different lobbying strategies and ten or twelve different lobbyists in the ten years between 1972 and 1982.

Experience

Experience counted heavily in the grass-roots election campaigns. By 1972, Phyllis Schlafly had been involved for two decades in state and national legislative politics. She first ran for congressional office herself in 1952, had a great personal effect in getting Barry Goldwater nominated the Republican candidate for President in 1964, and had worked intensively with Republican women's groups on both state and national campaigns. This experience gave her a wealth of practical understanding about how to organize at the district level. Almost as soon as she began organizing, state legislators, particularly in Illinois, began to feel STOP ERA as a constant presence. As one anti-ERA legislator put it,

> The STOP ERA forces were much better organized and did a better job lobbying. The pro-ERA forces are only visible when there's actually going to be a vote. Then they have a big hoopla and stage a rally, that sort of thing. The STOP ERA, Phyllis Schlafly, group is there all the time. They're always there, getting to know the legislators, developing a relationship with them, not necessarily harassing them, but constantly reminding them of their presence, maybe even talking to them about other issues, establishing that personal relationship.
>
> For example, on that first day when everyone, all the new people, are sworn into office—inauguration day—the STOP ERA forces always have a big reception. And they invite everyone. And that kind of constant contact makes their lobbying much more effective.

One legislative proponent believed that Schlafly gave the antis "a consistent plan," as opposed to the ERA supporters who "don't know how to help people get elected." Another strong ERA proponent in the legislature remarked, "The anti activists are much much much more political, much more highly organized. [STOP ERA] got the jump on us, and I would give a great deal of credit to Schlafly." Answering my question on the reason for the ERA's defeat, she concluded:

> I don't think we were political enough. I think that if we had worked in more political campaigns, early on, and could have built a kind of strong organization that gets candidates elected, and had been able to point to elections and say, "He is pro-ERA and we got him elected," those are the kinds of arguments that politicians pay attention to.[16]

Inexperience within the legislature worked against the ERA as much as inexperience without. In all the unratified states, supporters were faced with the unpleasant choice between giving the floor management of the ERA to powerful and experienced male politicians who did not care intensely about the issue or to less powerful and less experienced women who did care. The women supporters of the ERA had three strikes against them in the legislature. They were not only women but they were usually newcomers and "good government" idealists as well. In a legislature where many representatives see the democratic process as primarily a "fair fight" among contending interests rather than as "reasoning together" toward a common good, a reputation as a "goo-goo" (or "good-government") type tends to brand a legislator as someone who doesn't know what politics is all about. Such a person can be exluded from leadership, from unofficial information, and from the log-rolling that makes interest politics work.

In Illinois, women legislators originally sponsored the ERA in the House of Representatives. According to one leader, "There were no other options: it was felt that this was the girls' baby."[17] Yet having women sponsors might have hurt the ERA. Representative Alan Greiman, who followed Representatives Giddy Dyer and Eugenia Chapman to become the first male sponsor in 1977, said that

> the men's sponsorship was taken in a more serious vein. I got less catcalls, less sexist jokes, less abuse than Giddy and Eugenia. [JM:

What do you mean by catcalls?] You know, "yoo-hoo," crazy noises, that kind of thing. [JM: And abuse?] Being laughed at. . . . No one asked me if I was going to burn my bra. [JM: Did people ask Giddy and Eugenia things like that? Not on the floor, presumably.] No, not on the floor. But yes, they got a lot of abuse.

The early sponsors of the ERA in Illinois also made decisions that later Monday-morning quarterbacks considered mistakes of inexperience. Eugenia Chapman, one of the first sponsors, was an independent Democrat. In the late spring of 1972, when Chapman introduced the ERA for the second time, it could have passed, because the opposition was not yet organized. But, as one activist told me, Chapman "didn't believe in" the regular Democratic leadership, which was largely dominated by the Chicago machine. When Mayor Richard Daley, head of the machine, put himself forward to chair the Illinois delegation to the Democratic Presidential Convention, Chapman backed his opponent, Adlai Stevenson. To punish Chapman, Daley drew seven Democatic votes off the ERA and the Amendment failed.[18] In 1973, the independent Democrats ran Chapman for Speaker of the House, trying to take advantage of a split in the Republican ranks. The move eventually failed but it angered both Republicans and machine Democrats, and some people believed the anger at the sponsor hurt the prospects for the ERA.

Even in 1982, supporters were still criticizing the ERA's legislative sponsors in Illinois for not knowing how to "count." That is, the sponsors were not able to predict who would vote for and against the Amendment. One ERA Illinois leader recalled a "little discussion" she had had with one of the women sponsors of the ERA on the question of "who could count":

There was an incident last year, in June, when the vote came up. The vote was going to come up. And I was planning on coming down to Springfield because I wanted to be there when the vote was up. Giddy [Dyer, one of the sponsors] said she had the votes, she had so and so, so and so, and so and so. And so I called [my friend in the legislature] and told him that I was planning on coming down. And he said, "Why?" And I said, "I want to be there when the vote is taken. I want to see it pass." And he said, "Don't come then; you'll be disappointed."

And I didn't go down, and people said, "How did he know that it wasn't going to pass?" It's because he counts better than Giddy does. Giddy believed people when they said they were going to vote yes, and her yes's turned into no's. They were—they lied. It's as simple as that. They lied to her.

Because accuracy in predicting votes is an important measure of a politician's skill, the inability of ERA sponsors to "count" accurately lost them some respect among insiders in the legislature. Worse, it may have lost them occasional crucial votes, because some legislators will only take a political risk if they are assured that the cost to them in potential constituent anger will be balanced by the fact that with their vote a particular bill will pass. One pro-ERA legislator told me,

> Sooner or later if a guy sits in the General Assembly for ten years, I think it is crazy not to think that he is gonna make at least one judgment on, maybe, his principle. . . . [But] what good is it for me to sit there and vote what I feel would be my principle—in terms of the philosophy that I would have on how government ought to be run relating to an issue—and I voted against my constituency and voted my political philosophy, and then still when they took the tally, I was still on the losing side? . . . When you are really in a position where you can make it happen, *then* it would be rewarding enough to say, "I'll see you guys later; beat me in an election!" I don't care whatever it is, *that* is where it makes it worthwhile. Otherwise you are crazy, in my estimation.

When legislators are in this position, as some were with the ERA, getting each one to vote requires assuring each that the others will also vote this way. A reputation for not being able to count accurately makes such assurances worthless.

However, the ERA's problems in Illinois were caused only in part by inexperience. One year, for example, an ERA group hired two lobbyists with the reputation of getting matters taken care of with few questions asked. One of these "good old boys" made perhaps the worst single mistake in the ten-year campaign. That lobbyist

> is reputed to have said, in one of those closed rooms, "Never mind the Blacks; they don't have anywhere else to go. Of course they'll be with

us." That remark was repeated to the Blacks by someone who was in that room apparently. [As a consequence, that year] there were five Black Democratic votes that we'd always had before that didn't vote with us. And we fell two votes shy.

—ERA activist[19]

Ironically, this was a mistake that an "inexperienced" lobbyist—that is, a committed activist—would have been unlikely to make. As for experience in the role of sponsor, in 1980 the ERA was sponsored in the House by a man who had many years of experience. It failed by a few votes in that year as well.

The Result

The overall effect of all this effort was that the mainstream legislator in the average wavering state could end this ten-year period caring as little for the ERA as when he began, not having learned much about what the ERA would actually do, still as opposed as ever to significant changes in men's and women's roles, aware as always of local business support for generally conservative politics, and increasingly conscious of the political potential of his right-wing fundamentalist constituents. For him, the ERA looked bad both in principle and in practice. At the level of principle, it looked bad because it would give the Supreme Court, whose history of interpreting the Constitution he had grown to distrust, more words with which to play. On the practical, political level, it would subject him to the retribution of the newly active fundamentalist churches, to pressure from Schlafly's Eagle Forum, and, if he was a Republican, to possible retribution from his increasingly conservative party leadership.

Despite all their limitations, however, these middle-of-the-road conservative legislators could and should have been an important source of information to pro-ERA activists. While only a minority of these legislators voted on the basis of their views about what was best for the country, the attitudes they expressed in the course of the debate were not simply rhetoric designed to rationalize positions taken for other reasons. When these legislators said that the ERA would give the Supreme Court a "blank check," or open a "Pandora's box," or even when they said it was "unnecessary," they were implicitly saying that for them the important question was not what the ERA symbolized but what specific substantive effects it was likely to have.

Likewise, if the pro-ERA activists had taken the arguments of middle-of-the-road conservatives more seriously, they might well have avoided the "combat trap." When these legislators said they opposed the amendment because they feared it would send women into combat, they were faithfully mirroring their constituents' deep ambivalence about moving into a more androgynous society. Had the proponents of the Amendment recognized the strength of the popular resistance to such a change, they might well have been more willing to entertain a gradualist approach to ERA interpretation.

I do not mean to suggest that if activists had listened more carefully to their legislative opponents they would necessarily have swayed their opponents' votes. But more attention to their opponents' arguments would certainly have enabled them to mount a more effective campaign for the Amendment. It is true that ignorance and venality abound in state legislatures. It is also true that, for the many reasons that this chapter documents, legislators do not always vote their constituents' preferences or educate those constituents in a way that would serve the constituents' long-term interests. But the fact remains that legislators are better placed than almost anyone else in American society to think seriously about reconciling their constituents' current prejudices with the need to make public policy. Legislators must stay in touch with their constituents' feelings in order to get reelected. Their day-to-day job is to appraise legislative proposals and vote them up or down. Precisely because the two roles are hard to reconcile, attempting to do so can give legislators perspective on both their constituents and policy that activists are unlikely to have.

12 Organizing in Illinois: A Case Study

Both the pro-ERA and STOP ERA organizations always had to pursue two goals: surviving as organizations, and either passing or defeating the ERA. These goals often conflicted. The requirements of organizational survival forced both sides to recruit and retain activists for whom passing or defeating the ERA was only one of many goals, and whose activities occasionally did their cause more harm than good. Maintaining the commitment of these activists also required the organizations themselves to do things, like exaggerating the Amendment's probable effect, that sometimes hurt their cause. The need to maintain the activists' commitment to the organizations, moreover, shaped the day-to-day political tactics of the organizations on both sides, sometimes even bringing them into conflict with their nominal allies. This chapter examines how the demands of organizational survival influenced the tactics of NOW, ERA Illinois, and STOP ERA in Illinois.

Two Memberships: Two Tactics

To attract and keep their activists, the different pro-ERA organizations chose different ways of mobilizing public opinion and changing legislative votes. NOW, a national organization that had come to rely heavily on direct mail contributions, leaned toward tactics that would generate national media coverage—mass rallies, demonstrations, and television ads aimed at a national audience. Local groups picked other strategies. In Illinois, the statewide umbrella organization, ERA Illinois, depended on the energies of women who had long-standing interest in state politics. Accordingly, it leaned toward tactics that involved its members in the things they liked most—district-based local organizing, and building personal relationships with state leaders in the two political parties. Both strategies had their weaknesses and strengths. But in Illinois, as in the other states, those who practiced one tended to see the other as at best self-serving or deluded and at worst undermining the cause.

In 1982 NOW organized a mass demonstration at the Illinois state capitol in Springfield. Thousands upon thousands of women in white surged down the wide streets toward the capitol dome that towered against the blue midwestern sky, chanting over and over, "What do we want?" "ERA!" "When do we want it?" *"Now!"* Yet, far from rejoicing at this massive show of support, the members of ERA Illinois, who talked every day to the legislators, wrung their hands and agonized over the cumulative anger that these demonstrations were building up, even among sympathetic legislators, because these were the harried last days of the legislative session and the demonstrators demanded so much of the legislators' time that no ordinary business could get done.

May and June are always the best times for a demonstration. There is time for preparation over the fall and winter, and the demonstration provides a kind of culmination to the year's activities, which always dissipate during the members' scattered vacations during the summer and resume in the fall. More important, the warm weather of the oncoming summer will always lure outside many whose spirits have congealed during the winter months. But late spring and early summer are also frantic days for state legislators, whose work is underpaid and part-time, and who inevitably postpone the most difficult issues—budget, roads, taxes—until the last moment before they themselves go back to their neglected families and jobs for the summer.

So when another ERA demonstration loomed on the horizon, the legislators grumbled and cursed, building up vengeful feelings against the "goddamned women" who were invading their citadel again, bringing no new insights or information with them, just endless pestering and emotional displays. ERA Illinois members, with their fingers on the pulse of the few wavering legislators, worried desperately at the possibility that each new demonstration might be the last straw.

For their part, NOW leaders ground their teeth in frustration when the president of ERA Illinois (a Republican) and the vice-president (a Democrat), wearing ERA buttons, attended a fund-

raising dinner for Governor Thompson at which President Reagan
was the principal speaker. NOW members were picketing outside
the dinner, as they had picketed Reagan everywhere they could
throughout the state when he came to support Republican candidates for reelection. They were picketing to draw attention to the
President's opposition to the ERA and to his many national policies
that hurt the poor, who were primarily women. They had no qualms
about picketing Governor Thompson's fund-raising dinner, even
though he was a liberal Republican who nominally supported the
ERA, because he had also chosen a conservative Republican and
arch opponent of the ERA, George Ryan, as his running mate for
lieutenant governor. Ryan was the second speaker at the dinner.
Illinois was reducing the size of its legislature, which meant that
many incumbents would lose their seats.[1] If Thompson and Ryan
won the upcoming gubernatorial election, Ryan would play a piv-
otal role in redistricting, and thus in determining which legislators
lost their seats. No legislator in any but the safest seat wanted to be
on the wrong side of George Ryan, and Ryan had let it be known for
a long time that he detested the ERA. What, then, were the ERA
Illinois president and vice-president doing attending a $250-a-plate
fund-raising dinner for Thompson at which both President Reagan
and George Ryan would be honored speakers?

   Members of ERA Illinois, on the other hand, believed that
picketing Reagan would only generate national publicity and would
never persuade any Illinois legislator to vote for the ERA. They had
gotten the tickets to the fund-raising dinner free, they protested,
and had distributed pro-ERA literature around the tables. Most
important, it seemed clear to them that since the Republicans were
the majority party in the Illinois house, making the ERA a straight
Republican-Democratic issue would surely kill it. As one said,

> [NOW's leaders have] worked only with the Democrats and have
> simply almost ignored the Republicans, who are the majority party,
> and the leadership of the Republican Party, which has every preroga-
> tive to use the gavel in dozens of different ways to frustrate their
> efforts. . . . They must have ceased to believe that to keep communica-
> tions open was the better part of wisdom. It seems to me an unwork-
> able policy.

The two tactics developed quite naturally from the different
membership needs of the two groups. Each group attracted people

with different political sympathies, ages, and ways of life. ERA Illinois, a nonpartisan body, had for several years had a Republican president. When the president of ERA Illinois ran for state senate in 1982, her campaign literature pledged her to work for "public assistance only for those truly in need," and "a balanced state budget." The next president of ERA Illinois, a school teacher, commented at a meeting, "If the parents would teach their kids responsibility, respectability and religion . . . at home, we'd have no problem with them at school!" NOW, on the other hand, had a membership of liberals and radicals who were almost exclusively Democrats. Indeed, as one Illinois NOW leader put it, "Most of our members would identify themselves as socialist, without knowing what it meant."[2] NOW, working with Democratic politicians, developed ERA strategies that tended to benefit the Democrats, while ERA Illinois worked with Republicans.[3]

In part, the differences had to do with style. NOW members often thought of ERA Illinois as composed of ladies who sat with their hands in their laps expecting the Republican leadership to change because the ladies were so nice. The members of ERA Illinois were mostly over forty and thus older than most active members of NOW. ERA Illinois was also more sedate: in the first ERA Illinois meeting that I attended none of the women wore jeans, one wore a matched polyester pantsuit, and exactly half wore skirts—compared to half jeans and half slacks at my first local NOW meeting. More than half the women at ERA Illinois wore some kind of makeup compared to only one of the women at my NOW meeting. Ranging from the dumpy to the classically coiffed and tailored, the ERA Illinois women saw themselves as representing the grass roots. They laughed together, as they traded recipes during a potluck lunch, at the contrast their homey activity presented to the image they imagined state legislators had of the average ERA activist.

But notwithstanding the conservative sentiments of their presidents and their older, more local backgrounds, these women were genuine feminists. ERA Illinois meetings almost always began with someone passing around a news item about women or the ERA that had made them mad or telling a joke that spoke to women's plight. They welcomed a member's newborn to "his first feminist meeting," and in my later interviews every woman I talked with identified herself as a feminist. They simply had a different natural style.

One ERA Illinois leader responded with irritation to the charge of "niceness" by saying,

> I don't think niceness makes anybody change. But there is only one way to keep a rapport going with the people who are in a position to make or break a piece of legislation, and that is to keep communicating, to be sensitive to that person, to keep relaying what you know, what you hear, to other people in the party who have your best interest in mind, your issue in mind. And look for the moment when you might use some devious tactics to get what you need done. I don't think there is anything productive about making an enemy out of leadership unless you see a moment when some kind of extreme action is going to accomplish what you need accomplished.
>
> And this is what the NOW people are so annoyed about, is that they see us continuing to talk to Republicans and to Republican leadership, and they see us as traitors.[4]

But the NOW activists, eyeing the activities of some of the members of ERA Illinois, concluded that they were only trying to advance their careers in the Republican party.

Not only the age and style but the members' backgrounds in politics were quite different within the two groups. The typical NOW member had not been born in Illinois and did not necessarily expect to spend her life there. In my local NOW chapter, many of the members were recent migrants to the city,[5] at least half were under forty, several were lesbians, and many were unmarried. Recognizing their ignorance of state politics, one woman suggested at my first meeting that the chapter set up a "legislative task force" to learn more about the state legislature. One NOW leader summarized her constituency: "We have a lot of people who know about reproductive rights, affirmative action, and all the feminist issues— but they don't know a thing about street lights." While these NOW members might eventually settle in Illinois and become local political leaders, right now they were "cosmopolitans" who had joined the organization primarily to share their feminism in an atmosphere of mutual support.

This generalized feminist ideology made NOW a multi-issue organization. As a result, many legislators tied the ERA to other feminist causes, especially legal abortion. The NOW leadership was aware of this dilemma. In the major ratification push of 1980,

NOW's national office set up its ERA ratification project office in
Illinois several blocks away from the main NOW office, specifically
to insure that literature, posters, and other reminders that NOW
was a multi-issue organization would not be present. But while the
new direct-mail members of NOW often joined because of the
ERA, the active chapter membership was still concerned with the
full range of feminist issues. They had joined the organization to
find companions as well as to support the cause, and they often
resented the fact that NOW's national office was devoting time and
money to the ERA that they would rather have seen devoted to
preserving abortion rights or other feminist causes. Occasionally,
these members even responded to questions about the ERA's effect
on abortion by defending a woman's right to abortion rather than
taking the official NOW position that there was no connection
between the two issues. ERA Illinois, on the other hand, prided
itself in having engaged in its coalition a number of Roman Catholic
organizations, which opposed abortion as a matter of principle. The
leaders of ERA Illinois saw both NOW's support for abortions and
the generally distracting effect of other issues as hurting the ERA:

> NOW, for one thing, approaches ERA—especially within the last year
> and a half, two years, in this state—as one of *many* issues that are on
> their list of priorities, and I think after last session, after the failure of
> the successful roll-call on ERA [in 1980], they made a very conscious
> decision to continue to work on ERA but not at any more intense level
> than a lot of their other issues.
>
> And they also have, it appears, made a conscious decision to buck
> the system at all costs—to be making a statement, by bucking the
> system, which might be symbolic to the people, the onlookers, of the
> intensity with which they are going to approach all women's issues.
>
> And I honestly feel that they don't have the very best interest of
> the Equal Rights Amendment in mind as they implement this strategy.
> That they simply want to make their mark, that they want to, if
> possible, intimidate those people who seem to be the obstacles to
> implementing their women's program.

The active members of NOW did have a larger goal in mind
than simply ratifying the ERA. For many new members of NOW,
working for the ERA was a radicalizing experience. It opened their
eyes to the underlying attitudes of many of their legislators, friends,

families, colleagues, and bosses. For many, the ERA provided their first political activity. In a NOW bus going to Springfield in 1980 I interviewed one woman who had driven from Colorado to Illinois, using her entire yearly vacation from her secretarial job to work for the ERA. She had come in touch with the women's movement for the first time at her second job, when "the first issue of *Ms.* had come out, and someone was sharing the issue around the office." With no NOW chapter or any other women's group in her town, she became a direct-mail member of NOW, and for years was politically active only by sending postcards to legislators when the *NOW Times* sent out a call. But when the ERA began to falter, she moved into a political activity that absorbed her evenings, her weekends, and now her one vacation. Another woman, from a NOW chapter in a town of 25,000 in New Mexico, joined the chapter after listening to a feminist do an interview at the radio station where she worked. Her group had raised money to send her to Illinois to work for the ERA because she was the only one of them with no "8 to 5 job." An older black woman told me that she had watched on television the ERA demonstration organized by NOW in Chicago and had wanted to join in then, but this was the first time she had had the time to participate. Like almost everyone else on the bus, she had never been to Springfield before.

Knowing that work for the ERA was often the first step to committed feminism, both the leaders and most of the active members of NOW saw the ERA as only one battle in an ongoing, much longer war. They valued each demonstration, each phone call soliciting support, and each television ad, not just for its effect in passing the ERA itself but for its value in sensitizing all women to feminist political issues. Moreover, NOW was not just a local but a national organization, resting even more on its direct-mail membership than on its constituent chapters. Its political strength lay in attracting new members and in giving the present ones the feeling that the organization was doing something important. Once NOW became visibly involved in the national ERA struggle, its direct-mail membership began to increase dramatically.[6] This meant that the organization naturally leaned toward activities that had a national impact, like television ads and massive demonstrations that would get national media coverage rather than toward local organizing in districts with wavering legislators, many of which did not even have a NOW chapter.

While NOW had to rely on a group of people who had joined
the organization for a broad range of feminist reasons, ERA Illinois
depended largely on the energies of a few women who in their
unions, churches, or League of Women Voters chapters had followed state politics the way a fan follows baseball. At the first ERA
Illinois meeting I attended, the president spent more than two
hours giving an update on each of the state legislators, with a style
so informal in its references that at least half the time I did not
understand which legislator was being discussed. She caught the
meeting up on the legislators' personal and political fortunes, who
had said what to whom at what restaurant, who was getting divorced, who had a hard race ahead in the next election, who was
being maneuvered out of power by a group of local committeemen,
and how that all affected the probable line-up of votes on the ERA
in the upcoming legislative session. I was completely out of my
depth.

During a break in another meeting, I turned to a nurse from the
south side of Chicago who had been almost as quiet as I, and who I
thought might be almost as confused. Hoping to begin a tentative
alliance of the unsophisticated, I asked where she lived. "District
28," she replied, leaving me as ignorant as I was before. Had I asked
the same question at a NOW chapter meeting, it is inconceivable
that anyone would have described where she lived by naming her
legislative district. Indeed, few would even have known the number
of their legislative districts, must less expecting other people to
know where a district identified by a number really was. For the ten
or fifteen people who were extremely active in ERA Illinois, this
kind of response was second nature. As one member of the board
put it, they were "political animals."

Organizationally weak, ERA Illinois kept its larger membership by offering a nonradical way of supporting the ERA, and by
acting as the coalition that brought together all the state supporters
of the ERA—from unions to business. It attracted the energies of
its most active members by giving them a chance to live and breathe
intrigue, high drama and history-in-the-making, while also doing
good. Such a strategy produced active members who engaged in
what some ERA sponsors in the legislature considered counterproductive and naive meddling with the sponsors' legislative planning.
And in spite of the enthusiasm of its most active members, ERA
Illinois was not equipped to organize at the district level. It was an

unexciting, frequently disorganized umbrella organization, with few individual members. While its organizational membership included a number of large groups, none of these groups had much interest in trying to mobilize its membership to enter active politics in their home districts. There were simply not enough "political animals" to go around.

We need not assume that NOW and ERA Illinois consciously chose their tactics in the ERA struggle in order to attract and keep their membership. Both an invisible hand and self-selection were at work. The "invisible hand" ensures that if a voluntary association does not find viable ways of attracting and holding members, it goes out of business. Those that cannot adapt die off. Those that survive have, by definition though often by accident, characteristics suited to their particular ecological niche. Natural selection also operates through self-selection. People join organizations in search of others like themselves. If they do not find people like themselves they seldom try to change the organization; they just quit. The active membership of NOW was attracted to national media campaigns and nationally televised demonstrations not only because these events brought in new members but because they gave the old members the vital feeling of belonging to a larger, world-historical feminist cause. People who did not find such activities exciting were not very likely to join NOW. People who had joined because they resonated to such drama wanted more of it, even if it was not "cost effective" in terms of ERA ratification. "As for the value of our demonstrations," said one local NOW leader, "they were morale boosters for us." The active membership in ERA Illinois, by contrast, was attracted to one-to-one or small group meetings with individual legislators and to electoral campaigning. People who did not like that sort of thing simply fell away. These biases in self-selection made it hard for either organization to survey, "rationally," all alternative tactics for ratifying the ERA and choose among them solely on the basis of their payoff.

The Opposition

Within the anti-ERA movement, the need to attract members also influenced tactics. But here the tensions between groups recruited in different ways were not as visible, at least on the surface, partly because the movement did not have to be as large (and therefore heterogeneous) and partly because of Phyllis Schlafly's dominant role.

At the beginning of the anti-ERA campaign, Schlafly relied primarily on the highly committed conservative subscribers to *The Phyllis Schlafly Report* and on the Eagle Forum, a group formed from her supporters in the National Federation of Republican Women after the Republican establishment, suspicious of her extreme views and populist tactics, had maneuvered her out of NFRW leadership.[7] The women in the Eagle Forum had experience in local electoral campaigns and with state legislators. They also had an effective, though top-down, means of communication in *The Phyllis Schlafly Report,* and they had a war chest that Schlafly set up to receive donations for causes she took up in her newsletter.[8] But these women were widely viewed as extremists, and they were far too few to launch a national movement. When Schlafly tried to organize more widely among homemakers, she shifted her tactics to include activities that homemakers could do in interrupted time, like phoning talk shows, sending letters to the editor in local papers, and writing state legislators. But so long as the STOP ERA movement was composed primarily of the Eagle Forum and a few homemakers, it could not mount an impressive demonstration at the state capitol. In the early days of anti-ERA organizing, the STOP ERA women who went to Springfield were, by and large, older women whose children had left the home.

Beginning around 1976, however, the STOP ERA movement acquired a third constituency, as fundamentalist groups began to enter politics and focus on "women's issues" like the ERA. Many of these fundamentalist women were full-time homemakers. But unlike most homemakers, their church activities had given them experience speaking in public and approaching strangers. Their churches and their own convictions demanded an interventionist, missionary stance toward anyone who had not accepted Jesus Christ as a personal savior. While most Americans confronted with someone who does not share their religious or political views avoid the subject, missionary fundamentalists deliberately bring the controversial subject into conversation, challenge the unbeliever, present personal testimony, and work actively for conversion. These skills and the evangelical enthusiasm that gave them life made it relatively easy for such women to enter the political arena. Moreover, the churches were already organized. They had preexisting meeting places, buses, and claims on their members' time and money.

Neither the media, the American public, nor most legislators were aware that most of the women who demonstrated against the ERA at state capitols around the country in the last years of the ERA struggle were fundamentalists brought there by their pastors. While the male ministers and bus drivers sat outside in the yellow buses, the women did their work under the rotunda. There was enough central coordination so that the pamphlets the women brought with them were usually official STOP ERA literature, but in conversation they readily gave witness to their extreme fundamentalist beliefs. When I took part in NOW's June 1980 ERA demonstration at Springfield, for example, I had no way of telling visually that the counterpickets—some young, some grandmothers, all wearing white and red dresses and sporting the traditional red hexagonal Stop sign of the "anti" forces—were there under the auspices of their church. But when I asked them my introductory question of why and how they had become involved in activity against the ERA, all but one gave me some version of the response:

> Christian beliefs, mainly. I believe God made us different. . . . My religion strictly says women should submit to their husbands. It says so in the Bible, and you can't believe part of the Bible but not all. . . . So many people ask us why we do what we do—it's because of the Bible. Others don't know about the Bible, about the truth.

Or, as another explained,

> It was through a church group. . . . and of course there was a religious reason—I know that God gave men certain responsibilities and He gave women responsibilities. The men were to take care of the women. . . . "The husband is the head of the wife, as Christ is head of the Church."

Only one of the women I talked with that day was not from a fundamentalist church group, and she was firmly convinced that the ERA was a Communist plot sponsored by the Trilateral Commission.

Until I interviewed these women myself I had had no idea that the basis for their action was a literal belief in the Pauline passages from the Bible stipulating that women must be subject to men.[9] Nor did any of the reporters from national television or the Chicago newspapers who covered the demonstration that day know this, since they did not ask. Even a feminist reporter from one of the major television networks missed the religious motivation of the STOP ERA demonstrators. She had spent her time interviewing Phyllis Schlafly, and she, like everyone else, had assumed that the STOP ERA forces in the rotunda were the kinds of women Schlafly liked to claim as her troops—simply homemakers threatened by the potential loss of their special legal "protections" under the ERA. Fundamentalist church women also provided the bulk of the activists who attended STOP ERA demonstrations in the other unratified states on which I was able to gather information.[10]

The organizational base in church groups that developed about halfway through the ERA campaign gave the opposition an advantage in perceived longevity, at least among legislators who were aware of it, because these groups were all local and relatively stable. The legislators knew that they wouldn't go away, that they felt intensely, and that they would act politically on their feelings.

> The people who are anti-ERA in my district feel very, very intensely about it. And they will go out and they will work for or against people that are anti-ERA[sic]. . . . They will work very hard. The people who are pro-ERA, you know, they are "pro but so what." So it is intensity of feeling.
>
> . . . I have a district that contains a lot of very basic conservative religious groups. For example, the bastion of anti-ERA feeling in my district is concentrated mainly in the ——— and ——— county areas where we have what is called "the Bible Belt of the North." There are [unclear in tape] Apostolic Christians. I have areas in my district where some women do not even exercise their right to vote.
> —*Anti-ERA legislator*

However, the church groups, like NOW, had their own agenda, of which stopping the ERA was only a small part. As a result, while their tactics against ratification usually filled their own members' needs, they were often less effective with wavering legislators than NOW's activists. As we have seen, Phyllis Schlafly could not control what the fundamentalists said to legislators. Fundamentalist women sometimes told their legislators that they would literally go to hell, or must have been inspired by the devil, if they voted for the ERA. The legislators, in turn, became furious at having their religious commitment questioned.

Was Illinois Typical?

The Illinois experience was never exactly duplicated in other states. But the patterns of behavior I have described are not peculiar to Illinois or even to the struggle over the ERA. For example, few unratified states had as many problems as Illinois within their pro-ERA coalitions.[11] But every state had some coalitional problems, and those problems were often related to the kinds of incentives the different organizations offered their memberships.

Illinois was also atypical because Phyllis Schlafly lived there. Schlafly's organizing tactics, however, were no different in Illinois, only stronger and more visible. If in Illinois, despite Schlafly's long term contacts in the state Republican party, STOP ERA still had to rely heavily on the fundamentalist churches, this was likely to be even more true elsewhere.

Finally, unlike most states, Illinois had a rule requiring a three-fifths majority in both houses to ratify constitutional amendments— a requirement that was dropped soon after the ERA had died. Without the three-fifths rule, Illinois quite early would have become the thirty-sixth state to ratify the ERA. But the rule did not change the dynamics within the legislature or in the districts. It simply gave more power to the "downstate" and rural districts, making the balance of power on this issue closer to that in intrinsically more conservative states like Oklahoma and North Carolina. Thus, while the political situation in Illinois was certainly not typical, the processes at work in the state were probably quite typical.

13 A Movement or a Sect?

Like all social movements, both American feminism and Schlafly's brand of political fundamentalism faced a basic tension between reaching out and reaching in. To change the world, a movement must include as many people as possible. But to attract devoted activists, a movement must often promote a sense of exclusivity—"we few, we happy few, we band of brothers."[1]

If many forces in the ERA movement promoted inclusivity, other forces promoted the separatism, concern with purity, and homogeneity of thought associated with exclusivity. Despite their inclusive ideals, activists working for the ERA tended to maintain their own morale by dividing the world into "us" and "them," seeking doctrinal purity, and rejecting interpretations of reality that did not fit their preconceptions. The fundamentalist churches were, if anything, even more subject to this kind of tension, since they believed that impurity could lead not just to social exclusion but to personal damnation.

Us against Them

Rosabeth Moss Kanter's study of nineteenth-century communes found that when communes institutionalized exclusivity they were more likely to survive. The most successful communes discouraged relationships outside the group through geographic isolation, economic self-sufficiency, a special language and style of dress, and rules that controlled members' and outsiders' movements across the boundaries of the community. Three-quarters of Kanter's successful communes did not recognize the traditional American patriotic holidays. Half read no outside newspapers. More than a quarter specifically characterized the outside world as wicked.[2]

Although social movements are usually inclusive in their conscious aims, building an organization on belief in a principle can, when the world refuses to go along with that principle, produce a deep sense of "us" against "them." When two movements organized with ideological incentives are pitted against each other, reality will provide plenty of temptations to see the opposition as evil incarnate. For an opponent of the ERA, a photograph of two lesbians in cut-off shorts embracing in the middle of an ERA demonstration triggered the perception of evil. For proponents, a legislator's characterization of them as "bra-less, brain-less broads," patronizingly repeated time after time,[3] called forth equally intense hatred. Opponents' images of "libbers" and an "East Coast Establishment media blitz," and proponents' images of "right-wing crazies" or legislators conniving to kill the ERA in "smoke-filled rooms" all had elements of truth in them. The process of struggle accentuated the gulf. As a proponent, I found it impossible to sit in a legislative gallery, hear even a few legislators joke as they voted down equal rights for women, and not hate. And I have rarely seen such concentrated hate as I saw on the faces of some women in red when I stepped into an elevator in the state capitol on lobbying day wearing my green "ERA YES" button.

Like nationalism and some forms of religious conversion, some kinds of political activity engender a transformation of self that requires reconfiguring the world into camps of enemies and friends. Running for office or campaigning for social legislation is likely to have this effect. Other kinds of political activity, like holding political office, require people to break down such boundaries, or at least make them more subtle. The movements for and against the ERA had the same effects on participants as most struggles over social legislation, solidifying in-group ties without creating lines of dialogue with the "other." Political comradeship within the groups arose from mutual dependence and mutual respect, as proponents worked together late into the night preparing testimony or opponents piled into rented vans at 6:00 in the morning to negotiate icy roads to the state capitol.[4] Both sides also demanded sacrifice. The conviction that "if I don't do this, the cause may fail" brought many women for the first time in their lives to write out checks for fifty, one hundred, five hundred, or even a thousand dollars for a political cause. The people who experienced that solidarity and made that sacrifice often began to think of themselves as political beings, helping produce—not simply consume—the politics that affected them. But this admirable result frequently depended on a Manichaean vision of "us" and "them" to bring it about.

Doctrinal Purity

Once the necessary distinction has been made between "us" and "them," it follows that the less you are like "them," the more you are one of "us." Becoming "us" involves purifying your beliefs. The dynamic that binds activists to the movement entails idealism, radicalism, and exclusion. It works against the inclusive policy of accommodation and reform.

In organizations that have chosen ideological exclusivity as a means for building community, leaders are likely to be even more radical than their followers, for the leaders now serve not as intermediaries and ambassadors to the outside world but as moral exemplars whose function is inspiration. While traditional organizational theory predicts that leaders will grow more conservative than the rank and file, both Ellie Smeal of NOW and Phyllis Schlafly of STOP ERA—although undoubtedly less radical than some of their most active volunteers—were almost certainly further apart in their views than were the majority of people who gave time or money to their respective movements.[5]

Neither the pro- nor the anti-ERA movement seems to have pushed its adherents strongly toward internal disputes over purity, but some pressures were there on both sides. Among the proponents, for example, these pressures came out in the lawyers' decisions on combat and abortion.

Homogeneity

In groups that are building a sense of community, like attracts like, and potential deviants try to suppress their differences in order to belong. The internal homogeneity that the members create binds them to one another more fully.

The very inclusivity of a social movement paradoxically accentuates homogeneity. A social movement, unlike an organization, has no formal entrance requirements or certification of membership; its members define themselves and identify themselves to one another solely in terms of their ideology. You are a member of a movement to the degree that you believe what the other people in the movement believe. Once you stop so believing you are, by definition, no longer "in" the movement. All members know this, at least subconsciously. They also know that they have "joined" the movement in part to have the support of like-minded people—to make and keep friends. If deviating too far from the movement's current ideology will cause you to lose your friends, you will only move in this direction when you already feel estranged, or when you feel you have "no choice."

Among proponents, the pressure to conform was probably strongest in the radical women's movement, where "betraying the women's movement" by not taking the correct ideological line could be "as terrifying as betrayal of your family, your closest friends."[6] But even in the most conservative branch of the ERA movement in Illinois, ERA Illinois, I felt nervous about suggesting that we include in our 1982 testimony before the Illinois legislature a statement supporting the "deferential" interpretation on the military, which I had just discovered. As it turned out, the board of directors had no problem with my suggestion. My nervousness came from self-censorship and from fantasies of rejection, not from an accurate projection of what would happen. But inchoate fears of this kind are common among those whose particular access to information or experience leads them to contemplate deviations from "the party line." I have no direct evidence regarding such pressures among opponents, but it is hard to imagine that they were not equally intense. Indeed, since active opponents were by and large more rooted in small communities where they expected to spend the rest of their lives, and many were often more committed to their churches than feminists were to "the movement," the costs of challenging their co-workers were probably even higher.

Turning Inward: An Iron Law?

If social movements cannot reward their members materially, and if the activists must find their rewards in ideology and solidarity, we might expect such movements to follow an "iron law of involution," by which "every social movement tends to splinter into sects, unless it wins quickly, in which case it turns into a collection of institutions."[7]

The socialist movement in America illustrates this iron law. As Daniel Bell argues, it foundered on the tension between inclusion and exclusion.[8] The labor movement turned into an institution, while the Communist party turned into a sect. The party became ideologically exclusive, the very commitment of its members stemming in part from "that inward dread of not proving sufficiently revolutionary which hounds us all."[9] Its members also became social isolates, cut off from others, not only because others ostracized them but also because they needed isolation to avoid confronting the wide gap between their revolutionary expectations and their actual achievements. Their intense political commitment left little room for their jobs or families, and they felt uncomfortable with people who did not share their mission.[10] Said one member,

> When you are in the party for many years, as I have been, you develop warm bonds with your comrades. I have had a few friends outside the party, but they can never be as close friends. They can't be friends at all if they are hostile to the party. You never feel as comfortable with an outsider as you do with your comrades.[11]

All committed activists sense that their political commitment sets them apart from the great majority of citizens. The extreme case occurs when activism requires illegal action—as in Resist, a draft resistance group founded in 1967–1968, whose members had all committed the illegal act of burning or turning in a draft card.[12] With that one act the resisters became outlaws. But processes more common to all activists intensified their estrangement from the outside world. The resisters tended to feel both moral superiority and anger at having risked a great deal for the welfare of others without personally receiving anything in return.[13] As politics took up more of their identities, ideological disagreements with their former friends became harder to stand.[14] Finally, their decreasing interest in nonpolitical activities slowly eroded any ties outside the movement world,[15] while they built up an almost religious sense of community within.[16]

In the Black Power movement, activists struggled over the extent to which blacks should work with whites; in the Pentacostal movement, religious groups struggled over "whether or not a 'Spirit-filled' Christian should come out of the 'whore of Babylon' or remain within and try to redeem her."[17] In the women's movement, one activist concluded sadly of another group, "We saw them as not being as pure as we. They still exist, and we don't."[18]

The strengths of exclusivity are the strengths of a committed cadre. Exclusivity can produce a personal life that is intense, deep, and meaningful. Shared commitment and assumptions can also engender penetrating intellectual discourse, for the very intensity of the commitment urges one beyond both platitude and party line. Organizationally, an exclusive group can count on its members to do what needs doing.

By contrast, the strength of inclusivity is "the strength of weak ties."[19] Personally, a loose and inclusive organization makes possible the ego-strengthening retreat into apolitical sanctuaries like the family. Intellectually, it allows friendships that run the "whole gamut of political views."[20] Organizationally, it allows a host of different ties to the larger community. William Kornhauser, comparing the political and personal lives of liberal political activists affiliated with Americans for Democratic Action to those of Communist party members, concludes that "a liberal group finds strength in the multiple ties its members establish in the community."[21] Mark Granovetter, comparing two communities resisting urban renewal—one a tightly knit Italian neighborhood of long standing, the other a more loosely organized aggregation—argues that one reason the loose aggregation succeeded while the tightly knit community failed may have been that members of less exclusive and less tightly knit neighborhoods could use their many weak contacts with diverse organizations and individuals outside the neighborhood to further the neighborhood's interests.[22] As with contacts, so with information. Granovetter demonstrates that there is a

> structural tendency for those to whom one is only *weakly* tied, to have better access to . . . information one does not already have. Acquaintances, as compared to close friends, are more prone to move in different circles than one's self. Those to whom one is closest are likely to have the greatest overlap in contact with those one already knows, so that the information to which they are privy is likely to be much the same as that which one already has.[23]

So too with thinking itself. Acquaintances with different views and different structural roles can force us to articulate our hidden expectations and understandings, and even, on occasion, to negotiate, reflect, and make choices—all processes central to thinking well.[24]

Escaping the Iron Law

What conditions tend to turn a movement into a sect? Or, if we assume that the dynamics of recruiting are such as to turn every movement inward, what conditions impede this natural tendency toward exclusivity? The history of the ERA movement suggests three conditions: the likelihood of winning, the dependence of the movement on actors in different structural roles, and an explicitly inclusive ideology.

The ERA came extremely close to being ratified. Although no state ratified after 1977, the votes came so close in several states between 1977 and 1982 that even the sponsors were not able to predict beforehand which way the legislature would go. These conditions should have maximized the impact of political realism, by reducing both overconfidence and the temptation of the loser to retreat to purity. Because the goal of this particular social movement was to ratify a U.S. constitutional amendment, which requires a supermajority, the usual pressures for inclusivity—and therefore heterogeneity—in membership were increased.

The decentralized nature of the ERA movement also led to a division of labor between different states, between different communities within each state and between different constituencies on both the local and state levels. One organization within the movement would attract a more conservative membership, another a more radical one. Internally, this decentralization let members of each group feel more comfortable with one another. Externally, the division of labor made possible a "Mutt and Jeff" (or "good cop/ bad cop") act, in which the more conservative organization could tell relevant power holders that if certain concessions were not forthcoming it could not hold back the radicals much longer. But most important, the division of labor fostered distinctive perspectives that had the effect of undermining any unifying ideology. "Hydra-headed" organizationally, the movement was also "fly-eyed."[25] It depended on many different kinds of individual actors—

homemakers, secretaries, executives, writers, lawyers, academics, and politicians—almost all of whom remained in their other roles while working for the ERA. The distinctive incentives and exposures of their other roles gave these different members of the movement slightly different views of the common struggle, and these views produced different insights.

Finally, the ideology of the women's movement itself is inclusive, stressing the sisterhood of women of differing classes, ethnicities, regions, and traditional politics. That ideology requires women to listen to one another, on the grounds that each woman's story has its own validity and right to be heard. The first, simple statement of that ideology is that all women are sisters and fundamentally "on the same side." They are on the same side no matter what their class, their upbringing, or their politics, because structurally they have similar relationships to the world, and particularly to men. The "consciousness-raising group" of the women's movement typically did its work by allowing women who habitually sorted themselves by class, mores, and politics to see their similarities as women. It allowed each woman to hear other women talking about their lives as they had lived them, and to feel compassion for scenes never lived through, joy for memories mutually held but previously thought trivial, and the anger of recognition at events not shared until that moment. The movement's assertion that the "personal is political" means, among other things, that when women speak of what is important to them, those experiences often derive from common experiences in a world where men have most of the power. This means that it is a mistake not to listen and try to make sense of what other women say, even when one disagrees with them. In the ERA movement, no matter how involved any particular set of activists became with trying to persuade a legislator, organize a demonstration, or write a brief, the inclusive ideology of the broader women's movement was always there to push, gently, toward a strategy of listening to what other women—even in the opposition—had to say.

These forces in the ERA movement meant that if any movement could escape the iron law of involution, this would have been the one. That it did not fully escape means that no organization based on voluntary membership is likely to do so.

Social movements become "movements" only by building on common values and common dreams. They may hope to include everyone someday, but they cannot, by definition, do so today. To survive, they must balance the conflicting claims of pragmatism and purity, reaching out and turning in. Perhaps no social movement can maintain this balance for long, which may be why social movements are usually transitory. But some certainly maintain it longer than others, and exert more influence as a result. While the feminist movement that began in the late 1960s was often out of touch with middle-of-the-road legislators and with the millions of Americans whom they represented, it maintained a far better balance between reaching out and turning in than any of the other movements that began in the 1960s. This may help explain its longevity. Whether the conservative antifeminist movement of the 1970s and 1980s, with its renewed emphasis on traditional family values and sexual behavior, will prove equally resilient remains to be seen.

14 Requiescat in Pace

In January 1983, the ERA was reintroduced in the U.S. House of Representatives. After hearings in the spring, Republican representatives proposed a series of amendments to the ERA, providing that it would not require public funding for abortion, would not draft women, would not send women into combat, and would not jeopardize the tax-exempt status of all-male and all-female schools and colleges.[1] To avoid discussing or voting on these amendments, the Democratic Speaker of the House suspended normal rules when the issue came to the floor in November, limited debate to forty minutes, and barred any modifications of the measure on the floor. The Speaker took this action because, he said, he "doubted very, very much" that all of the proposed amendments could have been defeated.[2] In these circumstances the ERA garnered 278 votes for passage and 147 against. It thus fell six votes short of the two-thirds majority needed for a constitutional amendment. Since the Senate is currently more conservative than the House, and since state legislators are far more conservative than Congress on this issue, it seems clear that an ERA of the kind Congress passed in 1972 has virtually no chance of being ratified in the near future.

The political demise of the ERA poses a number of questions. First, with the wisdom born of hindsight, feminists must ask themselves a strategic question: Was the struggle worth the enormous effort they poured into it? Second, anyone involved in the political process can fruitfully ask tactical questions about the struggle: Were any "mistakes" made in the campaign from which all political activists can learn? Finally, there is the question of what to do in the future: Should feminists continue the struggle for the ERA, or abandon it, at least for the moment?

Was It All Worthwhile?

This book has documented the depth of American traditionalism, even in the midst of change. It has shown how hard it is to pass a constitutional amendment, and how lucky ERA proponents were to have gotten the ERA through most of the state legislatures before the opposition organized. It has described the difficulties proponents encountered when the Supreme Court's evolution made it harder to point to tangible benefits when proponents were pointing to tangible costs. Yet I will now argue that because the ratification campaign raised consciousness, helped women organize politically, and stimulated legislative and judicial action, that campaign was worth the effort put into it.

Although the ERA provoked little informed or subtle debate regarding its own impact, it did foster discussion of women's issues more generally. For ten years the ERA focused public attention on women's disadvantage in the workplace, the home, and the streets. The effect was probably greatest in those states that did not ratify, for issues like these had not previously had a large role in the public life of these states. As the campaign for the ERA became the visible symbol of demands for change in women's position in the workplace and the family, it forced Americans to keep thinking about these issues, in the same way that the more radical "women's liberation movement" had begun to do around 1968. When the ERA was in the newspaper, when a co-worker went to an ERA demonstration, or when advocates debated the ERA in the school gym, women who normally thought little about these issues seem to have begun to ask themselves about the amount of housework they were doing, about their pay, and about what kind of person they wanted to be. The result was both creeping feminism and creeping antifeminism. But most of those who pondered these issues have moved in a feminist rather than an antifeminist direction.[3] In the ten years that the ERA was before the states, ways of life that had never been questioned became issues on which women took a stand. Personal transformations took place in the heartland, even as feminists on the East and West Coasts imagined that the "women's movement" had died. In the middle part of the country, political work for the ERA kept upsetting the old order.

The ERA ratification campaign brought many women on the Left and the Right into active politics for the first time in their lives. It more than trebled the membership of NOW, making it stronger today than its counterpart in almost any other country. There is no chapter of the Democratic Socialists of America in Peoria, Illinois, but there is a chapter of NOW. The same is true in many other towns and small cities where NOW provides the only organized group more radical than the local Democratic party. At the same time, "family issues" like divorce, premarital sex, and abortion fed the growth of the new Right, and opposition to the ERA became an organizing tool for converting these previously apolitical concerns into political action. It is hard to predict the effects, either on individuals or on the larger polity, of inducting people into politics in the polarizing and polemical context of an issue like the ERA. But some, including myself, consider the politicizing effect of the campaign an overall benefit.

The attempt to put an ERA in the Constitution also produced important changes in political and judicial practice. At the federal level, the fact that Congress passed the ERA almost certainly encouraged the Supreme Court to interpret the Fourteenth Amendment as barring many varieties of discrimination against women, although uncertainty about the ERA's prospects for ratification may have later discouraged the Court from making gender a suspect classification.

On the state level, the campaign's impact varied greatly from one state to another. In many states, adopting a state ERA, or sometimes even ratifying the federal ERA, led the legislators to review state laws and rewrite them in "gender-neutral" form. The revisions, although sometimes prompted by the advances the Supreme Court was making under the Fourteenth Amendment, were faster and more thorough when a state had added an ERA to its own constitution. Reworking state legislation to eliminate distinctions based on gender often demanded a new analysis of what the legislation was intended to foster or prevent; it meant coming up with a functional equivalent of gender. The process raised the legislators' consciousness of women's problems, and usually helped women in substantive ways as well. While unthinking or vituperative legislators occasionally withdrew benefits from women without replacing them with a gender-neutral equivalent, such outcomes were rare. And as an educative tool, even replacing "his" with "his or her" and similar "cosmetic" changes probably had a useful impact on the way legislators, judges, and citizens thought about men and women. State ERAs also had an important though varying effect on judicial decisions in those states that, in the course of the national ERA ratification campaign, added an ERA to their own constitutions.[4] Of course, these developments encouraged judges to approach custody battles, among other things, in a more "gender-neutral" way, with the result that joint custody became more common. This was an extension of an earlier trend that worked against most mothers' interests. But in the progressive states—particularly Pennsylvania—state ERAs also led, directly or indirectly, to judicial initiatives that helped women—for example, by giving homemakers more credit for their contribution to a marriage.

Politically, in both federal and state legislatures the ERA struggles made representatives increasingly aware of the importance of women's issues and the potential organizing capacity of women on both the Left and the Right. In 1983, for example, the Illinois legislature considered a new Criminal Sexual Assault Act that made marital rape a crime and involved several other controversial changes. Several observers thought the bill passed in part because Illinois legislators either felt guilty about their hesitant support of the ERA the year before or feared the political retaliation that they knew organized women were now capable of mounting.[5]

The struggle over the ERA also coincided with, and probably helped cause, a marked increase both in the number of women deciding to run for legislative office and in the likelihood of their making "women's issues" prominent in their campaigns and on their legislative agendas. And it taught a lot of women how to organize politically in state legislatures, where many—perhaps most—issues affecting women are still decided.

The campaign had costs, but they were not excessive. Because the ratification campaign lost, feminists perhaps lost some political credibility. But the defeat came by a very narrow margin. At least in the key unratified states, legislators were impressed by the duration and intensity of the political effort that both sides mounted. And in choosing candidates for the 1984 Presidential election, the Democratic party seems to have taken NOW far more seriously as a political force than it had before the ratification battle began.

In some cases, no doubt, the ratification battle also diverted energy from other feminist causes. But there is no fixed supply of activist talent and energy that NOW or other groups can allocate as they see fit. The ratification campaign in the 1970s and early 1980s dramatically increased both the numbers of feminist activists and the money available to them. Legislative opposition to the ERA produced a sense of outrage in many women who did not even think of themselves as feminists. Precisely because it seemed to be no more than a matter of simple equal rights, as American and nonrevolutionary as apple pie, the ERA campaign produced support—and angry support, the kind that brings with it money and volunteered time—among women and men who had never belonged to a feminist, or even a reformist, organization. Having been touched by the ERA, these citizens began to pay more attention to other issues on the feminist agenda. On balance, therefore, the ratification struggle probably increased the energy and resources available for other feminist causes rather than harming those causes.

Organizational Lessons

All political activists will have gained something worthwhile from these ten years if the history of the ERA ratification campaign can teach more general lessons about politics and voluntary organizations. The major lesson of this book, which applies not only to women's groups but to all volunteers who work for a political cause, is that the very structure of a voluntary political organization tends to produce an inability to hear or understand what others are saying. This is, almost by definition, an unconscious error. And the first step toward correcting such errors is to make them conscious.

This book has shown how volunteer activity encourages ideological purity and allows individuals to make choices for which they are not accountable. It also has shown how decisions by accretion accentuate the impact of unconscious assumptions. Forewarned, anyone who volunteers for political activity can perceive, and begin to resist, the psychological temptations of dividing the world into the pure and impure. Activists can learn to ask to what degree their having freely volunteered their time exonerates them from accountability to others. And they can learn to watch for the inevitable tendency of every organization to drift into decisions without realizing that a decision is even being made.

Committed activists also need to question their almost automatic rejection of the muddled thinking and compromises that characterize mainstream discussions of most issues. The muddled middle is often muddled, not because it is composed of morons, lunatics, or unprincipled opportunists but because it is composed of people trying to reconcile conflicting principles and commitments that are all quite legitimate. Activists who are aware of the way their self-selection, sacrifice, and exposure to others like themselves encourages them to oversimplify should become more willing to listen to legislators, churches, and other groups that are sympathetic to their views but not totally committed to them.

We have seen, for example, how mutual suspicion made it hard for ERA Illinois and NOW to use each other's accumulated wisdom. The same kind of distrust, stemming in part from some pro-ERA activists' discomfort with organized religion, often kept the pro-ERA movement from listening to liberal churches whose leaders and congregations were sympathetic to the cause. Those churches could have provided both established organizational bases in many local districts and access to the insights of a relatively mainstream population. Again, the same kind of distrust kept feminists from listening to sympathetic legislators. At the beginning of the decade there were only a few women legislators, and they were often inexperienced. Had there been enough women legislators to encompass a fairly wide spectrum of personal styles and ideological views, those legislators could have constituted a forum for discussing the more problematic features of the ERA. As it was, the activists in Washington had to rely on legislators like Birch Bayh, who was himself inaccessible and had a male staff that did not even begin to understand the goals of the feminist movement.[6] This made discourse between legislator and activist almost impossible. This particular situation will become less common, both in Congress and in the states, as more women enter electoral politics. But the general problem of ensuring serious discourse between politicians and activists will persist.

Within the organizations central to a social movement, some institutional arrangements promote accurate information and internal dialogue better than others. On the organizational level, more democracy usually means better information. It helps to have flat hierarchies, rotation in office, career lines that run from field to headquarters, team or project organization, people at every level whose job it is to evaluate both the means and goals of particular policies, diverse channels for collecting and studying information, incentives for communicating outside the usual channels, contact with informed outsiders, and resources for research. Minimizing clandestine action and loyalty tests can also help.[7] In small group settings, better information comes from "brainstorming" sessions in which no new idea is quashed, and from encouraging minority members to speak.[8]

Any technique, of course, requires a will to use it. Discussing potentially controversial issues at every level of an organization takes time and often leads to conflict. These costs seem especially high when the organization is locked in conflict with others. Yet the benefits of openness are also high. Discussing a full range of options usually makes a decision more politically effective. For the participants, it also begins the process of understanding what they really want. Indeed, that process may be more important over the long run, both to the participants and to the organization, than almost any short-run gain.[9]

Because individuals cannot usually come to understand what they really want without the different options and perspectives provided by discussion, they need organizations. Moreover, although organizations have their faults—they can, undeniably, become rigid, self-absorbed, and deaf to the voices of the rank and file—they remain one of the few conduits through which the lessons of one experience can be applied to another. Although this book exemplifies one way of preserving useful history, it will reach only a few individuals. At least as long as the environment remains relatively stable, organizational memory, enriched by the details of what the participants are actually doing or can do at any given time, is a far more fruitful way of interpreting and applying the past. Because collective discussion rarely happens outside an ongoing organization, it is important that organizations, particularly those committed to internal democracy, reflect on the ways that they can foster discussion within their ranks in the face of all the unconscious and structural forces that tend to prevent it. We have seen how, at the beginning of the ERA movement, the pro-ERA organizations were either newly created or inexperienced in electoral politics. If those organizations can now survive in strength, supported not just by the most convinced activists but by a large number of newly politicized women, they will be in a position to apply the lessons of the past to future problems. If those organizations die, and new ones are established to deal with new issues, our collective memory will be impoverished.

Women's organizations are particularly weak because women do not have as much money as men, and because women are less likely to think of the money they have as "their own" money. Women have also learned the skills appropriate to the woman's economic role of careful buyer. Accordingly, wives are even more reluctant than husbands to give money away when this will produce no tangible return for their families. The dominant models of spending on politics and good causes are male: the "solid citizen" whose solidity is measured by the size of his donation; the corporate executive or small entrepreneur who contributes to political campaigns and worthy causes to grease the wheels of business and promote a good image; even the "big-time spender" whose masculinity is exemplified by his largesse. Before women's organizations can develop the longevity either to learn from their own past or to wield effective political power in adversary politics, they need adequate funding. This will require that individual women develop enough "class consciousness" to tithe regularly to political causes.

Despite the feminist movement's unusual openness to divergent opinions that seem to flow directly from women's own experience, the ERA provoked a debate in which, to an unusual degree, opponents simply talked past one another, each convinced that the other was deliberately violating the norms of fair play.[10] Trying to legislate a broad principle through the constitutional amendment process produced the kind of political question that is most difficult to resolve: basic issues were at stake; outcomes could not be broken down into subissues to allow each party in the conflict to gain something desirable; the action, once taken, was almost irreversible; and the final result had to be victory for one side and defeat for the other.[11] The institutions of adversary democracy, geared only to winning, losing, or bargaining,[12] provided few forums in which the issue could be discussed frankly, as among friends. In these circumstances, public debate led only to polarization.

However, while the battle over the ERA divided women deeply, it did not preclude alliances in its aftermath. In Illinois,

ERA legislative leaders joined forces with ERA opponents like Phyllis Schlafly to support the Criminal Sexual Assault Act mentioned earlier. This seemingly unlikely alliance sprang up only a year after the ERA's defeat. Although women, like men, often have conflicting political ideologies and economic interests, they also share some common interests that grow out of being women rather than men. Political ideology may sometimes blind women to these common interests, or make them reluctant to join forces even when they recognize a common interest, but the ideal of sisterhood in the feminist movement works to promote recognition of such interests. So does resistance to co-optation by the "New Right" in powerful segments of the anti-feminist movement. Phyllis Schlafly will not lend or sell her mailing lists to the direct-mail moguls of the New Right, for example, and "emphatically denies that [the STOP ERA members] are in any significant way adjuncts of 'the conservative movement.' "[13] This independence makes it easier for her to join with feminists on issues that benefit both groups. Such alliances depend on neither side succumbing fully to the habitual deafness of the activist life.

The Future

While the decade of agitation for and against the ERA on balance raised the consciousness of many Americans on matters relating to women as well as producing significant concrete gains, continuing this particular struggle now would probably yield diminishing returns and might become counterproductive.

This time, the ERA will not come close to ratification in the states. It is unlikely to pass in the states that tried to rescind their earlier ratifications, and, given the new potential connection with abortion funding, it is likely to have trouble in the many states that passed it handily in the years between 1972 and 1974. It will never again have a "honeymoon period" in which state legislatures will ratify without a hearing or in which only proponents show up at the hearings. A potential opposition is already organized in every state, in antifeminist or right-to-life groups, with bases in the fundamentalist and sometimes the Catholic churches. Moreover, this time it will be harder than in 1972 to spell out the concrete benefits of the ERA.

The first time, taking the ERA through Congress and to the

states encouraged the Supreme Court to speed up its consideration of gender discrimination. This is not likely today. While the Court still has to work out a way of interpreting the Fourteenth Amendment that makes women fully equal citizens under the law, the issues are now more complex than in 1972 and cannot in most cases easily be resolved by applying a gender-neutral formula. An unsuccessful political struggle over the ERA in the states will not encourage the Court to resolve these matters in ways that feminists would favor. This situation might change if a more conservative Court either overruled its recent interpretations of the Fourteenth Amendment on gender issues or refused to apply those interpretations consistently to new cases. If this were to happen, taking an ERA through Congress and to the states might be the best way to reinforce the Court's commitment to gender equality. But it is not easy to imagine specific decisions that the Court might make in this area that would arouse strong opposition among state legislators, so it is not easy to imagine that retrogression on the part of the Supreme Court would make it easier to pass an ERA.

Within the feminist movement, there are also reasons for laying the ERA temporarily to rest. Many women in the key unratified states and the major pro-ERA organizations staked a great deal on the ERA's passage. It is not easy to back away from commitments for which one has worked so hard. Just as soldiers find it hard to give up a hill for which some of them have died simply because the larger strategy of battle has changed, so those who in the years from 1972 to 1982 sacrificed much to ratify the ERA would find it hard to reevaluate its premises so long as the ratification campaign continued. Rather than resuscitating the ERA, the movement needs now a moratorium, in which its members can rethink their strategies and goals.

During this moratorium, feminists will need to discuss what would be best for all women in the realms of combat, school athletics, prisons, and sex-blind legislation generally. Since about 1980, as more women have experienced the results of gender-neutral legislation like no-fault divorce laws and joint custody, some feminists have begun to articulate a critique of egalitarianism that looks much like Marx's critique of bourgeois equality. They argue that in a society where one group holds most of the power, "neutral" laws usually benefit the powerful group.[14] From this perspective, a constitutional amendment that bars women from using their electoral majority and moral leverage to pass laws explicitly redressing the traditional balance of power may actually help maintain male supremacy. Although the ERA's direct legal mandate for gender neutrality would probably have been balanced by its indirect political mandate for legislation and judicial interpretations that benefitted women, its defeat still raises, in a different form, the questions that Florence Kelley raised in the 1920s. An open discussion of these issues among feminists would probably make some feminists more aware of the concerns that motivated mainstream legislators to vote against the ERA.

The political death of the ERA has in fact corresponded with a flowering in feminist thought. The renaissance had many causes. With the ERA struggle over, feminists may no longer have felt obliged to present a united front. The reaction of some women against the ERA, as well as against other feminist programs, also provoked feminist efforts to understand the sources of opposition. Advances in courts and legislatures in the ten years from 1972 to 1982 created a new situation in which old analyses were not always appropriate. Whatever the reasons, the years immediately after 1982 saw the start of a lively, thought-provoking debate among feminist lawyers on, among other issues, how thoroughly the law should embrace strict gender neutrality.[15] It also saw the publication of several books by feminists that took seriously the concerns of those who opposed traditional feminist positions.[16]

While trying to rethink the question of what will really benefit women, feminists could turn, politically, to more immediate, concrete matters: reforms in the divorce codes to provide better maintenance for divorced homemakers, adequate welfare for the many women who do not have enough income to support themselves and their children, good and affordable child care, stronger criminal assault laws, enforcement for existing equal pay laws, and protection for besieged abortion clinics, for example. Improvements in these areas all depend on effective political organization, particularly at the state and district level.

Equal rights advocates might also consider urging Congress to pass an Equal Rights Act.[17] Under Section 5 of the Fourteenth Amendment, Congress might be able to invalidate all state and local public policies that discriminate on the basis of sex. Paradoxically, such an Equal Rights Act could be stronger than the proposed Equal Rights Amendment would be without supporting legislation. Like the 1965 Voting Rights Act, an Equal Rights Act could restrict the states' ability to pass laws that are neutral on their face but have a discriminatory impact.[18] It could, for example, invalidate absolute veterans' preference without going into the question of whether such statutes involve any "intent" to discriminate against women. An Equal Rights Act could also spell out just what it would do in specific areas, reassuring the wary.

Most important, an Equal Rights Act would require only a bare majority in Congress and the signature of the President, or if the President vetoed the act, a two-thirds vote in each house of Congress. An Equal Rights Act passed by Congress could, of course, be repealed later by another Congress. But it has been hard to repeal the Voting Rights Act, and the fact that an Equal Rights Act could be repealed if it proved unsatisfactory might tempt some to vote for it who otherwise would not.

As for the ERA itself, proponents have two choices. The first is to cleave to a pure, egalitarian ERA, and to create for it an uncompromising legislative history. Although this stance will not succeed in ratifying the ERA, it is at least principled. One could even argue that, unratified, the ERA might stick like a burr in women's consciousness and help keep alive the organizations that fought for it, as did not happen when women won the suffrage in 1921.

The second choice is to accept the Republican amendments to the ERA. It is too late now to reassure conservative legislators in the states on issues like combat and abortion simply by writing the usual kinds of legislative history. It is conceivable that a formal agreement among the sponsors on conservative interpretations of these issues, specified in reports from the House and Senate Judiciary Committees and subscribed to publicly by legislators as they voted for the ERA, would do the trick. But probably the only effective way to reassure conservatives on these points now is to incorporate the required assurances into the language of the amendment itself.

If the choice now is between no ERA and an ERA with amendments, purity seems to me better than compromise. In ten or twenty years, full equality for women may not seem so threatening. Public opinion continues to shift in a progressive direction on a number of issues associated with support for the ERA (table A10). While the public has gotten more conservative on other issues, these are somewhat less related to support for the ERA (table A11). In ten or twenty years it may be possible to pass an ERA that expresses the principle of equality between the sexes in language as simple and unadorned as that of the Bill of Rights and the Fourteenth Amendment. It may even be possible at that time to develop a different legislative history that would exend the Amendment to prohibit some of the laws that discriminate in fact, and not just in intent, against women. But if this book indicates anything, it is that persuading state legislators to vote for such an Amendment would require a major change in political climate.

Appendix: Support for the ERA, 1970–1982

Nationwide Trends

As table A1 indicates, the first questions ever asked on the ERA, in 1970 and 1974, were never asked again. It is consequently hard to say anything with confidence about this early period. Nevertheless, question I (1970), question II (1974), and question III (1975) do not seem obviously biased in one direction or another. If we took questions I, II, and III as comparable, the data would suggest that public opinion followed the legislative fortunes of the ERA, soaring (perhaps) in 1972, when the Senate and the early state legislatures passed the ERA, and falling when the ERA lost legislative momentum. The data do not allow us to compare the ERA's legislative fortunes with public opinion at all accurately, because the first question on which we have comparable trend data (question III) was not asked until 1975. By then thirty-four of the thirty-five state legislatures that eventually ratified had already done so, some were already trying to rescind their earlier votes, and the tide had clearly turned against ratification.

The standard Gallup question (III), first asked in 1975, shows no trend from 1975 to 1981. Gallup changed the wording of this item in 1981 (to question IV), in a way that seemed likely to elicit more pro-ERA sentiment. But exactly 63 percent of those who had heard about the ERA favored the Amendment when each of the two wordings was placed in the same spot on simultaneous surveys. Gallup therefore concluded that question IV could be considered a fair continuation of the time series begun in 1975 with question III. (This argument was weak. Because of the small samples interviewed, the "true" difference in ERA support could have been 6 percent either way.) The new question implies some decline in support from July to December 1981, but no trend thereafter.

The NORC General Social Survey (GSS) question (V) shows a slight increase in support, from 67 to 69 percent, but this could easily be due to chance.[1]

NBC News and the Associated Press started asking question VI in 1980. This question shows a statistically reliable decline in support between July and August of 1980, perhaps associated with the Republican party dropping the ERA from its platform, but it shows no trend after August 1980.

The CBS News/*New York Times* survey (question VII) shows no trend.

The University of Michigan American National Election Survey (NES) changed its wording between 1976 and 1978. The only two NES surveys with comparable wording (question IX) show a very small increase, from 51 percent in 1978 to 53 percent in 1980, which could well be due to chance.

Taken together, the Gallup, GSS, NBC/AP, CBS/*NYTimes*, and NES results suggest no clear trend.

The Harris survey (question X) is the only survey to report a major change in 1982 in support for the ERA. There is no trend from 1975 to January 1982, but between January and April 1982 Harris recorded a large, statistically reliable increase in support, from 50 to 63 percent. As indicated in the text, this increase was very probably due to placing the traditional question after one generating commitment to the actual wording of the Amendment. Neither of the other two organizations polling continuously at this time recorded such an increase. Gallup recorded a statistically insignificant rise in support, from 55 percent in December of 1981 to 56 percent in June of 1982, while NBC/Associated Press recorded an equally insignificant decline from 54 percent in February of 1981 to 52 percent in June of 1982.

Correlates of Support for the ERA

Table A2 indicates that support for the ERA was hardly related to neither gender or with the traditional "New Deal" demographic variables. On three measures of class (income, job prestige, and education), there was

1. NORC did not ask question V in 1981; Gallup did. The drop in approval in that year is probably due to the fact that Gallup asked people simply whether they favored or opposed the Amendment, eliciting more "no opinion" responses than the GSS, which allowed respondents to favor or oppose the Amendment either "strongly" or "weakly." For simplicity, I have entered all the times that an identically worded question was asked on the same line of table A1, even when it was asked by different survey organizations, with different in-house procedures. However, the text compares only figures produced by the same survey organization.

almost no correlation with support for the ERA. Nor was ERA support stronger among whites or Protestants.

Table A3, however, indicates that ERA support was correlated with the demographic variables associated with the New Right.

Trends in the Unratified States

Table A4, based on Gallup data, indicates a statistically significant increase in opposition to the ERA in the unratified states between the years 1975–1976 and the years 1980–1981. The NES shows a statistically insignificant increase in support in the unratified states, from 42 percent in 1978 ($N = 650$) to 44 percent in 1980 ($N = 406$). The GSS cannot be analyzed by state, and other surveys were unavailable for analysis by state. It is difficult to gather data on whether opposition to the ERA in the unratified states rose and support declined in the early 1980s because data from national samples do not provide enough cases, and surveys in the individual states rarely asked the same question twice.

Table A5, based on Market Opinion Research data, indicates that in Illinois public support for the ERA declined from a relatively stable majority in 1976 and 1978 to a decreasing minority in 1981 and 1982. Additional data from Richard Day Research in Champaign, Illinois, suggest that among those with an opinion support for the ERA declined from 70 percent in 1976 to 64 and 66 percent in January and August of 1978 (N's = 413, 819, 811; wording "Do you support or oppose the Equal Rights Amendment?" identical at all three times; "don't know" opinions eliminated and irretrievable, except by paying their organization to reanalyze the data).

Table A6 indicates that in Oklahoma public opinion was probably evenly divided for and against the ERA from 1978 through 1981. On January 11 and 12, 1982, two days before the crucial vote in the Oklahoma senate, the *Daily Oklahoman*'s sample of 400 favored the ERA by 44–39. But, as the paper pointed out, all one can say with 95 percent certainty is that those numbers are correct within 5 percent; and if 5 percent were subtracted from forty-four and added to thirty-nine, the relationship would be reversed. In short, right before the vote the population might have been about evenly divided on the ERA. However, Oklahoma opinion seems definitely to have tipped against the ERA after the state senate voted the Amendment down.

I was not able to find even moderately comparable data over time for the other key unratified states.

In North Carolina, Harris results showing a rise in support in from 49 percent in 1979 to 61 percent in 1982 (*National NOW Times* [June/July 1982]. p. 1) are contaminated by introducing this question after a question using the ERA wording, in the same manner as the Harris results nationwide (see Chapter 2). The data library at the Institute for Research in Social Sciences at Chapel Hill shows no other surveys with comparable wording from 1972 to 1982.

In Missouri, the St. Louis *Globe Democrat* commissioned statewide surveys in 1975, 1976, and 1979. The results, using questions with different wordings each time, indicate some rise in opposition from 1975/1976 to 1979. A story of December 5, 1975, reports 56 percent in favor, 28 percent opposed, 16 percent not sure (no *N* given); a story of December 28, 1976, reports among registered voters 60 percent in favor, 27 percent opposed, 13 percent not sure (no *N* given); and a story of November 1, 1979, reports 54 percent in favor, 36 percent opposed, 10 percent not sure ($N = 1,012$).

In Florida, the statewide Florida Annual Policy Survey shows a statistically insignificant rise in opposition of two points between 1981 and 1982, and a corresponding decline in support ("Do you favor or oppose . . . the Equal Rights Amendment [ERA] to the Constitution which would give women equal rights and equal responsibilities?" February 1981: 59 percent in favor, 35 percent opposed, 6 percent no opinion [$N = 1019$]; January 1982: 56 percent in favor, 37 percent opposed, 7 percent no opinion [$N = 1086$]. I would like to thank Mark R. Daniels for providing the Florida data, originally supplied by Paul A. Beck).

Party Activism and Support for the ERA

Tables A7 and A8 indicate that in 1981 support for the ERA was highly polarized by party. Both in the United States as a whole and in California, the closer one came to being either a national or statewide Democratic or Republican party committee member, the more likely one was to take the party position on the ERA. The Republicans were less unified, however, because in the Democratic committees only about 10 percent defected from the official Democratic support of the ERA, while in the Republican committees about 30 percent defected from the official Republican opposition to the ERA.

Men, Women in the Labor Force, and Homemakers: Support for the ERA and New Roles

Table A9 indicates that the gap between women in the paid labor force and homemakers in attitudes toward social mores and gender roles grew wider during the years the ERA was before the states for ratification. The growth of that gap seems to be due primarily to the growing liberalism of women in the labor force, although some of it is due to the higher rates of conservative attitudes among the shrinking group who remained at home.

Trends in Selected "Liberal" and "Conservative" Attitudes

Table A10 indicates that on several attitudinal issues that are associated with support for the ERA the American public has been getting steadily more liberal over time. These issues include attitudes toward women's roles, racial roles, and sexual practices.

On other issues there has been a marked swing toward conservatism. Table A11 gives a few of the most dramatic examples, which deal with communism and crime. However, these attitudes correlate somewhat more modestly with attitudes toward the ERA than do attitudes on the issues in table A10. Nor, correlations aside, do attitudes on these issues appear likely to exert much causal influence on attitudes toward the ERA. They may be, in part, specific reactions to the stimuli of an increase in crime in the late 1960s and increases in FBI crime rates (though not in victimization) thereafter,[2] and to the Soviet attack on Afghanistan, the USSR's most public display of aggression since its 1968 invasion of Czechoslovakia.

2. U.S. Bureau of the Census. *Statistical Abstract of the United States 1984* (Washington, D.C.: Government Printing Office, 1984), tables 290–292 (on victimization), and table 285 (for official rates).

TABLE A1
Percent Favoring the ERA, 1970–1982
(Percent with "No Opinion" or "Not Sure" in Parentheses)

	1970	1974	1975	1976
I. Recently, it was proposed that an "Equal Rights" amendment be added to our Constitution. This amendment would guarantee that women would have all the rights that men have. Do you favor or oppose adding such an amendment to the Constitution?	56 (7)			
II. Suppose that on election day, November 5, you could vote on key issues as well as candidates. Please tell me how you would vote on each of these fourteen propositions. (Proposition 14, Equal Rights Amendment:) I favor a constitutional amendment which would give women equal rights and equal responsibilities. (Respondents also given the choice of "I oppose . . ." followed by the same wording.)		74 (5)		
III. Have you heard or read about the Equal Rights Amendment to the Constitution which would give women equal rights and responsibilities? (If yes:) Do you favor or oppose this amendment?			59 61 (9)(14)	60 (14)
IV. Have you heard or read about the Equal Rights Amendment to the Constitution which would prohibit discrimination on the basis of sex? (If yes:) Do you favor or oppose this amendment?				
V. Have you heard or read about the Equal Rights Amendment? (If yes:) Do you strongly favor, somewhat favor, somewhat oppose, or strongly oppose this amendment?				
VI. Have you heard or read enough about the Equal Rights Amendment to the Constitution, often referred to as the ERA, to have an opinion about it? (If yes:) Do you favor or oppose the Equal Rights Amendment to the Constitution?				
VII. Do you favor or oppose the Equal Rights Amendment—also known as the ERA—the constitutional amendment concerning women?				
VIII. An effort is being made to pass an amendment to the U.S. Constitution which would guarantee equal rights for all citizens regardless of sex. Do you approve or disapprove of the Equal Rights Amendment to the Constitution?				70 (14)
IX. Do you approve or disapprove of the proposed Equal Rights Amendment to the Constitution, sometimes called the ERA Amendment?				
X. As you know, the Equal Rights Amendment to the Constitution is being debated across the country. Let me read you the actual wording of that Equal Rights Amendment: "Equality of rights under the law shall not be denied or abridged by the United States or by any state on account of sex." Do you favor or oppose that Equal Rights Amendment to the Constitution?				

1977	1978	1979	1980	1981	1982
60 61 (12) (8)	55 58 61 60 54 (9)(11) (7) (8)(18)	55 (18)	58 (11)	63[a] (4)	
				63[a] 55 (7)(13)	56 (10)
67 (8)					69 (5)
			58 53 50 50 51 (10)(18)(18)(18)(16)	43 53 56 53 54 (18)(10)(10)(14) (9)	52 (6)
			54 51 54 50 51 53 53 (9)(10)(10)(10)(12)(14)(13)	57 (10)	54 52 (12)(13)
	51 (22)		53 (14)		
					73[b] (5)

TABLE A1 *(continued)*

	1970	1974	1975	1976
XI. Many of those who favor women's rights favor the Equal Rights Amendment to the Constitution. This amendment would establish that women would have rights equal to men in all areas. Opponents argue that women are different from men and need to be protected by special laws which deal with women's status. Do you favor or oppose the Equal Rights Amendment?			51 (13)	
XII. Many of those who favor women's rights favor the Equal Rights Amendment to the Constitution. Those who favor ERA argue that unless it is passed, women will continue to receive lower pay for the same work, receive fewer promotions to better jobs, and be discriminated against financially. Opponents argue that the special laws that now exist to protect women are sufficient and no new law is needed. Do you strongly favor, somewhat favor, somewhat oppose, or strongly oppose the Equal Rights Amendment?				

^aGallup split–sample survey: half the sample answered question II, half question III. ^bRespondents were asked all three questions, in the order X, XI, XII.

I. 1970, September: CBS News telephone survey, September 8–10, 1970 (*N* = 1312). Robert Chandler, *Public Opinion: Changing Attitudes on Contemporary Political and Social Issues* (New York: R. R. Bowker CBS News Reference Book, 1972).

II. 1974, October: Data from Mark R. Daniels, Robert Darcy and Joseph W. Westphal, "The ERA Won— at Least in the Opinion Polls" 15 *P.S.* (1982): 578–584, 579 (*N* = 2822). These data include a "don't know" category. Gallup reports a figure of 78% favor, with no "don't know" category (survey date, October 18–21, 1974 Gallup Public Opinion Referendum, Gallup Opinion Index #113 November 1974, and the Gallup Poll, vol. 1, p. 375).

III. 1975, March: Gallup face-to-face interview survey #925-k, March 7–10, 1975 (total *N* = 2762; 91% of this number had heard or read of the ERA): Gallup Opinion Index #118, April 1975, and the Gallup Poll, vol. 1, p. 447. There is some confusion regarding this poll, because the Gallup Poll reports 58% Favor, 24% Oppose, and 18% No Opinion, as "Asked of those who replied in the *affirmative*," while the Gallup Opinion Index reports the same percentages as "Asked of *everyone* after they were asked: 'Have you heard or read . .' (my emphases)." The Roper Center AIPO 925 Q 3 & 4 also reports "Ask everyone." In fact, the percentages that Gallup reported officially for this year are based on the *total sample* and not those who replied in the affirmative. However, the percentages reported in this table are percentages of those who replied affirmatively to the previous question on whether they had heard or read about the ERA.

1975, December: NBC News/Associated Press telephone survey, December 16–21, 1975 (total *N* = 2836; 88% of this number had heard or read of the ERA).

1976: Gallup face-to-face interview survey #947-k, March 19–22, 1976 (total *N* = 2798); 90% of this number had heard or read of the ERA): Gallup Opinion Index #128, April 1976, and the Gallup Poll, vol. 2, p. 684. As in 1975, the Gallup Opinion Index and the Roper Center AIPO 947 Q 6A & 6B report "Asked of everyone." And in fact the published responses, of 57% Favor, 24% Oppose, and 19% No Opinion, are based on the total sample. After noticing this, Gallup in 1981 for the first time began reporting retrospective 1976 results as "Based on all respondents" (see the Gallup Report 190, July 1981, p. 24, and the Gallup Report 203, August 1982, p. 28). It did not, however, report the 1975 results as based on all respondents. Like the 1975 and subsequent percentages reported in this table, the 1976 percentages are percentages not of the total sample but of those who replied "yes" to the previous question on whether they had heard or read about the ERA. (Analysis of the 1975 and 1976 data for respondents who replied in the affirmative to the

1977	1978	1979	1980	1981	1982

56 51	51 55	57	52	52	50 63[b]
(9)(16)	(15) (7)	(7)	(2)	(4)	(4) (3)

					63[b]
					(4)

first question was performed by the Roper Center. I would like to thank Ann Osborne of the Gallup organization for her help in straightening out these data.)

1977, January: NBC News/Associated Press telephone survey, January 24–25, 1977 (total N = 1600; 95% of this number had heard or read of the ERA).

1977, May: NBC News/Associated Press telephone survey, May 16–17, 1977 (total N = 1600; 90% of this number had heard or read of the ERA).

1978, March: NBC News/Associated Press telephone survey, March 21–22, 1978 (total N = 1604; 89% of this number had heard or read of the ERA). In this survey, the word "Constitution" was preceded by "U.S." or "United States."

1978, June: Gallup special telephone survey, June 4–12, 1978 (total N = 1010; 90% of this number had heard or read of the ERA): the Gallup Report #154 May (*sic*) 1978, and the Gallup Poll, release, July 16, 1978. The Gallup organization reports that its telephone surveys usually tap a more Republican sample than their face-to-face interviews. This feature would bias ERA approval rates downward.

1978, June: NBC News/Associated Press telephone survey, June 27–28, 1978 (total N = 1600); 94% of this number had heard or read of the ERA). In this survey, the word "Constitution" was preceded by "U.S." or "United States."

1978, August: NBC News/Associated Press telephone survey, August 7–8, 1978 (total N = 1600; 90% of this number had heard or read of the ERA). In this survey, the word "Constitution" was preceded by "U.S." or "United States."

1978, October-November: Attitudes toward Women and Work telephone survey, University of Illinois Survey Research Laboratory, October–November 1978 (total N = 2002; 90% of this number had heard or read of the ERA). I would like to thank Glenna Spitze of the State University of New York at Albany and Joan Huber of the University of Illinois at Urbana-Champaign for making these data available.

1979: December; NBC News/Associated Press telephone survey, December 11–12, 1979 (total N = 1595; 83% of this number had heard or read of the ERA).

1980: Gallup face-to-face interview survey #159G, July 11–14, 1980 (total N = 1548; 91% of this number had heard or read of the ERA). The Gallup Report #178 June (*sic*) 1980, and the Gallup Poll, Release July 31, 1980. This survey was taken during the week of the Republican Convention. On July 15, the Republicans adopted their 1980 platform, which for the first time in almost twenty years did not include a statement endorsing the ERA. This circumstance might conceivably have depressed ERA approval.

1981, July: Gallup telephone survey #177G, Form A, July 17–20, 1981 (weighted N = 1328; 90% of this number had heard or read of the ERA). Data from the Roper Center. (The Gallup Report #190, p. 24, reports slightly different N's and percentages.) Half the sample was asked this wording, half the new wording of Question III.

IV. 1981, July: Gallup telephone survey #177G, Form B, July 17–20, 1981 (weighted N = 1412; 87% of this number had heard or read of the ERA). Half the sample was asked this new wording, half the 1975–1980 wording.

1981, December: Gallup survey #187G, December 11–14, 1981 (total N = 1483; 83% of this number had heard or read of the ERA).

1982: Gallup face-to-face interview survey #196G, June 11–14, 1982 (total N = 1504; 90% of this number had heard or read of the ERA).

V. 1977: NORC General Social Survey, February–April 1977 (total N = 1530, of whom 224 were not used for the analysis because they had not heard or read of ERA, did not know if they had heard or read of it, or had no answer to either question).

1982: NORC General Social Survey, February–April 1982 (total N = 1506, of whom 160 were not used for the analysis because they had not heard or read of the ERA, did not know if they had heard or read of it, or had no answer to either question).

VI. 1980, July: NBC News/Associated Press telephone survey, July 8–9, 1980 (total N = 1947; 74% of this number had heard or read enough about the ERA to have an opinion on it).

1980, August: NBC News/Associated Press telephone survey, August 15–16, 1980 (total N = 2000; 73% of this number had heard or read enough about the ERA to have an opinion on it).

1980, September: NBC News/Associated Press telephone survey, September 22–24, 1980 (total N = 2393; 74% of this number had heard or read enough about the ERA to have an opinion on it).

1980, October: NBC News/Associated Press telephone survey, October 8–9, 1980 (total N = 2400; 74% of this number had heard or read enough about the ERA to have an opinion on it).

1980, October: NBC News/Associated Press telephone survey, October 22–24, 1980 (total N = 2405; 74% of this number had heard or read enough about the ERA to have an opinion on it).

1981, January: NBC News/Associated Press telephone survey, January 21–23, 1981 (total N = 2407; 72% of this number had heard or read enough about the ERA to have an opinion on it). In this survey, the second "Equal Rights Amendment" in the question was abbreviated to "ERA."

1981, February: NBC News/Associated Press telephone survey, February 23–24, 1981 (total N = 1597; 62% of this number had heard or read enough about the ERA to have an opinion on it).

1981, May: NBC/Associated Press telephone survey, May 18–19, 1981 (total N = 1599; 72% of this number had heard or read enough about the ERA to have an opinion on it).

1981, July: NBC News/Associated Press telephone survey, July 13–14, 1981 (total N = 1599; 74% of this number had heard or read enough about the ERA to have an opinion on it).

1981, December: NBC News/Associated Press telephone survey, December 14–15, 1981 (total N = 1602; 65% of this number had heard or read enough about the ERA to have an opinion on it).

1982: June: NBC News/Associated Press telephone survey, June 14–15, 1982 (total N = 1597; 69% of this number had heard or read enough about the ERA to have an opinion on it). I would like to thank Peggy Einnehmer of NBC News for supplying all NBC News/Associated Press data.

VII. 1980, February: CBS/New York Times, February 13–17, 1980 (N = 1536).

1980, March: CBS/New York Times, March 12–15, 1980 (N = 1968).

1980, June: CBS/New York Times, June 18–22, 1980 (N = 1517).

1980, August: CBS/New York Times, August 2–7, 1980 (N = 1769).

1980, September: CBS/New York Times, September 10–14, 1980 (N = 2062). From September 19–21, CBS/New York Times conducted a pre-Presidential debate survey of 817 respondents, of which 59% favored the ERA and 9% had no opinion. From September 23–25, they conducted a post-Presidential debate survey of 810 respondents. Of these, 55% favored the ERA and 10% had no opinion.

1980, October: CBS/New York Times, October 16–20, 1980 (N = 1539).

1980, November: CBS/New York Times, November 7–12, 1980 (N = 2651).

1981, April: CBS/New York Times, April 22–26, 1981 (N = 1439).

1982, January: CBS/New York Times, January 11–15, 1982 (N = 1540).

1982, June: CBS/New York Times, June 26–28, 1982 (N = 1174). I would like to thank Professor Robert Shapiro of Columbia University for supplying these data.

VIII. 1976; University of Michigan Survey Research Center, American National Election Study, November 3, 1976–January 15, 1977 (total weighted N = 2870, of whom 467 were excluded from the analysis because they had no postelection interview and thus were not asked the question, and 11 because they did not answer the question). These data derive from *The 1976 CPS American National Election Study: Introduction and Codebook* (Ann Arbor: University of Michigan, 1977),
p. 409.

IX. 1978: University of Michigan Survey Research Center, American National Election Study, ca. November 1978–January 1979 (total N = 2304, of whom 47 did not answer this question and were not used in the analysis).
 1980: University of Michigan Survey Research Center, American National Election Study, ca. November 1980–January 1981 (total N = 1614, of whom 206 were excluded from the analysis because they had no postelection interview and thus were not asked the question and 9 because they did not answer the question).

X. 1982, April: The Harris Survey, release May 6, 1982—see below, note to question XI.

XI. 1975: The Harris Survey, release May 19, 1975 (N = 1579; date "mid-April").
 [1976: Two Harris surveys, from August 18–30 (Harris #2624A1) and October 23–26 (Harris #2624L), have been omitted from this series. In both cases, the wording was different: "Do you favor or oppose . . . Passage of the Equal Rights Amendment putting women on an equal footing with men?" August: Favor 66%, Oppose 23%, Not Sure 11%; October: Favor 65%, Oppose 27%, Not Sure 8%.]
 1977, April: The Harris Survey, release April 28, 1977 (N = 1502; date "early April").
 1977, December: Harris Survey #2779, (N = 1259) data from the Institute for Research in Social Science, University of North Carolina at Chapel Hill.
 1978, January: The Harris Survey, release February 13, 1978 (N = 1259; date December 27, 1977–January 10, 1978).
 1978, July: The Harris Survey, release July 17, 1978 (N = 1502, date June 27–July 1).
 1979: Louis Harris and Associates (N = 1494, date November 30–December 2, 1979. Survey for the National Federation of Business and Professional Women). Due to rounding error, the Harris News release of January 30, 1980, reported ERA support as 56 percent.Data from the Institute for Research in Social Science, University of North Carolina at Chapel Hill. I would like to thank the National Federation of Business and Professional Women for permission to analyze these data.
 1980: The Harris Survey, release December 4, 1980 (N = 1199, date November 7–10, 1980).
 1981: The Harris Survey, release August 17, 1981 (N = 1252, date July 8–12, 1981).
 1982, January: The Harris Survey, no press release; reported in Release May 6, 1982 (N = 1256, date January 8–12, 1982).
 1982, April: The Harris Survey, release May 6, 1982 (N = 1258, date April 16–22, telephone). The survey asked all respondents all three questions, X, XI, and XII, in that order. Beginning with a question using the actual wording of the ERA, and asking in succession three different questions all with the same ending ("do you favor or oppose the ERA?"), undoubtedly pushed upward the approval rate on the traditional question XI and its successor, question XII. This data point is not, therefore, strictly comparable to the others in the series.

XII. 1982, April: The Harris Survey, release May 6, 1982—see above, note to question XI.

TABLE A2
Characteristics That Make Little Difference:
*Percent Favoring the ERA in 1982, by Gender, Race, Class,
and Catholicism/Protestantism*

	%	N
Gender:		
Male	70	(547)
Female	74	(732)
Race:		
Black	78	(129)
White	72	(1132)
Family income:		
Less than $10,000	74	(281)
$10,000–$20,000	73	(350)
$20,000–$35,000	74	(354)
More than $35,000	70	(200)
Occupational prestige:		
Low	75	(287)
Medium-low	72	(362)
Medium	73	(282)
High	70	(127)
Education		
Less than high school	71	(328)
High school	73	(458)
College	73	(399)
Graduate school	71	(90)
Catholicism/Protestantism		
Catholic	77	(307)
Protestant	68	(814)

Source: NORC General Social Survey: number of respondents in parentheses; "don't know" responses excluded.

TABLE A3
Characteristics That Make a Difference:
*Percent Favoring the ERA in 1982, by Religion, Number
of Children, Age, Rurality, and Region*

	%	N
Religion:		
Fundamentalist Protestant	61	(231)
Other Protestant	72	(522)
Catholic	77	(307)
Jewish	81	(36)
No religion	88	(101)
Church attendance:		
Several times a week	47	(104)
Every week	65	(255)
Once or several times a month	70	(257)
Rarely	80	(478)
Never	83	(175)
Number of children		
(among married or once-married only):		
6 or more	62	(65)
3–5	65	(324)
1–2	75	(531)
None	78	(357)
Age		
Over 65	63	(191)
56–65	68	(183)
46–55	59	(167)
36–45	77	(203)
26–35	80	(331)
18–25	81	(195)
Rurality:		
Open country	63	(233)
Suburbs, small cities	73	(673)
Cities of 50,000+	76	(373)
Region		
South	65	(399)
Midwest	72	(424)
East and West Coasts	79	(456)

Source: NORC General Social Survey: number of respondents in parentheses; "don't know" responses excluded.

TABLE A4
Support and Opposition to the ERA in Unratified States, 1975–1981

Year	Favor (%)	Oppose (%)	Hadn't Heard or Read of It or Don't Know (%)	N
1975	51	33	16	(861)
1976	53	27	20	(768)
1980	48	40	13	(778)
1981	47	38	14	(752)

Source: Daniels and Darcy, p. 583, using the Gallup surveys reported in table A1, Question III, but percentaging on the total sample, not just on those who replied in the affirmative.

TABLE A5
Support and Opposition to the ERA in Illinois, 1976–1982

Question	Year	Favor (%)	Oppose (%)	Don't Know/NA (%)	N
Do you think the Illinois Legislature should or should not pass the Equal Rights Amendment?	1976	58	27	15	(796)
Do you favor or oppose ratification of the Equal Rights Amendment?	Feb. 1978	54	28	18	(800)
Do you favor or oppose the Equal Rights Amendment?	Sept. 1978	58	29	13	(802)
Would you favor or oppose the State Legislature ratifying the ERA (Equal Rights Amendment)?	1981	48	42	10	(800)
Do you favor or oppose the State Legislature ratifying the ERA (Equal Rights Amendment)?	April 1982	45	41	14	(800)
	June 1982	38	45	16	(778)

Source: Market Opinion Research, registered voters only.

TABLE A6

Support and Opposition to the ERA in Oklahoma, 1978–1982

Year	Support (%)	Oppose (%)	Don't Know (%)	N
July 1978	45	36	19	(600)
October 1978	37	47	16	(600)
October 1981	41	50	9	(800)
January 1982	44	39	15	(400)
June 1982	31	48	20	(692)
August 1982	36	56	8	(581)

Source: Daniels and Darcy, p. 583, using Keilhorn and Associates, Inc. July 1978, October 1978, October 1981, August 1982, no question wording given; *Daily Oklahoman*, January 14, 1982, "Should Oklahoma approve the ERA?"; Ruddick Research International, "Oklahoma Opinion Profile," July/August 1982, "Do you favor or oppose the Equal Rights Amendment?"

TABLE A7

Party Activism and Support for the ERA Nationwide, 1981

	% Favoring the ERA
Democratic National Committee members	92
Democratic public	62
Republican public	46
Republican National Committee members	29

Source: *Public Opinion* (October/November 1981), p. 29; DNC $N = 324$, RNC $N = 150$, no public N given.

TABLE A8

Party Activism and Support for the ERA in California, 1981

	% Favoring the ERA
Democratic Committee members	90
Democratic contributors	80
Democratic public	74
Republican public	55
Republican contributors	43
Republican Committee members	29

Source: *Los Angeles Times* Poll, July 12–22, 1981, reported in Richard Bergholz, "Voters and Party Leaders Far Apart on the Issues," *Los Angeles Times*, August 2, 1981, p. 1. The story does not give the wording of the ERA question or the number of cases in the committee member or contributor samples. Total N, including non-party-identifiers, in the public sample was 1,304.

TABLE A9
Attitudes of Men, Women in the Labor Force, and Homemakers toward
the ERA and Nontraditional Roles, 1974–1982

		% Taking Traditional Position			Difference between Women in Labor Force and Homemakers
Question	Year	Men	Women in Labor Force	Homemakers	
Do you strongly favor, somewhat favor, somewhat oppose, or strongly oppose this amendment (ERA)? (Oppose)	1974	...	...	...	...
	1977	27	23	30	+7
	1982	30	21	31	+10
Do you think there should be laws against marriages between (Negroes/blacks) and whites? (Yes) [−.178]*	1974	33	30	42	+12
	1977	27	22	37	+15
	1982	28	21	45	+24
How about sexual relations between two adults of the same sex—do you think it is always wrong, almost always wrong, wrong only sometimes or not at all? (Always wrong) [−.251]*	1974	72	63	75	+12
	1977	77	74	84	+10
	1982	76	60	81	+21
Please tell me whether or not you think it should be possible for a pregnant woman to obtain a legal abortion if she is not married and does not want to marry the man? (No) [−.277]*	1974	50	46	54	+8
	1977	49	47	57	+10
	1982	51	43	60	+17
Would you be for or against sex education in the public schools? (Against) [−.174]*	1974	19	9	21	+12
	1977	22	13	27	+14
	1982	17	9	20	+11
Do you think birth control information should be available to teenagers who want it, or not? (Should not be available) [−.185]*	1974	21	11	24	+13
	1977	16	11	21	+10
	1982	10	7	18	+11
Most men are better suited for politics than most women. (Agree) [−.214]*	1974	48	42	51	+9
	1977	50	43	55	+12
	1982	39	26	50	+24
Women should take care of running their homes and leave running the country up to men. (Agree) [−.235]*	1974	36	24	43	+19
	1977	38	28	50	+22
	1982	27	16	38	+22
Do you approve or disapprove of a married woman earning money in business or industry if she has a husband capable of supporting her? (Disapprove) [−.166]*	1974	34	20	34	+14
	1977	32	27	43	+16
	1982	26	13	33	+20

TABLE A9 *(continued)*

Question	Year	Men	% Taking Traditional Position — Women in Labor Force	Homemakers	Difference between Women in Labor Force and Homemakers
If your party nominated a woman for president, would you vote for her if she were qualified for the job? (No) [−.308]*	1974	20	15	22	+7
	1977	18	14	32	+18
	1982	14	8	18	+10
Approximate number of cases, with some variations for nonresponse and no opinion.	1974	660	290	400	
	1977	600	380	330	
	1982	610	415	290	

Source: NORC General Social Survey; "don't know" responses excluded.
    *Correlation with support for the ERA.

TABLE A10
Liberal Trends, 1972–1985 (%)

	1972	1974	1976	1978	1980	1982	1985
Woman for President[a]	74	80	—	82	—	86	82
Premarital sex not wrong[b]	27	31	—	39	—	41	43
Black for President[c]	74	82	—	85	—	88	85
Legal for races to wed[d]	60	65	67	—	70	70	74
Married women's earning[e]	65	69	—	73	—	75	86

Source: NORC General Social Survey, 1972–1985: "don't know" responses omitted; N = +/−1500; — = not asked in that year.
    [a]If your party nominated a woman for President, would you vote for her if she were qualified for the job? (Yes) [.308]*
    [b]If a man and a woman have sex relations before marriage, do you think it is always wrong, wrong only sometimes, or not wrong at all? (Not wrong at all) [.250]*
    [c]If your party nominated a (Negro/Black) for President, would you vote for him if he were qualified for the job? (Yes) [.188]*
    [d]Do you think there should be laws against marriages between (Negroes/Blacks) and Whites? (No) [.178]*
    [e]Do you approve or disapprove of a married woman earning money in business or industry if she has a husband capable of supporting her? (Approve) [.167]*
    *Correlation with ERA support in 1982.

TABLE A11
Conservative Trends, 1972–1985 (%)

	1972	1974	1976	1978	1980	1982	1985
Communism worst[a]	—	51	52	—	59	61	59
Death penalty[b]	57	66	69	70	72	78	80
Courts harsher[c]	74	84	86	84	88	90	87

Source: NORC General Social Survey, 1972–1985: "don't know" responses omitted; $N = +/-$ 1500; — = not asked in that year.

[a]Thinking about all the different kinds of government in the world today, which of these statements comes closest to how you feel about Communism as a form of government? (It's the worst kind) [−.172]*

[b]1972–1973: Are you in favor of the death penalty for persons convicted of murder? (Yes) 1974–1985: Do you favor or oppose the death penalty for persons convicted of murder? (Favor) [−.150]*

[c]In general, do you think that courts in this area deal too harshly or not harshly enough with criminals? (Not harshly enough) [−.030]*

*Correlation with ERA support in 1982.

Notes

Preface

1. Pauline Bart and Linda Frankel, *The Student Sociologist's Handbook* (Cambridge, Mass.: Schenckman, 1971), p. 19. They cite Peter L. Berger, *Invitation to Sociology* (Garden City, N.Y.: Anchor Doubleday, 1963), p. 38, on this point.

2. The fieldwork on which part of this study is based consisted in part of twenty-eight in-person interviews, conducted in 1981 and 1982, with a sample of state legislators in Illinois (oversampled for women legislators and chosen randomly, three of the interviews being done by my research assistant, Deborah Gerner), eight in-depth, in-person interviews with activist women leaders in the ERA ratification campaign in Illinois, twelve shorter in-person interviews with rank and file activists in the ERA campaign, one in-person interview in Washington D.C. with an influential participant in the campaign, twenty-nine telephone interviews with activists and others outside Illinois, fourteen telephone interviews with lawyers outside Illinois whose work in some way affected the political fortunes of the ERA, and many discussions with friends who were in varying degrees part of the ERA campaign. I taped the in-person interviews and took notes on the telephone interviews. All those I interviewed in person and some of those I interviewed on the phone were guaranteed confidentiality. When interviewees are identified, they were either not guaranteed confidentiality or were contacted later and asked if I could make a particular statement public. All quotations not documented to a source derive from this fieldwork.

The work also included a history of participant observation, which began as participation pure and simple when in 1973 I organized a drive to collect signatures supporting the ERA from the women faculty of the University of Chicago and succeeded in getting 97 percent support. From 1973 on, I was a newsletter-receiving member of the organization that became ERA Central and then ERA Illinois. I was also an inactive member of the National Organization for Women. In the fall of 1980, I began my formal study of the ERA, turning my participation (which, except for the signature drive, monetary contributions, and attending one major demonstration, had been minimal) into participant observation and becoming at the same time an independent member of the board of directors of ERA Illinois. The board members knew my participation included collecting data for a book that would look at how the organizational incentives of the different pro-ERA groups affected their tactics. I was only a moderately active member of the board, occasionally helping to write public letters or statements on behalf of the group, agreeing to collect for a legislator who wanted it a list of the "laws the ERA would change" (a massive assignment that had major consequences for this book), and arranging (and in a few cases writing) testimony for the June 8, 1982, final hearings on the ERA before the Illinois House of Representatives. At the same time I was an inactive member of my local chapter of NOW, going to one meeting in which I briefly discussed my research and asked for responses to a questionnaire, attending two demonstrations (one with my local chapter), and attending the NOW state conference in June 1981.

Chapter 2

1. *S.J. Res. 21* and *H.J. Res. 75,* 68th Cong., 1st sess.

2. Eleanor Flexner, *Centuries of Struggle: The Women's Rights Movement in the United States* (Cambridge, Mass.: Harvard University Press, 1959), p. 328.

3. Josephine Goldmark, *Impatient Crusader: Florence Kelley's Life Story* (Urbana: University of Illinois Press, 1953), pp. 182, 183. See also Mary Van Kleek, "Women and Machines," *Atlantic Monthly* 127 (February 1921): 250–260, on the way "the women in the professions . . . have been willing . . . to offer up the present safeguards affecting their sisters in the factories—without consulting those sisters" (p. 254).

William Henry Chafe's account of the early ERA battles in *The American Woman: Her Changing Social, Economic and Political Roles, 1920–1970* (New York: Oxford, 1972), chap. 5 ("The Equal Rights Amendment"), does not capture the ways in which this dispute was a conflict among feminists. Nor does he distinguish adequately within the opposition to the Amendment between socialists like Florence Kelley and comparatively more conservative organizations like the League of Women Voters. Chafe's consistent opposition of "reformers" versus "feminists" implies that "reformers" like Kelley who opposed the ERA were neither true feminists nor as radical in their goals as the "feminists." For a detailed account more sympathetic to the "social feminists" than to the Woman's Party, see J. Stanley Lemons, *The Woman Citizen: Social Feminism in the 1920's* (Urbana: University of Illinois Press, 1973), chap. 7 ("Feminists against Feminists"). For a vivid picture of the divisive effect of this issue on international feminism, see Susan D. Becker *The Origins of the Equal Rights Amendment: American Feminism between the Wars* (Westport, Conn.: Greenwood Press, 1981), and "International Feminism between the Wars: The National Women's Party versus the League of Women Voters," in Lois Scharf and Joan M. Jensen, eds., *Decades of Discontent: The Women's Movement 1910–1940* (Westport, Conn.: Greenwood Press, 1983), pp. 222–242. For the way this issue divides feminists today, see below Chapter 11 n. 5.

4. Clement E. Vose, *Constitutional Change: Amendment Politics and Supreme Court Litigation since 1900* (Lexington, Mass.: D. C. Heath, 1972), p. 254. See also Esther Peterson, "The Kennedy Commission," in Irene Tinker, ed., *Women in Washington* (Beverly Hills, Calif.: Sage, 1983), p. 24; and Kathryn Kish Sklar, "Why Did Most Politically Active Women Oppose the ERA in the 1920's?" in Joan Hoff-Wilson, ed., *Rights of Passage: The Past and Future of the ERA* (Bloomington: Indiana University Press, 1986).

5. In response, twenty-seven national women's organizations and unions formed the National Committee to Defeat the Un-Equal Rights Amendment (Katherine Kraft, "ERA: History and Status," *Radcliffe Quarterly* 68 [1982]: 4). Chafe argues that after the Fair Labor Standards Act of 1938 established the precedent of wage and hour limitations for both men and women, "the protective legislation argument lost much of its force" (p. 131). But the Fair Labor Standards Act did not guarantee that protections for women would be extended to men. That issue remained live until 1970.

6. Marguerite Rawalt, "The Equal Rights Amendment," in Tinker, ed., p. 53.

7. Rawalt, p. 55.

8. Kraft, p. 5.

9. Rawalt, pp. 54–55. See also Gilbert Y. Steiner, *Constitutional Inequality: The Political Fortunes of the Equal Rights Amendment* (Washington, D.C.: Brookings Institution, 1985), p. 10.

10. Marguerite Rawalt, past president of the National Federation of Business and Professional Women (BPW) and later a founding member of the National Organization for Women (NOW), managed to persuade the commission to add the word "now" to its conclusion, so that in the end the phrase became "need not now be sought" (President's Commission on the Status of Women files, Esther Peterson Papers, Schlesinger library, cited by Kraft, p. 15). Kraft also points out that Esther Peterson, who urged Kennedy to appoint the Commission on the Status of Women and who

strongly opposed the ERA, lobbied intensively for the Equal Pay Act of 1963, an act that equalized pay rates for male and female workers doing the same job. See also Nancy E. McGlen and Karen O'Connor, *Women's Rights: The Struggle for Equality in the 19th and 20th Centuries* (New York: Praeger, 1983), p. 368; and Catherine East, "The First Stage," *Women's Political Times* (September 1982): 7.

11. Marguerite Rawalt indicates that NOW was founded by a group of women dissatisfied at the Interstate Association of State Commissions on the Status of Women for rejecting a resolution endorsing the ERA (Rawalt, p. 59). For the NOW Bill of Rights, see Robin Morgan, ed., *Sisterhood Is Powerful* (New York: Random House, 1970), pp. 512–514. For the union members' walkout, see the Minutes of the NOW annual meeting, November 19–20, 1967, Schlesinger Library, reported in France Kolb, "How the ERA Passed the Congress," *Radcliffe Quarterly* 68 (March 1982): 11. See also Judith Hole and Ellen Levine, *Rebirth of Feminism* (New York: Quadrangle Books, 1971), p. 68.

12. Peterson, p. 31. For pre-1970 court and EEOC activities, see Chapter 5 nn. 5–7. For the union position as of 1967, see Mary O. Eastwood, "Constitutional Protection against Sex Discrimination: An Informal Memorandum Prepared for the National Organization for Women Regarding the Equal Rights Amendment and Similar Proposals" (unpublished MS. in the files of Mary Eastwood).

13. Kolb, p. 11.

14. Marguerite Rawalt, Testimony, Equal Rights Amendment Hearings before the Committee on the Judiciary, Subcommittee no. 4, U.S. House of Representatives, March 25, 1971, p. 205.

15. Hole and Levine, p. 56. See also Rawalt, Testimony, p. 204.

16. The vote on this provision, proposed by Senator Ervin, was 36–33. A 50–20 majority also added a school prayer amendment, presumably intended to kill the ERA. The Amendment's supporters did not fight the school prayer amendment because they "felt that with the passage of the Ervin amendment we'd had it" ("Snarl in Senate All But Kills Women's Rights Amendment," *Washington Post,* October 14, 1970, p. 1).

17. *Congressional Record,* (hereafter *Cong. Rec.*), October 14, 1970, p. 36863.

18. Senator Birch Bayh, press interview, "Men's Lib Pending," *Washington Daily News,* October 15, 1970, p. 25.

19. See East, "The First Stage," p. 9. See also below, Chapter 5 n. 15.

The fact that Senator Ervin was reported as having "applauded the new language" (*Washington Post,* October 15, 1970, p. 1), and as having said that the substitute "would go a long way toward retaining the protective legislation which the states and the federal government have enacted" (*Evening Star,* Washington D.C., October 15, 1970, p. 5), confirmed the women's organizations in their suspicions of a sellout. I would like to thank Catharine East for providing the newspaper clippings referred to in nn 16–19.

20. Janet K. Boles, *The Politics of the Equal Rights Amendment: Conflict and the Decision Process* (New York: Longman, 1979), p. 39.

21. Catherine East notes that "the Judiciary Committee vote on the Wiggins version was, for the first time, along partisan lines. All the Republicans, except Congressman McClory of Illinois, had voted for the Wiggins version, whereas 13 of the 20 Democrats had supported the [original] ERA." Catherine East, "The ERA in Congress 1923–1972," unpublished MS., p. 15.

22. East, "The First Stage," p. 10.

23. Ibid.

24. Boles, *Politics,* p. 142.

25. Ibid., pp. 143–144.

26. Ibid., p. 72. See also pp. 62–66, and passim.

27. Gilbert Steiner (pp. 58–66) discusses in more detail the way abortion and the ERA became concatenated

28. In December 1974, Schlafly's banner headline proclaimed, "ERA Means Abortion and Population Shrinkage," *Phyllis Schlafly Report* 8, no. 5 (December 1974). Her accompanying story cited in support of this claim the arguments of Professor Charles Rice and Dean Clarence Manion of the University of Notre Dame Law School. A month later, Professor Joseph Witherspoon of the University of Texas telegrammed the Texas legislators: "Ratification of the ERA will inevitably be interpreted by the Supreme Court of the United States as an explicit ratification and an approval by the people of the United States of its 1973 decision invalidating state anti-abortion statutes . . ." (Professor Joseph Witherspoon, telegram to the Texas state legislators, January 9, 1975, cited in Phyllis Schlafly, *The Power of the Positive Woman* [New Rochelle, N.Y.: Arlington House, 1977], p. 88). And within two weeks Rice wrote the legislators in Indiana: "If the ERA were adopted, it would make clear beyond any doubt that the states would be disabled from prohibiting or even restricting abortion in any

significant way" (Professor Charles Rice, letter to Indiana state legislators, January 21, 1975, cited in Schlafly, *Power,* p. 88; see also Steiner, pp. 63–64). According to investigative work by the Lincoln, Nebraska, chapter of NOW, Dean Clarence Manion was a member of the John Birch Society National Council, and Professor Rice appeared with Phyllis Schlafly at a John Birch Society rally in July 1973 (Ann K. Justice, ed., "The Insurance Connection with STOP ERA Forces" [Lincoln, Nebr.: National Organization for Women, 1974], pp. 13, 33).

29. Although the ERA had no bearing on the legality of abortion per se, it did have potential relevance to the question of public funding for abortion. Once conservative legislators began cutting off public funds for abortions, liberal lawyers began looking for constitutional arguments that would make public funding mandatory. These arguments usually invoked the Fourteenth Amendment to the federal Constitution, but in addition they occasionally invoked state ERAs, and in Pennsylvania a lower court suggested that the state ERA would, in fact, require the state to pay for abortions on the same basis as other medical procedures. But all this came later; see Chapter 10.

30. I have taken this account largely from Boles, *Politics,* passim, and her table 1.1, pp. 2–3.

31. The states that refused to ratify were also relatively poor. See Chapter 4., n. 17.

32. *New York Times,* November 1, 1975, p. 61. The story does not give any further information on the percentages in the surveys or the names of the polling organizations.

33. For the New York vote, see "Voters Approved Charity Gambling," *New York Times,* December 16, 1975: 1,950,993 against the ERA; 1,470,213 for it. For the New Jersey vote, see "Election Results Certified by State," *New York Times,* December 9, 1975: 860,061 against the ERA; 828,290 for it. For the early returns, see Linda Greenhouse, "Equal Rights Amendments Lose in New York and New Jersey Voting," *New York Times,* November 5, 1975, p. 1.

34. John van Gieson, " 'Little ERA,' 7 More Revisions Rejected," *Miami Herald,* November 8, 1978, p. 21A. The story gives no further information on the percentages either in the survey or in the referendum. Gieson attributes the shift to a "last-minute campaign" in which opponents charged that the state ERA "would give homosexuals the right to marry and adopt children."

35. Survey reported in Laurence M. Paul, "Undecided May Hold ERA Fate," *Des Moines Sunday Register,* October 26, 1980, p. 6B, and

conducted by the Iowa Poll, October 1–4, 1980; $N = 1,204$; likely voters = 799; wording: "Do you favor or oppose the Equal Rights Amendment to the Iowa Constitution?" Among "all Iowans" the figures were 52 percent favor, 22 percent oppose, and 20 percent undecided. Paul also reported that "in the five years the poll has been asking Iowa's adults about the [Iowa] ERA, support consistently has been in the 60 percent range. In August 1979 the poll found that 60 percent favored the Iowa ERA, 30 percent opposed it and 10 percent had no opinion." The Iowa Poll also asked, "Do you favor or oppose the Equal Rights Amendment to the U.S. Constitution?" (Iowa had ratified the ERA two days after the U.S. Senate in 1972.) Among all adult Iowans, 50 percent favored, 29 percent opposed, and 21 percent were undecided; among likely voters, the percentages were 46, 34, and 20. Data on the referendum are not final but reported as "with nearly all of the states' precincts reporting," in Jim Healey and Tom Knudson, "Convention and the ERA Are Turned Down" (*Des Moines Register,* November 5, 1980, p. 1A). Healey and Knudson reported that the month between the poll and the vote had been marked by a bitter campaign in which opponents particularly linked the ERA with homosexuality and argued that the ERA would have allowed homosexual marriages, would have forced the state to pay for abortions on demand, and would have led to sexually integrated toilets, hospital rooms, and other facilities.

36. Market Opinion Research Job Number P34243, question 18: "If the election were being held today, would you be voting YES in favor of a state equal rights amendment or voting NO against the amendment?" Yes, in favor, 62 percent; No, against, 23 percent; Don't know/No answer, 15 percent ($N = 600$). Significantly lower approval rates are given by Pat Truman of Maine Stop ERA for the same week (October 3): 33 percent in favor, 34 percent against, and 33 percent undecided. Similarly, Sandra Faucher of Maine Right to Life gives figures from the next week (October 9) as 36 percent in favor, 40 percent against, 24 percent undecided. Because Maine Right to Life, which commissioned both the surveys, prefers that the wording and the survey organization involved remain confidential, and because the results differ so dramatically from those obtained by Market Opinion Research, it may be best to treat these results as the artifact of a particular wording. It is worth noting that according to Faucher even their wording produced, four days before the election (October 30), a response of 43 percent in favor, 43 percent against, and 14 percent undecided, which is still noticeably more supportive than the final 63–37 vote against the state ERA in the referendum itself. (The exact percentages in the referendum vary slightly in different reports, presumably due to time differences in the returns reported. I have taken the referendum figures from *Public Opinion* [December/January 1985]: 77: "No" 63.1 percent [333,998], "Yes" 36.9 percent [195,653], with a turnout of 62.5 percent; *Ms.* [December 1984]: 76, reports "No" 64 percent, "Yes" 36 percent.) Referenda votes do not, of course, measure the "true" desires of the public better than survey research. Referenda reflect the desires of those who turn out to vote in what

are often off-year elections. They are also extremely susceptible to the effects of short-run, dramatic, and extensive publicity. Moreover, they are notoriously conservative, at least on "social issues." The public's rule of thumb in a referendum seems to be, "When in doubt, vote no." David Butler and Austin Ranney, eds., *Referendums: A Comparative Study of Practice and Theory* (Washington, D.C.: American Enterprise Institute for Public Policy Research, 1978), pp. 16, 83–84.

37. In the *New York Times*/CBS survey of voters leaving the polls in the 1980 Presidential election ($N = 15,201$), 48 percent of the women supported the ERA (18 percent no opinion), compared to 44 percent of the men (16 percent no opinion). (In the twelve years from 1970 to 1982, men had moved slightly toward opposition, and women toward support. Compare this 48/44 ratio in the *New York Times*/CBS 1980 survey and the 70/74 ratio in the 1982 GSS [table A2] with the first poll on the ERA in 1970 [table A1, question I], in which only 47 percent of the women favored the ERA, compared to 66 percent of the men. Robert Chandler, *Public Opinion: Changing Attitudes on Contemporary Political and Social Issues* [New York: R. R. Bowker/CBS News *Reference Book*, 1972], p. 47.) In the 1980 *New York Times*/CBS survey, support for the ERA correlated with voting against Reagan .304 ($N = 5,743$) among women and .315 among men ($N = 5,989$). Attitudes toward the ERA account for less than half a point of the nine-point gender gap; interaction with variables including or mentioning the ERA account for another half a point. For a further discussion of these data, see my "Myth and Reality: The ERA and the Gender Gap in the 1980 Election," *Public Opinion* 73 (1985): 64–78. Val Burris, "Who Opposed the ERA? An Analysis of the Social Bases of Antifeminism," *Social Science Quarterly* 64 (1983): 305–317, table 1, also provides data that show a gender gap on the ERA only among people with high incomes and educations. In the middle- and lower-income groups, the relationship is reversed, with men supporting the ERA more than women.

38. U.S. Census of Population: 1970, Subject Reports, Industrial Characteristics, PC(2)–78, 362, table 45. Due to cutbacks in the census, comparable 1980 information is not available at this time.

39. In Texas, Tedin et al. found that in their sample of pro-ERA activists 56 percent had at least a college degree. In their anti-ERA sample, drawn from a group demonstrating at the state capitol and disclosed by their interviews to have been primarily fundamentalist women, only 16 percent had college degrees (Kent L. Tedin et al., "Social Background and Political Differences between Pro- and Anti-ERA Activists," *American Politics Quarterly* 5 [1977]: 395–408). In North Carolina, Theodore S. Arrington and Patricia A. Kyle ("Equal Rights Amendment Activists in North Carolina," *Signs* 3 (1978) 666–680) found that the ERA activist typically had at least a college degree and a professional occupation, and almost three quarters of the married ERA activists had spouses in the

professions. Iva E. Deutchman and Sandra Prince-Embury, interviewing six pro-ERA and six anti-ERA leaders, found that all but one of the pro-ERA leaders had graduate degrees, whereas only one of the antis (probably Phyllis Schlafly herself, from other evidence in the article) had a college education ("Political Ideology of Pro- and Anti-ERA Women," *Women and Politics* 2 [1982]: 39–55). Pamela Johnston Conover and Virginia Gray, *Feminism and the New Right: Conflict over the American Family* (New York: Praeger, 1983), table 5.4, produce similar educational comparisons for activists who combined both pro- or anti-ERA and abortion activities. See also Carol Mueller and Thomas Dimieri, "The Structure of Belief Systems among Contending ERA Activists," *Social Forces* 60 (1981): 657–675, table 1.

Among women state legislators (in one sense, the most active "activists"), the effect of education in 1977 was fairly dramatic: only 59 percent of the high school graduates ($N = 27$) supported the ERA, compared to 79 percent of those with some college ($N = 79$) and 92 and 90 percent, respectively, of those with a college degree and some graduate education ($N = 79; 160$). Joyce R. Lilie, Roger Handberg, Jr., and Wanda Lowrey, "Women State Legislators and the ERA: Dimensions of Support and Opposition," *Women and Politics* 2 (1982): 23–38, table 2 (61 percent return to a mail survey of the 688 women who in 1977 served in state legislatures). See also Joan S. Carver, "The E.R.A. in Florida" (paper presented at the annual meeting of the Southern Political Science Association, Gatlinburg, Tennessee, 1979, table 2), for the strong effect of education on legislators' votes for the ERA in the Florida House of Representatives from 1973 to 1979.

40. Although neither the Texas nor the North Carolina study looked at race and ethnicity, my own observation of more than a hundred ERA activists in Chicago, where blacks and Hispanics together constitute about half the adult population, turned up only one Hispanic and three black activists. The ERA activists I saw in Chicago were also almost all well educated and female.

41. For parallel findings on the lack of association of ERA attitudes with class, see Conover and Gray, table 6.6, using 1976 and 1980 NES data; and Glenna Spitze and Joan Huber, "Effects of Anticipated Consequences on ERA Opinion," *Social Science Quarterly* 63 (1982): 323–332, table 2, using a 1978 national probability sample. Spitze and Huber also document the small positive association between Catholicism and ERA support.

42. Louis Harris, "ERA Support Soars as Deadline Nears," a Chicago Tribune Syndicate, Inc., release, reprinted in *National NOW Times* (June 1982). See also "ERA Support Soars to a Six-Year High," *Chicago Sun-Times*, May 7, 1982, sec. 1, p. 36.

43. *Businessweek*, August 1, 1983: 92.

44. Gloria Steinem, "How Women Live, Vote, Think," *Ms.* (July 1984): 54.

45. The new question was the third question asked in April 1982 (table A1, question XII), and was worded:

Many of those who favor women's rights favor the Equal Rights Amendment to the Constitution. Those who favor ERA argue that unless it is passed, women will continue to receive lower pay for the same work, receive fewer promotions to better jobs, and be discriminated against financially. Opponents argue that the special laws that now exist to protect women are sufficient and no new law is needed. Do you strongly favor, somewhat favor, somewhat oppose, or strongly oppose the Equal Rights Amendment?
    —*Harris Survey release, July 16, 1984, telephone survey of "likely voters 18 and over" at 1,259 different sampling points.*

On the basis of the April 1982 sample, in which 63 percent of the public favored ERA on both the "traditional" question and this one, Harris might argue that the new question was a valid continuation of the traditional series. But in April 1982 respondents were answering for the third time in a few minutes the question of whether or not they favored the ERA. It is not surprising, once Harris moved away from the question that used the actual wording of the ERA, that the same people favored the ERA the third time they were asked as favored it the second time.

46. In Oklahoma in 1978, William J. Wiseman, a representative to the Oklahoma legislature from Tulsa County, reported that "my regular polling of the district I represent has indicated a remarkable shift over the past four years—from moderate support to strong opposition to the ERA." He testified in the federal hearings on ERA extension that this change in his constituency's opinion, coupled with his own change from believing that the ERA would make sex a suspect classification to believing that "it might also be interpreted to prohibit legal classifications based upon sex, a result which I would strongly oppose," had changed him from voting for ratification in 1974 and subsequent years to opposing it in 1977 and 1978 (statement of William J. Wiseman, Jr., on Equal Rights Amendment Extension, U.S. House of Representatives, Subcommittee on Civil and Constitutional Rights of the Committee on the Judiciary, May 17, 1978, pp. 212–213).
    In Illinois in 1977, Representative Griesheimer, a strong ERA opponent, claimed that "I've gone to [the people of my legislative district] three separate times in polls. . . . It's interesting to note that the first time they were polled in March they were in favor of the ratification of the Equal Rights Amendment, that's March of 1973. In July of 1975 they were still in favor of it; and in March of 1976 they turned around and said, 'No, do not ratify'." (Illinois House of Representatives, June 2, 1977, p. 55; see also June 7, 1978, p. 28).

In Illinois in 1978, Representative Mautino, an ERA supporter, reported that in his district "three years ago it was about 65 percent in favor of [the ERA], 35 percent opposed." By May 1978, he said, it was 50.1 percent in favor and 49.9 percent opposed. Mautino then concluded that "in all conscience from all of the information I have evaluated, I will be voting 'yes' on the Equal Rights Amendment" (Representative Mautino, Illinois House of Representatives, June 7, 1978, p. 41).

In Illinois in June 1982, only a few days before the final deadline, Representative Friedrich, an ERA opponent, stated that "the polls in my district have become more and more and more opposed to the ratification of this [the ERA]. The last one was 32 to 1. Before that it had consistently run 2 to 1" (Representative Friedrich, Illinois House of Representatives, June 22, 1982, p. 12).

Most of these representatives were probably referring not to professional surveys in their districts but to questionnaires mailed to their constituencies from their own offices. Such questionnaires are more likely to be returned by political activists than by representative members of the population, and, as we have seen, political activists usually take more extreme positions than the average citizen. Thus in a generally conservative district, one would expect an incumbent's mail-back questionnaire survey to overrepresent the anti-ERA positions of conservative activists. This kind of overrepresentation is also inevitable when a legislator sends a questionnaire, as some do, only to his or her own list. However, none of these considerations would explain either the reported shifts over time or the results in what ERA supporter Representative Mautino called his "middle-America" district.

47. Representative Barbara Currie, Illinois House of Represenatives, June 8, 1982, pp. 79, 81. These figures differ only slightly from those in Debra L. Dodson, "The Impact of Institutional Factors Upon the Ratification of the Equal Rights Amendment" (paper delivered at the 1982 Midwest Political Science Association meetings). Dodson's careful analysis indicates that the growth in Democratic support derived completely from changes in the "downstate" Democratic vote in the legislature—changes that I would explain by the "Dixiecrat" legislators in that area coming into line with their party's wishes. See also Carver, tables 3 and 4, for polarization in the Florida House, though not in its (much smaller) Senate, from 1973 to 1979.

At the same time, public attitudes toward the ERA were polarizing along party and ideological lines. In national NES samples, the correlations in the predicted direction between attitudes toward the ERA and feelings on a "feeling thermometer" toward "Republicans," "Liberals," "the Women's Liberation Movement," and "Civil Rights Leaders" increased noticeably between 1976 and 1980 (Conover and Gray, table 6.4).

48. The seminal article is Herbert McClosky et al., "Issue Conflict and Consensus among Party Leaders and Followers," *American Political Sci-*

ence Review 5 (1960): 406–427. For more recent work, see Norman H. Nie, Sidney Verba, and John R. Petrocik, *The Changing American Voter* (Cambridge, Mass.: Harvard University Press, 1976), pp. 200–205, and Sidney Verba and Gary Orren, *Equality in America: The View from the Top* (Cambridge, Mass.: Harvard University Press, 1985), chapter on representation, and citations therein.

Chapter 3

1. Although I have labeled these positions "traditional," a feminist could quite easily hold some of them. Given the state of day-care arrangements in the United States, a feminist could certainly argue that a preschool child is likely to suffer if his or her mother works. Given both the kinds of socialization men and women receive and the character of politics in the United States, a feminist could argue that most men are better suited emotionally for politics than most women. It is likely, however, that most people who gave what I have called "traditional" responses to these questions in fact held traditional values in these areas.

I am grateful to Sara Chamberlain, an undergraduate in my social science course at the University of Chicago in 1977–1978, for generating the original data analysis that I have adapted in table 1.

2. Only four of these questions were available for analysis in the 1982 NORC General Social Survey. As one might expect, in 1982 the percentage of the sample taking the traditional position on women's roles had in most cases decreased slightly: on women's emotional unfitness for politics (question 6), a decrease from 42 to 35 percent; on leaving running the country to men (question 7), a decrease from 37 to 26 percent; and on refusing to vote for a woman for President (question 9), a decrease from 20 to 13 percent. Regarding allowing legal abortion (question 5), there was a nonsignificant increase from 48 to 49 percent. However, a majority of the "traditional" group still supported the ERA in 1982 as in 1977 (63, 61, and 56 percent, respectively, in questions 5, 6, and 7), except, as in 1977, among the tiny minority who would not vote for a qualified woman for President, 38 percent of whom supported the ERA in 1982. Although by 1982 the percentage of the anti-abortion group favoring the ERA had declined from 68 to 63 percent, this decline is what one would expect given the opposition's increasing stress on the connection between the ERA and abortion as the decade progressed.

Susan Gluck Mezey's 1977–1978 interviews with forty-two men and women who had held state and local offices in Hawaii in 1974 and with one hundred men and women city council members in Connecticut suggest that even in an "elite" sample support for the ERA derived in large part from sources other than a commitment to feminist principles. Support for the ERA correlated only .47 with support for feminist policies in Mezey's Hawaii sample, and only .27 in her Connecticut sample. Susan Gluck Mezey, "Attitudinal Consistency among Political Elites: Implications of

Support for the Equal Rights Amendment." *American Politics Quarterly* 9 (1981): 111–125.

3. In the same way, supporters of the ERA were usually perplexed at the gap in public opinion regarding the words of the Amendment and the Amendment itself. See below n. 12.

4. 1930–1970 figures from U.S. Bureau of the Census, *Historical Statistics of the United States, Colonial Times to 1970* (Washington, D.C.: Government Printing Office, 1978, p. 133); the 1980 figure comes from the Bureau of Labor Statistics, as reported in *Public Opinion* (August/September 1981): 24.

5. NORC General Social Survey, 1972–1982; "don't know" responses included for comparison to earlier data (table A10 omits these). Wording: "If your party nominated a woman for president, would you vote for her if she were qualified for the job?" Data before 1972, with occasional differences in wording, derive from AIPO surveys: see bibliography in James Allan Davis, *General Social Surveys, 1972–1982: Cumulative Codebook* (Chicago: National Opinion Research Center, 1982).

6. Ibid.; "don't know" responses included (table A10 omits these). This question, worded "Do you approve or disapprove of a married woman earning money in business or industry if she has a husband capable of supporting her?" produces much more public approval of women working (65 percent in 1977) than does the similarly worded question imposing the condition of "a limited number of jobs" (36 percent approval in 1977). Data before 1972, with occasional differences in wording, derive from AIPO surveys: see bibliography in Davis 1982.

7. The question reads, "There has been much talk recently about changing women's status in society today. On the whole, do you favor or oppose most of the efforts to strengthen and change women's status in society today?" 1970 Harris release April 28, 1977; 1972 Harris release May 19, 1975; 1975 ibid.; 1977 Harris release April 28, 1977 ($N = 1,502$); 1980 Virginia Slims American Women's Opinion Poll (Roper Organization, late 1979, $N = 3,000$ women, 1,000 men, in-person interviews), reported in *The 1980 Virginia Slims American Women's Opinion Poll*, Philip Morris, Inc. (n.d.), 39 pp., and Fran Ambrosine and Susan Charles, "Traditional Roles of American Women Seen Changing in 1980 Virginia Slims Poll," *Women and Politics* 1 (1980): 85–87.

8. The first survey in this paragraph was conducted by the Roper Organization, *Roper Report*, January 10–24, 1981, pp. 81–82; second survey by Research and Forecasts, Inc., for Connecticut Mutual Life Insurance Company, September 1–November 15, 1980, p. 156. Both are reported and compared in *Public Opinion* (August/September 1981): 32. In

reporting survey research, I will sometimes use the word "public" to mean "representative sample of the public."

9. Research and Forecasts, Inc., *The Connecticut Mutual Life Report* (Hartford: Connecticut Mutual Life Insurance Company, 1981), pp. 182. 151 (survey dated September 1–November 15, 1980). Note: In this survey only 29 percent of the sample preferred "a traditional marriage in which the husband is responsible for providing for the family and the wife for the home and taking care of the children." See also a survey by Daniel Yankelovich (1980) showing a majority agreeing that "both sexes have the responsibility to care for small children." This was an increase of more than 20 percent since 1970 (reported in *Ms.* [June 1981]: 45).

10. Doyle Dane Bernbach, *Soundings*, no. 6 (September 1980): 2, 4.

11. In the spring of 1980, the Bardsley and Haslacher Survey Organization asked a sample of 615 Utah voters: "From what you heard, would you favor or oppose the State of Utah passing the Equal Rights Amendment?" Favor 29%, Oppose 65%, Undecided 6%. (Members of the Mormon church were more heavily opposed: Favor 18%, Oppose 76%, Undecided 6%. Members of other denominations had a majority in favor of the Amendment: Favor 57%, Oppose 37%, Undecided 6%.)

The organization then asked respondents how they would vote on this measure: "Equality of rights under the law shall not be denied or abridged by the United States or by a state on account of sex." Favor 58 percent, Oppose 32 percent, Undecided 10 percent. (On this wording, which differed from the text of the Equal Rights Amendment only by the substitution of the word "a" for "any" before "state," even a majority in the Mormon church approved the principle behind the ERA: Favor 51 percent, Oppose 38 percent, Undecided 11 percent. Members of other denominations were even more favorable: Favor 76 percent, Oppose 16 percent, Undecided 8 percent.) Source: J. Roy Bardsley, "Voters Opposed to ERA, But Support Its Concept," *Salt Lake Tribune*, May 11, 1980, p. A1.

12. On January 11 and 12, 1982, the *Daily Oklahoman* conducted a survey of 400 voting-age Oklahomans "designed by an independent polling service so that it has 95 percent reliability and no more than a 5 percent sampling error." Asked, "Do you agree with the statement, 'Equality of rights under the law shall not be denied or abridged by the United States or any state on account of sex?'" 81 percent of the sample agreed. Only 9 percent disagreed, and 11 percent were either uncertain or wouldn't say (percentages sum to 101 due to rounding). However, asked, "Should Oklahoma approve the ERA?" only 44 percent agreed, 39 percent disagreed, and 17 percent were uncertain or wouldn't say. *Daily Oklahoman*, January 14, 1982, pp. 1, 53. (Note: the 17 percent is composed of 15.1 percent "uncertain" and 2.0 percent "wouldn't say." Presumably, this is why Daniels and Darcy report 15 percent "don't know" in table A4.)

Similarly, while 98 percent of a sample of women on the boards of
Chicago suburban civic and women's organizations agreed that "the United
States and individual states should not deny any person his or her rights on
account of the person's sex," only 57 percent agreed that "the Equal Rights
Amendment should be ratified and become the law of the land" (Trudy
Haffron Bers and Susan Gluck Mezey, "Support for Feminist Goals among
Leaders of Women's Community Groups," *Signs: Journal of Women in
Culture and Society* 6 [1981]: 737–748, table 1, $N = 219$, no date given).
    Supporters of the ERA were often surprised at the gap between
support of the words or principle in the ERA and the ERA itself. See, for
example, "Surprisingly, there is a stronger positive response from people
when asked if they support the text of the Amendment as opposed to the
ERA" ("Women Can Make the Difference," NOW pamphlet [n.d.,;
probably late 1981]. p. 3); or " . . . when the polls are taken on the wording
of the Equal Rights Amendment, the polls come back strongly in favor of it.
When you have a poll saying, 'Do you support the ERA?', surprisingly the
results are different" (Representative Matijevich, Illinois House of Representatives, June 18, 1980, p. 114). Some ERA supporters, however, attributed the gap (only partly correctly, in my view) to the way the opponents
had been able to distort the meaning of the ERA in the public's mind. For
example, the U.S. Commission on Civil Rights, in a widely distributed
brochure entitled "The Equal Rights Amendment: Guaranteeing Equal
Rights for Women under the Constitution" (Washington, D.C.: Government Printing Office, 1981), commented that "the gap between reality and
myth concerning the meaning of the Equal Rights Amendment" is "illus-
trated by" the Utah poll showing strong support for the language of the
ERA but opposition to the ERA itself: ". . . such conflicting responses to
the two questions are not easy to reconcile" (pp. 1–2). The commission
pointed out that "this gap [between "reality and myth"] has significantly
interfered with efforts to add the amendment to our federal constitution"
(p. 1).

    13. These data derive from James W. Prothro and Charles M. Grigg's
classic, "Fundamental Principles of Democracy: Bases of Agreement and
Disagreement," *Journal of Politics* 22 (1960): 276–294, no exact date or
percentage given. I am not here arguing that Americans tend to endorse all
kinds of abstract principles but pull back from their practical implications.
Everything depends on the specific principle and the specific application.
Thus my argument is not at odds with findings that Americans favor
spending on specific welfare programs but also believe that "[s]ocial problems . . . could be solved more effectively if only the Government would
keep its hands off . . ." (Lloyd A. Free and Hadley Cantril. *The Political
Beliefs of Americans* [New York: Simon and Schuster, 1968], p. 24).

    14. *Roth v. U.S.,* 354 U.S. 476 (1957).

    15. *Mapp v. Ohio,* 367 U.S. 643 (1961); and *Miranda v. Arizona,* 384
U.S. 436 (1966).

16. *School District of Abington v. Schempp*, 374 U.S. 203 (1963).

17. *Green v. County School Board of New Kent County*, 391 U.S. 430 (1968).

18. *Roe v. Wade*, 410 U.S. 113 (1973).

19. See, for example, Robert G. McClosky. *The American Supreme Court* (Chicago: University of Chicago Press, 1960); or Alexander M. Bickel, *The Least Dangerous Branch* (Indianapolis, Ind.: Bobbs-Merrill, 1962).

20. Seymour Martin Lipset and William Schneider, *The Confidence Gap* (New York: Free Press, 1983), chap. 2.

Chapter 4

1. In 1964 the Gallup organization asked a sample of the American public. "Have you followed the discussion about presidential succession in the event President Johnson or a Vice President dies in office?"—Yes 53 percent, No 47 percent. Those who answered in the affirmative were asked, "It has been proposed that the Secretary of State succeed to the Office of the Presidency instead of the Speaker of the House, as at present. Would you favor such a change, or not?"—Favor 46 percent, Oppose 36 percent, No opinion 18 percent (Gallup survey no. 683–k, January 2–7, 1964, reported in the Gallup Poll, p. 1862).

2. Paul G. Willis and George L. Willis, "The Politics of the Twenty-second Amendment," *Western Political Quarterly* 5 (1952): 477.

3. AIPO survey of May 1947, reported in the Louisville *Courier-Journal* of March 7, 1951, and cited in ibid.

4. Interview dates February 16–21, 1941; March 5–10, 1948, and February 1–5, 1953, the Gallup Poll, vol. 1, pp. 271, 722; vol. 2, p. 1121. For opinions on the issue after ratification, see Louis Harris, "Growing Number of Whites Feel Demonstrators Hurt Rights Cause," *Washington Post*, July 12, 1965, p. A3.

5. Hazel Erskine, "The Polls: The Politics of Age," *Public Opinion Quarterly* 35 (1971): 482, 485–486.

6. Even the Eighteenth Amendment did not, by report, generate intense, organized opposition among the *public*. The United States Brewers' Association engaged in a massive and heavily funded campaign against the amendment, but the association focused on trying to bribe the state

legislators directly, engineer fraudulent elections, and boycott businesses that took protemperance positions. The heavily German association (most of the speakers in its opening convention made their remarks in German), already weakened by the strong anti-German sentiment that arose before and during World War I, lost even further legitimacy when its corrupt tactics resulted in indictment after indictment by state and federal grand juries. The antiprohibition public was unorganized (John Kobler, *Ardent Spirits: The Rise and Fall of Prohibition* [New York: G. P. Putnam's Sons, 1973], esp. pp. 95, 203–205).

7. See *Cong. Rec.*, May 27, 1924, p. 9598, for the text of the amendment; April 26, 1924, p. 7295, for the vote in the House of Representatives; and June 2, 1924, p. 10142, for the Senate vote.

8. Clement E. Vose, *Constitutional Change: Amendment Politics and Supreme Court Litigation since 1900* (Lexington, Mass: D. C. Heath, 1972), p. 249.

9. Lemons, pp. 216–225, documents the extensive red-baiting that the opposition engaged in, calling the amendment a "highly socialistic measure" inspired by "Bolshevism," and claiming, in Lemons's paraphrase, "that every communist in the nation was behind the child-labor amendment" (p. 222). These attacks were intertwined with attacks on the social feminists who promoted the amendment, as when one pamphlet argued that Florence Kelley was the chief promoter of communism in the United States, that Jane Addams was aiding the Communist cause, and that Carrie Chapman Catt's writings paralleled those of the Communist party, making her "intentionally or otherwise . . . a broadcaster for the Communists" (p. 224). On the child-labor amendment, see also Vose, pp. 247–252: and Stephen B. Wood, *Constitutional Politics in the Progressive Era: Child Labor and the Law* (Chicago: University of Chicago Press, 1968), pp. 300–301.

10. *United States v. Darby*, 312 U.S. 100 (1941), overruling *Hammer v. Dagenhart*, 247 U.S. 251 (1918). Public opinion polling had not been developed in the years between 1924 and 1937, when the child-labor amendment was before the states. But in 1939, "eight out of ten members of the public favored 'an amendment to the Constitution prohibiting child labor.' (Gallup: March 28, 1936)" (Lloyd A. Free and Hadley Cantril, *The Political Beliefs of Americans: A Study of Public Opinion* [New York: Simon and Schuster, 1968], p. 10).

11. *H.J. Res. 693*, 88th Cong. 1st sess. cited in Vose, p. 351.

12. Vose, pp. 351–352.

13. GSS 1974, 1976, 1978, 1982, and 1983.

14. The Harris Survey 1982, no. 20, ISSN 0273–1037, release March 11, 1982 (February 12–17, 1982; $N = 1,253$; telephone).

15. In 1979, Harris asked:

> Governor Jerry Brown of California has come out in favor of an amendment to the federal Constitution that would require the federal government not to spend more than it receives in revenues in any fiscal year—in other words, to have a balanced budget. Would you favor or oppose such a constitutional amendment?

Responses were: Favor 69 percent, Oppose 23 percent, Not sure 8 percent (January 17–22, 1979; $N = 1,498$; telephone; ABC News/Harris Survey. vol. I, no. 16. ISSN 1063–4846, release February 8, 1979). In 1981 Harris asked:

> The U.S. Senate has passed a new amendment to the constitution which would require that the federal government have a balanced budget each year—that the federal spending would not be greater than federal revenues. To make it difficult to spend more than the government takes in, deficit spending could be authorized by Congress only when 60 percent of the Congress favored such spending. The only exception would be a war-time emergency, when a majority of Congress could spend more money than the federal government takes in. In addition, the federal debt limit could be raised only by a 60 percent vote of the Congress. If Congress wanted to spend more money, it would have to raise taxes to pay for it.

Would you favor or oppose that constitutional amendment if it meant that [interviewer names in succession nine entitlement programs plus the present defense budget] had to be cut by 26 percent? [The figure of 26 percent was arrived at by taking the size of the current deficit and assuming that all government programs would be cut equally if the Constitution required a balanced budget.]

The highest percentage in favor came when the amendment meant cutting "the present defense budget": Favor 45 percent, Oppose 49 percent, Not Sure 6 percent. The lowest percentage in favor came when the amendment meant cutting "Social Security payments to the elderly": Favor 10 percent, Oppose 88 percent, Not Sure 2 percent. However, after two more questions on the balanced budget amendment, Harris asked,

> All in all, do you favor or oppose passage of a constitutional amendment to require a balanced, federal budget as an effective way to keep federal spending under control?

In response, a majority still favored the amendment: Favor 66 percent, Oppose 29 percent, Not Sure 5 percent (August 5–10, 1982: $N = 1,254$;

telephone; Harris Survey 1982, no. 69, ISSN 0273-1037, release August 30, 1982).

16. The survey data on these issues follows:

Representation as a state for the District of Columbia: "Do you favor or oppose your state voting for a new constitutional amendment that will let the District of Columbia (Washington, D.C.) elect two U.S. senators and a congressman?" Favor 57 percent, Oppose 32 percent, Not Sure 11 percent (December 21–26, 1978; $N = 1,498$; telephone; ABC News/Harris Survey, vol. 1, no. 14, ISSN 0163-4846, release February 1, 1979).

Presidential election by popular vote: "Would you favor or oppose having a President chosen by popular vote, instead of determining the outcome by electoral votes for each state?" Favor 77 percent, Oppose 21 percent, Not Sure 2 percent (December 3–6, 1980; $N = 1,200$; telephone; Harris Survey 1981, No. 4, ISSN 0273–1037, release January 12, 1981).

17. "Do you favor or oppose a constitutional amendment to ban legalized abortion?" Favor 33 percent, Oppose 61 percent, Not Sure 6 percent (February 12–17, 1982; $N = 1,253$; telephone; Harris Survey 1982, no. 2, ISSN 0273-1037, release March 15, 1982).

See also: "A 62–31 percent majority of Americans opposes a constitutional amendment to ban legalized abortion." Of those who opposed such an amendment, 27 percent would "certainly" and 36 percent would "probably" not vote for a congressional candidate whose views they mostly agreed with but who took a contrary stand on this issue. Of those who favored such an amendment, 32 percent would "certainly" and 39 percent would "probably" not vote for a candidate who took the opposite stand (July 9–14, 1982, $N = 1,250$; telephone; Harris Survey 1982, no. 64, ISSN 0273-1037, release August 12, 1982).

See also: "Now let me ask you about some specific policies included in the Republican 1980 platform adopted at the 1980 Republican convention and in Reagan's acceptance speech. For each, tell me if your own reaction was very favorable, moderately favorable, moderately unfavorable, or very unfavorable? . . . Advocating passage of a constitutional amendment making all abortions illegal." Favorable 35 percent, Unfavorable 61 percent, Not sure 4 percent (July 18–21, 1980; $N = 1,458$ "likely voters"; telephone; ABC News/Harris Survey, vol. 2, no. 93, ISSN 0163-4846, release July 13, 1980).

In 1980, when Gallup asked, "Now here are some amendments to the Constitution that are currently being talked about. Would you read down that list, and for each one tell me whether you would favor or oppose such an amendment?" 79 percent of the sample favored "an amendment to require a balanced national budget—to prevent the government from spending more money that it takes in, except in certain specified cases of crisis or emergency," 66 percent favored "an amendment to assure equal rights for women," 62 percent favored "an amendment to limit the number of employees government can have," but only 44 percent favored "an amendment to make abortions illegal unless the mother's life is in danger." *Roper Reports*, 80–8, (August 16–23, 1980; N = 2,001).

In 1984, surveys from the *Los Angeles Times* asked 7,310 voters as they left the voting booths on November 6, "Mark an 'x' if you approve of any of the following programs and leave it blank if you don't." Only 23 percent marked "approve of constitutional amendment to prohibit abortion" (*Public Opinion* [December/January 1985]: 37).

18. The correlation of an index of state legislative support for the ERA with annual median family income in 1975 is .50; with revenue from state and local taxes in 1972, .53; and with states' per pupil expenditure for education in 1975, .61. Other measures of state wealth follow this pattern. The correlation of state support for the ERA with percentage of votes for Wallace in the 1968 presidential election is -.63, and with percentage of population Baptist in 1971, -.54 (John S. Robey, Joe Lenart, Sharon Pruett, James Cox, and Frank von Menhaus, "American State Policies and the Women's Movement," *State Government* 54 [1981]: 62, 63). The correlation of state wealth with support of the ERA holds up quite well with southernness controlled (e.g., a reduction from .41 to .35) (Janet K. Boles, "Systematic Factors Underlying Legislative Responses to Woman Suffrage and the Equal Rights Amendment," *Women and Politics* 2 [1982]: 5–22, table 1, using percent of the legislature present and voting for the ERA and per capita income in 1970. As Boles indicates and one would expect, both the correlations are lower with dichotomous passage/rejection as the independent variable.) Note that while there is a strong correlation between state wealth and state legislative support of the ERA, there is no correlation between an individual's income and his or her support of the ERA (table A2). Refusal to ratify the ERA also has a statistically significant relation to the percentage of a state's population in eight major fundamentalist denominations and the Mormon church, to a state's degree of "conservatism" on the Albin Stein scale, to delay in adopting new policies generally on Walker's measure of state innovation, and to refusal to ratify the women's and eighteen-year-old suffrage amendments (Ernest H. Wohlenberg, "Correlates of Equal Rights Amendment Ratification," *Social Science Quarterly* 60 [1980]: 676–684). For more on the relation of ERA ratification to state innovation, see Mark R. Daniels, R. Darcy, and Joseph Westphal, "ERA: A Case of Arrested Diffusion" (paper presented at the annual meeting of the Midwest Political Science Association, Milwaukee, Wisc., 1982). In Boles's analysis, ERA ratification continues to have a significant relation to general innovation with southernness controlled. See also Ethel B. Jones, "ERA Voting: Labor Force Attachment, Marriage and Religion," *Journal of Legal Studies* 12 (1983): 157–168.

Chapter 5

1. Lisa Cronin Wohl, "The ERA: What the Hell Happened in New York?" *Ms.*, March 1976, p. 96.

2. See also:

JM: If you were to boil down all the arguments for the ERA to the most important, what is the one most important . . . ?
NOW OFFICIAL: The most convincing or the most important?
JM: Well, let's do both of them.
NOW OFFICIAL: I think the most convincing is, and one that should have been used much earlier, is the 59 cents argument, the equal pay argument—the equal money, the equal economic realities argument. Maybe it's also the most important.

3. See U.S. Bureau of the Census, "Money Income Households, Families, and Persons in the United States: 1982," *Consumer Income,* series P-60, no. 142 (Washington, D.C.: Government Printing Office, 1984), table 39. By 1981 the ratio was up to 60 cents, and by 1982 to 61 cents.

4. "ERA ERA ERA YES YES YES," NOW pamphlet (n.d.; probably 1980). See also "ERA and the 59 Cent Wage Gap," NOW pamphlet (1981).

5. See Carol Sherman, "Legal Memorandum to the Hon. Birch Bayh," *Cong. Rec.,* October 7, 1970, p. 35474.

6. See Susan Deller Ross, "Sex Discrimination and 'Protective' Labor Legislation, Part IV: The EEOC Record," in *Cong. Rec.,* October 7, 1970, pp. 35468–35470; and Brown et al., *Women's Rights,* p. 210.

7. See Susan Deller Ross, Ibid., "Part V: The Federal Court Approach"; and *Rosenfeld v. Southern Pacific Co.,* 444 F. 2d 1219 (9th Cir. 1971).

8. It is true that the Equal Pay Act, in combination with Title VII, can be interpreted by the courts in a way that allows employers still to pay men and women widely differing amounts through the strategem of designing jobs so that one small part of a job is something that, by and large, men are more qualified for, like heavy lifting. This technique could make legal different salaries based on job segregation even when the jobs are, in most respects, identical. See Barbara Allen Babcock, Ann E. Freedman, Eleanor Holmes Norton, Susan C. Ross, *Sex Discrimination and the Law: Causes and Remedies.* (Boston, Mass.: Little, Brown and Company, 1975), pp. 441–509. See also Wendy Williams, *Babcock, Freedman, Norton, Ross' Sex Discrimination and the Law Supplement* (Boston, Mass.: Little, Brown and Company, 1978), pp. 146–172.
The ERA would not have directly eliminated loopholes like this in the Equal Pay Act. Rather, as a general constitutional mandate for women's equality, it would have encouraged legislators and judges to look more

critically at the ways employers were using these loopholes to pay women less than men. However, even if all the loopholes were closed in the Equal Pay Act, this would not have significantly effected the gap between men's and women's wages.

9. Larry Suter and Herman Miller, "Income Differences between Men and Career Women," *American Journal of Sociology* 78 (1973): 962–968, table 1. For comparable, more recent findings, see Mary Corcoran, Greg Duncan, and Martha Hill, "The Economic Fortunes of Women and Children: Lessons from the Panel Study of Income Dynamics," *Signs* 10 (1984): 232–248. Corcoran et al.'s work indicates that about one-third of the gap between women's and men's wages is accounted for by differences in schooling, years of work experience, years in the labor force, and job interruption. More of the gap (at least a third, if Sutor and Miller's data are correct) may be accounted for by differential tracking into different occupations, which, since it is intimately related to the presumption of women's primary responsibility for child care, is a matter of both "choice" and discrimination. Finally, more of the gap may be accounted for by differences in the number of hours worked by "full-time" males and females, differences in the degree fields of college graduates, and differences in aspirations on the job. These "explanations" are, of course, themselves partly products of discrimination; they show only that the patterns of disadvantage both include and go far deeper than surface-level discrimination at the workplace. See also Earl F. Mellor, "Investigating the Differences in Weekly Earnings of Women and Men," *Monthly Labor Review* 107 (1984): 17–33; and Thomas N. Daymont and Paul J. Andrisani, "Job Preferences, College Major and the Gender Gap in Earnings," *Journal of Human Resources* 19 (1984): 408–428, and citations therein.

10. See Benson Rosen and Thomas Jerdee, "The Influence of Sex Role Stereotypes on Evaluations of Male and Female Supervisory Behavior," *Journal of Applied Psychology* 57 (1973): 44–48. See also G. W. Bowman, M. B. Worthy, and S. A. Greyser, "Are Women Executives People?" *Harvard Business Review* 43 (1965): 14–30, in which over two-thirds of the 1,000 male executives and nearly one-fifth of the 900 female executives interviewed reported that they themselves would not feel comfortable working for a woman.

The public, too, seems happier with men in positions of responsibility. In 1982, in a *New York Times* national survey, 49 percent of the women interviewed and 49 percent of the men said they would trust a man more than a woman to be their doctor (6 and 15 percent, respectively, said they would trust a woman more; 41 and 30 percent said it made no difference. Egalitarian sentiment was up from 1970, when 70 percent of the women and 66 percent of the men trusted a man, and only 18 and 28 percent said it made no difference). In the same survey, 49 percent of the women and 50 percent of the men said they would trust a man more to be their bus driver (13 and 9 percent said they would trust a woman more, while only 34 and 33 percent said it would make no difference) (*New York Times* telephone survey,

November 11–20, 1982; *N* women = 927, *N* men = 382. I am grateful to
Kathleen A. Frankovic, CBS News and consultant on this survey, for
providing these data).

11. Philip Goldberg, "Are Women Prejudiced against Women?"
Transaction 5 (1968): 28–30. Goldberg's study had an *N* of 40, all women.
His findings were in the expected direction for articles in all the fields he
tested but reached statistical significance only for articles on city planning,
linguistics, and law. Monica Morris, University of Southern California,
"Anti-Feminism: Some Discordant Data" (paper presented at the Pacific
Sociological Association Meetings, Anaheim, Calif., 1970), replicated the
study with an *N* of 90 men and women, with mixed and statistically insignificant results. In Morris' replication, the only instance in which differences in
attributed competences by gender reached statistical significance in either
direction was in the expected direction, in the article on law. Morris's
findings may have been weaker than Goldberg's because she announced to
her subjects before the exercise that she was investigating "the views of
college students regarding women's role in society."

12. *Dothard v. Rawlinson,* 433 U.S. 321 (1977).

13. In order to state a case for sex discrimination either under Title
VII or under the Fourteenth Amendment, it is necessary to prove that the
employment or other decision was based on gender. If the ERA were
ratified, it is most likely that the Court would continue its present tripartite
burden of proof rule, established for gender cases in *Texas Department of
Community Affairs v. Burdine*, 450 U.S. 248 (1981), that the plaintiff must
first prove a prima facie case of sex or race discrimination, the defendant
must then articulate a nondiscriminatory reason for his or her decision, and
the plaintiff must then show that the defendant's nondiscriminatory reason
was a "sham." The Court concluded in *Burdine* that the "ultimate burden
of persuading the trier of fact that the defendant intentionally discriminated
against the plaintiff remains at all times with the plaintiff" (ibid. at 253). At
the moment, this is as true with race cases as with gender cases. *McDonnell
Douglas v. Green,* 411 U.S. 792 (1973). Raising gender to the status of race
(making it a fully "suspect" classification) would thus have no effect on the
rule. For a discussion of the "suspect" versus a "prohibited" classification
with two exceptions, see below Chapter 6 n. 23.

14. For purposes of the equal protection and due process clauses, state
action exists when "a state has so far insinuated itself into a position of
interdependence with an alleged violator of a plaintiff's civil rights that it
must be recognized as a joint participant in the challenged activity . . ."
Bellnier v. Lund, 438 F. Supp. 47 (D.C. N.Y. 1977).

15. Beginning in 1974, the Court began to narrow its definition of state
action. First, it held that the actual action that is challenged has to be such
that it could "be fairly treated as that of the state itself." *Jackson v.*

Metropolitan Edison Co., 419 U.S. 345, 351 (1974). "The mere fact that a business is subject to state regulation does not in itself convert its action into that of the state. . . . Nor does the fact that the regulation is extensive and detailed. . . ." Ibid., at 350, citations omitted. This case also suggested that simple state approval or authorization of a practice would not constitute state action if the "initiative" did not come from the state and the state had "not put its weight on the side of a proposed practice by ordering it."

Two years later the Court narrowed the definition further by excluding the actions of enterprises that received state tax benefits or subsidies but would not be forced to stop the action by the state's revoking the benefit or subsidy. *Simon v. Eastern Kentucky Welfare Rights Organization*, 426 U.S. 26 (1976).

In 1982, the Court narrowed the definition further by saying that even if a state extensively regulates a particular enterprise, "state action" is involved only if the state regulations "require," or in other ways influence, the discriminatory act or if the state "is responsible for that decision" to perform the discriminatory act. *Blum v. Yaretsky*, 457 U.S. 991 (1982), at 1008. See also *Rendell-Baker v. Kohn*, 457 U.S. 830 (1982), and *Lugar v. Edmonson Oil Co.*, 457 U.S. 922 (1982).

It is not certain, of course, that the Supreme Court would apply to the ERA the standards of state action evolved under the Fourteenth Amendment. Looking at the legislative history, in which legislators often refer to women's economic disadvantage as one reason for bringing the ERA into existence, the Court might conclude that a more flexible set of standards should apply under the ERA. In 1968 the Court used the legislative history to interpret the Thirteenth Amendment in *Jones v. Alfred H. Meyer Co.*, 392 U.S. 409 (1968), to reach private discrimination in the sale or rental of housing.

The "state action" concept applies only to instances in which the Court would invalidate discriminatory practices under the constitutional mandate of the ERA. Beyond this, Congress could legislate under section 2 of the ERA, creating *statutory* bans on discrimination that the Court might well conclude could legitimately reach into the private sphere. No one has suggested, however, that in the area of employment Congress needs further enabling power beyond that already granted, in the Supreme Court's view, by a combination of section 5 of the Fourteenth Amendment and the interstate commerce clause. *Heart of Atlanta Motel Inc. v. U.S.*, 379 U.S. 241 (1964).

16. See decisions in *City of Los Angeles Department of Water and Power v. Manhart*, 435 U.S. 702 (1978); *Arizona Governing Committee v. Norris*, 463 U.S. 1073 (1983); and *Spirt v. Teachers Insurance and Annuity Association*, 475 F. Supp. 1298 (S.D. N.Y. 1979), aff'd in part, rev'd in part on other grounds, 691 F. 2d 1054 (2d Cir. 1982), vacated and remanded, 51 U.S.L.W. 3937 (1983). Title VII applies to employers and does not extend to individual consumers, who normally buy automobile and life insurance. For a discussion of the ERA's applicability to consumer insurance, see

Barbara A. Brown and Ann E. Freedman, "The Impact of the ERA on Financial Individual Rights: Sex Averaging in Insurance," in Equal Rights Amendment Project of the California Commission on the Status of Women, eds., *Impact ERA: Limitations and Possibilities* (Milbrae, Calif.: Les Femmes Publishing, 1976; hereafter, *Impact ERA*), pp. 127–138. Brown and Freedman do not address the issue of state action.

17. In 1980, a Pennsylvania Court held that governmental regulation of auto insurance rates did not constitute state action sufficient to maintain an equal protection challenge by male plaintiffs. *Murphy v. Harleysville Mutual Ins. Co.*, 282 Pa. Super 244, 422 A. 2d 1097, cert. denied 454 U.S. 896 (1980). In spite of the general narrowing of the definition of state action, however, two factors favor the possibility that insurance companies' use of gender-based rates could constitute state action. First, since *Wagner v. Sheltz,* 471 F. Supp. 903 (D.C. Conn. 1979), federal courts have considered the nature of the right violated when deciding on state action. Less state involvement might support a finding of state action if the ERA had passed and sex discrimination had been at issue.

Second, some state laws explicitly give their state insurance commissioner the authority to disapprove "discriminatory" policies. If the ERA were to be regarded as a public policy statement that distinctions by gender are discriminatory unless proven otherwise, then such laws might be held to bring the state into an active role regarding discrimination. Certainly an ERA would make it easier for a commissioner to hold gender-based rates discriminatory. For example, in 1984 the Supreme Court of Pennsylvania (which has adopted an absolute and far-reaching interpretation of its state ERA but in 1980 had ruled that auto insurance did not include enough state action to come under the equal protection clause) concluded that when the state's insurance commissioner ruled an insurance company's gender-based rates "unfairly discriminatory," he acted within his statutory authority under the state Rate Act, which forbade "unfairly discriminatory" rates. He did not "attempt to impose his personal theories and perceptions of social policy upon the insurance industry," because the state ERA "constrained" him to interpret the phrase "unfairly discriminatory" the way he did. *Hartford Accident and Indemnity Company v. Insurance Commissioner of the Commonwealth of Pennsylvania*, J-76-1984, reargued April 10, 1984, reprinted in *The Impact of the Equal Rights Amendment,* Hearings before the Subcommittee on the Constitution of the Committee on the Judiciary, U.S. Senate, 98th Congr., 1st and 2d sess., on S.J. Res. 10 (hereafter *Impact Hearings*), vol. 2, p. 763. The Court specifically said that "state action" in the federal sense was not an issue in this case.

18. Some feminist lawyers made a limited version of this argument in the 1983 Senate hearings on a new ERA but did not argue that the Court's adopting discriminatory impact interpretation of the ERA would affect the question of comparable worth. See below, Chapter 6 n. 26, for Brown et al.'s 1971 interpretation of disparate impact in the ERA, and n. 28 for the 1983 legislative history regarding disparate impact and the ERA.

19. See below, Chapter 6, discussion of *Washington v. Davis* and aftermath.

20. *Guardians Association v. Civil Service Commission of the City of New York,* 463 U.S. 582 (1983).

21. See, for example, Carolyn Shaw Bell, "Economic Realities Anticipated," in *Impact ERA.* Bell concluded that "ERA will have no impact one way or the other" on women's pay. See also Anne S. Miner, "The Lesson of Affirmative Action for the Equal Rights Amendment," ibid., p. 93: "Although it is commonly believed that the ERA will immediately affect employment opportunity for women, patterns of discrimination at work are actually the least likely to be *quickly* affected by the ERA."

22. September 19, 1945: "Do you think women should or should not receive the same rate of pay as men for the same work?" Should 76 percent, Should Not 17 percent, Don't Know 7 percent (AIPO files). See also Gallup Survey, no. 259-K, January 21–30, 1942: "If women replaced men in industry should they be paid the same wages as men?" Yes 78 percent, No 14 percent, Undecided 8 percent. Women were more likely to favor equal wages (85 percent) than men (71 percent) (*The Gallup Poll* [New York: Random House, 1972], p. 322). The percentages favoring equal pay were considerably lower if the question specified that the man but not the woman had children to support. Thus, September 19, 1945: "If a young single woman is doing exactly the same kind of work as a married man with children (and does the work equally as well), do you think she should (or should not) receive (exactly) the same rate of pay?" Yes 66 percent, No 28 percent No Opinion 6 percent (AIPO files). These answers indicate that while some respondents were simply sexist, others were thinking of distributing income on the basis of need as well as on the basis of work performed.

23. Gallup Survey, no. 530-K, May 2–7, 1954: "Do you approve of paying women the same salaries as men, if they are doing the same work?" Approve 87 percent, Disapprove and No Opinion (not disaggregated) 13 percent (*Gallup Poll,* p. 1240).

24. The last figures I have are from 1962, AIPO no. 660, June 28–July 3, 1962: "Do you approve or disapprove of paying women the same salaries as men, if they are doing the same work?" Approve 88 percent, Disapprove 10 percent, No Opinion 2 percent (AIPO files).

Chapter 6

1. I would like to thank Pamela Rothenberg, a student at the Northwestern University Law School, for careful comments on an earlier draft of this chapter and extensive work on nn. 43, 45, and 50.

2. Letty Cottin Pogrebin, "A Conversation with Pollster Dan Yankelovitch," *Ms.* (July/May 1982): 143.

3. *Frontiero v. Richardson,* 411 U.S. 677 (1973).

4. *Craig v. Boren,* 429 U.S. 190 (1976).

5. Representative Bluthardt, Illinois House of Representatives, June 18, 1980, p. 143; see also p. 144.

6. Representative Hudson, ibid., p. 136.

7. Representative Bluthardt, ibid., p. 144. Compare the early debate in the Illinois House of Representatives, June 7, 1972, p. 32, in which Representative Bluthardt, who changed his vote more than once, gave as reasons for his changing to opposition: (1) the resolutions at the International Women's Year conference in Houston, Texas; (2) proponents' boycotts of states that had not ratified the ERA; (3) vote-trading in the legislature for the ERA; and (4) "what the federal courts and many of their senile judges" had done with the Civil Rights Act and might do with the ERA.

The legislative debates in Illinois suggest that before 1980 (and possibly thereafter as well) the Supreme Court's evolution had not fully penetrated the consciousnesses of the legislative opposition to the ERA. In the 1978 debate, under a rule of debate that allowed only one proponent and one opponent, the single speaker chosen to represent the opposition documented his first and major point, that the ERA would "accomplish absolutely nothing," by saying:

> When the Congress of the United States a number of years ago voted on this issue, there were certain needs present and maybe necessarily ready for cure by a Constitutional Amendment. By and large the same constitutional lawyers who we refer to as Congressmen sold out to proponents shortly thereafter when they started passing every imaginable law to cure the very things that the Equal Rights Amendment was supposed to take care of. At the present time there are adequate federal laws to take care of every possible, conceivable area of discrimination.
>
> —*Representative Griesheimer, Illinois House of Representatives, June 7, 1978, p. 26*

If we ignore the seeming contradiction in acknowledging that in 1972 there were "needs" but describing the congressmen who met those needs as having "sold out," and ignore as well the slur on the congressmen's characters implied by the phrase "who we refer to as Congressmen," the main conclusion we can draw from these remarks is that two years after *Craig v. Boren* a leading opposition legislator could realize that there had been movement on women's issues since 1972, but ascribe these developments primarily, if not totally, to acts of Congress.

8. *Royster Guano Co. v. Virginia,* 253 U.S. 412, 415 (1919):

But the classification must be reasonable, not arbitrary, and must rest upon some ground of difference having a fair and substantial relation to the object of the legislation, so that all persons similarly circumstanced shall be treated alike.

9. *Goesaert v. Cleary,* 335 U.S. 464, 466 (1948). Michigan, the state in question, did not bar women from the less highly paid job of bar waitress.

10. *Korematsu v. United States,* 323 U.S. 214, 216 (1944).

11. *McLaughlin v. Florida,* 379 U.S. 184, 196 (1964). See also *Loving v. Virginia,* 388 U.S. 1, 11 (1967).

12. For a summary, see *Frontiero v. Richardson,* 411 U.S. 677, 682 (1973).

13. *Reed v. Reed,* 404 U.S. 71, 76 (1971), quoting *Royster Guano Co. v. Virginia.*

14. See, for example, the comments of Justice Brennan in *Craig v. Boren,* below.

15. *Craig v. Boren,* 429 U.S. 190 (1976). The constitutional status of this new "intermediate" test is unclear. The opinion of the Court (by Justice Brennan, joined by Justices White, Marshall, Powell, and Stevens) did not explicitly set forth a new standard in *Craig.* Rather, Brennan wrote that "previous cases established that classifications by gender must serve important government objectives and must be substantially related to the achievement of those objectives" (ibid. at 197). This wording and the opinion's subsequent use of *Reed* suggest that the Court was reinterpreting *Reed* as having always implicitly used this standard. Only the concurrences and dissents in *Craig* indicate that *Craig* could be thought of as setting forth a new "middle-tier" (Justice Powell, concurring in ibid., at 211) or "intermediate" (Justice Rehnquist, dissenting in ibid., at 218) level of scrutiny.

Moreover, even in *Craig* a majority of the Court did not adopt the new "intermediate" test. Of the five justices who made up the majority opinion in *Craig,* four had been willing to make sex a full "suspect" classification in *Frontiero v. Richardson* (see below, pages 6–16). Justice Powell, who joined the four in *Craig* and thus gave them a majority, wrote a special concurrence in *Craig* specifically disavowing the idea of a new "middle-tier" test, claiming that the case could be settled simply under the old "fair and substantial relation" wording of *Royster Guano v. Virginia* (1920), but also acknowledging that "candor compels the recognition" that the Court since *Reed* had subjected gender-based classification "to a more critical examination" with a "sharper focus" than in other, nonsuspect cases (*Craig v. Boren* at 211 and 210).

The content of the intermediate test is also unclear. For simplicity, I have followed in the text the suggestion of Nancy S. Erickson ("Equality between the Sexes in the 1980's," *Cleveland State Law Review* 28 (1979): 593 n. 5) that in *Craig* the Court characterized both the legitimacy of the governmental end and the relationship of the governmental means to that end as intermediate—falling between the test for suspect and the test for nonsuspect classifications. However, as Erickson points out, the Court had stated in a footnote in a case before *Craig* that the "state interest required has been characterised as 'overriding,' 'compelling,' 'important,' or 'substantial.' We attribute no particular significance to these variations in diction." *In re Griffiths*, 413 U.S. 717 (1973) at 722 n. 9, citations omitted. "Thus," Erickson concludes, "the 'ends scrutiny' may be the same under the *Craig* test as under the compelling state interest test."

Some commentators believe that the *Craig* "intermediate" test is really the suspect classification test in disguise, and they urge the Court to admit as much. See Ruth Bader Ginsburg, Brief for the American Civil Liberties Union as amicus curiae, *Wengler v. Druggists Mutual Ins. Co.* (1980), p. 49: " . . . while the court has not yet officially stamped sex classifications 'suspect,' all is in place save the seal." (Ginsburg cites in support of her contention "The Supreme Court, 1978 Term," *Harvard Law Review* 93 [1979]: 60, 130, 135, and n. 35.) Nevertheless, in *Wengler* the Court rejected this suggestion and continued to use the "intermediate" wording, stating explicitly that "gender-based discrimination must . . . satisfy the *Craig v. Boren* standard." *Wengler v. Druggists Mutual Ins. Co.*, 446 U.S. 142, 150 (1979). Other lawyers believe that the Court took a major step backward in *Craig* from the position of all-but-suspect-in-name that it had taken in *Frontiero*.

16. *Frontiero v. Richardson*, 411 U.S. 677 (1973).

17. *Vorchheimer v. School District of Philadelphia*, 532 F. 2d 880 (3d Cir. 1976), affirmed by an equally divided Court, 430 U.S. 703 (1977). Some think the court implicitly overruled *Vorchheimer* in *Mississippi University for Women v. Hogan* (1982) (see n. 19 below).

18. *Bernard Rostker, Director of Selective Service v. Robert Goldberg et al.*, 453 U.S. 57 (1981). See Chapters 7 and 8 for a fuller discussion of the relation of the ERA to women in the military.

19. *Michael M. v. Superior Court of Sonoma County*, 450 U.S. 464 (1981). This case upheld a California statutory rape provision that penalized only a male perpetrator and not his female counterpart. The Court

allowed the distinction to stand on the grounds that women are deterred by bearing the risk of pregnancy and that penalizing the female counterparts could deter them from reporting statutory violations.

20. *Parham v. Hughes*, 441 U.S. 347 (1979). This case held that a state could permit the mother of an illegitimate child to sue for the wrongful death of her child but permit the father to sue only if he had legitimated the child and the mother were dead or could not be accounted for.

21. *Heckler v. Matthews*, 465 U.S. 728 (1984). This case held that a temporary Social Security pension offset applicable only to men did not constitute gender-based discrimination under the equal protection component of the Fifth Amendment. This rule disadvantaged men compared to women. In the opinion of Jane Sherburne, an ERA proponent and former assistant director of the Social Security Administration, the Court would not overrule *Heckler* under an ERA because the discrimination was instituted for a limited period of time, was very narrowly drawn, and was necessary to protect legitimate expectations (*Impact Hearings*, vol. 1, pp. 57–58).

22. The best argument for the ERA's effects after 1976 is probably Ann E. Freedman's testimony in the 1983 house hearings on the ERA (Statement before the Subcommittee on Civil and Constitutional Rights of the House Judiciary Committee, November 3, 1983, printed in *Impact Hearings*, vol. 1, pp. 533–543). In that testimony Freedman argued:

> Three extremely important substantive areas in which the ERA would dictate different results than the equal protection clause are sex discrimination in the military, sex segregation in public schools, and overgeneralizations about individuals based on average physical differences between the sexes.
>
> —*P. 534*

As the next chapters (7 and 8) will indicate, there is little doubt that the ERA would have made women subject to the draft (*Rostker,* n. 18 above, thus would have been decided the other way), and would probably also, depending on the Court's interpretations, have allowed women volunteers in the military to be assigned to combat. As we will see, there are reasons to doubt that the Court would have decided that the ERA required women draftees to be sent into combat on the same basis as men, if the military opposed this plan, but even the limited moves of making women subject to the draft and allowing some women volunteers into combat positions would have had an important effect on the status of women in the United States. This, in my view, would have been the ERA's most important contribution.

Sex segregation in the public schools has been almost eliminated under the Supreme Court's rulings under the Fourteenth Amendment. *Mississippi University for Women v. Hogan,* 458 U.S. 718 (1982). The exception is *Vorchheimer* (n. 17 above, a case that does not set a precedent), which, after *Mississippi v. Hogan,* was overruled by a Pennsylvania lower court (Court of Common Pleas, Philadelphia County, Civil Division, no. 5822, August term, 1982, cited in *Newberg v. Board of Education, School District of Philadelphia* 478 A 2d 1353). In *Vorchheimer* the Supreme Court allowed gender segregation to stand under "intermediate" scrutiny, presumably because several members of the Court were persuaded that the education in the girls' school was as good as that in the boys' school. In view of recent evidence suggesting that both boys and girls, but especially girls, do better academically in schools that are segregated by gender (Helen Featherstone, "Single-Sex Schools," *Harvard Education Letter* 2 [1986]: 6), there might be some doubt as to how the Court would decide on this matter if, under an ERA, it had made gender a suspect classification. However, I think it highly likely, given the racial parallels, that under an ERA interpreted to make gender a suspect classification the Court, which needed only a one vote shift in *Vorchheimer,* would have decided both this and harder cases against gender segregation.

As for overgeneralizations based on average differences, the Court has already moved quite far under the intermediate standard on this front. *Caban v. Mohammed,* 441 U.S. 380 (1979). Using a "suspect" standard, the Court might well have decided differently in *Parham* (n. 20 above), and also in *Michael M.* (n. 19 above), although Freedman did not mention this case in her testimony. While the point of enunciating an intermediate standard is to make clear that there are differences between it and suspect scrutiny, a comparison of *Vorchheimer* with *Hogan* and of *Parham* with *Caban* suggests to me that the immediate, practical differences in these areas would be small.

The indirect, symbolic, and long-run effects of these differences might, of course, be much greater. For a persuasive argument that deciding *Michael M.* and similar cases differently would have had an important symbolic, indirect effect on judicial and public gender stereotyping, see Wendy W. Williams, "The Equality Crisis: Some Reflections on Culture, Courts, and Feminism," *Women's Rights Law Reporter* 7 (1982): 175–200. Other feminists agree. Sylvia Law writes that *Michael M.* "accepts and reinforces the sex-based stereotype that young men may legitimately engage in sexual activity and young women may not. . . . under the California law a young man is free to be sexual as long as he chooses a partner who is older than eighteen, while a young woman may not legally have sex with anyone, except her husband if she is married" ("Rethinking Sex and the Constitution," *University of Pennsylvania Law Review* 132 [1984]: 1001). See also Frances E. Olsen, "Statutory Rape: A Feminist Critique of Rights Analysis,"*Texas Law Review* 63 (1984): 387–432. However, there is no consensus among feminists on the degree to which women as a distinct group should have legal protection against specifically male sexual aggression.

For the parts of Ann Freedman's testimony that deal with the effects of interpreting the ERA to make gender a "prohibited" classification and extend its coverage to some cases of "disparate impact," see below nn. 26 and 32. For an analysis of the above cases, concluding that since 1971 "the

Supreme Court has been . . . achieving the same case results as if the ERA were already the law," see Leslie Friedman Goldstein, "The ERA and American Public Policy" (paper presented at the annual meeting of the American Political Science Association, Washington, D.C., 1984).

23. Barbara A. Brown, Thomas I. Emerson, Gail Falk, and Ann E. Freedman, "The Equal Rights Amendment: A Constitutional Basis for Equal Rights for Women," *Yale Law Journal* 80 (1971): 955–962. Hereafter, when I refer to the Yale authors' "absolute standard," making sex a "prohibited" classification, I will assume these two exceptions, following the most common exegesis of this article throughout the ratification campaign. The full story, however, is more complicated, because in the article itself and at different times thereafter the Yale authors used language suggesting from one to three exceptions. On page 890 they spoke of the "single" exception of unique physical characteristics, but on page 900 they introduced the "privacy qualification," and on page 904 an exception for affirmative action to make up for (specific acts of) past injustice. Through most of the debate they spoke of the "two narrow qualifications" of privacy and unique physical characteristics (e.g., Barbara A. Brown, Ann E. Freedman, Harriet N. Katz, and Alice Price, *Women's Rights and the Law,* [1977] p. 15), but by 1983 the two exceptions Freedman singled out for prominence had become privacy and affirmative action (Freedman, "Statement," in *Impact Hearings,* vol. 1, pp. 533–534). The authors presumably believed throughout that the courts should subject all three exceptions to strict scrutiny, but they stressed this point most with unique physical characteristics. (I am grateful to Leslie Friedman Goldstein for drawing to my attention the strength of the affirmative action exception in the original article.)

24. Some readers outside the legal profession have been taken aback by the way I write at various points of what the Supreme Court was "unlikely to do," or what it "probably," "very probably" or "almost certainly" would have done. My choice of words indicates that I do not claim perfect foresight into the future. On an issue like the ERA, however, lawyers, scholars, and political activists alike must try to predict what the Supreme Court will do. Indeed, such exercises in prediction are one of the major tasks of a practicing lawyer. The persuasive force of the prediction can derive only from the evidence marshaled to support it; the reader must consider that evidence and accept, modify, or reject the prediction accordingly.

25. The position I take here runs directly contrary to that of those who favor the prohibited classification. For example, Erickson, p. 595 n. 20: "The ERA would make sex a prohibited rather than a suspect classification"; Wexler, p. 1535: "An examination of congressional hearings and debates reveals that Congress adopted a strict interpretation of the Amendment, a position originally propounded by Professor Thomas Emerson and

three students from the Yale Law School"; Ralph Arditi, Frederick Goldberg, M. Martha Hartle, John Peters, and William Phelps, "Notes: The Sexual Segregation of American Prisons," *Yale Law Journal* 82 (1973): 1255: "The ERA's legislative history clearly indicated that Congress adopted [the] absolute interpretation. . . . Congress [gave] clear support for the absolute interpretation." See also citations in David Reid Dillon, "Congressional Intent and the ERA: A Proposed New Analysis," *Ohio State Law Journal* 40 (1979:636–661, n. 40. By 1983 the Yale position had become the official position of the pro-ERA organizations. See Ann Freedman, Phyllis Segal, and other proponents in the 1983 hearings (*Impact Hearings*, vol. 1, passim).

The most careful examination of the legislative history is, in my view, Dillon's "Congressional Intent." In particular, his fnn. 57, 78, and 79 suggest that in 1971, before the Senate hearings and the careful Senate Report, some representatives in the relatively brief debate before the House used language suggesting an absolute interpretation. He also points out (p. 643) that in 1972 Senator Bayh said on the floor of the Senate, "If the Supreme Court were to hold that discrimination based on sex, like discrimination based on race, is inherently 'suspect' . . . , then part of the reason for the amendment [the ERA] would disappear." This phrase indicates that Bayh believed that the ERA would do something more than make gender classifications suspect. Whether Bayh intended (as Dillon believes) an interpretation "almost identical" to the Yale article (p. 641), or intended (as I would guess) something vaguer, is impossible to tell from his words. Although Dillon argues that Congress intended an interpretation much like that of the Yale article, he is careful to point out that Congress proposed a "trinity of exceptions" (pp. 649–650), not just the two proposed by the Yale article. Indeed, the Senate Majority Report states that the ERA would "not prohibit the States from requiring a reasonable separation of persons of different sexes under some circumstances," and cites "two collateral legal principles" in this regard, the first being "the traditional power of the State to regulate cohabitation and sexual activity by unmarried persons" (p. 12). The report uses this principle to "permit the State to require segregation of the sexes for these regulatory purposes with respect to such facilities as sleeping quarters in coeducational colleges, prison dormitories, and military barracks" (ibid.), an end that the *Yale Law Journal* article had accomplished through the constitutional right to privacy.

Arditi et al. claim that the House of Representatives "indirectly rejected" the suspect classification, or compelling state interest test, because the " 'compelling state interest' test was embodied in the Wiggins Amendment" (p. 1255 n. 139). However, the rejected Wiggins Amendment in fact embodied a much lower standard: "any . . . law of the United States which reasonably promotes the health and safety of the people."

Law, p. 975 n. 68, writes, "The Yale ERA analysis, as presented to the Congress by Professor Thomas Emerson, was cited with approval by the congressional reports accompanying the proposed amendment." But the Judiciary Committee Reports that Law mentions did not, in fact, adopt the Yale interpretation. The Senate Report developed its own, similar but tripartite, interpretation, and, while it cited Professor Emerson in the Hearings, it never cited the *Yale Law Journal* article, which had appeared and had already been the subject of Senate discussion. Nor did the report ever use either the phrase "suspect classification" or the phrases "prohibited classification" or "absolute ban." One can only conclude that the report intended to avoid this point of potential contention.

As for the attitudes of the sponsors to the Yale article, there seems to be no doubt that, as Senator Ervin charged, Representative Martha Griffiths did send the article, when it came out, to all members of the House of Representatives with a note saying, "It will help you understand the purposes and effects of the Equal Rights Amendment. . . . The article explains how the ERA will work in most areas of the law." It may be worth wondering, since the article took a position opposite to hers at least in respect to job assignment in the military (see Chapter 7 n. 7), whether she had read the article carefully at the time. In any case, she did not defend the article subsequently on the floor of the House. This quotation from Griffiths, which many supporters of the absolute interpretation use to support their case, became part of the public record only when Senator Ervin cited it as part of his strategy to discredit the ERA. As for Senator Bayh's supposed endorsement of the Yale article, when in 1971 he asked permission to insert the article in the *Congressional Record,* he commented cautiously, "While I do not necessarily agree with every opinion expressed therein, I found it to be a masterful piece of scholarship which deserves to be brought to the attention of every Senator and the public." 117 *Cong. Rec.* 35040 (October 5, 1971). The caution stood him in good stead half a year later when, the implications of the Yale position having become clearer, Senator Ervin threw up to him his description of it as "a masterful piece of scholarship." At that point, Bayh asked to interrupt, and pointed out, "If the Senator will read the full context of the *Record* at the time I introduced the discussion to which he refers, he will see that I said that I did not agree with all the aspects discussed, or all the points and positions taken in the article." After a short interval of polite acrimony in which Ervin claimed that Bayh's original endorsement had had stronger connotations and Bayh denied it, the episode ended with Bayh referring his colleagues to the actual pages of the 1971 *Congressional Record,* so that they could confirm his testimony for themselves (*Cong. Rec.* 9083, March 20, 1972).

The conclusion I draw from Bayh's haste to dissociate himself from the Yale analysis, and from the silence on the subject in the Senate Report, is that the few people in Congress who were aware of the differences between the "suspect" position and the Yale article's "absolute" position preferred to keep the issue relatively unclear, leaving interpretation to the discretion of the courts.

The best evidence in legislative history for a prohibited classification interpretation derives, I believe, not from the debates but from the history of Senator Bayh's substitute version of the ERA in 1970. After the Senate had effectively defeated the ERA by adding amendments on school prayer and draft, Bayh proposed a new wording, patterned after the Fourteenth Amendment (see above, Chapter 2, p. 4 and accompanying notes). In a conciliatory letter to WEAL on October 29, Bayh indicated his willingness to make clear in the legislative history that his new wording was designed to ensure that the Supreme Court would treat sex under "the stricter doctrine of suspect classification" rather than under the present doctrine of "reasonable classification" (letter from the files of Catherine East).

ERA supporters rejected Bayh's proposed change in wording on the grounds that it weakened the original Amendment. However, the minutes of the November 2 meeting in which the leading supporters of the ERA took this decision do not suggest that they ever discussed whether or not the "suspect classification" standard itself was too weak. Interviews with two people who attended that meeting also indicate that they did not see themselves as explicitly rejecting a "suspect" for a "prohibited" interpretation. The minutes, the correspondence surrounding the decision, and those interviews seem instead to indicate that at that meeting many advocates of the ERA were afraid more of the explicit concessions that Bayh might write into the legislative history under the new wording than of that new wording itself.

It is conceivable that if the Court (1) assumed that Bayh's "equal protection" language was supposed to make sex a "suspect" classification, and (2) observed that proponents had rejected this language in favor of language that was supposedly stronger, it could conclude that Congress intended something stronger than a suspect classification, namely, a prohibited classification. However, it is more likely, as I indicate in the text, that the Court would see little in the congressional debates precisely on this point, and several instances, including the Senate Majority Report, in which legislative supporters of the ERA cited countervailing values (other than privacy and unique physical qualifications) that they expected the Court to take into account.

26. These issues were too subtle for most state legislative debates. I have found only one instance in the more than 700 pages of debate on the ERA in the Illinois legislature where the words "suspect classification" appear, and no instance of the words "prohibited classification" or "absolute ban." Unfortunately for clarity, the very representative who mentioned "suspect classification" (Illinois House of Representatives, June 2, 1977, p. 27) also said in a later part of the same speech that the ERA "bids us end discrimination and any classification by reason of gender" (ibid., p. 28), a wording that strongly suggests a prohibited classification. Although I did not ask a question on suspect classification in my 1981–1982 interviews, both my participant observation and subsequent interviews indicate that most, if not all, of the pro-ERA state legislators in Illinois thought that the ERA would make gender a suspect classification, not that it would create an absolute ban with two exceptions. For example, Eugenia Chapman, the primary sponsor of the ERA in the Illinois legislature, told me, "I thought very clearly that the ERA would make it [gender] suspect." When I asked

whether she had read the *Yale Law Journal*'s analysis suggesting an absolute ban with the two exceptions of privacy and unique physical characteristics, she answered,

> We [herself and Giddy Dyer, the other early and major sponsor in the legislature] quoted from that [the *Yale Law Journal*], but did not treat it in that absolute a fashion. We used it to deal with arguments that the ERA was entirely absolute. . . . We did not support it 100 percent. We thought of it as the opinion of writers from an eminent journal, that we could use to refute opponents. . . . we believed that the ERA would make it [gender] a suspect classification.

Susan Catania, another major legislative activist and sponsor, added that the ERA would make gender suspect, "as the Fourteenth Amendment did for race."

In 1983, some of these issues came up again in Congress. While in 1983 there was no legislative history in the strict sense because the House did not pass the ERA, it is worth noting that the fourteen members of Congress in the executive committee of the Congressional Caucus for Women's Issues put themselves on record as endorsing a summary of state experiences with ERAs that read, "The cases illustrate the common sense approach which the courts have taken to interpreting the ERA. Judges generally have stayed with familiar legal theories [by employing the strict scrutiny test] to review laws which classify persons on the basis of sex" (phrase in brackets in original Caucus Briefing Paper, presumably added by Caucus staff). Congressional Caucus for Women's Issues, *Equal Rights Amendment Briefing Paper*, November 1, 1983, in *Impact Hearings,* vol. 2, pp. 514–527, see esp. p. 518.

27. It would undoubtedly have resulted in the overruling of the *Vorchheimer, Rostker, Michael M., Parham, and Heckler* cases (nn. 17–21, above). Beyond these sorts of cases, Ann Freedman's 1983 testimony does not suggest that the ERA, even interpreted in an "absolute" way as making sex a "prohibited" classification, would have any further effect on laws or practices that explicitly distinguish between men and women. This does not mean that there might not be such effects, only that an important proponent of the ERA, identified more than any other person with the "absolute" interpretation, did not bring them to the attention of the Congress.

28. *Rostker v. Goldberg;* see Chapter 8.

29. Some lawyers, for instance, believe that the Court will, without any ERA, advance sex from an intermediate to a suspect classification. Others believe that the intermediate classification is actually the suspect classification in disguise and that the Court will really hold every law unconstitutional under the intermediate that it would under the suspect classification (e.g., Ruth Bader Ginsburg in n. 15 above). One or two

believe that the Court will begin to listen to Thurgood Marshall's dissents (e.g., *Mass. Board of Retirement v. Murgia,* 427 U.S. 307, 317 [1975]) and return to a simple "rational" test, making distinctions by defining what is rational rather than by distinguishing between demographic groups.

30. *Cong. Rec.* October 9, 1970, p. 35945; March 21, 1971, pp. 9320, 9321, 9331, 9333, 9335–9336, 9346, 9350, 9370, 9372, 9444, 9448; March 22, 1971, pp. 9544, 9549–9554, 9595–9596.

31. Barbara Brown, Thomas Emerson, Gail Falk, and Ann Freedman, authors of the original article interpreting the ERA in the *Yale Law Journal,* had suggested (at 898–900) that an ERA would require courts to look beyond "formally neutral laws which may have a discriminatory impact" into "the realities of purpose [i.e. intent], practical operation, and effect [i.e. impact]." Some combination of these would trigger strict scrutiny, and if a neutral classification were seen to "nullify the objectives" of the ERA, that classification would itself fall.

32. For this reason, several ERA proponents argued in the 1983 Senate hearings that the ERA should reach instances of disproportionate impact. In the most careful discussion of this issue, Ann Freedman (*Impact Hearings,* vol. 1, p. 539) and Phyllis N. Segal (Statement on the Impact of the Equal Rights Amendment on Veterans' Programs, in *Impact Hearings,* vol. 1, pp. 764–772, at 770) elaborated a standard whereby if a law (1) had a disparate impact on women and were both (2) traceable to and (3) reinforced or perpetuated discriminatory patterns, this would trigger strict scrutiny. At this point, the Court would uphold or strike down the law depending on (1) the severity of the impact upon the group adversely affected, (2) the importance of the statutory purpose, and (3) the necessity of achieving that purpose in the particular way chosen by the legislature. With this standard, Freedman and Segal moved beyond the "illicit intent" standard that the Court had enunciated in *Personnel Administrator of Massachusetts v. Feeney,* 99 S. Ct. 2282 (1979), but stayed far short of a simple "disparate impact" standard, which would have been so sweeping in its implications that neither the legislatures nor the courts would have adopted it. Their standard was designed not to go further in gender cases than in race cases, and was no more than the standard most liberal lawyers thought the Supreme Court should have enunciated under the Fourteenth Amendment in *Feeney.* (For a fuller elaboration, See Phyllis N. Segal, "Sexual Equality, the Equal Protection Clause, and the ERA," Buffalo Law Review 33 [1984]: 85–147.)

Other proponents in the 1983 hearings, sometimes people quite unconnected with the ERA movement, presented mixed testimony. One argued that it was "highly unlikely" that the Supreme Court would construe the ERA to invalidate statutes that simply had a disparate impact on women (Charles Shanor, associate dean of the Law School of Emory University, in *Impact Hearings,* vol. 1, p. 694). Another said that whether or not the ERA would touch disparate impact cases depended on what the 1983 Congress said it would do. (See Jane C. Sherburne, former assistant director of the Social Security Administration, testimony in *Impact Hearings*, vol. 1, p. 844: "I would certainly hope that the ERA would reach beyond facial discrimination. . . . that depends on the kind of legislative history that you [the Congress] develop and I would certainly encourage you to develop such a legislative history, and if it were up to me to develop that legislative history, I would make certain that it clearly reflected that the equal rights amendment would reach that kind of discrimination that disadvantages women.") A third said that the ERA could be interpreted either way, to incorporate a discriminatory intent or a disparate impact standard but that she advocated Congress's creating a legislative history in favor of a disparate impact standard. The disparate impact standard she had in mind was so far-reaching that it might even have invalidated a legislative decision to cut back a service, like AFDC benefits, that affected women disproportionately. Recognizing that the approach she advocated would provide a greater constitutional protection against gender-based discrimination than against discrimination based on race, she concluded that the added protection was "warranted in view of the social problems the ERA was designed to correct" (Judith Welch Wegner, professor at the University of North Carolina School of Law, testimony in *Impact Hearings*, vol. 1, pp. 878–892, at 878, 879, 890, and 892).

33. 426 U.S. 229 (1976).

34. *Personnel Administrator of Massachusetts v. Feeney*, 442 U.S. 256 (1979), at 272 and 269, n. 21.

35. *Frontiero v. Richardson*, 411 U.S. 677, 687–8 (1973).

36. Professor Kanowitz's prescient remarks, reprinted in *Cong. Rec.*, October 9, 1970, 35948–9, are worth quoting at length:

> There is one word of caution I would add at this point, however. And that is that this Committee and Congress, if it adopts the proposed Equal Rights Amendment as I hope it will do, will make sure that the record discloses that it does not thereby intend to discourage the United States Supreme Court from interpreting existing constitutional provisions—and especially the equal protection clause of the Fourteenth Amendment—so as to eliminate every sex-based discrimination in American law that cannot be sustained by overwhelming proof of functional differences between men and women.
>   I say this because there is a very real danger that if this is not done, the adoption of the Amendment at this time will ultimately represent a defeat rather than a victory for those of us who seek the eradication of irrational sex-based distinctions in American law and society. In the absence of such a clarifying declaration in the legislative history, the

Court, when faced with an equal protection or due process challenge to a sex-discrimination legal rule or official practice within the next few years, may be prompted to reason as follows: Since a coordinate branch of the federal government, the Congress, deemed it ncessary to adopt the Equal Rights Amendment, then it must have believed that existing constitutional provisions were inadequate to provide the needed relief in this area. Though such a view is not determinative, it is at least persuasive. As a result, deferring to Congress's apparent wishes in this respect, the Court could withhold any modification of the Muller principle and simply await the ratification of the Equal Rights Amendment before providing the needed relief in this area.

The problem of course is that one cannot be sure that the Equal Rights Amendment will be ratified by the requisite number of State legislatures. Even if it is eventually ratified, this may occur many years from now.

For these reasons, I believe it is of crucial importance that this Committee and Congress, in adopting the proposed Equal Rights Amendment, make clear their hope and expectation that forthcoming decisions of the United States Supreme Court will soon transform that Amendment into a constitutional redundancy.

37. *Frontiero v. Richardson,* at 688.

38. Ibid., at 691–692. It is true that Justice Powell also argued that the Court should "reserve for the future" any decision about sex being a suspect classification because the Court could hold the statutes challenged in *Frontiero* unconstitutional simply on the authority of *Reed v. Reed,* without setting forth any further reasoning. But he, and presumably the two justices who joined him, considered the fact that the ERA was before the states for ratification a "compelling" reason for not deciding in *Frontiero* that sex should be suspect *(Idem).*

39. *Cong. Rec.,,* March 22, 1972, p. 9553. See also *Cong. Rec.,* October 9, 1970, p. 35945, item 5.

40. *Cong. Rec.,* March 22, 1972, pp. 9350, 9544, 9549, 9595. See also *Cong. Rec.,* October 9, 1970, p. 35945, item 7.

41. *Cong. Rec.,* March 22, 1972, pp. 9321, 9370, 9544, 9549, 9551, 9552, 9553, 9596. See also *Cong. Rec.,* October 9, 1970, p. 35945, item 8.

42. *Cong. Rec.,* March 21, 1972, pp. 9320, 9336, 9372, 9444, 9448; March 22, 1972, pp. 9551, 9553, 9595. See also *Cong. Rec.,* October 9, 1970, p. 35945, item 6.

43. Title IX of the Education Amendments of 1972 made illegal those quotas and steeper entrance requirements that excluded women from

colleges, universities, and professional schools—schools that accepted federal financial aid. Title IX specifically exempted public elementary and secondary schools from its ban on public single-sex institutions. An ERA would probably have made single sex public schools unconstitutional at any level, but ERA proponents did not object to single-sex public schools in the Senate debate or elsewhere. Title IX did not forbid single-sex private colleges. Under the ERA, the Court probably would not have ruled that single-sex private colleges were unconstitutional, because the money these colleges accepted from the federal goverment and the tax exemptions they received from local or state governments would probably not have constituted enough "state action" to bring them under the jurisdiction of the ERA. Some scholars, however, believed that the eventual decision on private colleges could go either way (Barbara A. Brown, Ann E. Freedman, Harriet M. Katz, and Alice M. Price, *Women's Rights and the Law: The Impact of the ERA on State Laws* (New York: Praeger, 1977), p. 393 n. 92). Again, however, ERA proponents did not cite single-sex private colleges as an evil the ERA ought to abolish.

44. *Cong. Rec.*, March 22, 1972, pp. 9544, 9595. See also *Cong. Rec.*, October 9, 1970, p. 39549, item 1.

45. *Taylor v. Louisiana*, 419 U.S. 522 (1975), held that a state could not exempt all women from jury service, thus requiring those who wished to serve on juries to bear the extra burden of registering voluntarily. Automatic exemption and absolute prohibition from jury duty, also covered by *Taylor*, were the only evils relating to jury duty that were mentioned in the Senate debate. *Taylor* did not discuss child-care exemptions or the Massachusetts law that exempts women but not men who would be "embarrassed" by the nature of the prosecution. However, under its post-1976 *(Craig v. Boren)* interpretation of the Fourteenth Amendment, the Court would probably hold all such exemptions unconstitutional. Under both Taylor and its post-1976 interpretation of the Fourteenth Amendment, the Court probably would hold unconstitutional the Alabama law that allows women, but not men, to petition to be excused for good cause (see Brown et al., pp. 262–265). The ERA would probably have made all exemptions from jury duty that mentioned gender unconstitutional, but as the above indicates, it is not clear whether it would have had any more effect in this area than the Court's present interpretation of the Fourteenth Amendment.

46. *Cong. Rec.*, March 21, 1972, pp. 9320, 9331, 9336, 9372; March 22, 1971, pp. 9544, 9549, 9551, 9553–9554, 9595. See also *Cong. Rec.*, October 9, 1970, p. 39545.

47. *Cong. Rec.*, March 21, 1972, p. 9331; March 22, 1972, p. 9551.

48. By 1982, many of the gender distinctions made in the Social Security Act had been successfully challenged. In *Weinberger v. Weisen-*

feld, 420 U.S. 636 (1975), the Court, relying on *Frontiero v. Richardson,* held unconstitutional a provision of the Social Security Act (42 U.S.C. 402 [f] [1] [D]) which discriminated against female employees who contributed their earnings to social security by depriving their families of the same protections afforded to the families of male workers. In *Califano v. Goldfarb*, 430 U.S. 199 (1973), the Court found that federal Old Age, Survivors, and Disability Insurance (42 U.S.C. 401 et. seq.) denied equal protection to female wage earners. The program provided for survivors' benefits to be paid to the widow of a covered husband regardless of the degree of her dependency on her husband, while denying such benefits to the widower of a covered wife unless he could establish that he was dependent on his wife for at least one-half of his support. See also *Califano v. Silbowitz*, 347 F. Supp. 862 aff'd on appeal, 430 U.S. 924 (1977); and *Califano v. Jabcon* 399 F. Supp. 118 aff'd on appeal, 430 U.S. 924 (1977). One gender distinction retained in the Social Security Act, reviewed by the Court in *Califano v. Webster*, 430 U.S. 313 (1977), might have been struck down under the ERA. Relying on a benign discrimination rationale, the Court upheld a provision of the act (42 U.S.C. 415) under which a female wage earner could exclude from the computation of her "average monthly wage" three more lower earning years than a similarly situated male wage earner. The Court found that the provision served the important governmental interest of reducing the disparity in economic condition between men and women caused by the long history of discrimination against women.

49. *Cong. Rec.*, March 21, 1972, p. 9335; March 22, 1972, p. 9552, 9553, 9554, 9559, 9596. See also *Cong. Rec.*, October 9, 1970, p. 35495, item 2.

50. For cases holding different sentences for the same crime unconstitutional under the Fourteenth Amendment, see *U.S. ex rel. Robinson v. York*, 281 F. Supp. 8 (D.C. Conn. 1968); *Commonwealth v. Daniel*, 430 Pa. 642, 243 A. 2d 400 (1968); *Hobson v. POW*, 434 F. Supp. 362 (D.C. Ala. 1977). While a majority of the criminal statutes that make gender-based distinctions have been invalidated under the Fourteenth Amendment's equal protection clause, one such statute has been held constitutional even under the post-1976 interpretation of the Fourteenth Amendment. In *State v. Gurganus*, 39 N.C. App. 395, 250 S.E. 2d 668 (1979), the courts upheld as constitutionally valid a statute under which males over eighteen years of age may be imprisoned for as long as two years if they assault females, even though females may not be imprisoned for more than thirty days for most simple assaults. Following *Reed v. Reed* and implicitly *Craig v. Boren* the courts held that this law served the important governmental objective of protecting the physical integrity of the state's citizens and that the gender classification was substantially related to the achievement of such objectives. It is not clear whether the Supreme Court would have taken the same view. Nor is it clear whether either the lower courts or the Supreme Court would have taken a different view if the ERA had passed. Similar issues arise with regard to statutory rape, which is usually a crime that only men

can commit. The courts generally rely on a physical differences justification: "girls" need not be subject to criminal prosecution because the fear of pregnancy is a sufficient deterrent. *Michael M. v. Superior Court of Sonoma County,* 450 U.S. 464 (1981). Under the ERA it is possible that these gender-based distinctions in the criminal law would remain intact. Even if the ERA raised the level of scrutiny used by the Courts, the "physical differences" justification could still be relevant. Particularly where the crimes are related to the sexual act, the physical differences justification for different treatment of the sexes might be accepted.

More important than the handful of statutes that continue to recognize physical differences are those that, while neutral on their face, are enforced differently when violated by men or by women. This practice is particularly common with regard to charges of incest. See, for example, *People v. Boyer,* 63 Ill. 2d 433, 349 N.E. 2d 50 (1976); *Yocum v. Illinois,* 66 Ill. 2d 211, 361 N.E. 2d 1369 (1977) cert. denied 431 U.S. 941. The Courts have upheld the validity of giving males longer sentences in incest cases because fathers are typically dominant and can more readily coerce incestuous relationships, father-daughter incest occurs more frequently than mother-son incest, and father-daughter incest results in the more severe consequences of unwanted pregnancy and physical injury. *People v. Grammer,* 62 Ill. 2d 393, 342 N.E. 2d 371 (1976).

51. *Cong. Rec.,* March 21, 1972, pp. 9333, 9346, 9350; March 22, 1972, pp. 9551, 9552.

52. See Chapter 8.

53. *Cong. Rec.,* March 28, 1972, p. 10425.

Chapter 7

1. Barbara A. Brown, Thomas I. Emerson, Gail Falk, and Ann E. Freedman, "The Equal Rights Amendment: A Constitutional Basis for Equal Rights for Women," *Yale Law Journal* 80 (1971): 890–892.

2. Ibid., p. 977.

3. Ibid.

4. William Van Alstyne, Testimony on the Equal Rights Amendment Extension: Hearing before the House Subcommittee on Civil and Constitutional Rights of the House Committee on the Judiciary, 95th Cong. 1st and 2d sess. on *H.J. Res. 638* (1977–1978), November 8, 1977, p. 150. To show how the Court deferred to the military even under the First Amendment, Van Alstyne quoted from Justice Holmes's famous "clear and present danger" interpretation of the First Amendment:

When a nation is at war many things that might be said in time of peace
are such a hindrance to its effort that their utterance will not be
endured so long as men fight, and that no Court could regard as
protected by any constitutional right.
                    —Schenck v. U.S., *249 U.S. 47, 52 (1919)*

5. "Equal Rights for Men and Women," Report of the Senate Committee on the Judiciary, to accompany *S.J. Res. 8, S.J. Res. 9, H.S. Res.
208,* 92d Cong., 2d sess., 1972 Report no. 92-689, (hereafter Senate Report), p. 11; emphasis mine. It was probably no accident that while the
Senate Report cited Emerson's testimony, it never cited the *Yale Law
Journal* article in which Emerson, with the three other authors, had spelled
out his version of the implications of his testimony.

6. Senate Report, p. 13.

7. Ibid., quoting Representative Griffiths in *Cong. Rec.*, 35323 (October 6, 1971). In the sentences immediately before the three that end ". . .
the Army tells you where to go," Griffiths also implied a deferential
interpretation: "Now, all of this nonsense about the Army. . . . Has the
gentleman ever read any cases where anyone appealed to the Supreme
Court against Army regulations and asked that he be given equal treatment? Not one that I know of has ever won."

8. Ibid., quoting Representative Edwards in *Cong. Rec.* 35307 (October 6, 1971).

9. Idem.

10. *Cong. Rec.*, p. 9333 (March 21, 1972).

11. Ibid., p. 9349. See also p. 9335: "It is the prediction of the Senator
from Indiana that there is an extremely small likelihood that any [women]
will ever reach combat service."

12. Ibid., p. 9336.

13. *Cong. Rec.*, p. 9554 (March 22, 1972).

14. *Cong. Rec.*, p. 9350 (March 21, 1972).

15. Senator Cook, ibid., p. 9349.

16. The Ervin amendment read: "This article shall not impair the
validity, however, of any laws of the United States or any state which
exempt women from service in combat units of the Armed Forces" (*Cong.
Rec.*, 9317, March 1972). Of Senator Ervin's eight attempted amendments

to the ERA, this gathered the most support. See vote on Amendment 1066 (ibid., p. 9351). Amendment 1065, exempting women from compulsory military service, got the same number of favorable votes (18), but two more senators (73 total) voted against it (ibid., p. 9336).

17. See comment of Senator Cook, *Cong. Rec.*, p. 9576 (March 22, 1972).

18. However, see Judith Stiehm, "Public Opinion about Women in the Military," forthcoming, for the argument that "Congress was not so much opposed to women's registration as it was anxious to avoid the issue. . . . The result was probably less the product of majority rule than it was of deciding to avoid defining a majority which was likely to be slim, composed of disparate views, and confronted with intense opposition."

19. Van Alstyne, Testimony. Later, Van Alstyne again addressed the question of whether, if Congress sent qualified men into combat, the ERA would require sending qualified women too, and he concluded, "I am confident that it would not." He argued,

> . . . it is extraordinarily implausible, as well as remarkably unhistorical, to suppose that if the Congress and the President were mutually of the view that the insertion of women into combat infantry was not appropriate to the enforcement of [the ERA], but rather, that such a step would seriously compromise the related war powers entrusted to Congress and the President, then the Supreme Court would nonetheless presume to "overrule" their combined judgment on both matters at once.
>
> —*William Van Alstyne, "Commentary,"* Washington University Law Quarterly (1979): 193 n. 10

20. In 1979 and in early and late 1980, Gallup asked, "If a draft were to become necessary, should young women be required to participate as well

	Women Should Not Be Drafted	Women Should Be Drafted But Not Be Eligible for Combat	Women Should Be Drafted and Eligible for Combat	No Opinion[a]
1979	50	22	19	9
1980 (Feb.)	45	28	21	6
1980 (July)	47	25	22	6

Source: Gallup Surveys, no. 122-G, March 2–5, 1979; no. 148-G, February 1–4, 1980; no. 159-G, July 11–14, 1980.

[a]"No Opinion" includes both those with no opinion on whether women should be drafted and those who thought women should be drafted but had no opinion whether they should be eligible for combat.

as young men, or not?" Those who said young women should be required to participate were asked, "Should women be eligible for combat roles or not?" See unnumbered table above for the combined results of these two questions.

In early 1980, after asking, "Do you favor or oppose all women being registered for the draft and then being subject to the draft later on?" (Favor 50%, Oppose 41%, No opinion 9%), the Harris organization asked a sample of "likely voters," "Do you favor or oppose women in the military being assigned to combat units?" Twenty-nine percent answered "Favor," 69 percent "Oppose," and 3 percent "Not Sure." Source ABC News/ Harris Survey, vol. 2, no. 29, ISSN 0163-4846, release March 7, 1980, telephone survey, January 31–February 4, 1980, N = 1,198 "likely voters."

The context of these questions might well have led respondents to think that the questions referred to women draftees. Unfortunately, no survey of the American public has ever made the distinction between women *volunteers* being *allowed* to serve in combat and women *draftees* being *forced* to serve in combat. In 1982 the National Opinion Research Center (NORC) put the following question to a sample of the American public: "I'm going to read you a list of jobs that people might have in the armed forces. Please tell me whether you think a woman should or should not be assigned to each job, assuming that she is trained to do it?" Only 35 percent answered that a woman should be assigned to the job of "soldier in hand-to-hand combat." See James A. Davis, Jennifer Lauby, and Paul B. Sheatsley, *Americans View the Military: Public Opinion in 1982*, Technical Report no. 131 Chicago: National Opinion Research Center, 1983). When Charles Moskos and I replicated this question a year later with a group of 353 Northwestern University students, 28 percent thought women should be assigned to the job of soldier in hand-to-hand combat. But when the question was rephrased to read, "whether you think a woman volunteer should or should not be permitted to serve in this capacity, assuming that she wanted to serve in this capacity, volunteered to serve in this capacity, qualified on the appropriate physical and psychological tests, and was trained to do it," 57 percent—more than a majority—thought that women should be assigned to the job of soldier in hand-to-hand combat. The twenty-nine-point difference in evaluation was presumably produced primarily by the difference in reaction to women *volunteers* being allowed to serve in combat and women *draftees* being assigned to combat.

In the same year, when a small sample of Maryland residents were asked, "Do you think that young women should be allowed to volunteer to fight in combat in the armed forces, or not allowed to volunteer to fight in combat in the armed forces, or don't you have any opinion on this?" 65 percent—considerably more than a majority—answered that women should be allowed to volunteer for combat. Maryland Poll 1983, Survey Research Center of the University of Maryland, telephone interview March/April 1983, randomly designated householders at randomly generated phone numbers of households, N = 265; N responding to questions and having an opinion = 231. I am grateful to Kathy Gravino, who developed this question, for these data.

On the issue of women in combat, young people are somewhat less conservative than their elders. Although the group of Northwestern students Moskos and I questioned were less likely (28%) than the national average (35%) to think that women should be assigned to the job of soldier in hand-to-hand combat, in Davis et al.'s national sample 46 percent of the eighteen- to thirty-four-year-olds took this position. In 1980, 34 percent of a representative sample of the Yale student body ($N = 390$) answered "yes" to the question, "If women were drafted, do you believe they should serve in combat?" In 1980, 42 percent of a random sample of the University of California—Berkeley student body ($N = 365$) answered "yes" to the question (which did not specify draftees), "Should women in the Armed Forces be available for combat roles?" In 1978, of a Gallup sample of American youth aged thirteen to eighteen, 53 percent—more than a majority—answered "should" to the question (which implied volunteers and used the choice-oriented word, "permitted"), "Do you feel that women who are in the Army and Marines should or should not be permitted to serve as combat soldiers or marines—that is, to fight in combat units alongside men in the case of war?" (I would like to thank Karla Goldman of the 1980 Yale College Council Polling Task Force for providing me with the original report, which she summarized in testimony to the United States House of Representatives, Committee on Armed Services Subcommittee on Military Personnel, concerning proposed changes in the Military Selective Service Act, *H.R. 6569,* March 5, 1980. I would like to thank Judith Stiehm for providing a copy of Marcelo Rodriquez, "Students Oppose Draft Plan," *Daily Californian*, February 19, 1980, p. 7, and Mr. Shriver of the Gallup Youth Survey for providing the exact wording of the Gallup question.)

21. *Cong. Rec.*, 9333 (March 21, 1972). For repetitions of this list of deadly weapons, see pp. 9333 (again), 9350, 9507. For repetitions of an abbreviated variant in which "the daughters of America" are "sent into battle to have their fair forms blasted into fragments by the bombs and shells of the enemy," see pp. 9080, 9089, 9100, 9103.

22. Hearings before the Subcommittee on the Judiciary, Illinois House of Representatives, 1978.

Chapter 8

1. Interview with Judy Topinka, 1981.

2. As far as I know, this useful term has not yet been adopted by political scientists. Carol Weiss, an organizational theorist, coined the term, identifying decisions by accretion as follows:

[In] large organizations, policies often come into being without . . . systematic consideration. No problem (or opportunity) is identified as an explicit issue, no identifiable set of authorized decision makers meets, no list of options is generated, no assessment is made of relative advantages and disadvantages, no crisp choice is made. Yet the onrushing flow of events shapes an accommodation—and a pattern of behavior—that has widespread ramifications. It may in time be ratified by conscious policy action, but in the crucial formative states, it just seems to happen. Without conscious deliberation, the policy *accretes*.
—*Carol H. Weiss, "Knowledge Creep and Decision Accretion,"* Knowledge 1 (1980): 381–382

See also Howard S. Becker, "Notes on the Concept of Commitment," *American Journal of Sociology* 66 (1960): 32–40, for the similar concept of "commitment by default." For the related concept of "nondecision," see Peter Bachrach and Morton Baratz, "Decisions and Non-decisions." *American Political Science Review* 57 (1963):632–642; and Morris Zeldich, Jr., William Harris, George M. Thomas, and Henry A. Walker, "Decisions, Nondecisions, and Metadecisions," in Louis Kriesberg, ed., *Research in Social Movements: Conflicts and Change* (Greenwich, Conn.: Jai Press, 1983), pp. 1–31.

3. For a comparison of the goals of BPW and NOW with those of younger, more "socialist" or more "radical" women's organizations, see Jo Freeman, *The Politics of Women's Liberation* (New York: David McKay, 1975); and Alison M. Jaggar, *Feminist Politics and Human Nature* (Totowa, N.J.: Roman and Allenheld, 1983).

Early in the decade, radical and socialist feminists had doubted the wisdom of investigating energy in the ERA. In 1970, "Emma Goldman," "Sarah Grimke," and "Angelina Grimke," from Washington, D.C., Women's Liberation, testified in the Senate Hearings that although they had come there to support the ERA, "the amendment cannot guarantee real equality." Even equal pay, they argued, is "only an equal right to be exploited in a market economy based on profit and not on human needs." The society needed cooperative responsibility for children, free health care, safe contraception, abortion on demand, a just international policy, and a less repressive judicial system, but "constitutional amendments will not make any difference to these things: only revolutionary change can meet the demands that women are making today." Crying, "Free our sisters, free ourselves, all power to the people," the three walked out, leaving behind them a hearing room packed with supporters cheering and screaming, and a confused collection of senators. (Hearings before the Subcommittee on Constitutional Amendments of the Committee on the Judiciary, U.S. Congress, on *S.J. Res. 61*, May 5, 1970, pp. 78–79; interview with Joan E. Biren, one of the participants, November 1985. The anti-individualist ethos of the early radical women's movement led the participants to choose not to use their real names.) The Feminists, a radical feminist group, sent the Hearings an even more negative statement that began, "We feel it is our responsibility to denounce the proposed Equal Rights Amendment, and to caution the Women's Movement against squandering invaluable time and energy on it." (Hearings before the Committee on the Judiciary, U.S. Senate, *S.J. Res. 61 and S.J. Res. 231,* September 15, 1970, pp. 398–400).

4. For a fuller discussion of legalistic equality, see Chapter 14 n. 4.

5. "Women in the Military," Hearings before the Military Personnel Subcommittee of the Committee on Armed Services, House of Representatives, 96th Cong., 1st and 2d sess., November 13, 1979, p. 45. The conclusion that women marines could only "try" to defend their charges seems particularly gratuitous.

6. Phyllis Schlafly, "The Right to be a Woman," *Phyllis Schlafly Report* 6 (March 1972): 4.

7. Senator Ervin, *Cong. Rec.*, 9092 (March 20, 1972), quoting in full the five stanzas of John Charles McNeill's "The Bride."

8. National Organization for Women, "Position Paper on the Registration and Drafting of Women in 1980," p. 2 (hereafter, NOW Position Paper).

9. James A. Davis, et al.

10. Illinois House of Representatives, April 4, 1973, pp. 112–113, 125, 127.

11. NOW Position Paper, p. 3, quoting WEAL's "Women and the Military," 1979.

12. This was the position of Eleanor Smeal, national president of NOW. Pacifist feminists also made the argument that the necessity of inducting women for combat would make the nation's leaders think twice before committing themselves to a war. Unfortunately, wavering legislators in the key unratified states (Illinois, Oklahoma, Florida, and North Carolina) were likely to be dismayed at this potential outcome, seeing it as "weakening the nation's will to fight." Similarly, the feminist argument that women members of the armed forces would have more respect for human life and be less interested in fighting for its own sake had a political double edge. The possibility tended to frighten mainstream legislators, who saw such anti-aggressive sentiment as undermining the fighting spirit of the troops.

13. Martin Binkin and Shirley J. Bach, *Women and the Military* (Washington, D.C.: Brookings Institution, 1977), p. 32, fig. 4-1.

14. NOW Position Paper, pp. 6–7. Forty-three percent of these jobs were directly combat related.

15. Carol Parr, executive director of the National Coalition for Women in Defense, in "Women in the Military," Hearings before the Military Personnel Subcommitee of the Committee on Armed Services, House of Representatives, 96th Cong., November 16, 1979, p. 203.

16. Ibid., p. 206.

17. Ibid., p. 253.

18. Carter's statement reads,

My decision to register women is a recognition of the reality that both women and men are working members of our society. It confirms what is already obvious throughout our society—that women are now providing all types of skills in every profession. The military should be no exception. In fact, there are already 150,000 women serving in our armed forces today, in a variety of duties, up from 38,000 only 20 years ago. They are performing well, and they have improved the level of skills in every branch of the military service.

There is no distinction possible, on the basis of ability or performance, that would allow me to exclude women from an obligation to register. I am very much aware of the concern that many Americans feel about the issue of women in combat. There are also as many job categories in the military services as there are in civilian life, and many of these categories do not involve combat. In the All-Volunteer Force, women are successfully carrying out tasks which, in the event of hostilities, would involve deploying them in or near combat zones. But women are not assigned to units where engagements in close combat would be part of their duties, and I have no intention of changing that policy.

   —*Statement by the President, February 8, 1980, in Hearings on Military Posture and HR 6495 before the Committee on Armed Services, House of Representatives. 96th Cong., 2d sess. February 19, 1980, p. 135.*

19. NOW Position Paper, pp. 6, 8.

20. Ibid., p. 2.

21. Supreme Court of the United States, October Term 1980, *Bernard Rostker, Director of Selective Service v. Robert L. Goldberg, et al.*, Brief for

Amici Curiae, Women's Equity Action League Educational and Legal
Defense Fund, et al., 29 pp., available from WEAL. In support of its
position, the brief quoted the lower court in *Korematsu v. U.S.*:

> It would be an incorrect and dangerous concept for the judiciary to
> apply a less stringent test to possible violations committed by the
> Congress or the Executive in exercising the war powers. That power is
> precisely the power which historically can infringe most substantially
> on the civil rights of citizens and therefore may be the one most in need
> of an appropriate check and balance.
>
> —*P.17*

This position was also the one taken by counsel for Goldberg et al., who
were, among others, Diana Steele and Isabelle Katz Pintzler of the ACLU
Women's Rights' Project, and Lawrence Tribe of Harvard. Their two briefs
argued that the First Amendment military precedents, in which the Supreme Court had justified a reduction in First Amendment rights on
grounds of military discipline and morale, were inapplicable because they
"involved matters *wholly internal* to the military," whereas the Selective
Service law regulates only civilians (Supreme Court of the United States,
October Term 1980, *Bernard Rostker, Director of Selective Service, v.
Robert L. Goldberg et al.*, Motion to Affirm Judgement, Harold E. Kohn et
al., pp. 32–33). They also agreed that "there is no military exception to the
standard of review otherwise applicable in cases of explicit gender-based
classifications," on the grounds that "if the power to raise armies or wage
war justifies a lower standard of review for gender classifications it would
justify a lower standard for racial classifications as well. Even a registration
law excluding blacks might be permissible on the grounds that minorities
are already over-represented in the armed forces, thus making it unnecessary to draft them and 'rational' not to." Supreme Court of the United
States, October Term 1980, *Bernard Rostker, Director of Selective Service,
v. Robert L. Goldberg et al.*, Brief for the Appellees, Harold E. Kohn et al.,
pp. 16, 17. Before the case was decided, a Note in the *Harvard Law Review*
by one of Tribe's students ("Women and the Draft: The Constitutionality
of All-Male Registration," *Harvard Law Review* 94 [1980]: 406) argued
that "although the Supreme Court has . . . set aside an area of military
competence in which the judiciary will not apply the level of constitutional
scrutiny applicable to similar governmental actions in other contexts" (p.
421), "deference is inappropriate when invalidating the challenged action
does not require judicial intervention to . . . an extraordinary degree" (p.
423). After the case was decided, Lawrence Gene Sager, writing in "The
Supreme Court, 1980 Term," *Harvard Law Review* 95 (1981): 91, concluded, "The Court's stated rationale is unacceptable because special
deference was unwarranted" (p. 108). With all this unanimity on the issue
among the liberal legal intelligentsia, it would have been almost impossible
for a feminist lawyer to raise the possibility of a deferential, war-powers
interpretation of the ERA even if the idea had occurred to her.

22. Brief for Amici Curiae, WEAL, pp. 23, 25.

23. Supreme Court of the United States, October Term 1980, *Bernard Rostker, Director of Selective Service, v. Robert L. Goldberg. et al.*, Brief for Amicus Curiae, National Organization for Women, pp. 3, 15. Note that the NOW brief does not make an argument for hand-to-hand combat but implicitly argues for women's participation in the many other positions that bear a "combat" label.

24. Eleanor Smeal, telephone interview, May 24, 1984.

25. See, even at the time, E. V. Rostow, "The Japanese-American Cases—Disaster," *Yale Law Journal* 54 (1945): 489.

26. Brown et al., p. 871.

27. Brown et al., p. 977. Bella Abzug repeated this language almost exactly on the floor of the House: *Cong. Rec.*, 35311 (October 6, 1971).

28. For example, Mariclaire Hale and Leo Kanowitz, "Women and the Draft: A Response to Critics of the Equal Rights Amendment," *Hastings Law Journal* 23 (1971): 199–220, esp. pp. 201, 216, 219–220.

29. Joan Wexler, "The ERA and the Military," *Yale Law Journal* 82 (1973): 1537. For a similarly conceived feminist view, see Jill Laurie Goodman, "Women. War and Equality: An Examination of Sex Discrimination in the Military," *Women's Rights Law Reporter* 5 (1979): 243–269.

30. Telephone interviews, June 1982.

31. Caroline Bird and the members and staff of the National Commission on the Observance of International Women's Year, eds., *What Women Want* (New York: Simon and Schuster, 1979), p. 122.

32. Common Cause, "What Happens If a Man Leaves the Picture?" pamphlet (n.d.), p. 7.

33. Ibid.

34. National Federation of Business and Professional Women (National BPW), "ERA at a Glance." 2 pp. (n.d.), p. 2 (mimeographed).

35. National BPW, "How and Why to Ratify the Equal Rights Amendment." pamphlet, 4 pp. (n.d.), p. 2. For similar wording, see National BPW. "Equality ERA, the Equal Rights Amendment," pamphlet, 4 pp. (n.d.), p. 2. See National BPW, "What is Your ERA IQ?" pamphlet (October 1978), p. 2, for the phrase, "Combat qualifications are determined by separate armed services needs and regulations."

36. National BPW, "Who Will Defend America," pamphlet, 1 p. (n.d.).

I have not been able to find a NOW pamphlet addressing this issue. Like all of the ERA organizations, NOW dispensed the pamphlets that different pro-ERA groups put out.

The National Women's Party, once the militant wing of the post-suffrage women's movement, answered the question, "Will women be assigned combat duty?" with the ambiguous answer, "Every man is not assigned combat duty, so there is no reason to assume women will be," and then argued that because almost nine out of ten military jobs are noncombat, and because women would receive the same exemptions and deferments as men, "it seems improbable that anyone, men or women, not desiring to serve (as in the case of some men now) would serve in a capacity they didn't wish to." National Women's Party, "A/Q: Answers to Questions about Equal Rights Amendment," pamphlet, 8 pp. (1976), pp. 5–6.

The League of Women Voters also tended to skirt the question of combat. In a one-page summary of the Amendment's effects on the military, the League talked almost exclusively about discrimination in the volunteer army. Then in one short paragraph it concluded,

> The Equal Rights Amendment would require that women be allowed to participate in the Armed Services on the same basis as men. The question of equal participation in the military is often obscured by irrelevant emotional issues. The issue is not whether war is desirable—it clearly isn't. The issue isn't whether men are more capable than women—because it varies from individual to individual. The issue isn't whether the life of a woman is more important than the life of a man—that's indefensible on its face. The fact is that true equality does require that all persons accept the responsibilities as well as the rights of citizenship. Nowhere are both the benefits and responsibilities of full citizenship so demonstrable as in the military.

While this statement captured many valid arguments for sending qualified women into combat, it was also vague enough not to have left a casual reader with the impression that the ERA required involuntary combat for women, even if a future Congress decreed that fate for equally qualified men. Mary E. Brooks and Susan Tenenbaum, League of Women Voters of the United States, 1976, revised 1977.

The 287-page book put out by the Equal Rights Amendment Project of the California Commission on the Status of Women, entitled *Impact ERA* and funded by the Rockefeller Foundation "with the goal of promoting public understanding of the issues involved," devoted just over one page to "the impact of the ERA on women and the military service." This section, written by a sociologist rather than a lawyer, concluded vaguely that "as long as traditional stereotypes of women and men are maintained, the likelihood of Congress 'forcing' women into direct military combat is minimal." Eloise C. Snyder, "Legal Change and Social Values," in *Impact ERA*, pp. 148–149.

37. It is not as if the pamphlets never brought up complex legal arguments. Proponents often rebutted the opponents' charges regarding the husband's duty of support (see Chapter 9) by citing *McGuire v. Mc-Guire,* Supreme Court of Nebraska (1953), 157 Neb. 226, 59 N.W. 2d 336, and the charges regarding unisex toilets (see Chapter 9) by citing the "right of privacy" that the Supreme Court created in *Connecticut v. Griswold,* 381 U.S. 479 (1965). See, for example, "What Happens If This Man Leaves the Picture . . ." ERAmerica and Common Cause 8 pp. (n.d.) (ca. 1980), p. 2; and "Equality/Equality," National Federation of Business and Professional Women, 2 pp. (n.d.) (c. 1980), p. 2.

38. For example, Professor Emerson from the Yale Law School testified at Connecticut's 1977 recision hearings, criticizing a brochure widely distributed in Connecticut by the Connecticut Committee to Rescind ERA. Emerson analyzed the seventeen statements in the brochure one by one, proving ten of them totally false, six of them false in part, and only one of them correct. The brochure's single correct statement was:

> ERA will make women subject to the draft on an equal basis with men in all our future wars. ERA will make women and mothers subject to military combat and warship duty.

To this, Emerson responded,

> This statement is substantially correct. Under the ERA, men and women, in accordance with their individual capacities, will have equal obligations to protect the country against foreign foes in time of war. They would also have equal opportunity to secure the advantages of service in the military forces, during both war and peace.

Above statement by Thomas I. Emerson was given before the Government Administration and Policy Committees of the Connecticut General Assembly on Proposed Resolution to Rescind Connecticut's Ratification of the Equal Rights Amendment, 13 pp., p. 8, (mimeographed); from the University of California at Santa Barbara Women's Center ERA files.

39. See testimony of Eugene Weedoff and Kathleen Carpenter, Hearings before the Illinois General Assembly, June 8, 1982, pp. 33, 19–22. 98–116. Earlier, Colorado legislators, who eventually passed the ERA heard testimony explicitly pointing to a deferential interpretation. Statement of Catherine East on the Equal Rights Amendment before the Committee on the Equal Rights Amendment of the Colorado Legislature, October 23, 1975 (from the files of Catherine East).

40. Illinois House of Representatives, June 18, 1980, p. 109–161.

41. *Phyllis Schlafly Report* 6, no. 4 (November 1972).

42. *The Times*, London, June 24, 1982, p. 12.

43. Illinois House of Representatives, testimony against ERA, June 8, 1982.

44. Carol Felsenthal, "How Feminists Failed," *Chicago Magazine* (June 1982), p. 157.

45. Jane O'Reilly, "The Mysterious and True Story of the ERA in Oklahoma," *Ms.* (July 1982), p. 124. Others echoed this sentiment. A leader in WEAL commented, "It [combat] was critically important. It caused a lot of the real opposition to the ERA, apart from the emotional shift. Dear thoughtful folks who opposed the ERA did so for one of two reasons. First, they were against a sweeping law. They were not comfortable erasing all gender-based differences. Second, combat. This was more than just emotional. They could not accept that degree of equality." A feminist in the Department of Defense added, "This was a major issue for them [the legislators] . . . I think it was terribly important." The political scientist who has written most extensively on the ERA concluded, "The question of altered conditions of military service for women under the ERA is one which has given proponents the most difficulty" (Boles, *Politics*, p. 171).

46. See Sarah Ruddick, "Drafting Women: Pieces of a Puzzle," Working Paper MS-5, Center for Philosophy and Public Policy, University of Maryland, July 19, 1982; Judith Stiehm, "Women and the Combat Exemption," *Parameters* 10 (1980): 51–59; and essays in Nancy Loring Goldman, ed., *Female Soldiers—Combatants or Noncombatants?* (Westport, Conn.: Greenwood Press, 1982). See also Catherine A. MacKinnon, "Towards a Feminist Jurisprudence," *Stanford Law Review* 34 (1982): 703–737; and Michael Walzer, "The Obligations of Oppressed Minorities," in *Obligations* (Cambridge, Mass.: Harvard University Press, 1970).

The question of class interests in mandating gender equality in the military also has not been looked into carefully. Charles Moskos, interviewing forty-one enlisted women and seven women officers ("virtually the entire complement of women") at two United States Army installations in Honduras in 1984, found that "about half the enlisted women said women should not be allowed in combat units, reflecting the status quo; about half opined that women who were physically qualified should be allowed to volunteer for combat roles." On the other hand, "about half the women officers believed qualified women should be allowed to volunteer for combat units, as did half of the female enlisted; the remainder said women should be compelled to go into combat units in the same manner as men—a viewpoint held by none of the enlisted women" (Charles C. Moskos, "Female GIs in the Field," *Society* 22 [1985]: 32). If Moskos's small sample is at all representative, we might postulate that the enlisted women, who were high school graduates (half white, one-third black, the rest principally

Hispanic) hoping to leave the army after an appropriate time and use the army benefits to pursue a college degree, had material interests in this decision different from those of the women officers, whose upward mobility would be helped by being able to enter combat specialities and command female or mixed fighting units in wartime. If the Equal Opportunity Officers in the Department of Defense talked primarily with women officers about the issue of mandating qualified women in combat, they may have received an incorrect impression of the preferences and possibly the interests of the enlisted women.

47. An all-woman unit might also have greater positive effects on both the women's own feelings of competence and on breaking down nationally held stereotypes of women than would women in mixed units.

The fact that women receive a radically different socialization from men also poses problems when one uses a constitutional amendment to end sex stereotyping. American women are less likely than American men to murder or harm others physically, and they are more likely to disapprove of war, capital punishment, and other causes of death. When asked about the reasons why they might not want to join the armed forces, collegiate women and men differed significantly in only one respect: only 63 percent of the men answered, "I might be in a position where I would have to kill others," but 91 percent of the women gave this answer (Moskos and Mansbridge, Survey, 1983). Such differences are obviously not a sensible reason for excluding women volunteers from combat, but they do suggest that combat might be an even greater burden for female draftees than for male draftees.

In theory, the military could perhaps select combatants so as to ensure that women who ended up in combat were no more averse to violence than men. In practice, however, selecting combat troops on the basis of their subjective feelings about violence would encourage everyone who wanted to survive to claim they hated violence.

Regarding other potentially unforeseen effects, the one time that Israel put some of its women into hand-to-hand combat, military strategists claim to have discovered that having women opponents made the Arabs fight harder, because the prospect of surrender to women was unthinkable. On the domestic front, the presence of women in combat might reduce the incentive for men to enlist, by diminishing the "macho" component of the event, and it might undermine civilian morale in wartime by exposing more women prisoners of war to rape. While these domestic effects would gratify those of us who believe there are few (if any) just wars, the nonpacifist population might not want to have them removed from the field of policy choice by a constitutional amendment.

48. See Chapter 6. By "presumptively" unconstitutional, I mean highly likely, in the opinion of most lawyers in the field, to be declared unconstitutional under existing precedents if the case were taken to the federal courts.

49. For types of membership incentives, see Chapter 9, especially n. 1.

50. For examples, Representative Wincup, in Women in the Military: Hearings before the Military Personnel Subcommittee of the Committee on Armed Services, House of Representatives, 96th Cong., 1st and 2d sess., November 13–16, 1979, and February 11, 1980, p. 11.

51. By the time of the 1983 Senate Hearings on the impact of the ERA, the feminist lawyers' position on women draftees in combat had become the official ERA movement's position. Antonia Handler Chayes, former Under Secretary of the Air Force and a liberal feminist lawyer who worked with the Women's Equality Action League (WEAL) in preparing her testimony, testified in those hearings: "With this adoption of the ERA, explicit gender-based exclusions would fail. . . . any classification based upon sex, just as race, will be unacceptable" (*Impact Hearings*, vol. 1, pp. 301–302, November 1, 1983).

Chayes admitted four exceptions to this general rule. She singled out "two rare and narrowly circumscribed circumstances" in which the government could employ gender-based classifications (p. 367): first, gender-based classifications "carefully employed to remedy past gender discrimination" (a position consonant with the proponents' 1983 interpretation generally), and second, regulations based on unique physical characteristics, which would be subject to strict scrutiny. In addition, I have derived inferentially from her testimony two other exceptions: first, policies designed to accommodate constitutionally protected privacy rights, so long as those policies were "drawn as narrowly as possible so as to assure that they do not serve to curtail women's participation by perpetuating past exclusions" (p. 369), and second, a transition period:

> I do not believe that the courts would construe the ERA to preclude legitimate transitions. . . . There may be reasons to provide transitions to ameliorate sociological problems. It will be necessary to develop understanding of the impact of large numbers of women generally, and in fields presently closed to them.
>
> —*P. 302*

Chayes specifically rejected the suggestion of Senator Dennis DeConcini, an ERA supporter and Judiciary Committee member, that "under the Constitutionally-based doctrine of 'military necessity,' the courts have generally deferred to the Congress and the Executive on matters of national security" (p. 367). This is the first time, in my reading, that a member of Congress explicitly raised this possibility. Chayes responded to Concini by making the parallel to race, arguing that racially segregated units would "now be considered indefensible," and concluding that "the same thing would be true under the ERA. Explicit exclusionary policies on the basis of sex would be prohibited under the ERA; and, in fact, are completely unnecessary to any national security interest" (p. 367). Chayes also explicitly repudiated the suggestion of the International Women's Year Commission (see n. 31 above) that women would not be assigned to combat duty. "Explicitly gender-based assignment policies," she stated, "would not be tolerated after the ERA" (p. 365).

As we have seen, no official report came out of either the House or the Senate Judiciary Committees. Nor were these issues debated at all in the Senate, or more than briefly in the House. Consequently, we cannot know what position congressional proponents of the ERA would have taken on these issues in 1983. What is clear is that in 1983—as opposed to the period from 1971 through 1982—the proponent organizations consciously chose to reject the deferential interpretation.

Chapter 9

1. The case cited in every text on family law is *McGuire v. McGuire*, 175 Neb. 226, 59 N.W. 2d 336 (1953). See also Herma Kay, *Sex-based Discrimination*, 2d ed. (1981) pp. 190–191.

2. After the U.S. Supreme Court struck down the Alabama statute requiring husbands but not wives to pay alimony, the Alabama court's remedy was to extend the alimony requirement to the wife in cases where she was able to pay and he was unable to support himself. See *Orr v. Orr*, 351 So. 2d 906 Ala. Civ. App. (1979). The U.S. Department of Labor followed the same logic when it concluded that limitations on women's hours and weight-lifting violated the Equal Pay Act of 1963. Its remedy was to extend these limitations to men, not to eliminate them for women.

3. See, for example, the Alabama statute held unconstitutional under the Fourteenth Amendment in *Orr v. Orr*, 440 U.S. 268 (1979).

4. See the statutes of Colorado, Georgia, and Pennsylvania, in *People v. Elliott*, 186 Colo 65, 525 P. 2d 457 (1974); *Dill v. Dill*, 232 Ga. 231, 206 SE 2d 6 (1974); *Conway v. Dana*, 456 Pa. 536, 318 A. 2d. 324 (1974). For the evolution in judicial interpretation of these statutes before 1972, see Charles M. Walker, "Domestic Relations: The Expanding Role of the Mother in Child Support," *Arkansas Law Review* 27 (1973): 157–161.

5. For data on the extraordinarily low levels of alimony and child support ordered by courts, and the even lower levels actually paid, see U.S. Bureau of the Census, *Current Population Reports*. Series P-23, no. 112, "Child Support and Alimony: 1978" (Washington, D.C.: Government Printing Office, 1978).

6. See Brown, Freedman, Katz, and Price, pp. 136–145, on the harsh impact on women of the "model" no-fault Uniform Marriage and Divorce Act, and their policy recommendations for eliminating present statutory restrictions on maintenance, and basing maintenance payments on, among other things, the ages of the parties, their past contributions to the marriage

(including interruption of personal careers or educational opportunities), and their present earning capacities.

7. Foote, Levy, and Sanders, *Cases and Materials on Family Law* (1966), pp. 320–321, cited in Barbara Allen Babcock, Ann E. Freedman, Eleanor Holmes Norton, and Susan C. Ross, *Sex Discrimination and the Law* (Boston: Little, Brown, 1975), p. 604.

8. The husband's "ownership" was not complete, except in a handful of "title" states like Mississippi. In most states, during a marriage neither spouse could sue the other, and at divorce a wife might be given property held in the husband's name.

9. See Lenore Weitzman, "The Economics of Divorce: Social and Economic Consequences of Properties, Alimony and Child Support Award," *UCLA Law Review* 28 (1981): 1264–1265, on the negative impact on women of California's "equal division" rule for property. See also Rhode, p. 25, and citations therein.

10. For example, by being held legally to assume her husband's domicile, a wife could be subjected to unfavorable state income tax treatment, have to pay nonresident tuition if she attended a university in her home state, and lose her right to run for office in the state where she actually lived. In a number of states, a wife's refusal to move when her husband moved also created the presumption that she had deserted him, but not vice versa. In Louisiana, a husband could sue for divorce in a place other than the one in which the couple had lived without offering proof of his wife's misconduct, but a wife had to prove her husband's misconduct under comparable circumstances. Leo Kanowitz, *Women and the Law* (1969), pp. 46–52; and *Craig v. Craig*, 365 So. 2d 258 (La. 1979).

11. *Forbush v. Wallace*, 341 F. Supp. 217 (N.D. Ala. 1971) Aff'd per curiam, 405 U.S. 970 (1972).

12. Kanowitz, p. 10.

13. See *Orr v. Orr*.

14. *Stanton v. Stanton*, 421 U.S. 7 (1975).

15. See *People v. Elliott* and *Dill v. Dill*.

16. *Kirschberg v. Feenstra*, 450 U.S. 455 (1981).

17. Judith Areen, *Cases and Materials on Family Law*, 2d ed. (Mineola, N.Y.: Foundation Press, 1985). p. 596.

18. See *Samuel v. University of Pittsburgh*, 375 F. Supp. 1119 (W.D.

Pa. 1974), for a case dealing with out-of-state tuition; and *Craig v. Craig*, 365 So. 2d 1298 (La. 1979), for a case dealing with differences in the rules governing choice of a forum for a divorce suit. See also *Crosby v. Crosby*, 434 So. 2d 162 (La. 1983), in Areen, p. 255.

19. *Forbush*; and *Whitlow v. Hodges*, 539 F. 2d 582 (6th Cir. 1976), cert. denied 429 U.S. 1029 (1976), cited in Areen, p. 95.

20. See argument in *Dunn v. Palermo*, 522 S.W. 2d 679 (Tenn. 1975), and other cases cited in Areen, p. 95.

21. Kay, p. 165. The exception is Arkansas, which still allows women to marry without parental consent at sixteen while requiring men to be seventeen. In most cases these laws were changed by the relevant legislature, though in Illinois and perhaps a few other states they were struck down by state courts under the state ERA. See *Phelps v. Bing*, 58 Ill. 2d 32, 316 N.E. 2d. 775 (1974).

22. See *Stanton*.

23. Deborah L. Rhode, "Equal Rights in Retrospect," *Law and Inequality* 1 (1983): 18. Rhode's article presents a larger analysis quite similar to mine.

24. Dating the "modern" women's movement is obviously somewhat arbitrary. In 1963, Betty Friedan published *The Feminine Mystique* (New York: Dell, 1963). In 1964, Ruby Doris Smith Robinson presented to a staff retreat at the Student Non-Violent Coordination Committee (SNCC) a paper entitled "Women in the Movement" (Sara Evans, *Personal Politics: The Roots of Women's Liberation in the Civil Rights Movement and the New Left* [New York: Vintage, 1979] 1980, p. 85; and Hole and Levine, p. 110). In 1965, Casey Hayden and Mary King circulated among members of the Students for a Democratic Society (SDS) "A Kind of Memo," drawing attention to women's issues (Evans, pp. 99–101; and Freeman, pp. 57–58). Professional women in the mid-1960s were reaching similar conclusions, and on June 30, 1966, the last day of the Third National Conference for Commissions on the Status of Women, a small group of nationally prominent women formed the National Organization for Women (NOW). The mass media discovered what was happening in 1968 and 1969; after that "women's liberation" became a mass movement.

25. Hole and Levine, p. 85

26. For example, "We believe that proper recognition should be given to the social value of homemaking and child-care . . ." (ibid.)

27. Ibid., pp. 77–166, and Freeman, passim, for descriptions of the spectrum of women's organizations in the early days of the modern Amer-

ican women's movement, and for the gradual movement toward more radical principles in NOW.

28. Freeman, p. 58.

29. See Chapter 5 n. 9.

30. Disadvantaged groups become increasingly underrepresented as one moves higher and higher on the ladder of success. This phenomenon has an easy statistical explanation. If the attributes that produce a given variety of success are more or less normally distributed, and if the dispersions are the same for both groups, raising the cut-off point for inclusion in a given elite will reduce the percentage of the disadvantaged group that ends up in the elite faster than it reduces the percentage of the advantaged group.

For example, if women's primary responsibility for child care puts them at a slight disadvantage vis-à-vis men, this disadvantage will have greater and greater repercussions as the positions to which both sexes aspire become more select. If an elite is fairly large (e.g., includes 30 percent of the population), then there will be almost as many women in that elite as men. But if the elite is quite small (e.g., includes only 5 percent of the population), then there will be many fewer women in that elite than men. Thus, it is no accident that there are smaller percentages of women in highly competitive state legislatures, where one representative has many constituents, than in less competitive state legislatures, with low representative/constituent ratios (Irene Diamond, *Sex Roles in the State House* [New Haven: Yale University Press, 1977]). Similarly, the percentage of women in the U.S. Senate is smaller than in the House of Representatives, and smaller in the Presidency than in the Senate. The economic hierarchy is also characterized by declining percentages of women as one nears the top.

31. Freeman, p. 55. I am using the word "professional" loosely here, to cover nuns, union officials, and appointees to state commissions on the Status of Women.

32. Pat Mainardi, "The Politics of Housework," reprinted in Robin Morgan, ed., *Sisterhood is Powerful* (New York: Vintage/Random House, 1970), pp. 447–454.

33. Leaflet by The Feminists (written for a demonstration at the Marriage License Bureau, New York City, Winter 1969), reprinted in Morgan, ed., p. 536. The Feminists also distributed the following:

THE FEMINISTS v. THE MARRIAGE LICENSE
BUREAU OF THE CITY OF NEW YORK

WHEREAS it is common knowledge that women believe the conditions of the marriage contract to be positive and reciprocal feelings between the two parties (known as "love and affection"); and

WHEREAS the marriage contract in fact legalizes and institutionalizes the rape of women and the bondage of women, both their internal (reproductive) and external (domestic labor) functions; and

WHEREAS the marriage contract, known as "license," fails to list the terms of that contract, a failure which would automatically nullify the validity of any other important contract

THEREFORE, WE, THE FEMINISTS, do hereby charge the city of New York and all those offices and agents aiding and abetting the institution of marriage, such as the Marriage License Bureau, of fraud with malicious intent against the women of this city.

September 23, 1969   —*Morgan, ed., p. 537*

34. "Confront the Whoremakers at the Bridal Fair," February 1969, reprinted in Morgan, ed., p. 543.

35. "Mother's Day Incantation," WITCH (Women Interested in Toppling Consumption Holidays [The WITCH acronym changed references according to the topic of attack]), reprinted in Morgan, ed., p. 550.

36. For examples of women's culture, see, among many others, Marlene Dixon, Kathy Sarachild, Peggy and Dianne and others, *It Ain't Me Babe* 1 (April 7, 1970): 5, 8, 9; or Jane Alpert, "Mother Right," in *Off Our Backs* 3 (May, 1973): 6 ff. For an example of the feminist sympathy to motherhood, see Pauline Bart, "The Loneliness of the Long-Distance Mother," in Jo Freeman, ed., *Women: A Feminist Perspective* (Palo Alto, Calif.: Mayfield Publishing, 1975). For more recent discussions, see Jean Bethke Elshtain, *Public Man, Private Woman* (Princeton: Princeton University Press, 1981), chap. 5; or Betty Friedan, *The Second Stage* (New York: Summit, 1981), chaps. 1 and 2.

37. *Phyllis Schlafly Report* 5, no. 7 (February 1972): 3, 4.

38. Representative Henry J. Hyde, Illinois House of Representatives, May 16, 1972, p. 202. For another example of the unblushing, jocular, and subtle misogyny of some of the ERA's opponents, see the comment of Representative Hyde, the first and principal speaker against the ERA, the first time the ERA was brought to the Illinois House. Representative Hyde began his speech: "Mr. Speaker, Ladies and Gentlemen of the House, they say that diamonds are a girl's best friend. You know what man's best friend is, don't you? It's his dog. And I think that indicates in some manner the disparity that nature and society in custom has built up in the essential differences between man and woman" (ibid., p. 197).

39. For example,

"This is a direct blow against the home and the family and could be disastrous to our country."
                                    —*Representative Webber Borchers, Illinois House of Representatives, May 16, 1972, p. 213.*

The family unit made this country great and if you want to see something destroyed, the family unit, pass ERA. Put it on the heads of your children and your grandchildren and watch and witness the decline of the United States of America, a great country that was founded on the principle of family units. In Colorado, where they have ERA, men want to marry horses. Homosexuals marry homosexuals there. This is what you're talking about with ERA.
                                    —*Representative Hanrahan. Illinois House of Representatives, May 1, 1975, p. 36*

I have nothing against the ERA, except I believe that the hoards of kooks and carpetbaggers who have swarmed into Illinois on its behalf, to stampede its passage in recent days, represent a considerable threat to that grand American tradition called "Family and Home." You and I know that the honored head of that block of the national foundation is the wife of the breadwinner, the mother of the children, the queen-bee around whom all life can happily revolve. And yet the grand madame of ERA, one Gloria Steinem, has often publicly described these extraordinary housewives and mothers as "prostitutes." On behalf of my mother, my wife, my daughters and yours, I resent Gloria Steinem, her ilk, and every alien philosophy that they espouse. I have never met a rabid gung-ho "libber" who was happily married, and that somber fact, that somber fact should be noticed to the thousands of dedicated ladies, albeit misguided, in the State of Illinois . . . who have striven so mightily for ERA's ratification. . . ."
                                    —*Representative Cunningham, ibid., p. 45*

40. CBS/*New York Times* poll, cited in Keith T. Poole and L. Harmon Zeigler, "The Diffusion of Feminist Ideology," *Political Behavior* 3 (1981): 244.

41. Philip E. Converse et al., *American Social Attitudes Data Sourcebook 1947–1978* (Cambridge, Mass.: Harvard University Press, 1980), p. 106, tables 3.7 and 3.8: "Did your wife/Did you (wife) do any work for money during the previous year?"; 1962 grade school $N = 153$, high school $N = 208$, college $N = 130$; 1978 grade school $N = 229$, high school $N = 1,006$, college $N = 648$; all N's weighted, intervening years omitted. The growth in employment among highly educated women was accompanied by growth in the percentage of working women who said they worked because they enjoyed it, not just for the money (pp. 119, 120, tables 3.26, 3.28. Here too there is a growing class gap, but the N's are too small to say much about the group of women with a grade school education working for pay [$N =$

13]). Because Converse at al. did not specify how they created the variables reported in these tables, I was not able to replicate their analysis exactly. However, in an analysis that approximated their results, controlling for age did not greatly reduce the relationship between education and working outside the home.

42. Ibid., p. 110, table 3.15: "Different people feel differently about taking care of a home—I don't mean taking care of the children, but things like cooking and sewing and keeping house. Some women look on these things as just a job that has to be done—other women really enjoy them. How do you feel about this?"; 1957 grade school (76.7 percent) $N = 287$, high school $N = 455$, college $N = 118$; 1976 grade school (76.3 percent) $N = 198$; high school $N = 500$, college $N = 217$; all N's weighted, intervening years omitted.

43. Ibid., p. 113, table 3.19: "Have you ever wanted a career?": 1957 grade school $N = 288$, high school $N = 455$, college $N = 118$; 1976 grade school $N = 119$, high school $N = 501$, college $N = 217$; all N's weighted, intervening years omitted. See also pp. 115, 116, tables 3.21, 3.23: "Are you planning to go to work/thinking of getting a job in the future?"; rise from 16.6 percent in 1957 to 29.9 percent of homemakers overall, with a drop among the homemakers with a grade school education from 12 percent in 1957 ($N = 282$) to 6 percent in 1976 ($N = 199$), and a rise among the college educated homemakers from 20 percent in 1957 ($N = 115$) to 44 percent in 1976 ($N = 216$).

44. One possible indication of this loss of status in society at large is that from 1968 to 1980, the percentage of women reporting themselves as housewives to the Michigan CPS surveys fell from 49 percent to 27 percent, while the percentage of women reporting themselves in the work force rose only 41 percent to 50 percent. The residual category of "other" (temporarily laid off, unemployed, retired, permanently disabled, and student) thus rose from 10 percent to 23 percent in a way that seems to reflect at least in part respondents' decisions not to identify themselves as housewives. For this point, see Keith T. Poole and L. Harmon Zeigler, "Gender and Voting in the 1980 Presidential Election" (paper presented at the annual meeting of the American Political Science Association, Denver, Colo., September 1982, p. 2).

45. Barbara Ehrenreich, *The Hearts of Men* (New York: Anchor/ Doubleday, 1983), especially "Backlash," her chapter on the ERA.

46. Ibid., p. 146.

47. Schlafly, *Power,* p. 76.

48. Quoted by Jane O'Reilly, in *The Girl I Left Behind* (New York:

Macmillan, 1980), p. 189, punctuation edited. Ehrenreich (pp. 148–149) drew my attention to both of these quotations.

49. Rhode, p. 8.

50. Dr. Joyce Brothers, quoted in Carol Felsenthal, *Sweetheart of the Silent Majority* (New York: Doubleday, 1981), p. 287. Schlafly's snappy reply was: "Forty million women are being supported by their husbands today" (ibid.).

51. In the 1977 and 1982 NORC General Social Surveys, homemakers were more likely than women in the paid labor force to say that the nation was spending "too little on welfare" (r = .14 in 1977, .09 in 1982; there were essentially no differences between the two groups on questions regarding spending on improving the conditions of blacks and on improving and protecting the nation's health. On the other hand, in 1982, 52 percent of homemakers who claimed they had voted in 1980 (N = 134) said they had voted for Reagan, compared to 49 percent of women in the labor force (N = 262). In both 1977 and 1982, women in the labor force were somewhat more likely than homemakers to say that the nation was spending "too little" on improving and protecting the environment," "solving the problems of the big cities," and "improving the nation's education system." Women in the labor force were also slightly more likely to say the nation spent "too much" on "the military, armaments and defense." But none of these differences were more than a few percentage points. Men whose wives worked in the paid labor force were also slightly more likely than men whose wives were homemakers to take a liberal position on all these measures except welfare. On welfare there was no difference between the two groups of men.

52. The GSS for 1977 shows differences between women in the paid labor force and homemakers comparable to those in table A9 (GSS 1982), as does the NES for 1976, 1980, and 1982. However, in 1981, Gallup recorded "no significant differences in attitude toward the amendment [ERA] between working men and women and those not employed outside the home." Gallup News Release, reported in Santa Barbara, California *News-Press*, August 9, 1981.

A regression analysis using the 1977 and 1982 GSS indicates that 99 percent of the difference between homemakers and working women on the ERA can be explained by age and attitudes toward permissiveness in sexual relations, including interracial marriage.

53. NOW data reported in Freeman, p. 91; U.S. data from GSS 1974; 793 respondents coded as female, of whom 412 answered the question, "Last week were you working full time, part time, going to school, keeping house or what?" with the answer, "Keeping house." See the numbers of cases in table A9 for the declining numbers identifying themselves as homemakers in 1974, 1977, and 1982.

54. Freeman, p. 91.

55. "What's Wrong with 'Equal Rights' for Women?" *Phyllis Schlafly Report* 5, no. 7 (February 1972). Many commentators have repeated Schlafly's story about how she had no interest in the ERA until December 1971, when a friend insisted she learn something about it (Felsenthal, *Sweetheart,* p. 240). When she did turn to it, however, she had a reservoir of bitterness on the subject dating from at least two months earlier, when "the tight little clique running things from the top" [of the National Federation of Republican Women] had "presented speaker after speaker to promote the Equal Rights Amendment, but gave no 'equal rights' to delegates who wanted to speak against it" ("What's Wrong . . . ," p. 3). This was the very group of liberal Republican Women who had, in a "tumultuous . . . bitter . . . maligning and vilifying" internal battle, prevented Schlafly from being elected president of the Federation (Felsenthal, *Sweetheart,* pp. 179 ff).

In her next newsletter on the subject ("The Fraud Called the Equal Rights Amendment," *Phyllis Schlafly Report* 5, no. 10, sec. 2 [May 1972]), Schlafly reported that her February issue ("What's Wrong . . .") had drawn "[t]he biggest response in the five-year history of this newsletter." Her subsequent appearance, April 19, on the Phil Donahue Show, convinced her that "the live studio audience was 98 percent against women's lib and the Equal Rights Amendment," and so was the "flood of fan mail that resulted from the show." Schlafly had walked into the biggest issue in her career.

56. "The Right to be a Woman," *Phyllis Schlafly Report* 6, no. 4 (November 1973).

57. See table A9; and also Mark R. Daniels, Robert Darcy, and Joseph W. Westphal, "The ERA Won—at Least in the Opinion Polls," *PS* 15 (1982): 580.

58. Paul A. Freund, "The Equal Rights Amendment Is Not the Way," *Harvard Civil Rights—Liberties Law Review* 6 (1971): 240. In his testimony to the Senate Judiciary Committee, Freund was equally careful. He said, "let us see whether the analogy to race is a satisfying one. . . . The strict model of racial equality . . . would require that there be no segregation of the sexes in prisons, reform schools, public restrooms, and other public facilities" (Equal Rights 1970, Hearings before the Committee on Judiciary, U.S. Senate, 91st Cong., 2d sess., on *S.J. Res. 61* and *S.J. Res. 231* [Washington, D.C.: Government Printing Office, 1970], September 9, 1970, p. 74). Freund's hypothetical became, in Schlafly's words, "Professor Paul Freund at the Harvard Law School testified that the ERA would be absolute and 'would require that there be no segregation of the sexes in prison, reform schools, public restrooms, and other public facilities' " ("The Fraud . . ." p. 2). Similarly, in the same hearings Professor Philip B. Kurland testified that "if all classification by sex was [sic] made invalid," laws requiring separate restrooms would be nullified. He added, however,

that although he believed that the language of the Amendment was absolute, "I would have to submit that the judiciary does not conclude that
because the language of legislation is a clear mandate that they are not free
to indulge in other devices for its construction" ("Equal Rights . . .,"
September 10, 1970, p. 94). Schlafly reported his words without the dis-
claimer ("The Fraud . . .," p. 2).

59. Lisa Cronin Wohl, "The ERA: What the Hell Happened in New
York," *Ms.* (March 1976): 64, 65.

60. In the NORC General Social Survey, February–April 1982, respondents were asked, after a favor/oppose ERA question, "Why do you
(favor/oppose) the Equal Rights Amendment?" and were probed for three
reasons. After three probes, only 2.8 percent of the opponents ($N = 353$)
gave reasons relating to unisex bathrooms. In the same three probes, 21
percent gave reasons relating to women being drafted or sent into combat,
and 15 percent reasons relating to the ERA's promoting abortions. In July
17–20, 1981, the Roper organization asked a national sample, after a
favor/oppose ERA question, "Why do you feel this way?" There were no
probes. Seventeen percent of those opposed (weighted $N = 771$) volunteered that they were opposed to military service for women. Six percent
gave miscellaneous uncoded reasons, among which were presumably abortion funding and unisex toilets (AIPO 177G, forms A and B; data run by the
Roper Center, University of Connecticut).

61. In a Harris survey for the National Federation of Business and
Professional Women, November 30–December 2, 1979 ($N = 1494$), 18
percent of the total answered that if the ERA were passed it would be
"more likely to happen because of the Equal Rights Amendment" that
"separate public toilets for men and women would not be allowed"; 76
percent said it "won't happen"; 1 percent volunteered that it had already
happened; and 5 percent were not sure. (29 percent of those opposed to the
ERA [$N = 502$] thought that unisex toilets would be more likely to
happen.) For comparison, 55 percent of the total sample thought that it
would be more likely because of the ERA that "women will be drafted to
serve in combat," and 53 percent thought that "abortions will become more
common."

62. For North Carolina, see Donald G. Mathews and Jane De Hart
Mathews, "The Cultural Politics of ERA's Defeat," *Organization of American Historians Newsletter* (November 1982): pp. 14–15. I would like to
thank Donald Mathews for bringing to my attention the almost mythic
salience of the "potty" issue to North Carolina activists. I have no data on
Florida, but in Tedin's representative Texas sample ($N = 351$, date: Spring
1977), 25 percent of the public thought that the ERA was "likely" or "very
likely" to "require unisex toilets." This is higher than Harris's 13 percent
nationwide, presumably because Texas is a southern state where the issue

of integrating toilets still had great resonance from the civil rights era, and because the survey was taken at the height of the campaign to rescind Texas's earlier ratification of the ERA. Among members of the public who opposed the ERA, the percentages would undoubtedly have been even higher. (In the same survey, 69 percent of the Texas public thought it likely or very likely that under an ERA "women will be drafted." Tedin did not ask about abortions.) Kent L. Tedin, "If the Equal Rights Amendment Becomes Law: Perceptions of Consequences among Female Activists and Masses" (paper presented at the annual meeting of the Midwest Political Science Association, Chicago, Ill., April 1980).

63. Tedin, for example, compares his Texas public in 1977 to his study the same year of 335 Texas anti-ERA and antifeminist activists, 85 percent of whom believed that the ERA was "likely" or "very likely" to "require unisex toilets." (91 percent thought it likely or very likely that women will be drafted.) Tedin concludes that while the general public distinguished among the more and less plausible consequences of the ERA, the anti-feminist activists' beliefs were part of a "ritualistic" response in which "the attitude is causing the belief" (ibid., p. 6).

64. Illinois House of Representatives, June 8, 1982, p. 138.

65. For example, Professor Thomas Emerson testifying in Connecticut: see above, Chapter 8 n. 38. Emerson further concluded that the opposition to the ERA in Connecticut, in all respects other than their treatment of the combat issue,

> has been characterized by a degree of misrepresentation and distortion of fact that is virtually unprecedented in the annals of public debate. And the falsifications have been constantly repeated despite the fact that time after time the errors have been called to the attention of those who insist on spreading them.

Above statement by Thomas I. Emerson was given before the Government Administration and Policy Committees of the Connecticut General Assembly on Proposed Resolution to Rescind Connecticut's Ratification of the Equal Rights Amendment, 13 pp., p. 8, from the University of California at Santa Barbara Women's Center ERA files (mimeographed).

66. Debrah Bokowski, "State Legislator Perceptions of Public Debate on the Equal Rights Amendment," paper presented at the annual meeting of the American Political Science Association, Denver, Colo., September 1982. There is a parallel to the ideological distance between opposition legislators and opposition activists in the arguments that differently educated members of the public made against the ERA. In the 1982 GSS sample, among the college and graduate school educated ($N = 58$) 43 percent volunteered as a reason for their opposition that the ERA

was not needed, compared to 18 percent of those with high school degrees or some college ($N = 196$) and only 7 percent of those with less than a high school degree ($N = 85$). On the other hand, in the least educated group 31 percent volunteered some version of the idea that women simply were not equal, compared to 19 percent of those with high school or some college, and only 7 percent of those with college or graduate degrees. Thus the most and least educated had very different reasons for opposing the ERA. There was some difference between the more and less educated supporters of the ERA: the college and graduate educated gave more reasons of principle (23 percent, $N = 146$) than those who had not finished high school (18 percent, $N = 225$), and fewer economic reasons (28 compared to 37 percent). But the overlap between classes, as measured by education, was much greater than among the opponents.

67. Boles, *Politics*, p. 7.

Chapter 10

1. James Q. Wilson, "Incentive Systems: A Theory of Organization," *Administrative Science Quarterly* 6 (1961): 129–166 (with Peter B. Clark); *The Amateur Democrat* (Chicago: University of Chicago Press, 1962), esp. pp. 156–163; and *Political Organizations* (New York: Basic Books, 1973), introduced to political science the kind of analysis I employ here. In his terms, the ERA movement relied primarily on "purposive" and secondarily on collective "solidary" incentives. Because the movement combined what Wilson terms "goal-oriented," "ideological," and "redemptive" purposes, it suffered from the inherent contradictions of such a combination. In sociology, Amitai Etzioni's *Comparative Analysis of Complex Organizations* (New York: Free Press [1961], 1975) earlier introduced a similar classification of organizations into those which rely on "coercive," "utilitarian," and "normative" compliance, with the "core" organizations of social movements usually depending heavily on normative compliance (p. 41).

2. Mancur Olson, *The Logic of Collective Action* (Cambridge, Mass.: Harvard University Press, 1965). Many analyses of social movements have used Olson's analysis, almost always pointing out that social movements, precisely because they rely on ideological (or "purposive") and solidarity incentives, fall into a category of organizations that Olson himself decided not to analyze. See, for example, Bruce Fireman and William Gamson, "Utilitarian Logic in the Resource Mobilization Perspective," in Mayer M. Zald and John D. McCarthy, eds., *The Dynamics of Social Movements* (Cambridge, Mass.: Winthrop, 1979); Maren L. Carden, *Feminism in the Mid-1970's* (New York: Ford Foundation, 1977); Ralph Turner and Lewis M. Killian, *Collective Behavior* (Englewood Cliffs, N.J.: Prentice-Hall, 1972); Anthony Oberschall, *Social Conflict and Social Movements* (Englewood Cliffs, N.J.: Prentice-Hall, 1973); J. Craig Jenkins, "Sociopolitical

Movements," in Samuel Long, ed., *The Handbook of Political Behavior,* vol. 4 (New York: Plenum Press, 1981); Norman Frohlich, Joe A. Oppenheim, and Oran R. Young, *Political Leadership and Collective Goods* (Princeton: Princeton University Press, 1971); and Mary Douglas and Aaron Wildavsky, *Risk and Culture* (Berkeley: University of California Press, 1982). For an excellent review of the literature, see David Knoke and Christine Wright-Isak, "Individual Motives and Organizational Incentive Systems," *Research in the Sociology of Organizations* 1 (1982): 209–254. For an analysis of the anti- and pro-ERA movements and the anti- and pro-abortion movements in Olson's terms, see Conover and Gray, who point out (table 5.7) that in their small sample of activists all twenty-eight members of New Right organizations and all 8 members of liberal organizations gave personal principles or ideology as their primary motive in joining the organization. For the tactics of women's groups trying to represent a diffuse interest with few selective benefits, see Anne E. Costain, "The Struggle for a National Women's Lobby: Organizing a Diffuse Interest," *Western Political Quarterly* 33 (1980): 476–491.

3. *Roe v. Wade*, 410 U.S. 113 (1973).

4. The eventual ACLU decision to stress autonomous decision making free from state intervention rather than sex discrimination in the federal abortion funding case was, however, made on the basis of "what argument was most likely to win. . . . The ERA was not a consideration in how that case was argued—not at all" (telephone interview with Ruth Bader Ginsburg, November 7, 1985). See also Law, pp. 981–982.

5. *Hawaii Right to Life, Inc. v. Chang, Director of Social Services and Housing*, Civ. No. 53567, Memorandum in Support of Motion to Intervene, p. 1, cited in *Impact Hearings* vol. 1, pp. 562, 659–660.

6. *Harris v. McRae*, 448 U.S. 297 (1980), at 325, 326. The state case was *U.S. v. Zbaraz*, 448 U.S. 324 (1980).

7. "From the Executive Director's Desk," *Docket* (newsletter of the Civil Liberties Union of Massachusetts), paper 1980, in *Impact Hearings,* vol. 1, p. 657.

8. *Moe v. Secretary of Administration and Finance*, 417 N.E. 2d 387 (Mass. 1980), quoted in part in *Impact Hearings*, vol 1, p. 657.

9. *Rosie J. Doe et al v. Edward Mahler et al.*, Superior Court, Judicial District of New Haven, Memorandum of Decision on Motions for Class Certification, Motion for Temporary Injunction and Certain Other Motions. October 9, 1981, in *Impact Hearings,* vol. 1, pp. 655–656.

10. John A. MacPhael, Judge of the Commonwealth Court of Penn-

sylvania, Opinion in *Fischer v. Department of Public Welfare*, 283 C.D. 1981, heard February 7, 1984, in *Impact Hearings*, vol. 1, p. 641.

11. Ann Freedman argued in the 1983 hearings that the Supreme Court would interpret the ERA, as the *Yale Law Journal* article and subsequent expansions of that theory in *Gilbert* argued it should, to prohibit absolutely legislative classification by gender except in cases of privacy, unique physical characteristics, and temporary compensatory treatment to make up for past discrimination. These three exceptions would be subject to strict judicial scrutiny.

She then argued that the ERA would not raise the standard of scrutiny in abortion funding cases beyond the standard the Court had already used in *Harris v. McRae*. This argument assumed that the Court in *Harris* had used a strict scrutiny standard, on the grounds that abortion legislation involves the fundamental right of privacy and the Court uses strict scrutiny in cases that involve a fundamental right *(City of Akron v. Akron Center for Reproductive Health)*. Ann Freedman, Testimony in *Impact Hearings*, vol. 1, pp. 451–454; summarized p. 502; and Letter to Representative John Edwards, Nov. 7, 1983, in *Impact Hearings*, vol. 1, pp. 624–625. Freedman particularly pointed out in her letter to Representative Edwards that if the Supreme Court in *Harris* had wanted to see abortion funding as raising an important issue of sex discrimination, the Court would have used the middle-tier standard it had already created in *Craig v. Boren*, and would have asked whether the Hyde amendment was "substantially related to an important government interest." "Instead," Freedman noted, "the Supreme Court decided the case entirely on privacy grounds and dismissed the sex discrimination argument." *Impact Hearings*, vol. 1, p. 625.

Other lawyers believed that the Court would not feel required by an ERA to change its abortion funding decisions because funding issues preeminently involve the equal protection of the laws: if the state funds one class, it must also fund the others. Under this reasoning, abortion funding issues are essentially Fourteenth Amendment issues.

12. Ann Freedman, Testimony in *Impact Hearings*, vol. 1, pp. 490–491. See also p. 506, where Freedman pointed out that the legislative history had to be made by "a senatorial or congressional proponent." Opponents of the ERA, like Senator Hatch, often suggested incorrectly that arguments by feminist lawyers in the state courts, by feminist organizations, and by opponents in the Congress constituted legislative history.

Senator Hatch, in a particularly distasteful piece of manipulation, claimed that the 1983 legislative history indicated an ERA-abortion link because "Senator Tsongas had the opportunity to disclaim [the ERA-abortion funding link] and failed to" (p. 507). But anyone reading Tsongas's remarks would understand that he intended no such thing. Completely unprepared and on his way to a plane, Tsongas at first answered vaguely to almost every question on the effect of the ERA, suggesting (in words that would later be used against the ERA) that all of these matters would "be settled in the courts." Later, when he began to see the trap that Hatch had led him into, he began to backtrack, saying, "I will answer all of your questions in writing" (p. 31), "Why were not these questions submitted when we would have a chance to review them and give you detailed answers?" (p. 32), and "I simply am asking that the committee give me the right to look at [these questions on the effect of the ERA] and respond to you. I did not anticipate the questions; I did not anticipate the tactics" (p. 39). Out of this material, Senator Hatch's Subcommittee on the Constitution created the following misleading summary:

Legislative History

The most compelling legislative history on the meaning of an amendment comes from its Congressional proponents. In responding to the alleged ERA/abortion connection, the Senate co-sponsors of the ERA stated as follows: (Sen. Robert Packwood) "I'm not sure how a court would come out on it." (Sen. Paul Tsongas) "This issue would be resolved by the courts."

—Impact Hearings, *vol. 1, p. 548*

13. Opponents also picked up a feminist law professor's use of the ERA to support abortion rights in an article in *Ms.* magazine after the 1982 deadline. That article argued that "the separation of abortion from the campaign for the ERA has jeopardized abortion and produced a truncated version of liberation." Rhonda Copelon, "Abortion Rights: Where Do We Go From Here?" *Ms.* (October 1983): p. 146, reprinted in *Impact Hearings,* vol. 1, p. 639. The ERA-abortion link had a continuing impact, for example on U.S. Representative James Oberstar who voted for the ERA when it came before the U.S. House in November 1983 but changed his mind later, saying he would now support the ERA only with an amendment stating that it did not pertain to abortions *(Eleanor Smeal Report,* April 19, 1984, p. 4).

14. In the 1982 GSS, 52 percent of the people who favored the ERA answered "no" to the question, "Please tell me whether or not you think it should be possible for a pregnant woman to obtain a legal abortion if the woman wants it for any reason." See table 1 in Chapter 3 for support for the ERA from those who took traditional positions on women's roles.

15. See Chapter 6, esp. n. 14.

16. Statement of William J. Wiseman, Jr., on Equal Rights Amendment Extension, U.S. House of Representatives, Subcommittee on Civil and Constitutional Rights of the Committee on the Judiciary, May 17, 1978, pp. 212–213. For wording, see Chapter 12 n. 12.

17. "The Legality of Homosexual Marriage," *Yale Law Journal* 82 (1973): 573.

18. "The legislative history of the Amendment clearly supports the interpretation that sex is to be an impermissible legal classification . . . [and] a statute or administrative policy which permits a man to marry a woman, subject to certain regulatory restrictions, but categorically denies him the right to marry another man clearly entails a classification along sexual lines" (ibid., p. 583). See also, "It was the clear intent of Congress to forbid classifications along sexual lines regardless of the countervailing government interests which might be raised to justify such classification" (p. 585), and "The legislative history supports this proposition that the new Amendment represents an unqualified prohibition—an absolute guarantee" (p. 585). As in other Yale articles on the ERA in this period, the argument for this version of the legislative history relies heavily on the words "sex should not be a factor" in the Senate (and House) Judiciary Committee reports and on the House rejections of the Wiggins amendment (see above, p. 51 n. 25; p. 62 n. 5). This article adds, and makes its first argument, the statement by Senator Stevenson, one of the many cosponsors of the Amendment, "There is but one principle involved . . . sex, by and of itself cannot be used as a classification to deny or abridge any person of his or her equal rights under the law." 118 *Cong. Rec.*, 54571, March 21, 1972.

19. *Cong. Rec.*, 54389, March 21, 1972. Perkins and Silverstein admitted that Bayh's opinion should be given considerable weight in determining the legislative intent, but concluded that "it cannot be seen as controlling unless it is at least reasonably consistent with established Constitutional doctrine and the more general interpretation of the proposed Amendment as evidenced in the legislative history" (pp. 583–584). By "established constitutional doctrine" the authors mean *Loving v. Virginia*, 388 U.S. 1 (1967), in which the Court ruled that a marriage license cannot be denied merely because the applicants are of different races. This case can be interpreted in the way that Senator Bayh and Thomas Emerson, two proponents of the ERA, interpreted it, as well as in the way Perkins and Silverstein interpreted it, drawing on the conclusions of two opponents of the ERA, Senator Ervin and Professor Paul Freund. By the "more general interpretation of the legislative history" the authors mean the Yale interpretation.

20. The only ERA supporters I know who suggested publicly that the ERA might provide the basis for a court's ruling unconstitutional prohibition on homosexual marriages are Barbara Allen Babcock, Ann E. Freedman, Eleanor Holmes Norton and Susan C. Ross, who said only, "The effect that the Equal Rights Amendment will have on discrimination against homosexuals is not yet clear. The legislative history suggests that it was not the intent of Congress to prohibit such discrimination. On the other hand, it is hard to justify a distinction between discrimination on the basis of the sex of one's sexual partners and other sex-based discrimination" *(Sex Discrimination and the Law* [Boston, Mass.: Little, Brown, 1975], p. 180, footnotes and citations omitted). The position of the NOW Legal Defense

and Education Fund, for example, was that "the equal rights amendment does not reach discrimination on the basis of sexual preference" *Impact Hearings,* vol. 2, p. 87). ERA supporters usually cited *Singer v. Hara,* 11 Wash. App. 247, 522 p. 2d 1187 (1974), in which a state court of appeals held that the ERA in the constitution of the state of Washington did not invalidate a state law prohibiting same-sex marriages. They could also have pointed out that in the case law developed for interpreting Title VII, discrimination based on sex is a basis for Title VII coverage, while discrimination based on sexual preference is not (Karen J. Lewis, Congressional Research Service, "A Legal Analysis of the Potential Impact of the Proposed Equal Rights Amendment [ERA] on Homosexuals," October 12, 1983, in *Impact Hearings,* vol. 1, p. 1017–1018).

21. Berenice A. Carroll, "Direct Action and Constitutional Rights: The Case of the ERA," *Organization of American Historians' Newsletter* 11 (1983): 18–21, lists several other instances of direct action in support of the ERA. Carroll, a member of the "Grassroots Group of Second-Class Citizens," which chained itself to the railings before the Illinois State Senator Chamber, concludes that NOW "informally discouraged" civil disobedience and that "in the major ERA campaign organizations" direct action "was viewed with much doubt, if not hostility." In the discussions in which I participated, I sensed caution but support rather than hostility and, among many, active enthusiasm. In any case, as Carroll reports, direct action provoked "much debate on its wisdom and effectiveness." For the difficulties of controlling autonomous direct action that had potentially negative effects on public opinion, see Rhode, pp. 59–61.

22. In June 1982, when seven women were protesting nonratification through a public fast in the rotunda of the state capitol which seriously weakened their health, Market Opinion Research asked a sample of Illinois voters, "Do you approve or disapprove of the efforts of women's groups over the past two weeks to get the ERA ratified? Sixty-seven percent of the voters opposed those efforts, with only 23 percent favoring them and 11 percent having no opinion ($N = 79$). Women were slightly more likely to oppose (69 percent) than men. Even among ERA supporters, 54 percent opposed.

23. *Phyllis Schlafly Report* 9, no. 11, sec. 2 (June 1976).

24. See comments on Georgia in Boles, *Politics,* pp. 76–77.

25. See Luther P. Gerlach and Virginia H. Hine, *People, Power, Change: Movements of Social Transformation* (Indianapolis: Bobbs-Merrill, 1970), pp. 34—78, esp. pp. 63 ff.: "The Adaptive Functions of Decentralized, Segmented, Reticulate Structure." Manfred Kocken and Karl W. Deutsch, "Toward a Rational Theory of Decentralization," *American Political Science Review* 63 (1969): 734–749, point out that decentral-

ized structures are more likely to act with speed, accuracy, innovation, and adaptability. Herbert A. Simon, *Administrative Behavior* (New York: Macmillan. 1960), p. 238, recommends decentralization for speed. Warren G. Bennis and Philip E. Slater, *The Temporary Society* (New York: Harper and Row, 1969), indicate that structures in which participants autonomously determine much of what they do are likely to be innovative and adaptable. Amitai Etzioni, p. 71, citing a study of the League of Women Voters, points out that in organizations where the incentives for participation are nonmaterial (or moral, solidary, purposive, or ideological, depending on one's terminology), high control leads to less loyalty, while decentralization leads to more loyalty.

26. Having paid a price, emotionally or otherwise, people often upgrade in their minds the worth of the good they have paid for. See Leon Festinger, *A Theory of Cognitive Dissonance* (Evanston, Ill.: Row, Peterson, 1957); E. Aronson and J. Mills, "The Effect of Severity of Initiation on Liking for a Group," *Journal of Abnormal and Social Psychology* 59 (1959): 177–181; and, for a recent summary and critique of the literature, Hal R. Arkes and John P. Garske, *Psychological Theories of Motivation,* 2d ed. (Monterey, Calif.: Brooks/Cole Publishing, 1982).

27. The same person told me that "there is always a temptation in a movement, where there's a lot of emotionalism and so on, to take the reins as a charismatic leader and get everybody marching with you, and to order them here and there. And that ability to influence people is heavy stuff, and I think all of us appreciate the dangers in that, and we find ourselves liking it too much. We begin to back off." This recognition and conscious avoidance of the seductions of power was common among the participatory democrats of the American 1960s and 1970s. See my chapter, "The Lust for Power," in *Beyond Adversary Democracy.*

28. Felsenthal, *Sweetheart,* p. 261.

29. Ibid., p. 267–268.

30. Representative Brummer, Illinois House of Representatives, Judiciary I Committee, Hearings on House Resolution CAI [ERA], April 30, 1980, and Illinois House of Representatives, June 18, 1980, p. 151.

31. See also Mueller and Dimieri, p. 662, for the tension and lack of communication between anti-ERA groups in Massachusetts in 1976. STOP ERA was hierarchical internally but had the problems of coalitions that all groups experience.

32. ERA Illinois Decision Analysis, Part A: Comparison of Alternatives, p. 11. Completed by members of the Executive Committee of ERA Illinois and interested board members on September 6, 1980, and compiled

by Gloria Phillips, Federally Employed Women. Cost was not the only reason for not stressing the research effort. As Part B (Adverse Consequence Analysis) of the ERA Illinois Decision Analysis pointed out, there were problems in disseminating information once the information had been collected. Moreover, by the end of the ten-year struggle, few voters or activists seemed to be interested in education. They wanted action.

33. The organization was poor enough that when an employee at the Post Office lost or intentionally mislaid a major mailing of the newsletters containing both information on how each state representative had stood on the last ERA vote and a special code to try to trace which members had not paid their dues, ERA Illinois simply could not afford to duplicate the mailing.

34. Correspondence from the files of Barbara D. Haas, past president, Women in Communications, Inc.

35. NOW Legal Defense and Education Fund and Women's Law Project's ERA Impact Project, *ERA Impact Clearinghouse Index and References.*

36. In early 1982, I experienced the effects of the mindset, when, in response to a request from an Illinois legislator to ERA Illinois for a list of discriminatory laws to insert in her speech during the final legislative debate on the ERA, I agreed to try to compile such a list. The list ERAmerica had sent me, information from Women in Communications, and the U.S. Commission on Civil Rights brochure, "The Equal Rights Amendment: Guaranteeing Equal Rights for Women Under the Constitution" (Washington, D.C.: Government Printing Office, 1981), which spent fifteen of its twenty-nine pages on the positive practical effects of the Amendment, together produced a list of only twenty-five discriminatory state laws that (1) seemed important enough to mention in debate, (2) were still on the books, and (3) had not yet been declared unconstitutional. When two feminist lawyers scrutinized my list, they told me they considered only three or four of those twenty-five laws still constitutional in the light of the Supreme Court's expanded interpretation of the equal protection clause. No doubt, mine was a very incomplete list of laws. Moreover, since it was clear by 1982 that the ERA was not going to pass, the lawyers I consulted had a stake in the broadest possible interpretation of the Fourteenth Amendment. Nevertheless, I realized later, by 1982 even a more exhaustive search and a more restrictive interpretation of "equal protection" would not, as the aide at LDEF suggested, have produced an impressive list.

37. Lisa Cronin Wohl, "The ERA: What the Hell Happened in New York?" *Ms.* (March 1976): 65, 92.

38. Ibid., p. 65.

39. Ibid., p. 66.

40. Cited in Justice, ed., p. 17.

41. Cited in Ellen Goodman, "At Large," *Boston Globe,* reprinted in *National NOW Times* (January/February 1984): 9.

42. "ERA ERA ERA YES YES YES," NOW pamphlet (n.d., probably 1980). See also "ERA and the 59 Cent Wage Gap," NOW pamphlet (1981): "The ERA will be an important legal weapon to counter sex-based discrimination in employment regardless of the political climate. The ERA will provide for more effective and aggressive enforcement of anti-discrimination laws. The ERA will create a uniform standard that all courts must apply when they decide cases raising problems of sex discrimination in employment and education."

43. Wohl, p. 65.

44. Boles, *Politics,* pp. 17–18, applying to the ERA the characterizations of "community conflict" of James S. Coleman, *Community Conflict* (New York: Free Press, 1957), and Robert L. Crain et al., *The Politics of Community Conflict* (Indianapolis: Bobbs-Merrill, 1969).

45. Bokowski, "State Legislator Perceptions," fig. 2.

Chapter 11

1. It is also possible that, in spite of court surveillance of the districting process, the way many states were divided into districts favored the rural, conservative legislators at the expense of those more likely to support the ERA. I do not have the detailed district by district public opinion data that would be necessary either to test this hypothesis or to estimate the number of districts in which a majority either favored or opposed the ERA.

2. Kathy A. Stanwick and Katherine E. Kleeman, "Women Make a Difference" (New Brunswick, N.J.: Center for the American Woman and Politics, Eagleton Institute of Politics, Rutgers University, 1983), pp. 13–14. The exact figures for all the state legislatures are 77 percent of the women ($N = 499$) compared to 49 percent of the men ($N = 267$). These figures derive from a mail-back questionnaire to all women state legislators and a systematic sample of male legislators, with a 57 percent response rate from the women and a 52 percent response rate from the men. The percent "strongly" agreeing with ERA ratification show an even greater gender difference, of 62 percent of the women legislators compared to 26 percent of the men. (I would like to thank Wendy Strimling, of the Center for the American Woman and Politics, for providing the original tabulations from which I could calculate both the numbers of cases reported above and the

percentages strongly agreeing.) In Illinois, the 1982 role call on the ERA found 75 percent of the women representatives voting for the ERA compared to 55 percent of the men ("How House Members Voted on ERA Ratification," *Chicago Tribune*, June 23, 1982, p. 5) See also Shelah Gilbert Leader, "The Policy Impact of Elected Women Officials," in Louis Maisel and Joseph Cooper, eds., *The Impact of the Electoral Process* (Beverly Hills, Calif.: Sage, 1977), pp. 265–284: 68 percent of the women legislators in unratified states voted for the ERA compared to 42 percent of the men (as of July 1976, using roll call votes in states where both houses of the legislature had voted on the ERA). In ratified states the figures were 86 percent of the women compared to 79 percent of the men. Also Marilyn Johnson and Susan Carroll, *Profile of Women Holding Office, 1977* (New Brunswick, N.J.: Center for the American Woman and Politics, Eagleton Institute of Politics, Rutgers University, 1977): 67 percent of women office-holders (primarily local council members) agreeing that the ERA should be ratified compared to 48 percent of a sample of comparable men (mail-back questionnaire survey). In Mezey's 1974 Hawaiian sample of local and state public officeholders (not state legislators), the women did not differ from comparable men in their support for the ERA. Lilie, Handberg, and Lowrey found that 72 percent of the women legislators who returned their 1977 survey supported the ERA. The longer a woman legislator had served in the legislature, the more likely she was to favor the ERA (table II).

The irony is that among the population as a whole women did not differ greatly from men in their support of the ERA (table A2, and Chapter 2 n. 36). The different balance in the legislature presumably derives both from pro-ERA constituencies being more likely to elect women, and from the women legislators occasionally acting as "trustees" and voting for their constituents' real interests against their expressed preferences.

3. In the present U.S. House of Representatives, however, gender does not seem to be an independent factor when controlling for incumbency and other relevant political variables. See Carol Uhlaner and Kay Lehman Schlozman, "Candidate Gender and Congressional Campaign Receipts," *Journal of Politics* (February 1986).

4. For the many connections between high executives in the insurance industry and the anti-ERA forces, including the Radical Right, see Ann K. Justice, ed., *The Insurance Connection with STOP ERA Forces* (Lincoln, Nebr.: National Organization for Women, 1974).

5. The industry would only lose if such shifts reduced overall demand for insurance. Nor is it clear whether women would gain or lose. "Whole life" insurance would cost women less, but "term" life would cost them more. In principle, men might withdraw from the "whole life" life insurance market and begin saving money to provide insurance for themselves, but this is not very likely in practice.

6. In May 1983, for instance, the American Council of Life Insurance

voted "overwhelmingly" to support rates based on sex, and fourteen members, including Aetna, Nationwide, Fireman's Fund, Allstate and Traveller's, produced a budget of $500,000 to influence public opinion on this issue. The campaign included newspaper and radio advertisements, and a mailing to more than 500,000 constituents of fifteen House members and sixteen senators (Robert D. Hershey, Jr., "Insurance Lobbying Draws Ire," *New York Times,* May 20, 1983, sec. 1, p. 18; and Michael de Conrey Hinds, "Gender as an Insurance Issue Faces Showdown in Congress," *New York Times,* May 17, 1983, sec. 1, p. 16). In Montana in 1985, State Farm Insurane sent 92,000 letters to its policyholders forcasting large rate increases if "unisex" insurance legislation were to be allowed to go into effect. Aetna, U.S. Fidelity, and Guarantee telephoned their customers to get their signatures on letters against the legislation (Mike Dennison, "First Time for Unisex Insurance," *In These Times,* May 22–28, 1985, p. 7).

7. In 1974, the *Wall Street Journal* reported that "21 of the 58 members of the current Illinois state senate are licensed insurance brokers, agents, or both, as are 40 of the 174 members of the house. An estimated two dozen more legislators have other direct ties to the industry, serving as officers or directors of insurance companies or representing them as lawyers" (Jonathan Laing and Frederick Klein, "Industry Lobbies Are Active and Powerful at the State Level," *Wall Street Journal* 83, June 6, 1974, p. 1). The percentage of legislators actually connected with insurance may be as high in the other key nonratifying states. Certainly the percentage listing their occupation as "insurance" in the Illinois state legislative directory *(The Illinois Blue Book* [Springfield: Secretary of State, 1979], pp. 68–185) in 1979–1980 was about the same (6 percent, or 14 of 223) as in North Carolina (11 percent, or 19 of 172), *North Carolina Manual* [Raleigh, N.C.: Secretary of State, 1979], pp. 320–413) and Oklahoma (5 percent, or 8 of 149, *Directory of Oklahoma* [Oklahoma City: Secretary of State, 1979] pp. 115–123, 142–159). The Florida legislative directory did not list occupations in 1979. A 1977 analysis of legislators' occupations, "reviewing publications and other information that were obtained in each of the states," finds 5 percent of all legislators giving their occupation as "insurance" *(Occupational Profile of State Legislatures* [New York: Insurance Information Institute, 1977], cited in William J. Keefe and Morris S. Ogul, *The American Legislative Process* [Englewood Cliffs, N.J.: Prentice-Hall, 1981], p. 125). The pressure from insurance people could be extremely effective in an indirect way. For example, one Republican committeeman in Illinois, a lobbyist for an insurance company, reportedly refused to slate anyone for the state legislative elections who was not opposed to the ERA, even though his district was relatively liberal.

8. One Pro-ERA leader in the legislature put it this way:

The groups they [the antis] turned out initially, it was simply women whose children were raised, women who stayed at home all day, who had free time. And they were grim-faced, older women, usually of about the age of 50, and often above the age of 60, who came to oppose the ERA.

Now, since the opposition has been able to develop the fundamentalist religious types, you are seeing young women, women with babies, women with children, bearing their children. And so there has been a development of the base by the opposition, and there has been no corresponding development at the base by the proponents of the Equal Rights Amendment.

Another pro-ERA legislator noticed only the more superficial changes:

The antis, women who are antis, have changed to some degree. The ones who go to Springfield have changed over the last four or five years. The women who come to Springfield now against ERA are a trifle more—well, chic isn't the right word—they're a little more chic than they were. Let's put it this way: you see, they seem to be a little more—they're younger women. Some younger women and some women who are a little better dressed.

For a description of members of the prefundamentalist STOP ERA (in Connecticut, 1973), see Susan and Martin Tolchin, *Clout: Womanpower and Politics* (New York: Coward, McCann and Geogheghan, 1974), chap. 4.

9. 1976 SRC American National Election Study, as analyzed in Debrah Bokowski and Aage R. Clausen, "Federalism, Representation, and the Amendment Process: The Case of the Equal Rights Amendment" (paper presented at the annual meeting of the Midwest Political Science Association, Chicago, 1979).

10. Women were slightly less negative on this point (61 percent of all voters, 51 percent of ERA supporters). The fact that voters thought that a candidate's position on the ERA should be a "factor" in the upcoming election did not, of course, necessarily mean that they thought it should be an important, much less a decisive, factor. It would be a mistake to conclude from these figures that 25 percent of the Illinois electorate (those who said the ERA should be a factor) expected to decide for or against a candidate on the basis of that candidate's stand on the ERA. A more detailed analysis of public opinion and the ERA in this election appears in Mansbridge, "The ERA and the Gender Gap in Illinois" (paper presented at the annual meeting of the Midwest Political Science Association, Chicago, 1982). Data from Market Opinion Research; registered voters only. I would like to thank Frederick T. Steeper of Market Opinion Research for providing these data.

11. Representative Emil Jones, Illinois House of Representatives, June 18, 1980, p. 160.

12. Barbara Brotman, "Did ERA Groups Just Throw Money at Politicians?" *In These Times,* December 10–16, 1980, p. 5 (also Barbara Brotman and Marianne Taylor, "If Your Hear That Money Alone Has Swung Legislators' Votes, Reconsider," *Chicago Tribune,* November 2, 1980, sec. 12, p. 1). On the basis of campaign disclosure reports filed with the Illinois Board of Elections, Brotman concluded that STOP ERA, the major anti lobbying group, did outspend pro-ERA groups in the month before the 1980 election ($37,000 compared to $18,000). However, in the four years between 1976, when ERA contributions began to flow, and 1980, "the two sides were dead even: Pro-ERA groups contributed $114,109 in Illinois; anti-ERA groups, including conservative lobbies known to contribute to anti-ERA candidates, gave $115,660."

Judson H. Jones, comparing the same disclosure reports with consistent and inconsistent votes on the ERA in the 1977 and 1978 elections, produces a similar picture of most anti-ERA voters in the Illinois house receiving at least $150 contributions from STOP ERA, either as a reward for voting or as an inducement to shift (the timing is unclear). Seventy-four percent of the 57 consistent anti voters got such contributions, while only 30 percent of the 47 consistent pro voters got contributions of $150 or more from the pro-ERA organizations. Of the 42 *inconsistent* voters in 1977, six got STOP ERA contributions of $150 or more, and five got pro-ERA contributions of $150 or more. Five of the six who got STOP contributions of $150 or more moved in an anti-ERA direction in 1978, but only one of the five who got pro-ERA contributions of $150 or more moved in a pro-ERA direction. While Jones concludes, undoubtedly correctly, that "campaign financing did influence legislators' voting" (p. 84), the data he presents do not show any clear causal relation (Judson H. Jones, "The Effect of the Pro- and Anti-ERA Campaign Contributions on the ERA Voting Behavior of the 80th Illinois House of Representatives," *Women and Politics* 2 (1982): 71–86.

13. In 1982 NOW reported spending a great deal more than STOP ERA reported spending. NOW spent a total of $6 million from January to June 1982, while STOP ERA reported only about $200,000 (Jane O'Reilly, "The Big-Time Players Behind the Small-Town Image," *Ms.* [January 1983]: 59). See also Mueller and Dimieri, p. 662, comparing pro-ERA expenditures of $66,000 and anti-ERA expenditures of $5,000 in Massachusetts in 1976. In other states and years (e.g., Maine, 1984) the anti-ERA organizations spent a great deal more.

14. See also an ERA Illinois member:

We have only been working, you know, since 1978 and '80—perhaps '78 marginally—and '80 was the first time we really launched any meaningful campaign efforts. And Phyllis was back there in the precincts in 1974 and she beat us with money and door knockers. She bought it. You look at the disclosure statements back from 1974, and she bought and paid for her people then. . . . That's why we missed it years ago, by not getting politically active early enough. And I just was thinking that last night. Dang, if only I had known in 1976 what I know now.

A NOW leader agreed:

The antis knew all along where to work. The pros didn't. And it took [us] until 1978. . . . Phyllis [Schlafly] has been on the inside all along and knows it very well—or at least sort of semi-inside. In the years to come we'll do better at it.

A pro-ERA legislator had the same analysis:

A lot of these men I know that I have talked to over the phone, he took a position and got some help from the antis, because, very frankly, he didn't think about it much one way or another. The antis got to him first. And now he feels somewhat obligated to them.

15. Boles, *Politics,* pp. 62–66.

16. See also another pro-ERA leader in the Illinois legislature: "The pros have been much more naive than the antis, quite obviously, much less able to understand the political process, and still don't understand the political process."

17. Boles, *Politics,* p. 147; see also pp. 145–170 on problems with ERA sponsorship, committee consideration, etc., in the state legislatures. Deborah Rhode points out (p. 9) that Eugenia Chapman and Giddy Dyer, the two original women sponsors in the 1972 Illinois House of Representatives, "declined assistance" from the ninety-three male representatives ("comprising a larger than necessary constituency for passage") who offered to co-sponsor the measure. Rhode also documents (pp. 64–65, and citations therein) several other instances in which "ERA sponsors in contested states displayed singular mismanagement at certain critical junctures."

18. Eugenia Chapman, who does not see the issue this simply, told me, "I'm not a bit convinced it was seven votes. When I was pressured to vote for Daley, I was told that some people would be angry with me and not vote for the ERA. I asked, 'If I support Daley, will the ERA be passed?' But I didn't get that commitment. The way Daley operated was not to give but to take. I don't think they had any intention of letting the ERA pass, but they were using it to muscle me. And I had no intention of being muscled."

19. One of the black legislators described the incident this way: "The ERA people's lobbyist had gotten involved in the internal politics here in the House, which was affecting me and several other legislators, so I didn't

vote." Others indicated that the action involved an internal Black Caucus dispute over a leadership position.

Chapter 12

1. Illinois voters had approved a referendum reducing the number of legislators by one-third, thus requiring complete redistricting throughout Illinois. This issue too had divided the ERA forces in Illinois. NOW and most of the ERA Illinois leadership (at least half of whom were liberal Republicans) favored the traditional Illinois district system, which provided three representatives from each district, one of whom had to be, by law, a member of the district's minority party. The traditional system guaranteed that the electorate would return a fair number of liberal Republicans in otherwise Democratic districts. The large number of Representatives in the legislature under the traditional system also meant that the proportion of women legislators would probably be greater than in the new, smaller system. (In fact, because women were entering the political system at this time, the percentage of women in the old, larger House of Representatives—15.3 percent in 1981–1982—did not decline but increased slightly in the new, smaller house—16 percent in 1983–1984. However, in the same years, the number of women in the Illinois senate doubled from four to eight, increasing the percentage in that body from 6.7 to 13.5. The rapid increase of women in the senate, combined with the research indicating higher percentages of women in the larger legislatures, suggests that the percentage in the Illinois house might have grown a good deal larger had not the size of the legislature been reduced. I am grateful to Representative Barbara Currie for providing these data. See Diamond (1977) for the positive effect of large legislatures on the percentage of women representatives; and Frank M. Bryan, *Yankee Politics in Rural Vermont* [Hanover, N.H.: University Press of New England, 1974], for the positive effect of unequal districting.) Particularly, it seemed clear that in the new system the two key sponsors of the ERA—Susan Catania, a liberal Republican in a Democratic District, and Eugenia Chapman, an independent Democrat in a Republican district—would both lose their seats. Finally, no change was popular with the incumbent legislators, who had been elected under the old system. Because the change had originated with "the ladies" of the League of Women Voters, ERA supporters believed, correctly, that some legislators would blame them all for it and possibly hurt the ERA in the process. Nevertheless, the League of Women Voters, whose members for years had studied the issue of size and composition of the Illinois legislature, had come out solidly for the new system on the grounds that it would be cheaper and more efficient than the old. This "apolitical" business-management reasoning drove some of the more "political" women mad.

This chapter focuses on NOW and ERA Illinois. NOW was the most influential group in the ERA struggle in Illinois, and ERA Illinois was the only group focused solely on the ERA. A full history of the issue in Illinois would include analyses of the role of the League of Women Voters in particular, and of the Federation of Business and Professional Women, American Association of University Women (AAUW), Homemakers for ERA (HERA), church groups, and other groups that at various points became active in the struggle. For a short history of the AAUW's ERA efforts in Illinois, see Nancy Douglas Joyner, "Coalition Politics: A Case Study of an Organization's Approach to a Single Issue," *Women and Politics* 2 (1982): 57–70.

2. My experience confirms this analysis. At one statewide Illinois NOW conference, a speaker asked if there were any Republicans in the audience of about sixty. When no hands were raised, delighted laughter erupted from the floor. In one of the NOW buses I rode down to Springfield, someone, giving directions to the driver, shouted out, "Turn right!" And the answering shout came from somewhere in the bus, "Never turn right; always turn left!" In Arrington and Kyle's North Carolina sample, only three of the thirty-seven pro-ERA women identified herself as a Republican (Arrington and Kyle, table 1).

3. See, for example, the disagreement between these two groups on whether to stress getting the 107 votes needed for a three-fifths vote in the Illinois house, or to try instead to get the eighty-nine votes needed to change the three-fifths rule that the Illinois constitution required for constitutional amendments. The Republican Speaker upheld the three-fifths rule, and the Democrats' proposed change to a majority rule came in a package that would otherwise benefit the Democrats. Democratic ERA supporters thus pressed for the adoption of the Democratic package; Republican supporters tried to garner the full 107 votes. Neither group was able to find sufficient votes to succeed.

In this account, when I refer to ERA Illinois "members" and "meetings," I mean members of the ERA Illinois board of directors and meetings of that board. From 1980 to 1982, when I was a member, ERA Illinois had a complex structure, evolved from a tumultuous history. It was a coalition of organizations that endorsed the ERA in Illinois. Any of these organizations could petition the board for one of the forty places on the board reserved for organizations, and the board would vote to give that organization's representative one of those places. As a matter of course, the board always voted any major organization a place. In addition, twelve places were reserved for individual members, of which I was one, upon a vote of the board. In practice, many of the legal representatives of the constituent groups did not attend the meetings, so that much of the hard work of the board was done by seven or eight representatives of organizations along with the seven or eight individual members. ERA Illinois also had at-large members whose connection with the organization consisted primarily of paying dues, receiving the newsletter, and sending letters to their state representatives, although they were authorized and encouraged to attend the organization's yearly meeting and to become members of the board. I would estimate that among the members of the board about half were Republicans and half Democrats.

4. As another ERA Illinois leader described it:

The strategy that we have evolved was to work with the leadership of both sides. That meant making friends with the enemy, while never forgetting that the enemy, in the person that was Speaker of the House, George Ryan, was indeed anti-ERA. You just *never* turn your back on him. But it meant making a working relationship with him. And I think, if I had to make a guess, I'd say that NOW considered that a sell-out.

5. A leader in Illinois NOW described its members as "very mobile. I'm one of the few Illinois born and raised." In Arrington and Kyle's North Carolina sample, only 14 percent of the sixty-two pro-ERA activists were presently living in the area in which they were reared, compared to 44 percent of the anti-ERA activists who answered this question (Arrington and Kyle, p. 676).

6. Janet Boles points out that due to the 1977–1979 "shift in focus to a national campaign instead of one centered on the legislatures in unratified states," NOW's annual budget soared from $700,000 in 1977 to $8,500,000 in 1982, and its membership from 55,000 to 210,000 ("Building Support for the ERA: A Case of 'Too Much, Too Late,' " *PS* 15 [1982]:576). See also "The staff of NOW says it has received $1.3 million a month since last December through its direct mail, phone banks and television appeals," Jane Perlez, "NOW's Funds Soar Suggesting Extent of Women's Power," *New York Times,* May 20, 1982, sec. 3, p. 1.

7. Felsenthal, *Sweetheart,* chap. 12, passim.

8. Ibid., p. 195.

9. St. Paul, Letter to the Ephesians 5.22-23: "Wives, be subject to your husbands, as to the Lord. For the husband is the head of the wife, as Christ is head of the church;" and "As the church is subject to Christ, so let wives be subject in everything to their husbands." See also 1 Timothy 2.11–12: "Let a woman learn in silence with all submissiveness. I permit no woman to teach or to have authority over men; she is to keep silent." These passages were a central inspiration in the fundamentalist opposition to the ERA. One of the attractions of the fundamentalist churches to their women members was the emphasis these churches placed on the husband's responsibility for family and children, and for the hard work, sobriety, and respectable behavior entailed by that responsibility. The wife's part of the bargain was to obey. The Mormon church, whose teaching stresses a traditional role for women, also derives some of its attraction from its great emphasis on the family.

10. Kent L. Tedin, "Religious Preference and Pro/Anti Activism on

the Equal Rights Amendment Issue," *Pacific Sociological Review* 21 (1978): 55–66, indicates that more than three-quarters of the anti-ERA women who attended the Texas legislature's 1975 hearings on rescinding the ratification of the ERA were members of Mormon, Baptist, or fundamentalist churches. Sixty percent were members of the fundamentalist Church of Christ. See also David W. Brady and Kent L. Tedin, "Religion and Political Ideology in the Anti-ERA Movement," *Social Science Quarterly* 56 (1976): 564–575. In Arrington and Kyle's tiny sample of female North Carolina anti-ERA activists (*N* = 14), 69 percent were members of a fundamentalist church (Arrington and Kyle, p. 674). See also Felsenthal, *Sweetheart,* pp. 263–264.

Many legislators were aware of the frequent explicit fundamentalist activities against the ERA. The media gave extended coverage to the political rallies of the Moral Majority and other fundamentalist groups, and legislators heard from these groups frequently. My point is that beyond their overt influence, the fundamentalist churches also provided most of the troops for demonstrations and legislative visits that both the media and legislators interpreted as composed simply of homemakers.

11. It is too late now for ERA, but I hope that someone will use the laboratory of fifty states to study the dynamics of effective coalition building on other issues, like abortion, now before our state legislatures.

Chapter 13

1. William Shakespeare, *Henry V,* act 4, scene 3, line 60. I take the terms "exclusive" and "inclusive" from Mayer M. Zald and Roberta Ash, "Social Movement Organizations: Growth, Decay and Change," *Social Forces* 44 (1966): 330–331. I will distinguish the "ERA movement" from the feminist movement, of which it was a part, because it involved a somewhat different spectrum of people, particularly in the smaller towns and in the Midwest and the South. I call it a "movement" rather than a coalition of interest groups because of the extent to which it conjured up feelings of positive solidarity among people who were not members of any affiliated organization and involved them in political participation, often in unorthodox or "counterinstitutional" forms, like demonstrations.

2. Rosabeth Moss Kanter, *Commitment and Community: Communes and Utopias in Sociological Perspective* (Cambridge, Mass.: Harvard University Press, 1972), p. 92, table 3.

3. Representative Hanrahan, Illinois House of Representatives, May 16, 1972), p. 208; May 8, 1975, p. 37; June 2, 1977, p. 39.

4. I take these details from Felsenthal, *Sweetheart,* pp. 259–260.

5. Robert Michels, *Political Parties* (Glencoe, Ill: Free Press, 1949),

first postulated that leaders in democratic movements would become more conservative than the rank and file. Zald and Ash, recognizing that the opposite sometimes holds, postulate that a decline in member interest may produce a leadership cadre more radical than the membership (p. 399). The causes of more radical leadership are, in my view, quite complex, but include prominently the mutually reinforcing demands of ideological incentives for participation and exclusivity in organization. Sidney Verba and Gary R. Orren, *Equality in America: A View from the Top* (Cambridge, Mass.: Harvard University Press, 1985), document the relative distance of the feminist leadership in the United States from the opinions of the citizenry, compared to that of the black and union leadership that they selected from more governmentally connected or mainstream sources.

6. Michelle Harrison, Beth Horning, Gail Koplow, Mary Lowry, Ellie Siegal, and Laura Zimmerman, "Feminist Writers: 'All of Us Have Censored,'" *Sojourner* (September 1984): 14–16.

7. I am indebted to Arthur Stinchcombe for the original version of this formulation. See also Earl D. C. Brewer, "Sect and Church in Methodism," in Ralph H. Turner and Lewis McKillian, eds., *Collective Behavior* (Englewood Cliffs, N.J.: Prentice-Hall, 1957), pp. 482–493. Like all social movements, the ERA movement had within it not only core organizations but sect-like as well as institutional components. All of these components, however, could be greatly influenced by the trends toward sect or institutional behavior in the movement as a whole.

8. Daniel Bell, "The Background and Development of Marxian Socialism in the United States," in Donald D. Egbert and Stow Persons, eds., *Socialism and American Life,* vol. 1 (Princeton, N.J.: Princeton University Press, 1952), p. 217.

9. Irving Howe and Lewis Coser, *The American Communist Party: A Critical History 1919–57* (Boston: Beacon Press, 1957), p. 39.

10. William Kornhauser, "Social Bases of Political Commitment: A Study of Liberals and Radicals," in Arnold M. Rose, ed., *Human Behavior and Social Processes* (London: Routledge and Kegan Paul, 1962), pp. 321–339, see esp. p. 326.

11. Ibid., p. 326.

12. Michael Useem, *Conscription, Protest, and Social Conflict: The Life and Death of a Draft Resistance Movement* (New York: Wiley, 1973), p. 239 and passim, stresses the "external estrangement" that members of Resist felt vis-à-vis the outside world.

13. "For a while I felt closer to people who had turned in their cards

and more distant from people who hadn't. It was that simple. I respected those people who had made the gesture, and those who hadn't were cowards" (ibid., p. 240; see also p. 244).

14. "I would say [the experience] sensitized me to [my friends'] insensitivities, and this has not abated. I am no longer as close to them and see them much less now" (ibid., p. 246).

15. "I began to feel that my interests and those of my friends in graduate school were not on the same paths and were increasingly farther apart. We had chemistry to talk about, but I was becoming far less interested. . . ." (ibid., p. 248; also p. 237).

16. "The day I did it [turned in my draft card], I accepted myself as part of the movement. . . . I felt very close to my friends who had resisted, the Resistance, and the Movement in general" (ibid., p. 235). Barrie Thorne, who studied both Resist and the Boston Draft Resistance Group (BDRG), a more liberal counseling group, poses the exclusivity versus inclusivity problem as one of "protest" versus "credibility." The strategy of Resist's members was to set themselves apart, "establishing a visible alternative and evoking a partisan response," while that of the BDRG was to "minimize differences between themselves and those they hope[d] to reach" (Barrie Thorne, "Protest and the Problems of Credibility: Uses of Knowledge and Risk-taking in the Draft Resistance Movement of the 1960's," *Social Problems* 23 (1975): 117). In Thorne's view, neither strategy succeeded very well. In the "inclusive" group, BDRG, many activists concluded that their political purposes had been unduly compromised by their efforts to gain credibility, while in the more exclusive Resist, the members found that their policy of forcing choices usually led outsiders to choose against resisting the draft. Thorne concludes that a comparison of the implicit strains in these two groups highlights a dilemma many protest movements have experienced: gaining legitimacy involves the risk of compromising the movement's beliefs and political goals, but staying apart and true to the group's differences with the existing culture may limit the movement's effectiveness.

See also Lewis Coser, "Sects and Sectarians," *Dissent* (Winter 1954): 360–369, reprinted in Lewis A. Coser, *Greedy Institutions: Patterns of Undivided Commitment* (New York: Free Press, 1974). John Wilson, *Introduction to Social Movements* (New York: Basic, 1973), pp. 167–168, presents the issue succinctly:

Organizing collective effort to change the world demands acceptance of part of that world as a constraint upon one's own behavior, especially if one belongs to a minority. Social movements are forced to adapt themselves to present social norms and institutions in the ambient society, and yet they must maintain their own sense of apartness and purity, their own distinct social identity, to retain membership commitment and avoid the dilution of co-optation.

17. Luther P. Gerlach and Virginia H. Hine, *People, Power, Change: Movements of Social Transformation* (Indianapolis: Bobbs-Merrill, 1970), p. 54. See also their discussion of commitment mechanisms requiring the cutting of family and friendship ties, pp. 114–117. However, they document their commitment discussion with examples from only the Pentecostal and not from the Black Power groups.

18. M. Galper and C. K. Washburne, "A Women's Self-Help Program in Action," *Social Policy* 6 (1976): 108, cited in Stephanie Riger, "Vehicles for Empowerment: The Case of Feminist Movement Organizations," in J. Rappaport, C. Swift, and R. Hess *Studies in Empowerment: Steps toward Understanding and Action* (New York: Haworth Press, 1984), p. 108. See also Ralph H. Turner, "Determinants of Social Movement Strategies," in Tamotsu Shibutani, ed., *Human Nature and Collective Behavior: Papers in Honor of Herbert Blumer* (Englewood Cliffs, N.J.: Prentice-Hall, 1970), p. 150; Michael Lipsky, "Protest as a Political Resource," *American Political Science Review* 62 (1968): 1148; and Douglas and Wildavsky, pp. 114–121.

19. Mark Granovetter, "The Strength of Weak Ties," *American Journal of Sociology* 78 (1973): 1360–1380.

20. Kornhauser, p. 335.

21. Ibid., p. 333.

22. Granovetter, "The Strength of Weak Ties."

23. Mark Granovetter, *Getting a Job: A Study of Contacts and Careers* (Cambridge, Mass.: Harvard University Press, 1974): 52–53. See also Granovetter, "The Strength of Weak Ties: A Network Theory Revisited," in P. Marsden and N. Lin, eds., *Social Structure and Network Analysis* (Beverly Hills, Calif.: Sage, 1982), pp. 105–130.

24. See Rose Lamb Coser, "The Greedy Nature of *Gemeinschaft*," in Walter W. Powell and Richard Robbins, eds., *Conflict and Consensus* (New York: Free Press, 1984), pp. 226, 230–233.

25. I take these terms from Jessica Lipnack and Jeffrey Stamps, *Networking* (New York: Doubleday, 1982). The more common academic term for "hydra-headed" is "polycephalous" (e.g., Gerlach and Hine).

Chapter 14

1. "Nothing in this article shall be construed to grant or secure any right relating to abortion or the funding thereof"; "Nothing in this article shall be construed to affect any law, regulation or policy relating to the draft

for military service"; and "Nothing in this article shall be construed to affect any law, policy or regulation relating to the utilization of persons in military combat."

2. William E. Farrell, "U.S. Amendment on Equal Rights Beaten in House," *New York Times,* 16 November 1984, p. 1.

3. See Table A10.

4. The differences among states arose both from the different wordings of the 16 state ERAs and from different judicial interpretations. For a thorough treatment of the state reforms as of 1977, see "State Reform" sections of Brown et al., *Women's Rights.* (For a cursory treatment, see Paul M. Kurtz, "The State Equal Rights Amendments and Their Impact on Domestic Relations Law," *Family Law Quarterly* 11 [1977]: 101–150.) For a study of the different standards of review under the different state ERAs, see Lujuana Wolfe Treadwell and Nancy Wallace Page, "Equal Rights Provisions: the Experience under State Constitutions," *California Law Review* 65 (1977): 1086–1112. For a continuing analysis, see ERA Impact Project, NOW Legal Defense and Education Fund, 132 West 43rd Street, New York, N.Y. 10036. For a recent analysis of the effect of state ERAs on family law, see Judith I. Avner and Kim E. Greene, "State ERA Impact on Family Law," *Family Law Reporter* 8 (1982): 4023–4035.

5. For example, Julie Hamos, Legislative Liaison for the Cook County State's Attorney's Office, comments:

> Those of us who were in Springfield for that whole period of time (I was there from 1976 to 1984) noticed an increased responsiveness to legislation dealing with women after the legislature had failed to pass the ERA. Anti-ERA legislators were concerned about being branded "anti-woman." They needed to prove to themselves and their constituents that it was, somehow, just the Equal Rights Amendment that they opposed, and not all legislation relating to women. So we saw a proliferation of bills dealing with women that were both introduced and passed as a legacy of the Equal Rights Amendment.
>
> Legislators went out of their way to point out that even though they had voted against the ERA the year before, they were now prepared to vote for a lot of issues benefitting women. Many of the lobbyists and legislators [in Springfield] noticed and commented on this phenomenon.

6. East, "The First Stage," p. 8.

7. I take all these suggestions from Harold Wilensky, *Organizational Intelligence* (New York: Basic, 1967), esp. pp. 75–78.

8. Panajiota A. Callaros and Lynn R. Anderson, "Effects of Perceived Expertness upon Creativity of Members of Brainstorming Groups," *Journal of Applied Psychology* 53 (1969): 159–163; and Jay Hall, "Decisions," *Psychology Today* 5 (1971): 51–88.

9. See Claus Offe and Helmut Wiesenthal, "Two Logics of Collective Action: Theoretical Notes on Social Class and Organizational Form," in Maurice Zeitlin, ed., *Political Power and Social Theory,* vol. 1 (Greenwich, Conn.: JAI Press, 1980), pp. 67–115. They conclude that "those interests that are exposed to structural ambiguities, and which require a collective discourse for their articulation and an ongoing dialogical pattern of communication between leaders and those whom they represent in order to become 'true,' are less likely to be articulated with equal accuracy [compared to capitalist interests] within the framework of [liberal democratic] political forms" (p. 94).

10. William Gamson uses the word "rancorous" to describe such exchanges. See Carol Mueller, "Rancorous Conflict and Opposition to the ERA," *New England Sociologist* 3 (1981): 17–29.

11. Anthony Obershall, *Social Conflict and Social Movements* (Englewood Cliffs, N.J., 1973), pp. 49–64, cited in Mueller. Obershall also lists another condition, not so related to political institutions, that there be doubt as to the precise result of the legislation. As Mueller indicates, this condition also fits the ERA neatly. David Braybrooke and Charles Lindblom, *A Strategy of Decision* (London: Collier-Macmillan, 1963), pp. 66–70, point out that decisions that are designed to achieve large changes but are not guided by high predictive capacity are, almost by definition, most likely to generate unanticipated consequences. As we have seen, this was the basis of one of the most effective conservative critiques of the ERA.

12. See my *Beyond Adversary Democracy,* passim.

13. Alan Crawford, *Thunder on the Right* (New York: Pantheon, 1980), p. 35.

14. Catharine A. MacKinnon, however, further argues that neither the egalitarian nor the special benefits (or "difference") approach challenges the gender hierarchy that defines men as the standard and women as different. See her *Sexual Harassment of Working Women* (New Haven: Yale University Press, 1979); "Toward Feminist Jurisprudence," *Stanford Law Review* 34 (1982): 703–737; "Feminism, Marxism and the State: An Agenda for Theory," *Signs* 7 (1982): 515–544; "Feminism, Marxism and the State: Toward Feminist Jurisprudence," *Signs* 8 (1983): 1–24.

15. For example, Sylvia A. Law, "Rethinking Sex and the Constitution," *University of Pennsylvania Law Review* 132 (1984); 955–1040; Wendy W. Williams, "Equality's Riddle: Pregnancy and the Equal Treatment/Special Treatment Debate," *Review of Law and Social Change* 13 (1984/1985): 325–380, and "The Equality Crisis: Some Reflections on Culture, Courts, and Feminism," *Women's Rights Law Reporter* 7 (1982): 175–200; Frances E. Olsen, "The Family and the Market: A Study of Ideology and Legal Reform," *Harvard Law Review* 96 (1983) 1497–1578, and "Statutory Rape: A Feminist Critique of Rights Analysis," *Texas Law Review* 63 (1984): 387–432; Ann E. Freedman. "Sex Equality, Sex Differences, and the Supreme Court," *Yale Law Journal* 92 (1983) 913–968; Herma Hill Kay, "Models of Equality," *University of Illinois Law Review* 1 (1985): 39–88, and "Equality and Difference: The Case of Pregnancy," *Berkeley Women's Law Journal* 1 (1986): 1–37; and Ann C. Scales, "Towards a Feminist Jurisprudence," *Indiana Law Journal* 56 (1981): 375–444.

16. For example, Barbara Ehrenreich, *The Hearts of Men* (New York: Anchor/Doubleday, 1983); and Kristen Luker, *Abortion and the Politics of Motherhood* (Berkeley: University of California Press, 1984).
This debate on fundamentals touched on commitments so deep that some of the participants, in the classic manner of sectarians, tried to read one another out of the feminist movement. In 1983, for example, Catherine MacKinnon, Andrea Dworkin, and other feminists began pressing various municipalities to institute "antipornography" ordinances—legislation allowing women to sue on a tort basis (by claiming personal harm) the manufacturers or sellers of material that "subordinated" women in a "sexually graphic" manner. The suggested legislation was explicitly not gender neutral; it addressed itself only to men's oppression of women. Moreover, although it built on classic tort law rather than on the "obscenity" tradition, it raised for many feminists—particularly civil liberties lawyers and writers—the frightening possibility that ordinances like this might begin to legitimate censorship. While the issue sometimes divided friend from friend, however, the major feminist institutions played a moderating role. Rather than taking sides, they called for open debate and mutual understanding. In these "postwar" years, the internal debate that the ERA struggle had closed off revived without destroying the movement.

17. In this analysis, I follow the suggestion of Gayle Binion, in "The Case for an Equal Rights Act," *Center Magazine* (November/December 1983):2–7, and "Sex Bias Can Be Treated as Racial Bias Is: By Law," *Los Angeles Times*, 5 September 1982, pt. 4, p. 5. It is not certain, however, that the Supreme Court would hold constitutional an Equal Rights Act based on sec. 5 of the Fourteenth Amendment, particularly after the defeat in the states of an Equal Rights Amendment. In *Oregon v. Mitchell* 400 U.S. 112 (1971), the Court held that Congress did not have power under sec. 5 of the Fourteenth Amendment to lower the voting age in state

elections to eighteen, because the legislation was not aimed at eliminating racial discrimination (see Committee on Civil Rights and Special Committee on Sex and Law, Association of the Bar of the City of New York, cited in Babcock, pp. 143–144). Of course, if the Supreme Court were to disallow an Equal Rights Act, this itself might produce a more favorable climate for an Equal Rights Amendment.

18. Gayle Binion suggests that an Equal Rights Act "should require that the disadvantageous effects or impacts that follow from a law or policy must be justified as essential to the achievement of a significant governmental objective" ("The Case . . . ," p. 6).

Index

AAUW. *See* American Association of University Women

Abortion, 13, 27, 34, 86, 89, 99, 109, 110, 113, 118, 122, 123, 127, 169, 170, 223, 225, 230, 289; feminist stand on, 3, 122–28; public funding for, 124, 125, 126, 127, 187, 224, 288

Absolute ban. *See* Prohibited classification

Abzug, Bella, 269

ACLU. *See* American Civil Liberties Union

Activists, x–xi, 3, 15, 22, 45, 59, 68, 80, 83, 84, 88, 114, 118, 123, 130, 131, 132, 142–45, 151–52, 153, 165, 168–69, 176, 182, 189, 229, 302–3; as perceived by legislators, 146–47

Addams, Jane, 235

Affirmative action, 39, 250, 251

Age, 16, 168, 169

Agnostics, 16

AIPO survey, 234, 244, 284

Alabama, 96, 275

All-Volunteer Force, 72, 73, 74, 75

Alpert, Jane, 279

American Association of Retired People, 119

American Association of University Women, 73, 75, 301

American Bar Association Special Committee to Oppose Ratification, 31–32

American Civil Liberties Union, 73, 76, 125, 126

American Jurisprudence, 110

Americans for Democratic Action, 183

Anderson, Lynn R., 308

Andrisani, Paul J., 240

Anti-abortion movement, 34

Antipornography ordinances, 309

Arditi, Ralph, 251

Areen, Judith, 276

Arizona Governing Committee v. Norris, 242

Arkansas, 98, 277

Arkes, Hal R., 292

Armed forces and women. *See* Military, women in

Aronson, E., 292

Arrington, Theodore S., 226, 301, 302

Ash, Roberta, 303

Attitudes, 23, 70–71, 89, 105, 107,
    109, 205, 229; ambivalence
    of, 22–23, 26–27; polarization
    of, 18–19. *See also* Surveys
Attitudes toward Women and
    Work survey, 209
Authority, women in positions of,
    38–39, 70, 72–73, 79, 190,
    192, 230, 240
Avner, Judith I., 307

Babcock, Barbara Allen, 238,
    276, 290
Bach, Shirley J., 267
Bachrach, Peter, 265
Baratz, Morton, 265
Bardsley and Haslacher Survey
    Organization, 232
Bart, Pauline, ix, 219, 279
Bayh, Birch, 10, 12, 63–64, 129,
    135, 192, 222, 251, 252, 290;
    substitute ERA, 11, 252–53
BDRG. *See* Boston Draft Resist-
    ance Group
Beck, Paul A., 204
Becker, Howard S., 265
Becker, Susan D., 221
Bell, Carolyn Shaw, 244
Bell, Daniel, 182, 304
Bellamy, Carol, 145
Bellnier v. Lund, 241
Benefits, individual. *See* Public
    good
Benefits, intangible, as incentive
    for volunteers, 3, 47, 87–88,
    118–22, 130–32, 147, 165–77,
    191–92. *See also* ERA, possi-
    ble effects of
Bennis, Warren G., 292
Bernbach, Doyle Dane, 232
Bers, Trudy Haffron, 233
BFOQ. *See* Bona fide occupa-
    tional qualification

Bible, 175–76, 302
Bickel, Alexander M., 234
Bill of Rights, 61, 77, 85
Bill of Rights for Women, 10
Binion, Gayle, 309–10
Binkin, Martin, 267
Bird, Caroline, 269
Biren, Joan E., 265
Black Power movement, 182
Blackmun (Justice), 50, 56, 124
Blacks, 10, 54. *See also* Race
Blum v. Yaretsky, 242
Bluthardt, Edward, 70, 245
Bokowski, Debrah: "Federation,"
    297; "State Legislator
    Perceptions," 146, 285
Boles, Janet K.: "Building Sup-
    port," 302; *Politics,* 146, 223,
    224, 286, 291, 294, 299
Bona fide occupational qualifica-
    tion, 40
Borchers, Webber, 70–71, 280
Boston Draft Resistance Group,
    305
Bowman, G. W., 240
BPW. *See* National Federation of
    Business and Professional
    Women
Brady, David W., 303
Braybrooke, David, 308
Brennan (Justice), 55, 56, 246
Brewer, Earl D. C., 304
Brooks, Mary E., 270
Brothers, Joyce, 282
Brotman, Barbara, 155, 156, 298
Brown, Barbara A.: "The Equal
    Rights Amendment," 51, 61,
    77–79, 243, 250, 255, 260,
    269; "The Impact," 243;
    Women's Rights, 239, 258,
    275
Brown v. Board of Education,
    141

Brummer (Representative), 292
Bryan, Frank M., 300
Burger (Justice), 50, 56
Burris, Val, 226
Business Week, 17–18
Butler, David, 226
Byrne, Jane, 154

Caban v. Mohammed, 249
Califano v. Goldfarb, 259
Califano v. Jabson, 259
Califano v. Silbowitz, 259
Califano v. Webster, 259
California, 204, 215
California Commission on the
   Status of Women, 139
Callaros, Panajiota A., 308
Cantril, Hadley, 233, 235
Carden, Maren L., 286
Careers, interruptible, 100
Carpenter, Kathleen, 136, 271
Carroll, Berenice A., 291
Carroll, Susan, 295
Carter, James, 65, 73, 86, 88, 267
Carver, Joan S., 227, 229
Catania, Susan, 134, 254, 300
Catholics, 15, 31, 195, 203
Catt, Carrie Chapman, 235
CBS News/New York Times sur-
   vey, 16, 202, 208, 210, 226,
   240–41, 280
Celler, Emanuel, 10, 32
Chafe, William Henry, 220
Chandler, Robert, 208, 226
Chapman, Eugenia, 134, 160, 161
   253–54, 299, 300
Chayes, Antonia Handler, 274
Child Labor Amendment, 31–32,
   234, 235
Children, 38, 92, 93, 100, 230
Churchgoers, 16
*City of Akron v. Akron Center for
   Reproductive Health,* 288

*City of Los Angeles Department
   of Water and Power v. Man-
   hart,* 242
Civil disobedience, 130–31
Civil Rights Act of 1964, 111,
   112; Title VI, 42; Title VII,
   10, 37–42, 55, 242, 291
Civil Service protection, 39
Class divergence, 105–7, 227, 278,
   280
Clausen, Aage R., 297
Coalitions, NOW decision on, 131
Cognitive dissonance, 292
Coleman, James S., 294
Colorado, 97, 275, 280
Combat. *See* Military, women in
Commission on Civil Rights
   (U.S.), 233, 293
Commission on the Status of
   Women, 9
Committee on the Judiciary, 12
Common Cause, 82
Common law, 92, 108
Commonwealth v. Daniel, 259
Communist party, 182, 183
Community conflict, 146
Comparable worth, 41–42
Compromise, 3, 47, 77, 78, 88,
   89, 132, 192, 198, 302
Congress (U.S.), 2, 73, 74, 198,
   251, 254. *See also* House of
   Representatives; Senate
Connecticut, 9, 126, 230, 271, 285
Connecticut Committee to Re-
   scind ERA, 271
Connecticut v. Griswold, 271
Conover, Pamela Johnston, 227,
   229, 287
Conservatives, 5, 10, 13, 34, 109,
   111, 150, 151, 186, 195, 204,
   205, 218
Constituent opinion, 149–52, 154,
   228, 229

Constitutional amendments, 8, 28, 87, 194, 222, 234, 235; controversial, 29; history of, 29, 30, 31, 34; opposition to, 29–30, 31, 34

Contributions, political, 155–57, 158, 179–80, 194, 299

Converse, Philip E., 106, 280, 281

Conway v. Dana, 275

Cook (Senator), 64, 261, 262

Copelon, Rhonda, 289

Corcoran, Mary, 240

Coser, Lewis, 304, 305

Coser, Rose Lamb, 306

Costain, Anne E., 287

Cox, James, 238

Craig v. Boren, 46, 50, 53, 55, 77, 141, 151, 245, 246, 247, 258, 259, 288

Craig v. Craig, 277

Crain, Robert L., 294

Crawford, Alan, 308

Criminal Sexual Assault Act, 190, 195

Crosby v. Crosby, 277

Cunningham (Representative), 280

Currie, Barbara, 229, 300

Daily Oklahoman, 203, 215

Daley, Richard, 161, 299

Daniels, Mark R., 204, 208, 214–15, 232, 238, 283

Darcy, Robert, 208, 232, 238, 283

Davis, James Allan, 231, 263, 266

Daymont, Thomas, 240

Debate, national, on ERA, 3, 47, 84–86, 118, 130, 138–47, 153, 184–86, 188–95, 252; on tactics, 122–32, 135–37

Decision by accretion, 68, 191, 264–65

Decentralization, 115; advantages, 131, 184, 193; "participating

decentralization," 122–33. *See also* Hierarchy

DeConcini, Dennis, 274

Deferential interpretation, 68, 71, 75–77, 79, 80–85, 88, 261, 274

Democrats, 9, 19, 89, 154, 157, 161, 167, 168, 191, 204, 215, 229

Demographic factors, 14–15, 202, 212, 213, 226

Demonstrations, 102, 103, 113, 130, 131, 154, 158, 166, 167, 176, 291, 303

Dennison, Mike, 296

Department of Labor, 10, 37

Deutchman, Iva E., 227

Deutsch, Karl W., 291

Diamond, Irene, 278, 300

Dianne (author), 279

Dill v. Dill, 276

Dillon, David Reid, 251

Dimieri, Thomas, 227, 292, 298

Direct mail, 6, 109, 170, 171

Disability benefits, 53

Disadvantage, women's, increasing with competition, 278

Discourse. *See* Debate

Discrimination, 38–39, 45–46, 50–51, 54, 57, 72–73, 75, 139, 140, 240, 241, 243, 246, 247

Discriminatory intent, 42, 54–55. *See also* Laws neutral on their face

Disparate impact, 94, 243, 256. *See also* Discriminatory intent; Laws neutral on their face

Divorce, 57, 92, 93, 94, 108

Dixon, Marlene, 279

Dodge, Mrs. Arthur, 31

Dodson, Debra L., 229

Donahue, Phil, 135, 283

Dothard v. Rawlinson, 241

Douglas (Justice), 55, 56
Douglas, Mary, 287, 306
Draft, 3, 11, 46, 47, 50, 52, 58,
    61–63, 71, 74–76, 80, 86, 87,
    187, 262–63. *See also* Mili-
    tary, women in
Duncan, Greg, 240
Dunn v. Palermo, 277
Dworkin, Andrea, 309
Dyer, Giddy, 134, 160, 161, 254,
    299

Eagle Forum, 135, 144, 163, 174
East, Catherine, 12, 222, 223, 271
Eastwood, Mary O., 222
Education Amendments of 1972,
    Title IX, 257
Educational level, effects of, 15,
    105, 106, 107, 226–27, 280–81
Edwards, Don, 63, 261
EEOC. *See* Equal Employment
    Opportunity Commission
Egalitarian interpretation, 61, 63,
    68, 76, 79–85, 87–89. *See also*
    Prohibited classification
Ehrenreich, Barbara, 108, 281,
    309
Eisenhower, Dwight, 9
Elshtain, Jean Bethke, 279
Emerson, Thomas I., 51, 61, 77–
    79, 84, 250, 261, 271, 285,
    290
Equal Employment Opportunity
    Commission, 10, 37
Equal Pay Act, 37, 38, 55, 238
Equal rights, principle of, 9–10,
    26–27
Equal Rights Act, 197–98
Equal Rights Amendment:
    amendments to, 12, 64–65,
    77, 88, 187, 198, 252–53,
    261–62, 306–7; complete text
    of, 1; effects of campaign for,
    55–56, 188–90; failure of, ix,

x, 1, 2, 4, 67, 89, 98, 116–17,
    127, 128, 142, 147, 149, 158,
    187, 197; history of, 1, 2, 8–
    19, 170, 184, 187, 265; in-
    direct effects of, 42, 88, 93,
    94; possible effects of, 2, 4,
    40–43, 45, 47, 52–55, 57, 59,
    60, 84–87, 96, 98, 118, 124,
    136, 138–45, 188, 244, 248–
    50, 254, 294, 307; potential
    radicalism of, 3, 20, 52, 59,
    60, 65, 67, 68, 85, 88, 98,
    109, 110–13, 129; ratification,
    probability of, ix, 1, 2, 4, 12,
    13, 16, 60, 61, 147, 177, 184,
    195, 199; wording of, 11, 12,
    14, 17, 61, 89, 253, 306–7
Equal Rights Amendment Project
    of the California Commission
    on the Status of Women,
    139, 243, 244, 270
Equal Rights for Men and
    Women. *See* Senate Majority
    Report
ERA. *See* Equal Rights Amend-
    ment
ERA Coalition, 36
ERA Illinois, 121, 131, 138, 165–
    73, 181, 219, 292, 293, 300–
    301
ERA Impact Clearinghouse Index
    and References, 139, 293
ERAmerica, 121, 122, 139
Erickson, Nancy S., 247, 250
Erskine, Hazel, 234
Ervin, Sam, 11, 12, 63–66, 69, 77,
    111, 222, 223, 261, 266, 290
Etzioni, Amitai, 286
Evans, Sara, 277

Fair Campaign Practices Commis-
    sion, 144
Fair Labor Standards Act, 32, 221
Falk, Gail, 51, 61, 77–79, 250

Family law, 57, 91, 96, 275, 276;
    alimony obligations, 92, 93,
    96; child support, 93, 97; cus-
    tody, 93, 95, 97; domicile,
    95, 97, 276; marital property,
    93, 94, 97; marriage age, 95–
    96, 98, 277; name, 95, 98;
    parental obligations, 92, 97;
    support obligations, 92, 93,
    96, 108, 109. See also Home-
    makers
Farrell, William E., 307
Faucher, Sandra, 136, 225
Featherstone, Helen, 249
Federal Women's Bureau, 9
Federally Employed Women, 75
Feigen, Brenda, 145
Felsenthal, Carol, 272, 282, 283,
    292, 302, 303
Feminism, 2, 68, 69, 71, 73, 76–
    79, 80, 81, 84, 86, 89, 98, 99,
    100, 101, 104, 109, 123, 124,
    125, 128, 168–69, 170, 171,
    178, 186, 188, 190–91, 196,
    197
Feminists, The (group), 102, 103,
    266, 278–79
Festinger, Leon, 292
FEW. See Federally Employed
    Women
Fifth Amendment, 74, 75, 124,
    125, 248
First Amendment, 43, 62, 260,
    268
Fischer v. Department of Public
    Welfare, 288
Flexner, Eleanor, 220
Florida, 14, 114, 136, 149, 204,
    227, 229, 266
Florida Annual Policy Survey, 204
Fong, Hiram, 64
Forbush v. Wallace, 267, 277
Fourteenth Amendment, 2, 11,

42, 45, 46–48, 53–54, 55, 57,
    60, 74–75, 77, 87, 91, 124,
    125, 141, 142, 151, 189, 196,
    197, 224, 241, 243, 248, 256,
    258, 259
Frankel, Linda, ix, 219
Free, Lloyd A., 233, 235
Free rider, 119
Freedman, Ann E., 51, 61, 77–79,
    127, 238, 243, 248–51, 254,
    255, 258, 275, 276, 277, 288,
    290, 309
Freeman, Jo: Politics, 265, 277,
    278, 282, 283; Women, 279
Freund, Paul, 110, 111, 113, 283,
    290
Friedan, Betty, 135, 277, 279
Friedrich (Representative), 229
Frolich, Norman, 287
Frontiero v. Richardson, 46, 53,
    55, 56, 77, 245, 246, 247,
    256, 257, 259
Fundamentalists. See Religious
    fundamentalists

Gallup surveys, 16, 30, 201, 202,
    203, 208–10, 234, 235, 237,
    244, 262–63, 264, 282
Galper, M., 306
Gamson, William, 308
Garske, John P., 292
Gatekeeping, 80
Gender-based classifications, 41,
    46, 49–52, 55, 56, 60, 128,
    241, 243, 246, 247, 248, 249,
    250, 251, 252, 253, 258, 259,
    260, 274, 288, 290. See also
    Discrimination: Prohibited
    classification; Suspect clas-
    sification
Gender gap, 15, 226
Gender neutrality. See Laws,
    gender-neutral

Gender roles, 1, 75, 93, 100, 103, 109, 249, 278, 279, 302
General Social Survey of the National Opinion Research Center, 20, 201, 202, 203, 210, 217, 218, 230, 231, 235, 263, 282, 284, 285, 289
Georgia, 97, 142, 275
Gerlach, Luther P., 291, 306
Gerner, Deborah, 219
Gieson, John van, 224
Ginsburg, Ruth Bader, 247, 254, 287
Globe Democrat, 204
Goesaert v. Cleary, 246
Goldberg, Frederick, 251
Goldberg, Philip, 241
Goldman, Nancy Loring, 272
Goldmark, Josephine, 220
Goldsmith, Judy, 74
Goldstein, Leslie Friedman, 250
Goldwater, Barry, 110
Goodman, Ellen, 294
Goodman, Jill Laurie, 269
Granovetter, 306
Gray, Virginia, 227, 229, 287
Green v. Country School Board of New Kent County, 234
Greene, Kim E., 307
Greenhouse, Linda, 224
Greiman, Alan, 160
Greyser, S. A., 240
Griesheimer (Representative), 228, 245
Griffiths, Martha, 10, 63, 252, 261
Grigg, Charles M., 233
GSS. *See* General Social Survey of the National Opinion Research Center
Guardians Association v. Civil Service Commission of the City of New York, 244
Gurney (Senator), 64

Haas, Barbara D., 293
Hale, Mariclaire, 269
Hall, Jay, 308
Hammer v. Dagenhart, 235
Hamos, Julie, 307
Handberg, Roger, Jr., 227, 295
Hanrahan (Representative), 280, 303
Harris, Louis, 16, 18, 227. *See also* Harris organization surveys
Harris, William, 265
Harris organization surveys, 16–19, 23, 26, 30, 202, 203, 211, 228, 231, 234, 236, 237, 284
Harris v. McRae, 125, 126, 287, 288
Harrison, Michelle, 304
Hartford Accident and Indemnity Company v. Insurance Commissioner of the Commonwealth of Pennsylvania, 243
Hartle, M. Martha, 251
Hatch (Senator), 288, 289
Hawaii, 125, 230
Hawaii Right to Life, Inc. v. Chang, 125, 287
Hayden, Casey, 277
Hayden rider, 9
Healey, Jim, 225
Heart of Atlanta Motel Inc. v. U.S., 242
Heckler v. Matthews, 248, 254
HERA. *See* Homemakers for ERA
Hershey, Robert D., Jr., 296
Hierarchy, 115, 122–38, 193. *See also* Leadership
Hill, Martha, 240
Hine, Virginia H., 291, 306
Hines, Michael de Conrey, 206
Hober, Mary, 144
Hobson v. POW, 259

Hoff-Wilson, Joan, 221
Hole, Judith, 222, 277
Holm, Jeanne M., 82
Holmes (Justice), 260
Homemakers for ERA, 301
Homemaking as a full-time
    career, 5, 90–112, 190, 204,
    216–17, 281
Homosexuals, 109, 128–29, 136–
    37, 144–45, 224–50, 280, 289
Horning, Beth, 304
House Judiciary Committee, 10,
    11, 32
House of Representatives (U.S.),
    x, 9, 10, 51, 127, 187
Housework, 92, 101–2
Howe, Irving, 304
Huber, Joan, 227
Hudson (Representative), 245
Humphrey (Senator), 64
Hyde, Henry J., 279

Ideology, 68, 76–77, 81, 131, 178–
    79, 180–84, 191
Illinois, 34, 86, 114, 130, 134,
    136, 142, 147, 149, 151, 153,
    154, 155, 156, 158, 159, 160,
    161, 162, 166, 167, 177, 190,
    194, 203, 214, 228, 229, 233,
    245, 266, 277, 300
Impact ERA. See Equal Rights
    Amendment Project of the
    California Commission on the
    Status of Women
Impact of the Equal Rights
    Amendment, The, 243, 248,
    250, 254, 255, 256, 274, 288,
    289, 291
Impact Hearings. See Impact of
    the Equal Rights Amendment,
    The
In re Griffiths, 247
Incentives. See Benefits, in-
    tangible

Information and misinformation,
    138–45, 148, 151–52, 153–54,
    183, 192–93, 293
Insurance industry, 41, 149, 150,
    151, 242–43, 295–96
Integration of sexes, 85–86
Intermediate test, 50, 52, 56, 60
Involution, iron law of, 181–82,
    184, 185
Iowa, 14, 225
Israel, women in the defense
    forces of, 63–64

Jackson v. Metropolitan Edison
    Co., 241–42
Jaggar, Alison M., 265
Japanese-Americans, internment
    of, 48–49, 77
Jenckins, Craig J., 286
Jensen, Joan M., 221
Jerdee, Thomas, 240
Jewish religion, 16
John Birch Society, 224
Johnson, Marilyn, 295
Jones, Emil, 297
Jones, Ethel B., 238
Jones, Judson H., 298
Jones v. Alfred H. Meyer Co.,
    242
Joyner, Nancy Douglas, 301
Judicial review, 48–49
Jury service, 258
Justice, Ann K., 224, 294, 295

Kanowitz, Leo, 56, 95, 256, 269,
    276
Kanter, Rosabeth Moss, 178, 303
Katz, Harriet N., 250, 258
Kay, Herma, 275, 277, 309
Kelley, Florence, 8, 197, 235
Kellog, Verna, 82
Kennedy, John, 9
Killian, Lewis M., 286

King, Mary, 277
Kirschberg v. Feenstra, 276
Kleeman, Katherine E., 294
Klein, Frederick, 296
Knoke, David, 287
Knudson, Tom, 225
Kobler, John, 235
Kocken, Manfred, 291
Kolb, France, 222
Korematsu v. United States, 246, 268
Kornhauser, William, 183, 304, 306
Kraft, Katherine, 221
Kurland, Philip, 110, 283–84
Kurtz, Paul M., 307
Kyle, Patricia A., 226, 301, 302

Labor unions, 9, 10, 182
Laing, Jonathan, 296
Lauby, Jennifer, 263
Law, Sylvia, 249, 251, 287, 309
Laws, 2, 37, 45–46, 47–48, 50–52, 53, 54, 57, 58, 61, 68, 85, 90, 91, 128, 138, 139, 189, 190, 256, 260; constitutionally suspect, 49, 52, 91, 138, 139, 140, 142, 255, 293; gender-neutral, 197, 220–22; neutral on their face, 52–55, 94, 198, 255–56
Lawyers, 31, 129, 142; feminist, 3, 75, 76–81, 122–28, 132, 197
LDEF. *See* Legal Defense and Education Fund
Leader, Shelah Gilbert, 295
Leadership, 133–38, 146, 160, 166, 170, 180, 190, 292, 304. *See also* Hierarchy
League of Women Voters, 121, 122, 270, 300
Legal Defense and Education Fund, NOW, 139, 291, 293

Legislative intent, 54–55, 65, 127, 251–54, 288–90. *See also* Equal Rights Amendment, history of
Legislators, 2–4, 6, 46–48, 64–65, 85, 104, 116, 128, 141, 143, 146–47, 149–64, 166, 189–90, 192, 227, 228–29, 250–56, 288, 294, 295, 296, 300; material rewards for, 155; trustee theory, 153–54
Lemons, J. Stanley, 220, 235
Lenart, Joe, 238
Lesbian participation in demonstrations, 130–31
Levine, Ellen, 222, 277
Lewis, Karen J., 291
Libertarian issues, 22
Lilie, Joyce R., 227, 295
Lindblom, David, 308
Lipnack, Jessica, 306
Lipset, Seymour Martin, 234
Lipsky, Michael, 306
Louisiana, 97
Loving v. Virginia, 246, 290
Lowrey, Wanda, 227, 295
Lowry, Mary, 304
Lugar v. Edmonson Oil Co., 242
Luker, Kristen, 309

MacKinnon, Catherine A., 266, 272, 308, 309
MacPhael, John A., 287
Mainardi, Pat, 101–2, 103, 278
Maine, 14, 136, 137
Majority, three-fifths required in Illinois, 156, 177
Male protection, 68–69
Manion, Clarence, 223, 224
Mansbridge, Jane J., ix, 292, 297, 308
Mapp v. Ohio, 233
Market Opinion Research, 203, 214, 225, 291

Marriage, 92, 94, 99, 101, 102,
    103, 109, 232
Marshall (Justice), 55, 56, 246,
    255
Maryland, 144, 263
*Mass. Board of Retirement v.
    Murgia,* 255
Massachusetts, 126
Mathews, Donald G., 284
Mathews, Jane De Hart, 284
Matijevich (Representative), 233
Mautino (Representative), 229
Maximum hour law, 8
McCalls, 109
McCarthy, John D., 286
McCloskey, Herbert, 229, 234
McGlenn, Nancy E., 222
McGuire v. McGuire, 271, 275
McLaughlin v. Florida, 246
McNeill, John Charles, 266
Mellor, Earl F., 240
Menhouse, Frank von, 238
Methods, 219–20
Mezey, Susan Gluck, 230, 233,
    295
*Michael M. v. Superior Court of
    Sonoma County,* 247, 249,
    254, 260
Michels, Robert, 303
Michigan, 246
Middle class, 15
Military, women in, 58, 60–89,
    111, 136, 248, 260–75
Miller, Herman, 240
Mills, J., 292
Miner, Anne S., 244
Minimum wage law, 8
Miranda v. Arizona, 233
*Mississippi University for Women
    v. Hogan,* 247, 248
Missouri, 14, 204
*Moe v. Secretary of Administra-
    tion and Finance,* 126, 287

Moral exhortation, 119–20. *See
    also* Benefits, intangible
Moratorium, 196
Morgan, Robin, 222, 278, 279
Mormon church, 34, 232, 238,
    302–3
Morris, Monica, 241
Moskos, Charles, 263, 272
Motherhood, 13, 230, 280. *See
    also* Homemaking
Ms. magazine, 17–18, 104, 110
Mueller, Carol, 227, 292, 298, 308
*Murphy v. Harleysville Mutual
    Ins. Co.,* 243

National Association of Manufac-
    turers, 32
National Association of Women
    Lawyers, 9
National Association Opposed to
    Women Suffrage, 31
National Child Labor Committee,
    31
National Coalition for Women in
    Defense, 73, 267
National Commission on the
    Observance of International
    Women's Year, 82
National Committee to Defeat the
    Un-Equal Rights Amend-
    ment, 221
National Conference for Commis-
    sions on the Status of
    Women, 277
National Consumers' League, 9
National Federation of Business
    and Professional Women, 9,
    22, 68, 72, 73, 75, 82, 121,
    122, 265, 269, 284, 301
National Federation of Republi-
    can Women, 135, 174
National NOW Times, 203

National Opinion Research Center. *See* General Social Survey

National Organization for Women, 10, 13, 36, 37, 43–44, 67, 68, 70, 71, 73, 74, 75, 76, 80, 84, 88, 99, 101, 109, 120–21, 122, 123, 130, 131, 137, 143, 158, 165, 166, 167, 172, 222, 265, 270, 277, 282, 300–301; membership, 168–71, 173, 189, 302

National Plan of Action, 82

National Woman's Party, 8, 270

National Women's Conference, 82

NBC/Associated Press survey, 16, 202, 208, 209, 210

NCLC. *See* National Child Labor Committee

Nebraska, 144

NES. *See* University of Michigan American National Election Study

New Jersey, 14

New Right, 4, 5, 16, 110, 189, 195, 203

New York (State), 14, 36, 144

Newberg v. Board of Education, School District of Philadelphia, 249

NFRW. *See* National Federation of Republican Women

Nie, Norman H., 230

NORC GSS. *See* General Social Survey of the National Opinion Research Center

North Carolina, 80, 114, 149, 177, 203, 226, 227, 266, 301

Norton, Eleanor Holmes, 239, 276, 290

NOW. *See* National Organization for Women

NOW Legal Defense and Education Fund (NOW LDEF). *See* Legal Defense and Education Fund

NOW Position Paper. *See* Position Paper on registration and the draft

Obershall, Anthony, 286, 308

Oberstar, James, 289

Occupational segregation, 38, 41, 100

O'Connor, Karen, 222

Offe, Claus, 308

Oklahoma, 26, 86, 136, 149, 177, 203, 215, 228, 232, 266

Old Radical Right, 5

Olsen, Frances E., 249, 309

Olson, Mancur, 286

Oppenheim, Joe A., 287

Opposition to the ERA, 3, 5–6, 9–10, 12–13, 18–19, 20, 31, 34, 46, 65–66, 67–68, 86, 90, 91, 98, 104, 109–10, 112, 114, 115–18, 127, 131, 133, 135–37, 143–45, 150–53, 173, 189, 195, 203, 228, 229, 279, 288–89; exaggerations, 144–45, 279–80, 283, 284, 285, 296–97

Oregon v. Mitchell, 309

O'Reilly, Jane, 272, 280, 298

Organizations, image of, ix, 6–7, 119–20, 132, 160, 173, 178–79, 180, 183–85, 191–93, 291–92, 304–5, 308

Orr v. Orr, 275, 276

Orren, Gary, 230, 304

Pacifists, 71

Packwood, Robert, 289

Page, Nancy Wallace, 307

Paid labor force, women in, 100, 102, 104, 107–8, 204, 216–17, 280–81, 282

Pamphlets, on ERA's effect on
    military, 81–84; on 59¢, 37,
    294
Parents of illegitimate children,
    50, 248
Parham v. Hughes, 248, 249, 254
Parr, Carol, 267
Participatory decentralization,
    122–23, 131, 133, 291–92
Party politics, 19, 154–55; polar-
    ization, 18, 223
Paul, Alice, 8
Paul, Laurence M., 224
Peggy (author), 279
Pennsylvania, 126, 190, 224, 243,
    275
Pentacostal movement, 182–83,
    306
People v. Boyer, 260
People v. Elliott, 275, 276
People v. Grammer, 260
Perkins, Samuel T., 129, 290
Perlez, Jane, 302
*Personnel Administrator of Mas-
    sachusetts v. Feeney,* 54, 255,
    256
Peters, John, 251
Peterson, Esther, 221, 222
Petrocik, John R., 230
Phelps, William, 251
Phelps v. Bing, 277
Phillips, Gloria, 293
Physical abilities, 62, 70–71, 72,
    73, 74, 78, 83
Pintzler, Isabelle Katz, 268
Pogrebin, Letty Cottin, 45, 245
Poll data analysis. *See* Surveys
Poole, Keith T., 280, 281
Popular opinion. *See* Public
    opinion
Populist tradition, 34
Position Paper on registration and
    the draft, NOW, 69, 71, 74,
    75, 266, 267

Powell (Justice), 50, 56, 246, 257
Powell, Walter W., 306
Pregnancy, 78, 124
Presidential elections, 15, 190,
    226
Presidential tenure, 29–30
Pressing public necessity. *See* Sus-
    pect classification
Prestige, social, 107–8
Price, Alice, 250, 258
Prince-Embury, Sandra, 227
Prison sentences, 58, 142, 259,
    260
Privacy, as exception to ERA
    coverage, 51, 61, 113, 250
Private sector versus public sec-
    tor, 39, 41. *See also* State ac-
    tion
Pro-choice movement, 34. *See
    also* Abortion
Progressive movement, 9, 31
Prohibited classification, 50–52,
    61, 128–29, 274. *See also*
    Egalitarian interpretation
Protectionism, 68
Protective legislation, 8, 37–38, 68
Protestants, 15, 203
Prothro, James W., 233
Pruett, Sharon, 238
Public good, 118–19
Public opinion, 14, 34, 198, 201–
    5, 225–26, 231, 235, 297. *See
    also* Surveys
Purity, doctrinal, 180

Race, 15, 48–49, 114, 141, 227,
    290
Radical Right, 16, 150, 151. *See
    also* New Right; Old Radical
    Right
Ranney, Austin, 226
Rape, 69, 78, 190. *See also* Statu-
    tory rape
Rawalt, Marguerite, 221, 222

Reagan, Ronald (President), 15, 66, 86, 88, 166
Redbook, 109
Reed v. Reed, 49, 246, 247, 257, 259
Referenda, 14, 225–26
Registration. *See* Draft
Rehnquist (Justice), 246
Religious fundamentalists, 5, 6, 15–16, 34, 152, 174–76, 178–79, 195, 238, 297, 302–3
Rendell-Baker v. Kohn, 242
Republicans, 9, 18–19, 89, 135, 155, 156, 161, 167, 187, 202, 204, 215, 301
Research, lack of, 18, 23, 138–39. *See also* Information
Research and Forecast, Inc., survey, 231, 232
Resist (group), 182, 305
Retirement benefits, 53
Rhode, Deborah, 277, 282, 291, 299
Rice, Charles, 223, 224
Richard Day Research, 203
Riger, Stephanie, 306
Right to Life movement, 136. *See also* Abortion
Right to privacy, 13, 127. *See also* Privacy
Robbins, Richard, 306
Robey, John S., 238
Robinson, Ruby Doris Smith, 277
Roe v. Wade, 13, 124, 127, 234, 287
Roosevelt, Eleanor, 9
Roosevelt, Franklin, 29
Roper Organization surveys, 231, 284
Rosen, Benson, 240
Rosie J. Doe et al. v. Edward Mahler et al., 287
Ross, Susan C., 239, 276, 290
Ross, Susan Deller, 239

Rostker v. Goldberg, 74–76, 79–80, 81, 84, 247, 248, 254, 267, 268, 269
Rostow, E. V., 269
Roth v. U.S., 233
Royster Guano Co. v. Virginia, 246, 247
Ruddick, Sarah, 272
Ryan, George, 167, 302

Sager, Lawrence Gene, 268
Samuel v. University of Pittsburgh, 276–77
Sarachild, Kathy, 279
Scales, Ann, 309
Scharf, Lois, 221
Schenck v. U. S., 261
Schlafly, Phyllis, 29, 33, 67, 69, 86, 92, 98, 103–4, 108, 109, 110–15, 133–37, 145, 155, 159, 174, 176, 177, 180, 195, 227, 284, 298–99; *A Choice, Not an Echo,* 110; *Phyllis Schlafly Report,* 86, 90, 104, 110, 112–13, 174, 223, 266, 279, 283, 291; *The Power of the Positive Woman,* 223, 224, 280
Schlozman, Kay Lehman, 295
Schneider, William, 234
School District of Abington v. Schempp, 234
School Prayer Amendment, 32–33
SDS. *See* Students for a Democratic Society
Segal, Phyllis N., 251, 255
Senate (U.S.), 9, 51, 56–59, 127, 187
Senate Majority Report, 12, 51, 62–63, 82, 83, 113, 261
Sentinels of the Republic, 31
Sex-based classifications. *See* Gender-based classifications

Sex segregation in education,
    248–49, 258
Sex stereotypes. *See* Gender roles
Shakespeare, William, 303
Shanor, Charles, 255
Sheatsley, Paul B., 263
Sherburne, Jane C., 248, 256
Sherman, Carol, 239
Siegal, Ellie, 304
Silverstein, Arthur J., 129, 190
Simon, Herbert A., 292
*Simon v. Eastern Kentucky Wel-
    fare Rights Organization,* 242
Singer v. Hara, 291
Sisterhood, 185, 195
Sklar, Kathryn Kish, 221
Slater, Philip E., 292
Smeal, Eleanor, 76, 80, 125, 135,
    136, 137, 143, 180, 266, 269,
    289
SNCC. *See* Student Non-Violent
    Coordinating Committee
Snyder, Eloise C., 270
Social movements, ideology of,
    178–79, 180–81, 182, 183,
    184–85, 192–93, 286–87,
    304–5
Social Security system, 50, 52–53,
    57–58, 248, 256, 258, 259
Socialists, 8; participation in dem-
    onstrations, 130–31
*Spirt v. Teachers Insurance and
    Annuity Association,* 242
Spitze, Glenna, 227
Stamps, Jeffrey, 306
Stanton v. Stanton, 276, 277
Stanwick, Kathy A., 294
State action, 40, 241–42
State v. Gurganus, 259
Status degradation. *See* Home-
    makers
Statutory rape, 50, 247–48, 259
Steele, Diana, 73, 268

Steinem, Gloria, 228
Steiner, Gilbert, 221, 223
Stevens (Justice), 246
Stevenson, Adlai, 161, 290
Stiehm, Judith, 262, 272
Stinchcombe, Arthur, 304
STOP ERA, 34, 122, 133, 135,
    136, 137, 152, 159; mem-
    bership, 174–76, 292; training
    of activists, 135
Strict scrutiny. *See* Suspect clas-
    sification
Student Non-Violent Coordinat-
    ing Committee, 101, 277
Students for a Democratic Soci-
    ety, 99, 101, 277
Subcommittee on Constitutional
    Amendments, 11
Supermajority, required for con-
    stitutional amendments, 6,
    29, 34–35, 184. *See also*
    Majority, three-fifths
Support, husband's entry of, 90–
    92. *See also* Family law
Support of the ERA: by women,
    14–15; federal, 10, 56–57;
    organizational, 9, 10, 68, 84,
    189, 291, 300–301; public, x,
    2, 14–15, 16, 17, 45, 129,
    130, 171, 188, 191, 202, 228,
    233; state, 12–13, 126, 128,
    166, 238
Supreme Court (U.S.), x, 1, 4–5,
    13, 27, 28, 40–41, 45–59, 60–
    62, 74–75, 91–98, 124–27,
    128, 141, 189, 196, 197, 250,
    259, 288; legislative suspicion
    of, 4, 5, 27–28, 85–86, 163
Surveys: on abortion, 21, 127,
    284, 289; on actual words of
    ERA, 16–17, 26, 232–33; on
    attitudes to ERA, 14–19, 20–
    22, 136, 201–16, 225–26, 228–

29, 285–86, 294–95, 297; on civil disobedience, 291; on equal pay for equal work, 44, 244; on housework, 105–7, 109, 280–81, 282; on information about ERA, 153–54; on integrated toilets, 114, 234; on liberal and conservative ideas, 218, 282; on other abstract principles, 233; on other potential amendments, 29–34, 235–38; on sexual relations and women's roles, 20–25, 109, 204, 216–17, 230–32, 240–41; on women in military, 65–66, 70, 81, 262–64, 272–73, 283–84
Suspect classification, 48–52, 55–56, 60, 128
Suter, Larry, 240
Symbol, ERA as, 87–88, 132. *See also* ERA, indirect effects

Tactics, political, 165, 166, 167, 187–88, 192–93, 301–2
Taylor v. Louisiana, 258
Tedin, Kent L., 226, 284, 285, 302, 303
Tender years presumption. *See* Family law, custody
Tenenbaum, Susan, 270
Texas, 226, 227, 284, 285
Texas Department of Community Affairs v. Burdine, 241
Thirteenth Amendment, 242
Thomas, George M., 265
Thorne, Barry, 305
Title VII. *See* Civil Rights Act
Tolchin, Martin, 297
Tolchin, Susan, 297
Toilets, public, integration of, 90, 91, 112–16, 144, 225, 271. *See also* Privacy

Topinka, Judy Baar, 67, 68, 264
Traditionalists, 13, 20–21, 23, 70, 98, 100, 230, 302–3
Treadwell, Lujuana Wolfe, 307
Tribe, Lawrence, 268
Trilateral Commission, 175
Truman, Pat, 225
Tsongas, Paul, 288, 289
Turner, Ralph H., 286, 306
Twenty-fourth Amendment, 30
Twenty-sixth Amendment, 30–31

U.S. ex re. Robinson v. York, 259
U.S. v. Zbaraz, 287
Uhlaner, Carol, 295
Uniform Marriage and Divorce Act, 275
United Auto Workers, 10
United Nations charter, 9
United States Brewers' Association, 234
United States v. Darby, 235
University of Michigan American National Election Study, 202, 203, 211, 229, 297
Useem, Michael, 304, 305
Utah, 232, 233

Van Alstyne, William, 62, 65, 79, 80, 260, 262
Van Kleek, Mary, 220
Verba, Sidney, 230, 304
Vietnam War, 30, 63, 66, 68
Virginia Slims American Women's Opinion Poll, 231
Volunteers, ideology of, 3, 6, 118, 119, 147, 148, 191. *See also* Benefits, intangible
Vorchheimer v. School District of Philadelphia, 50, 247, 248, 249, 254
Vose, Clement E., 221, 235

Voting, 1, 14, 15, 30, 149, 154, 161, 162, 225–26, 299
Voting Rights Act, 198

Wages, 2, 36–44, 53, 72, 145, 244; gap between men's and women's, 36, 100, 143, 238, 240. *See also* Protective legislation
Wagner v. Sheltz, 243
Wake Up, 143–44
Walker, Charles, 275
Walker, Henry A., 265
Walters, Barbara, 135
Walzer, Michael, 272
War power clauses, 61, 62, 75, 77, 78, 79, 81, 83, 268
Washburne, C. K., 306
Washington v. Davis, 54, 55, 56, 94, 244
WEAL. *See* Women's Equity Action League
Weedoff, Eugene, 271
Wegner, Judith Welch, 256
Weinberger v. Weisenfeld, 258–59
Weiss, Carol H., 264–65
Weitzman, Lenore, 276
Wengler v. Druggists Mutual Ins. Co., 247
Westphal, Joseph W., 208, 238, 283
Wexler, Joan: *The ERA and the Military,* 79, 83, 84, 269
White (Justice), 55, 56, 246
Whitlow v. Hodges, 277
Wiesenthal, Helmut, 308
Wife, 53, 91, 92, 93, 94, 98, 100
Wiggins amendments, 11, 251, 290
Wildavsky, Aaron, 287, 306
Wilensky, Harold, 307

Williams, Wendy, 239, 249, 309
Willis, George L., 234
Willis, Paul G., 234
Wilson, James Q., 286
Wilson, John, 305
Wincup (Representative), 274
Wiseman, William J., Jr., 228, 289
WITCH. *See* Women Interested in Toppling Consumption Holidays
Witherspoon, Joseph, 223
Wohl, Lisa Cronin, 238, 284, 293, 294
Wohlenberg, Ernest H., 238
Woman for President, 21, 22, 38
Woman Patriot, 31
Womanhood, image of independent, 93
Women in Communications, 138
Women in positions of authority. *See* Authority, women in positions of
Women in the military. *See* Military, women in
Women Interested in Toppling Consumption Holidays, 103, 279
Women's Equity Action League, 70, 72, 73, 75, 76, 268–69
Women's liberation movement, 13, 99, 101, 104, 277, 303
Women's organizations, 8, 9, 68, 71, 72, 73, 75, 79, 88, 194, 265, 287; expenditures, 156, 298, 302
Women's suffrage, 8
Wood, Stephen B., 235
Work force. *See* Paid labor force
Working class, 8, 15
Worthy, M. B., 240
Wright-Isak, Christine, 287

Yale article, 51, 61–62, 77–79, 84, 111, 113, 128, 251–52, 255, 260, 261
Yankelovitch, Daniel, 45, 232
Yocum v. Illinois, 260
Young, Oran R., 287

Zald, Mayer M., 303
Zeigler, L. Harmon, 280, 281
Zeldich, Morris, Jr., 265
Zimmerman, Laura, 304